TEACHERS OF YOUNG CHILDREN

TEACHERS OF YOUNG CHILDREN

THIRD EDITION

Robert D. Hess

Stanford University

Doreen J. Croft

De Anza College

HOUGHTON MIFFLIN COMPANY   BOSTON

Dallas   Geneva, Illinois

Hopewell, New Jersey   Palo Alto   London

Illustrations for the cover and the text by Marcia R. Smith

Photo Credits

p. 2 Lynn McLaren, Photo Researchers, Inc. / p. 7 Brown Brothers / p. 7 Culver Pictures, Inc. / p. 7 The Bettmann Archive / p. 8 Culver Pictures, Inc. / p. 8 The Bettmann Archive / p. 8 The Bettmann Archive / p. 46 Alice Kandell, Photo Researchers, Inc. / p. 51 Leonard Freed, Magnum Photos / p. 57 Rose Skytta, Jeroboam, Inc. / p. 64 Elizabeth Hamlin, Stock Boston / p. 67 Anestis Diakopoulous, Stock Boston / p. 81 Suzanne Wu, Jeroboam, Inc. / p. 89 Bohdan Hrynewych / p. 99 Peeter Vilms, Jeroboam, Inc. / p. 106 Elizabeth Hamlin, Stock Boston / p. 128 Woodfin Camp and Associates / p. 134 Peeter Vilms, Jeroboam, Inc. / p. 140 Suzanne Arms, Jeroboam, Inc. / p. 140 Kent Reno, Jeroboam, Inc. / p. 155 Yves DeBraine, Black Star / p. 158 Elizabeth Crews, Stock Boston / p. 209 Bohdan Hrynewych / p. 216 Mike Mazzaschi, Stock Boston / p. 239 Mike Mazzaschi, Stock Boston / p. 252 Ken Korre, Stock Boston / p. 261 The National Foundation March of Dimes / p. 284 Cary Wolinsky, Stock Boston / p. 305 Burt Glinn, Magnum Photos / p. 316 Elizabeth Hamlin, Stock Boston / p. 324 A. J. Sullivan / p. 324 Laszlo Hege, Photo Researchers, Inc. / p. 333 Betsy Cole, Stock Boston / p. 351 Charles Gatewood / p. 356 Terry McKoy, The Picture Cube / p. 368 Lynn McLaren / p. 368 Erika, Peter Arnold, Inc. / p. 369 Jack Prelutsky, Stock Boston / p. 369 A. J. Sullivan / p. 369 Julie O'Neil / p. 369 Peter Vandermark, Stock Boston / p. 388 Terry McKoy, The Picture Cube / p. 406 Rick Friedman, The Picture Cube

Picture song card on p. 231 reprinted with the permission of Holt, Rinehart and Winston, Inc., from *The History of Education: Socrates to Montessori*, p. 537. Copyright 1950 by Rinehart and Company, Inc.

Printed in the U.S.A.

Library of Congress Catalog Card Number: 80-81928

ISBN: 0-395-29172-0

CONTENTS

v

PREFACE

The third edition of *Teachers of Young Children* is an introductory text for students who are preparing to work in the field of early education and child care. It is intended to provide knowledge about characteristics of children during the preschool years, to describe the curriculum elements that are used in preschool programs, and to offer information and suggestions about career development in the field.

ORGANIZATION

Twenty-five chapters are organized into eight parts: "The Expanding Field of Early Education and Child Care," "Preparing to Teach in the Classroom," "Health and Safety in the Preschool," "Helping Children Learn," "Gathering and Using Data about Children and Their Families," "The Family and the Preschool," "Administration of Preschools," and "Some Personal Matters." A prologue opens each part, outlining the major themes of the chapters that follow. The style of the prologues is more informal and personal, and because they are directed to the individual reader, they should not be overlooked in reading assignments.

Each chapter begins with an outline of the major topics covered. The chapters include boxed inserts that offer specific suggestions for classroom teaching, summaries of pertinent studies, and expanded coverage of selected topics discussed in the text. The material in each chapter covers matters that concern the teacher as a professional who is developing a career; knowledge about children, the field, and the curriculum that is needed to become a competent professional; and the application of such knowledge in specific classroom situations.

AUDIENCE AND POINT OF VIEW

The text is written for the beginning student in the field—typically an undergraduate in a four-year or community college—although some chapters may be more useful in more specialized courses. Examples of situations that the teacher will meet are included; specific points are identified, especially in suggesting how the material may be used in interacting with parents, children, and staff members. Marginal notes offer excerpts of opinions and perspectives that the student may encounter as well as comments that illustrate, sometimes by contrast, the material in the chapter. The writing style of the text is generally informal, but a glossary at the end of the book defines terms that may be unfamiliar to some readers.

The perspective of the book is eclectic but with sympathetic consideration of a cognitive developmental slant. We see theories, programs, and techniques as tools to use in the classroom, not as doctrines to be promoted or defended.

PEDAGOGICAL FEATURES

Several features of the third edition are intended to make the material useful for the beginning student. There is a strong orientation toward classroom practice and research. We have made relevant studies more practical by suggesting applications of the material for classroom use. Illustrations and examples are included to show how principles in the field can be applied in a given situation.

The text reflects a concern with both early education and child care. The field is diverse, but there is a great deal of overlap in the types of competence needed in these two major areas. The materials are prepared to include both child care and educational settings.

The text also focuses on career development. Some students who use this book will soon seek careers in early education and child care. The final part may hold special interest for the young professional. The topics discussed in that section include getting a job, dealing with stress and burn-out, and evaluating personal growth in the early stages of a career.

The third edition includes more practical suggestions for using knowledge about children in designing the curriculum. The companion volume, *An Activities Handbook for Teachers of Young Children*, presents many specific ideas about how to help children learn. *Teachers of Young Children* expands on those ideas and also discusses principles of classroom management, administration of preschools, and collaboration with parents to teach them to be effective in working with young children.

ACKNOWLEDGMENTS

We wish to extend our thanks to those reviewers whose criticism and suggestions helped refine the manuscript. They include Robert Granger, Georgia State University; Georgia Houle, Rhode Island Junior College; Finton Kavanagh, Marywood College; Samuel Meisels, University of Michigan; Carole Schwartz, University of South Florida; June Sciarra, The University of Cincinnati; and Ann Williams, Ball State University. We also would like to acknowledge the following people for their help in preparing this third edition: Geraldine Alvarado, Anne Arnold, Shirley Baskette, Jalane Christian-Stoker, Deborah Dale, Anne Kirby, Shirley Lee, Margaret Obenour, Anne Schneider, and Jane Warner. We are grateful for their interest and assistance.

R.D.H.
D.J.C.

TEACHERS OF YOUNG CHILDREN

PART ONE

THE EXPANDING FIELD OF EARLY EDUCATION AND CHILD CARE

A PROLOGUE You probably have some personal reasons for reading *Teachers of Young Children*. You may be thinking seriously of entering the field, or you may simply be curious about child care. Perhaps you have been told that you are good with children. Maybe you're a homemaker who wants to return to the labor market or a young man who believes that child care is the responsibility of both men and women. Whatever your reasons, you will see the field through the lens of your own experience and needs.

Several questions may come to mind as you approach the study of early childhood education. Foremost among them may be, "Should I choose a career in early education?" Although your present motives are a good base on which to form your answer, your ideas are likely to change as you learn more about young children, the various kinds of jobs that will be available, and the conditions under which you will work. The field is diverse and challenging, and new career options will appear as your training continues.

One chapter in the text explores the question, "Is child care good for children?"; you may also ask, "Is child care good for *me*?" Perhaps you should also ask, "Will I be good for child care?" If you enter the field of early education, you should be prepared to contribute. *Teachers of Young Children* is intended to help you prepare to offer the field the professional competence and skills that are needed.

In order to help you begin to answer the questions you may have, Part

One provides some background on the history of child care, the need for early education in this society, and the growth of the field.

Imagine your situation five years in the future. You will have completed your training and gained experience. You will be making decisions about the role you want to play in the field. What images come to mind? Will you be a teacher in a large day care center? Serve as a curriculum coordinator in a multicultural school district? You might see yourself directing a chain of franchised preschools, or operating a day care home with a small group of children. These goals are within reach. They take planning, work, and determination. They are rarely achieved through luck. The knowledge now available makes it possible for you to develop basic skills that will help you deal effectively with young children.

In our society, few adults are professionally trained to work with young children. Those who are, hold a special place. If early education is your choice, your influence will reach far into the future.

CHAPTER 1

THE NEED FOR CHILD CARE

A GLIMPSE AT HISTORY

Every weekday morning, hundreds of thousands of parents leave their young children in the care of relatives, friends, preschools, day care centers, or day care homes. The proportion of parents who rely on others to care for their children has grown rapidly. The number of day care centers and day care homes tripled between 1967 and 1975, from 35,000 to 116,000. During the same period, the proportion of children enrolled in preschool programs increased more than 50 percent (Snapper and Ohms, 1977).

Child care and early education constitute a large and growing industry. How did it begin? Why is it growing so rapidly?

Early Forms of Preschool Education

The preschool movement began more than three hundred years ago. In 1657, a Czech named Comenius published a book, *The Great Didactic*, in which he argued that the first schooling should be at home—a sort of "School of the Mother's Knee"—where, during the first six years of life, children would be taught by their mothers so that when they reached school age they possessed simple facts and skills that prepared them for more formal learning. A year later, Comenius published a picture book for children to supplement a course of study he had prepared twenty years before. His curriculum covered names of parts of the body, colors, plants, and animals, as well as religious and moral training.

About 150 years later, a Swiss educator, Johann H. Pestalozzi, created preschools for young children. His interest in early schooling came from a deep love for children and a concern that their spirit and growth were threatened by factories, industrialized cities, and neglect by working parents. In 1801 he wrote *How Gertrude Teaches Her Children*, in which he described his philosophy and methods. Simple and perceptive, they are still applicable. Children were taught to observe things around them—the number of panes in a window, the number of steps in a stairway, and specific things in the natural world. Pestalozzi believed such attentiveness would lead to heightened awareness in a child, promoting speech and academic skills (Braun and Edwards, 1972).

In 1842, one of Pestalozzi's students, a German, Frederick Froebel, founded the *kindergarten*, or "children's garden." The garden was intended as a sanctuary for children, where the pressures of the family and the school could not enter. Froebel used "gifts" of soft felt balls, blocks, and sticks and various activities such as painting, sewing, paper cutting, marching, dancing, and singing. School work in the form of classroom materials, books, writing or reading exercises was forbidden; the focus was on play. The teacher, through careful supervision, helped the child combine play and

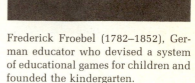

John Amos Comenius (1592–1670), Czech educator who wrote first text using pictures for teaching children.

Johann H. Pestalozzi (1746–1827), Swiss educational reformer who emphasized use of objects at early age to develop powers of observation and reasoning.

Frederick Froebel (1782–1852), German educator who devised a system of educational games for children and founded the kindergarten.

work. According to Froebel, the work of young children was play; it was from play that they were to learn (Braun and Edwards, 1972).

In the United States, the kindergarten movement grew as the result of the efforts of Elizabeth Peabody who started the first private English-speaking kindergarten in Boston in 1860. (The first kindergarten was actually started by Mrs. Carl Schurtz in Watertown, Wisconsin, in 1855. A student of Froebel, Mrs. Schurtz opened the school in her home mainly for her own children.) Young children, as viewed by Elizabeth Peabody, were self-centered, aware of their senses and experiences. Left at home, the child could become selfish. The kindergarten could provide a place where this early concentration on the self would be balanced by learning to take a place in a group.

Early Education as Social Reform

Initially, the first kindergartens were expensive and were used primarily by affluent families. In both Europe and the United States, however, they came to be seen as a way of helping children escape the evils of the industrial age.

At the turn of the century, a major force in early childhood education emerged in the slums of Rome. Maria Montessori, a feminist and the first woman to earn a degree in medicine in Italy, began her work with retarded children as an intern at the University of Rome. She developed materials and methods suitable for teaching these children, and in 1907 she was asked to

Jean Jacques Rousseau (1712–1778), French philosopher who believed education should start at birth and continue through the twenty-fifth year.

Elizabeth Peabody (1804–1894), American educator who emphasized Froebel's theories in championing the cause of kindergartens in the United States.

Maria Montessori (1870–1952), Italian physician who created instructional materials that used motion and manipulation to train the senses.

Kindergartens were originally supported by private foundations. They were first included in public schools in St. Louis in 1873.

organize a school in a tenement in Rome. Ironically, the motivation for the school sprang from the desire of the Roman Association of Good Building to prevent children from vandalizing the tenements while their parents were away at work. Montessori opened the *Casa dei bambini* for children between the ages of two and one-half and seven, with hours from 8 a.m. to 6 p.m. (Braun and Edwards, 1972). Montessori's genius was her ability to design materials for training. She created materials that were self-administered and self-correcting and that used motion and manipulation to train the senses. She wanted materials to be inherently interesting, simple, and thoroughly comprehensible to the teacher. Although the movement she founded is criticized by some as insufficiently oriented toward social and linguistic development, Montessori's work continues to have significant impact on the field (Hunt, 1964).

Underprivileged children also received attention in the United States. About twenty years after Elizabeth Peabody established her kindergarten in Boston, Kate Douglas Wiggin, author of *Rebecca of Sunnybrook Farm*, became excited over the prospect of planting one of the ''children's gardens'' in the ghettoes of San Francisco for nurturing children who were underfed, neglected, and vulnerable. She started a settlement kindergarten in the early 1870s.

In this way, kindergartens and, later, preschools were used as instruments for social reform. They provided special educational and nurturing climates for children from low-income backgrounds who were thought to have special needs (Lazerson, 1970). Schools have been used for such social goals and purposes for a long time and are still seen as routes to social improvement.

Nursery Schools

Nursery schools appeared in the United States much later than kindergartens. The influence of Montessori led to the establishment of the first nursery school in New York City in 1915, under the auspices of the Child Education Foundation. That same year, a group of faculty wives at the University of Chicago organized a cooperative preschool.

In 1919, Caroline Pratt founded a nursery school in New York City under the direction of the Bureau of Educational Experiments. This school eventually became a demonstration center for the Bank Street College of Education. Teachers College of Columbia University began another school in 1921. The Merrill Palmer Institute organized a nursery school in Detroit in 1922 to provide "a laboratory for training young women in child care" (Braun and Edwards, 1972). Nursery schools gained immediate popularity. Within a few short years, more than two hundred schools were established (Davis, 1932).

The first organization of nursery schools was sparked by Patty Smith Hill in a meeting at Teachers College in 1925. This organization, the National Association for Nursery Education, later became the National Association for the Education of Young Children (NAEYC).

Origins of Child Care in the United States

In contrast to kindergartens and nursery schools, which were established for the benefit of the child, child care has been oriented toward the needs of working adults. In the 1850s, for example, child care was provided for employed mothers, especially those who had been deserted or widowed. The first facilities were set up in 1854 and by 1897 there were 175. During World War I, child care centers were established to accommodate children of women who were employed to assist in the war effort (Pidgeon, 1953). During the depression of the 1930s, child care centers were established as part of the Work Projects Administration (WPA) to serve a dual purpose: to furnish day care for children of working parents and to provide jobs for unemployed teachers (Rothman, 1973). Women were recruited during World War II to work in factories and offices to replace men who were called for active military service. Through federal funds authorized by the Lanham Act of 1940, child care centers were established to serve working women. Industries sometimes provided their own baby-sitting and day care services. Many of these child care centers disappeared after the war when men replaced

"I worked in a shipyard child care center in 1942, and I still recall having the full responsibility for eighteen children, ages two and one-half to six. Sometimes, the best I could do was to let a child hang on to part of my skirt and follow me around while I attended to the needs of the children as best I could."

Teacher

WHAT ARE THE DIFFERENCES BETWEEN
KINDERGARTEN, NURSERY SCHOOL,
AND *DAY CARE CENTER?*

The distinctions among the terms *kindergarten, nursery school*, and *day care center* are not always clear. The definitions overlap and their meanings change over time. These terms may be more closely related to the historical roots of a particular movement than to a strict definition of the program and structure.

In the United States, *kindergartens* are most often associated with the education of five-year-old children in the year prior to entering the first grade. *Nursery schools* generally serve youngsters who fall within the two- to five-year age range; they offer services for only part of a day—usually either morning or afternoon. *Day care* centers usually provide full-day care for preschoolers of all ages and after-school care for elementary school children.

---

women in the factories. A few states—California is an example—continued to support the children's centers with tax funds.

RECENT GROWTH OF EARLY EDUCATION AND CHILD CARE

Extensive growth has taken place in the field of early education and child care since 1965. Today, there are roughly 20 million children under six years of age in the United States, many of whom are in some kind of educational or day care program. In 1975, about 1.3 million children were enrolled in licensed day care centers or family day care services (Senate Committee on Finance, 1977). In addition, almost 5 million children between the ages of three and five attended kindergartens or nursery schools (see Table 1.1). The figures in Table 1.1 do not include the many children under six who were cared for by relatives, unlicensed day care homes, or "block mothers" who volunteer to be homes of reference to children whose parents are at work. The increase in enrollment shown in Table 1.1 underestimates the actual rate of expansion since the total number of three- to five-year-old children in the United States was declining at the same time—from more than 12 million in 1967 to less than 10 million in 1976. The percentage of children enrolled in preschools doubled during this period.

TABLE 1.1

Number of Children Enrolled in Nursery School and Kindergarten, 1968–1978

Year	Nursery School			Kindergarten		
	Public	*Private*	*Both*	*Public*	*Private*	*Both*
1968	268,000	554,000	816,000	2,709,000	559,000	3,268,000
1969	245,000	615,000	860,000	2,682,000	594,000	3,276,000
1970	333,000	763,000	1,096,000	2,647,000	536,000	3,183,000
1971	317,000	749,000	1,066,000	2,689,000	574,000	3,263,000
1972	402,000	881,000	1,283,000	2,636,000	499,000	3,135,000
1973	400,000	924,000	1,324,000	2,582,000	493,000	3,074,000
1974	423,000	1,184,000	1,607,000	2,726,000	526,000	3,252,000
1975	574,000	1,174,000	1,748,000	2,851,000	542,000	3,393,000
1976	476,000	1,050,000	1,526,000	2,962,000	528,000	3,490,000
1977	562,000	1,056,000	1,618,000	2,665,000	526,000	3,191,000
1978	587,000	1,237,000	1,824,000	2,493,000	496,000	2,989,000

Source: U.S. Department of Commerce, Bureau of the Census, *School Enrollment—Social and Economic Characteristics of Students: October 1978*, Current Population Reports, Population Characteristics, Series P-20, No. 335 (Washington, D.C.: Government Printing Office, April 1979), p. 42.

The rapid expansion of child care and early education in the past fifteen years is a new trend. Unlike the proliferation of child care centers and nursery schools in the first half of this century, this new growth is not in response to a national emergency. It represents several changes in our society that have increased the demand for child care and preschool programs.

The Demand for Early Education

Welfare mothers can receive Aid to Families with Dependent Children (AFDC) for child care services. In 1975 there were 2.8 million AFDC children under 6 years of age.

The recent growth of early educational programs in the United States was stimulated by several factors. One was the recognition of the effects of racial discrimination and proverty on young children and their educational opportunities. Head Start, for example, began in 1965 with the purpose of providing preschool experience and training for children from low-income backgrounds. Another impetus for expansion was the Soviet launching of *Sputnik* in 1957. A desperate scramble ensued in the American scientific and educational communities to catch up with the technical progress of the Soviet Union. At about the same time, behavioral scientists in the United States published data suggesting that children's early cognitive growth and performance indicated their level of achievement later in school. Two books written in the early 1960s had a dramatic effect on the field: *Stability and Change in Human Characteristics* (Bloom, 1964) and *Intelligence and Experience* (Hunt, 1961). Early years and early learning were both considered crucial in intellectual development and academic achievement. These and other publications initiated a national effort to introduce education during the preschool years. The preschool and the teacher took a central role in this attempt to prepare children for successful performance in school. Instruction in school-related tasks became a reasonable goal. Schools had the curricula, the equipment, and the staff of trained professionals.

The Need for Child Care

"In 1978, there were 5,819,000 mothers with children under six in the labor force."

Bureau of the Census

Increase in Employment of Married Women   The major reason for the recent growth in child care is the increasing number of married women who have young children and are working outside the home. Some women choose to work because they enjoy the stimulation and contact with other adults. Some are returning to school to prepare for a career. Others are continuing careers that would suffer if they stayed out of their chosen

FIGURE 1.1

Changes in Percentage of Women Who Have Children under Six and Are Working Outside the Home

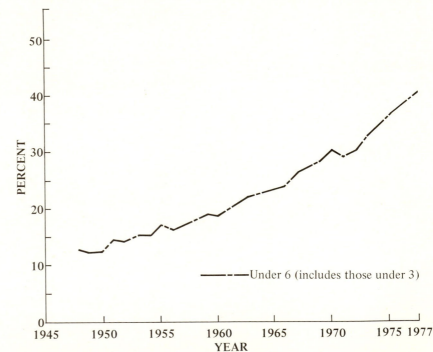

Source: Adapted from National Academy of Sciences, *Toward a National Policy for Children and Families*, Advisory Committee on Child Development, Assembly of Behavioral and Social Sciences, National Research Council (Washington, D.C.: National Academy of Sciences, 1976), p. 16. Updated to 1977 from U.S. Department of Commerce, Bureau of the Census, *Perspectives on American Husbands and Wives*, Current Population Reports, Special Studies Series P-23, No. 77 (Washington, D.C.: Government Printing Office, 1979), p. 26.

"Having a job means money of my own to spend. Besides, I was getting 'flabby' intellectually and physically just sitting at home and watching TV!"

Working Mother

"I'm really a 'closet mother.' I'd rather stay home and take care of the baby, but we need two incomes to survive."

Mother

By 1976, there were more than half as many divorces as marriages.

field until their children were in school. For many, additional income is a necessity.

The increased demand for child care reflects these and other changes in the lives of the women who traditionally provided the care they now seek from other sources. In 1978, 40 percent of mothers with children under six years of age were working (see Figure 1.1). In 1978, more than one-half (60 percent) of married women with children between ages six and seventeen were working or seeking work. Most had full-time jobs. Many of these women were married to men whose incomes were relatively low. For mothers with young children, the economic pressures to work are often intense.

Changes in Divorce Rates   The incidence of divorce has been increasing over the past century, with the most rapid rise occurring in the past ten years. The number of women who have been divorced has risen almost tenfold since 1890. In the period between 1965 and 1975, the number of divorces doubled (see Figure 1.2). In 1978 there were 1,122,000 divorces or annulments, involving roughly one million children. In 1975 more than one child

FIGURE 1.2

Number of Divorces and Estimated Number of Children Involved in Divorce, 1953–1975

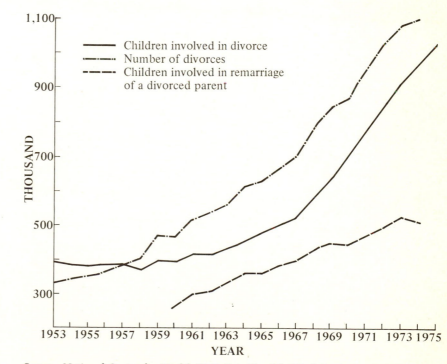

Source: National Center for Health Statistics, *Monthly Vital Statistics Reports: Final Divorce Statistics, 1953–1975*, U.S. Department of Health, Education, and Welfare (Washington, D.C.: Government Printing Office, 1976).

in six under age eighteen was living in a single parent household. This was almost double the figure for 1950, only twenty-five years earlier.

The economic loss that results from divorce affects the need for child care. Economic need brought on by divorce forces many women with children under school age to work outside the home. A father who decides to divorce and then to remarry faces the prospect of having to support two families. It is highly unusual for his income to provide adequately for both. Indeed, the wife of a new marriage may feel obligated to get a job to supplement her husband's income, reduced because of child support and/or alimony payments. Her children may then need child care. A change in family patterns thus can have several interlocking consequences on income.

Other Factors in Growth of Child Care   After-school care is needed by working parents. The school day ends in midafternoon, but working parents often do not reach home until much later. There are several possibilities open to such families. They may make arrangements for a baby sitter in the neighborhood or send the child to a day care center during the after-school hours. The child may check in with neighbors and use their house as a base from which to play at a local park or with friends. The child may have a key to his or her own house and stay home unsupervised. The number of such "latchkey children" appears to be growing. About 1 million school-age children have no care between the end of the school day and the time parents return from work (National Research Council, 1976).

The growing need for child care is not simply economic. The spirit of women's liberation touches a wide range of behavior of both women and men. This is reflected in the desire of many women to take a paying job outside the home and in a new view of the role that men might play in child care. The increase in public funds for child care over the past decade also represents, in part, some acceptance of the concept that child care services should be provided at public expense to families with young children.

REFERENCES

Bloom, B. S. 1964. *Stability and Change in Human Characteristics*. New York: John Wiley & Sons.

Bradbury, D. E. 1962. *Five Decades of Action for Children*. Rev. ed. U.S. Department of Health, Education, and Welfare, Social Security Administration, Children's Bureau, Publication No. 358. Washington, D.C.: Government Printing Office.

Braun, S. J. 1966. "Nursery Education for Disadvantaged Children: An Historical Review." In *Montessori in Perspective*. Ed. L. Perryman. Washington, D.C.: National Association for the Education of Young Children.

Braun, S. J., and E. P. Edwards. 1972. *History and Theory of Early Childhood Education*. Worthington, Ohio: Charles A. Jones Publishing Company.

Bremner, R. H., et al. 1970–1974. *Children and Youth in America: A Documentary History*. 3 vols. Cambridge, Mass.: Harvard University Press.

Davis, M. D. 1932. *Nursery Schools, Their Development and Current Practices in the United States*. U.S. Office of Education, Bulletin No. 9. Washington, D.C.: Government Printing Office.

Froebel, F. 1903. *The Education of Man*. New York: Appleton-Century-Crofts.

Hunt, J. McVicker. 1964. Revisiting Montessori: Introduction.'' In *The Montessori Method*. New York: Schocken Books.

Hunt, J. McVicker. 1961. *Intelligence and Experience*. New York: The Ronald Press Company.

Kamerman, S. B. 1975. *Child Care Programs in Nine Countries*. U.S. Department of Health, Education, and Welfare, Office of Child Development, Office of Human Development, Publication No. OHD 30080. Washington, D.C.: Government Printing Office.

Lazerson, M. 1970. ''Social Reform and Early Childhood Education: Some Historical Perspectives.'' *Urban Education*, 5, No. 1 (April), 84–102.

Pestalozzi, J. H. 1898. *How Gertrude Teaches Her Children*. 2nd ed. Trans. Lucy E. Holland and Francis C. Turner. Ed. Ebenezer Cooke. Syracuse, N.Y.: C. W. Bardeen.

Pidgeon, M. E. 1953. *Employed Mothers and Child Care*. U.S. Department of Labor, Bulletin of the Women's Bureau, No. 246. Washington, D.C.: Government Printing Office.

Rothman, S. 1973. ''Other People's Children: The Day Care Experience in America.'' *Public Interest*, 30 (Winter), 11–27.

Snapper, K. J., and J. S. Ohms. 1977. *The Status of Children 1977*. U.S. Department of Health, Education, and Welfare, Office of Human Development Services, Administration for Children, Youth, and Families, Research and Evaluation Division, DHEW Publication No. OHDS 78-30133. Washington, D.C.: Government Printing Office.

U.S. 95th Congress, 1st Session, Senate Committee on Finance. 1977. *Child Care: Data and Materials*. Publication No. 79-578. Washington, D.C.: Government Printing Office.

U.S. Department of Commerce, Bureau of the Census. 1979. *Marital Status and Living Arrangements: March 1978*. Current Population Reports, Population Characteristics. Series P-20, No. 338. Washington, D.C.: Government Printing Office.

CHAPTER 2

IS CHILD CARE GOOD FOR CHILDREN?

SOURCES OF CONCERN ABOUT CHILD CARE

Marianne wiped away a tear as she drove her car out of the parking lot of the child care center. She tried to concentrate on the day ahead—doing the billing and payroll for the Anderson Company—but the image of Jon would not leave her mind.

She had tried not to look back, but she couldn't resist a quick parting glance as she walked away resolutely from his imploring cries. She could see the tears rolling down his chubby cheeks, his arms reaching for her skirt, his whole body pleading not to be left behind. All he wanted was to be with her. And all she really wanted was to be with her child. Nothing mattered quite as much to her as Jon—just toddling now and learning to say a few words.

The tears welled up again and she took a deep breath. If only he wouldn't cry so. The teacher had reassured her that Jon stopped soon after she was out of sight, but lately he had started to cry even before they left home. Yes, books, teachers, and friends had told her this was "normal," but that didn't help her this morning. She was already looking forward to the end of the day when she could pick Jon up, give him a big hug, and reassure him.

As she drove along the freeway, Marianne reflected on how she had gotten into such a situation. Maybe if she hadn't gotten the divorce she wouldn't be working. No, that wasn't true. Even before Jon was born, she and Dan both had to work to make ends meet. Maybe she should move back to her parents' home in Iowa. No, her independence was too important; she had to make it on her own. But in the many lonely moments—like now—Marianne wondered how she would have done things differently if she had them to do all over again. Would she have had Jon? The thought snapped her back to reality. She felt guilty. And sad. How much longer would she have to leave her baby with someone else? Would these experiences be harmful to him? Would she have to share him with other caregivers for the rest of his early years? Would they come to mean more to him than his own mother?

"My daughter can hardly wait to get to school in the morning. She doesn't seem to miss me at all. On the one hand I'm relieved, but on the other, I feel a bit jealous of the teacher."

Mother

Marianne's anxieties are shared by thousands of parents who have to leave their children in someone else's care. Most parents do not want their children to be cared for outside the home on a full-day basis for long periods of time. The family offers a continuity of warmth, experience, and emotional ties that is almost impossible to match. Whatever the reasons for leaving their children in the care of others, parents ask themselves how the separation and the experience will affect their children and the parent-child relationship. These important and reasonable questions are being raised not only by parents but also by professionals in child development and policy makers who provide financial support and regulate child care. In order to understand the basis for such questions, we must first look at several main sources of concern about the effects of child care.

Parents, especially mothers, are expected to put the child's interests above almost every other demand, certainly above their own personal interests. This expectation is so strong that many parents feel guilty about leaving their children even when it is necessary. They worry about whether the child is receiving the kind of care he or she needs. It is especially important for parents to know what effect, if any, child care may have on children.

For some, the idea of institutional care suggests neglect or abandonment. These fears may be attributed to tales of abuse in nineteenth-century orphanages or homes for waifs established to provide care. Although child care today has little in common with the facilities of a century ago, prejudice lingers in the public's mind.

Child care, particularly when it is supported by taxes, also evokes images of government interference in family life. In 1971 Congress passed the Child Care and Family Services Act, which received a great deal of support as well as sharp criticism. President Nixon's veto message (see page 385) reflects the intense opposition to government-sponsored day care that is shared by many people.

Some of the opposition to child care has an economic basis. Care for young children is costly; the annual expense for a child in an infant-toddler center can approach the tuition charges at a major private university. Some taxpayers resist the use of public funds to support an expensive service that, they believe, should be offered by the family.

Perhaps the most serious concern is raised by theory and research on the attachment bond that normally develops between mothers and infants. Some believe that this bond is threatened by prolonged or frequent separation from the mother (or mothering figure) during the early years of the child's life. We will discuss this issue later in the chapter.

Child care outside the home thus raises significant issues. It involves questions of policy and economics about which there is disagreement within the community. The long-term effects of child care on children and their families is not well known. Before effective and meaningful public policies can be developed, we must know much more about the impact of child care than we do at the present time.

THE VARIETY OF CHILD CARE

The term *child care* covers a range of conditions (see Figure 2.1). The Saturday night baby sitter provides child care, as does the older brother or sister left with a three-year-old. Children receive care in a nursery school or a Montessori class. Head Start cares for children while providing them with

"Children are quick to sense a parent's guilt feelings; this makes separation more difficult. When the parent has no choice but to leave, I usually recommend that they do so matter-of-factly. They can phone me to be reassured that the child is OK."

Teacher

FIGURE 2.1
Arrangements for Daytime
Care of Children with
Mothers in the Labor Force
(February 1975)

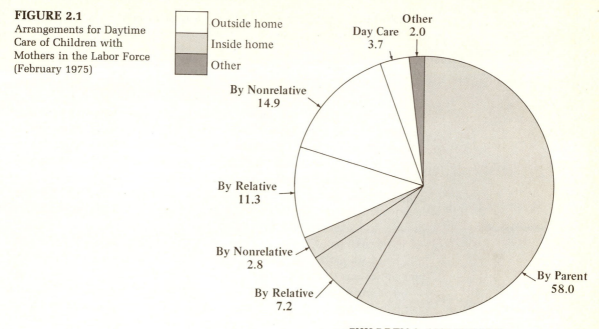

CHILDREN 3–6 YEARS OLD

The different types of care parents use for their three- to six-year-olds are shown in the pie graph. Notice that centers and day care homes account for a relatively small part of the total. Most families leave their youngsters with relatives and friends; many children are cared for in their own homes. There is almost no research on these types of care or their effects on young children. Research that is available concentrates on children in centers and also deals predominantly with youngsters three years of age and younger.

Source: U.S. Department of Commerce, Bureau of the Census, *Status: A Monthly Chartbook of Social and Economic Trends* (Washington, D.C.: Government Printing Office, October 1976), p. 54.

comprehensive services—educational, social, nutritional, medical, diagnostic, and the like.

The question stated in the title of this chapter does not specify the type of care involved. A university experimental day care program, for example, has a budget, staff, facilities, and professional resources far beyond the resources of most nonprofit schools. Care in these settings is obviously not equivalent to that offered in the struggling parent co-op on the other side of town, or in an urban, low-income area.

Child care varies greatly from one center to another and from one type of care to the next. Any conclusions or assessment of the effects of care must take this into account. A number of studies have used children in experimental, high-budget programs and their results may not apply to cen-

Price is not always a sign of quality in either food or child care.

ters with more modest resources. Research is incomplete; reports should be taken as estimates, providing partial answers. Read them with caution.

PROBLEMS IN EVALUATING CHILD CARE

It is difficult to conduct research on child care in a systematic way. The variables involved are complex and it is not easy to measure the nuances of human interaction. If several studies report similar results, confidence in the validity of the research data will increase. As an analogy, consider the variables involved in comparing the quality of food in the restaurants of New York, Omaha, and San Francisco. Each meal can provide a useful report on a particular restaurant, but one needs to sample many different restaurants in order to make statements about the general quality of the city's cuisine. As in research on preschools, such a study would be further complicated by differences in individual taste and differences in any given chef's ability to prepare various entrées.

So when you read the results of studies on the effects of child care, note carefully the kind of program under examination. A half-day nursery school offers a different kind of child care than a center at a camp for children of migrant workers where the children are brought at five in the morning and put back to bed for a nap before breakfast is served. A center with a child-to-adult ratio of 4 to 1 offers a different experience than one with a ratio of 8 to 1. The effects of care may be very different for infants than for four- or five-year-old children. In this field, you should keep careful mental (or actual) notes and reserve judgment until a clear picture begins to emerge.

CURRENT RESEARCH ON THE EFFECTS OF CHILD CARE

"I resent people saying that day care is just baby-sitting. We have a very strong educational component in our center. Maybe we should change our name to the 'Pre-Kindergarten Center.' "

Day Care Worker

Studies of preschool experience outside the home can be divided into two major groups: (1) those that examine the effects of educational programs and (2) those that examine the effects of full day care. Such distinctions are somewhat artificial. Day care programs often include educational components, and those that do not formally devote parts of their curriculum to cognitive development still offer stimulation and experience from which young children can learn. Educational programs also offer a range of services, which are sometimes very comprehensive. The distinction between educational and day care programs is one that is not rigid or formal but is often made for convenience.

We will first look at the effects of preschool education programs and their impact on the intellectual development and social and emotional growth of young children. A discussion of the effects of day care will follow.

Effects of Preschool Education Programs

A spirit of social reform characterized early childhood education programs of the 1960s. Preschool programs were established to provide equal educational opportunities for children from low-income and minority backgrounds. Head Start, created in 1965, is the federal government's contribution to these educational programs. As discussed in Chapter 1, it evolved from a concern for educating very young children and from a hope that educational programs would protect children from the dangers of an urban, industrialized society. The television series "Sesame Street" is another expression of this optimistic view of the promise of early intervention.

Although some of the early educators—Comenius, Pestalozzi, Froebel, and Montessori—had worked out their own approach to education and early learning, it was not until the 1960s that early childhood education was designed on a scientific research base. Educational programs were planned using principles of human learning (Bereiter and Engelmann, 1966, is one of the first examples) and theories of the growth of mental capacities and operations (Piaget and his followers were actively involved).

Although early schooling focuses on mental development, its impact is often considered under two general types of outcome: (1) intellectual and (2) social and emotional.[1]

The Department of Health and Human Services often commissions researchers to review the latest early education programs. Copies of these reviews can be obtained from the Administration for Children, Youth, and Families, Washington, D.C. 20201. Another excellent source is the ERIC Clearinghouse on Early Childhood Education, University of Illinois, 805 West Pennsylvania Ave., Urbana, IL 61801

Growth of Intellectual and School-Related Skills   Since 1960, the influence of preschool educational experience on the intellectual growth of young children has been the subject of much research. Educators who review these studies complain justifiably about inadequacies in the design and instruments used. Some of these deficiencies can be attributed to the fact that research in classrooms and schools is so extraordinarily difficult. The results of the research are not entirely consistent, but several reviews of the literature point to some general conclusions that apply to the various studies (Bronfenbrenner, 1974; White, 1973; Lazar et al., 1979; Goodson and Hess, 1978).

Research has focused largely on programs designed to provide special mental and verbal stimulation for young children from low-income homes. The purpose of these programs was to offer children, and sometimes parents, experiences in school-related activities that might enhance achievement in school. These programs were designed with a particular group of families in mind. Their immediate effect was to raise the mental test scores of children who participated. When compared to children from similar backgrounds who were not in such special programs, participants often performed at higher

[1]This discussion does not include the extensive evaluation conducted for the largest program of all, Project Follow Through. Follow Through was developed to continue the special educational resources that Head Start had provided. It has concentrated on the primary grades and thus deals with a level of schooling not considered in this chapter.

levels on letter recognition, ability to label colors, recognition of shapes, ability to count, and the like. Such skills were most likely to appear in programs having specific educational goals and instruction.

Many studies reported that these gains did not last more than a year or two after the children left the program and entered the public schools (Bronfenbrenner, 1974). This "fade out" of gains did not always occur, however. A group of researchers examined the school performance and social behavior of children several years after they had participated in these special programs. They found that children with educationally based preschool experiences showed higher performance in school when compared to other children (Figure 2.2). They were less often retained in grade, were less often assigned to special education classes, and seemed to perform better on achievement tests, including standard IQ measures, than children who did not participate in early intervention programs (Lazar et al., 1979; Weikart et al., 1978).

Social and Emotional Development   Social and emotional behavior are also influenced by educationally based preschool programs, according to follow-up studies. Children adapt better to school, show more interest in school-related tasks, and display greater spontaneity in interaction with adults and other children. They are also less likely to be involved in disciplinary encounters in schools (Lazar et al., 1979; Weikart et al., 1978).

It is difficult to find measures to assess accurately the social and emotional development of young children. Researchers are busy, however, studying these areas of child development, and more precise measures and data may be available soon. The 1960s and early 1970s were a period of concentration on cognitive development; the 1970s and possibly the 1980s may yield significant research on social and emotional development.

Implications of Studies of Preschool Education   Some important ideas about early development have been changed as a result of research on preschool education. Some assumptions that were popular in early Head Start days are no longer tenable. The belief that children from low-income backgrounds or minority families come to school with a linguistic deficit has been discarded. Head Start and the research it stimulated have led to dramatic changes in our thinking on language development.

Educators had also assumed that programs of intervention for preschool children could easily affect mental development and quickly raise the performance level on school-related skills. Some early reports in the 1950s and 1960s suggested that lack of experience with basic school materials and school-related tasks—reading, drawing, scribbling, playing with specially designed materials—was the central educational problem of children from low socioeconomic backgrounds. They needed time to catch up. Head Start was born of this idea and designed as a summer program. It was soon obvious, however, that the impact of poverty and discrimination went much

"No matter how good or expensive the program, schools can't be expected to perform miracles. It should be no surprise that 'enrichment' has to be carried out consistently throughout all aspects of the child's life."

Head Start Director

FIGURE 2.2

Effects of Four Early
Intervention Programs

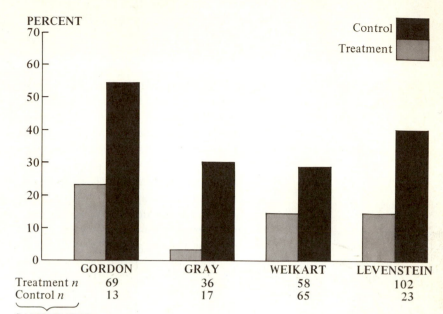

	GORDON	GRAY	WEIKART	LEVENSTEIN
Treatment *n*	69	36	58	102
Control *n*	13	17	65	23

SAMPLE SIZE

This figure shows the results of follow-up studies of several programs begun in the 1960s to facilitate the progress of disadvantaged children in the public schools. The height of the screened bar for each program indicates the percent of participating children who were placed in special education classes at some time during their elementary school years. The solid bars show the percent of children in special education classes of comparable (control) groups who had not been enrolled in intervention programs. Although initial gains in IQ faded after the end of the program, there were long-term positive effects on school performance.

Source: Irving Lazar et al., *Summary Report: Lasting Effects After Preschool*, U.S. Department of Health, Education, and Welfare, Office of Human Development Services, Administration on Children, Youth, and Families (Washington, D.C.: Government Printing Office, 1979), p. 7.

deeper. When it became apparent that summer programs alone were insufficient, Head Start programs were extended to full-year sessions. Convincing proof now exists that no single dimension of any program can deal adequately with educational disadvantage. To achieve real gains there must be a multiplicity of efforts, which include health services, interaction with families, economic support, and community involvement, along with direct instructional services.

The studies previously described reported on programs designed to promote school-related skills; most were conducted by specialists in child development. Attempts have been made to adapt special programs for more general use. One must realize, though, that an innovative program meeting with success in an experimental setting cannot be implemented in other centers like an electric appliance that is purchased and plugged into a socket. A curriculum, in a sense, is what the staff does in interacting with the children. It is not merely a plan described in a manual that sits on the director's desk. A new program, or curriculum plan, is inevitably modified by the style and philosophy of the staff that adopts it. In this process, it may become quite different from the original "successful" program.

Neither the title of a program nor its source of funds describe the curriculum or indicate whether it has the cognitive elements needed to produce gains in school-related skills. Head Start, for example, was intended to provide verbal and cognitive experience, but the term *Head Start* does not reveal what goes on daily in the preschools that operate on Head Start funds.

It is reasonable to say, then, that preschool programs *can* enhance school achievement, but this does not mean that *any* preschool program *will* do so. There is a growing conviction, however, as illustrated by the comments of Edward Zigler (1978), the first director of the Office of Child Development, that preschool programs often have positive effects on mental development.

"The evidence from these projects (evaluations of preschool intervention) allows for but one conclusion: there are long-lasting positive effects from early intervention programs."

Zigler (1978, p. 73)

Effects of Day Care

The second major area of research concerned with preschool experience outside the home examines the effects of full-time day care. Although many day care programs are designed to include educational components, their primary objective is to provide care. Activities intended to promote cognitive growth are sometimes a significant part of the program (and should be), but they may be secondary or omitted completely. Because day care is an experience very different from care by a family member in the child's home, there is a legitimate concern among professionals and parents about its effects on young children.

Studies of day care programs usually deal with one or more of the following questions: (1) What is the effect on intellectual development? (2) How does it affect the relationship between the mother and child (attachment)? and (3) What is its influence on social development?

As mentioned earlier, research on the effects of day care experience generally reports on very young children, rather than three- to five-year-olds.

Intellectual Development   Only a few studies are available on the cognitive outcomes of day care experience, almost too few to use in drawing conclusions. The results of these studies show no differences in measures of intellectual growth among children receiving family day care, center day care, and home care (Bronfenbrenner et al., 1976; Ricciuti, 1976).

Attachment to the Mother   The effect of day care on the relationship between parent and child is currently the focus of a considerable amount of research. The concern about emotional and social development of young children in day care comes in part from the writings of a British psychiatrist, John Bowlby (1969). His theories are based on observations of children who had been placed in institutions as infants as well as on his other clinical experience. He believes that an affective bond or *attachment* to the parents is the most crucial factor in the child's early social and emotional development. Bowlby and some other writers also believe that a lengthy separation of the infant from the mother is likely to make this attachment *insecure*, undermining the child's confidence in the mother as a source of nurture and care.

Children who are insecurely attached may exhibit one of two clusters of behavior. Children in one cluster cling to the mother and experience negative reactions during even brief separations. They express excessive fear of strangers and hesitate to explore new settings. Children who fall into the other cluster show more aggressive behavior; they avoid the mother after a separation, appear to be indifferent, and have little trust or confidence in other caregivers. Interaction with others is often aggressive, uncooperative, and angry, and there is a great deal of exploration in a new environment.

Some writers believe that frequent separations of the child from the mother, as in a full-day child care situation, may damage the child's attachment to the mother. This is most likely to occur during the period when attachment is forming—beginning at about six months and continuing for roughly a year.

Research on the effects of day care experience on attachment between mother and child is not, at this writing, conclusive. Some researchers have reported that children in day care arrangements show negative effects, but other studies report no difference between day care and home-based children (Bronfenbrenner et al., 1976; Portnoy and Simmons, 1978).

"My older child stayed with my parents during his preschool years. I sent the second child to a child care center. I think the second child is more outgoing and flexible than the older one."

Father

Social Development   The real test of the impact of day care is to study its effects on the behavior of children as they move into later periods of development and into new school experiences. We may expect studies that follow children into the primary grades, using their adjustment to the classroom and the teacher as one measure of the influence of early out-of-home child care. Some follow-up work has already been done. In the most comprehensive study reported to date, Schwarz and associates (1974) describe the school behavior of two groups of nineteen three- to four-year-olds with varying levels of day care experience in social and motivational areas. Nineteen children who had been placed in group care at about nine months of age were compared to nineteen children from similar backgrounds who had received care at home. At the time of the study, the home-reared children had just been enrolled in a day care center for the first time.

Compared to the home-reared children, the day care group was more aggressive, physically and verbally, toward both peers and adults. They

"My daughter has become aggressive and demanding since she started attending the center. I'd like to complain, but there's a waiting list and they wouldn't care if I left."

Parent

engaged in more running around and were generally less cooperative. Day care children interacted more with peers and spent more time in the large-muscle activities and less in expressive and cognitive areas of the center. Other studies support these findings and suggest that day care children tend to be more aggressive and assertive, less conforming than children with little or no day care experience (Raph et al., 1968; Lippman and Grote, 1974).

Some children seem especially resilient in responding to new experience and separation from the mother. The ease with which children adjust to change may be influenced by their relationship with their parents before the new experience began. Heinicke et al. (1973) describe an "adaptation syndrome"—the ability to move comfortably into new relationships and experiences. In their view, children who display this syndrome have more positive relationships with their parents.

"I think I've been lucky because my son has had the same teacher for three years at the children's center. He hasn't had to adjust to new teachers or different settings like most of the other children."

Mother

Another aspect of assessing the impact of a program is the degree to which the program is flexible or structured. Prescott and her associates (1973) found that children in open programs were more active physically; those in closed situations were more compliant.

"I hope that someday when I have children of my own, I won't have to leave them in a center like the one I work in."

Student Teacher

It may be that day care is so much affected by the behavior of each center's staff that no safe generalizations can be made. Recent studies (Hess et al., 1979; Hess et al., 1980; Kagan, 1976; Winetsky, 1978) suggest that child care staffs are more permissive than parents, tolerate more aggression, and are less likely to urge self-control. Some of the reported findings regarding aggressive behavior may be a reflection of staff standards and not a result of the separation of the child from the mother.

HELPING PARENTS ADJUST TO CHILD CARE

"I know my child is better off with his teachers than with me. They have training, experience, and PATIENCE!"

Mother

Teachers of young children will often be called on to deal with concerns of parents like Marianne. Here is a mother who feels guilty about leaving her child, who, if given a choice, would choose to take care of Jon herself rather than entrust him to a caregiver. Is Marianne hurting Jonathan by leaving him with someone else? Is there good reason for her to feel the experience might be harmful?

"One of the best things I ever did was to design a brochure with a section that discusses parents' feelings—some of their most common questions, and a list of helpful suggestions. Some parents tell me they read the booklet and refer to it frequently just for reassurance."

Director

The answers are not simple. But there are some things the teacher should keep in mind. The parent's frame of mind is of great importance. How parents feel about themselves, their jobs, their relationships to others—their general sense of well-being and optimism about the world—all these influence the way in which they approach the experience of leaving their children in someone else's care. Young children can sense their parents' attitude. Parental behavior can leave a child feeling either uncertain or confident. It is healthier for parents and teachers to convey to a child that their situation is an unavoidable fact of life ("Mother goes to work; Jon goes to school").

Marianne's wishes and regrets are not useful feelings, since neither Jon nor his mother can do anything about their situation.

Sometimes this means parents must force themselves to act as if they are comfortable with the decision to leave their children. The parents' words, tone of voice, body language, and actions give a message that they know what is best for parent and child. Their choice is deliberate, considered, and confident. They reassure the child matter-of-factly that they will be back and then go on with their commitments. This confident attitude is more helpful to a child and the teacher than one that causes confusion and sadness. The attitudes of the parent give meaning to the experience of preschool and day care.

How the parent and child feel about the center and the caregivers also plays a role. If the child likes the teacher and looks forward to school and if the parent genuinely supports the program and likes what the staff is doing, chances are that the experience will be a useful one for both parent and child.

But what if Marianne could stay home with Jon? Would this be better for him than the child care center? We can only be certain it would be different. She would be spending more time with him. His social experiences would probably be limited to fewer children. He would be playing on different kinds of outdoor equipment under different circumstances, or he might watch TV much of the day. The point is that the home and center offer different things and Jon's experiences, whatever they are, will influence his development.

REFERENCES

Bereiter, C., and S. Engelmann. 1966. *Teaching Disadvantaged Children in the Preschool.* Englewood Cliffs, N.J.: Prentice-Hall.

Bowlby, J. 1969. *Attachment.* Attachment and Loss, Vol. 1. New York: Basic Books.

Bronfenbrenner, U. 1974. *Is Early Intervention Effective? A Report on Longitudinal Evaluations of Preschool Programs.* Vol. 2. U.S. Department of Health, Education, and Welfare, Office of Child Development. Washington, D.C.: Government Printing Office.

Bronfenbrenner, U., J. Belsky, and L. Steinberg. 1976. "Day Care in Context: An Ecological Perspective on Research and Public Policy." Unpublished paper. Washington, D.C.: U.S. Department of Health, Education, and Welfare.

Brown, B., ed. 1978. *Found: Long-Term Gains from Early Intervention.* Boulder, Colo.: Westview Press.

Gold, D., and D. Andress. 1978. "Developmental Comparisons Between Ten-Year-Old Children with Employed and Nonemployed Mothers." *Child Development,* 49, 75–84.

Goodson, B. D., and R. D. Hess. 1978. "The Effects of Parent Training Programs on Child Performance and Behavior." In *Found: Long-Term Gains from Early Intervention.* Ed. B. Brown. Boulder, Colo.: Westview Press.

Heinicke, C. M., F. Busch, P. Click, and E. Kramer. 1973. "Parent-Child Relations, Adaptation to Nursery School, and the Child's Task Orientation: A Contrast in the Development of Two Girls." In *Individual Differences in Children*. Ed. J. C. Westman. New York: Wiley Intersciences.

Hess, R. D., W. P. Dickson, G. G. Price, and D. Leong. 1979. "Some Contrasts Between Mothers and Child Care Staff in Interaction with Four-Year-Old Children." *American Educational Research Journal,* 16, 307–316.

Hess, R. D., G. G. Price, W. P. Dickson, and M. Conroy. 1980. "Different Roles for Mothers and Teachers: Contrasting Styles of Child Care." In *Advances in Early Education and Child Development*. Ed. S. Kilmer. Greenwich, Conn.: Johnson Associates.

Hetherington, E. M., M. Cox, and R. Cox, 1978. "Family Interaction and the Social, Emotional, and Cognitive Development of Children Following Divorce." Paper prepared for the Symposium on the Family: Setting Priorities, May 1978. Washington, D.C.: Institute for Pediatric Service (Johnson & Johnson Baby Company).

Hoffman, L. W. 1974. "Effects of Maternal Employment on the Child: A Review of the Research." *Developmental Psychology,* 10, 204–228.

Kagan, J. 1976. "The Effect of Day Care on the Infant." Unpublished paper. Washington, D.C.: U.S. Department of Health, Education, and Welfare.

Lazar, I., V. R. Hubbell, H. Murray, M. Rosche, and J. Royce. 1977. *Summary Report: The Persistence of Preschool Effects*. U.S. Department of Health, Education, and Welfare, Office of Human Development Services, Administration on Children, Youth, and Families. Washington, D.C.: Government Printing Office.

Lippman, M. A., and B. H. Grote. 1974. *Socio-emotional Effects of Day Care: Final Project Report*. Washington, D.C.: Office of Child Development.

Portnoy, F. C., and C. H. Simmons. 1978. "Day Care and Attachment." *Child Development,* 49, 234–242.

Prescott, E., E. Jones, S. Kritchevsky, C. Molich, and E. Hasselhoef. 1973. "Who Thrives in Day Care?" Part 2 of final report *Assessment of Child Rearing Environments: An Ecological Approach*. U.S. Department of Health, Education, and Welfare, Office of Child Development, Children's Bureau. Washington, D.C.: Government Printing Office.

Raph, J. B., A. Thomas, S. Chess, and S. J. Corn. 1968. "The Influence of Nursery School on Social Interactions." *Journal of Orthopsychiatry,* 38, 144–152.

Ricciuti, H. N. 1976. "Effects of Infant Day Care Experience on Behavior and Development: Research and Implications for Social Policy." Unpublished paper. Washington, D.C.: U.S. Department of Health, Education, and Welfare.

Schwarz, J., R. Strickland, and G. Krolick. 1974. "Infant Day Care: Behavioral Effects at Preschool Age." *Developmental Psychology,* 10, 502–506.

U.S. Department of Commerce, Bureau of the Census. 1976. *Status: A Monthly Chartbook of Social and Economic Trends,* October 1976. Washington, D.C.: Government Printing Office.

U.S. Department of Health, Education, and Welfare. 1977. *Policy Issues in Day Care: Summaries of Twenty-One Papers*. Washington, D.C.: Government Printing Office.

Weikart, D. P., A. S. Epstein, L. Schweinhart, and J. T. Bond. 1978. *The Ypsilanti Preschool Curriculum Demonstration Project: Preschool Years and Longitudinal*

Results. Monographs of the High/Scope Educational Research Foundation, No. 4. Ypsilanti, Mich.: High/Scope Educational Research Foundation.

White, S. H. 1973. *Review of Evaluation Data for Federally Sponsored Projects for Children*. Federal Programs for Young Children: Review and Recommendations, Vol. 2. Cambridge, Mass.: The Huron Institute.

Winetsky, C. S. 1978. "Comparisons of the Expectations of Parents and Teachers for the Behavior of Preschool Children." *Child Development,* 49, 1146–1154.

Zigler, E. 1978. "The Effectiveness of Head Start: Another Look." *Educational Psychologist,* 13, 71–78.

CHAPTER 3

TRAINING AND CAREER OPPORTUNITIES

PROGRAMS OF TRAINING

The first time you visited a child care center or early education classroom, could you tell who was head teacher, assistant, or volunteer? Most preschool programs are designed around team teaching, requiring cooperative interaction among staff members. The training and duties of each adult may not be clear to the casual observer, but there are certain roles each must fill.

Preschool and child care certification requirements are not uniform. There are a number of ways to qualify for jobs in early education. Qualifications for a head teacher, for example, may differ from the training needed to become a director. Can an assistant teacher with an associate's degree be promoted to a director's position? What courses must child care workers complete in order to qualify for their work? To answer these questions, let's examine a typical training pattern for various professional steps in early education.

In New York, a child care center head teacher must be at least 21 years old, have a high school diploma, and teaching experience.

In North Dakota, a teacher in a child care center must be at least 16 years old, be able to read and write, and have some training or demonstrated ability in working with children.

Figure 3.1 shows some common training levels in early childhood education. These levels are not rigidly defined. An individual who wants to start a school can, in many locales, meet the necessary requirements with a certificate of completion that includes a course in administration and supervision. A teacher with an Associate of Arts (A.A.) degree from a community college might qualify for a director's position. Job qualifications are flexible and depend a great deal on the standards of the hiring agency. Each state and local district has its own regulations governing degree requirements, unit hours of supervised practicum, years of experience, and transfer credits. If you are taking courses to fulfill certain local guidelines but plan to seek employment in another state, you should inquire about requirements of agencies in the area of your choice. The hiring facility, local college, or licensing agency will provide such information.

Degree programs and classes leading to a certificate of completion or proficiency are offered in several different departments. In some colleges, these courses are listed under psychology, education, home economics, arts and sciences, humanities, or child development. Courses often are available in a number of related areas:

Child Development or Psychology
Language Development
Child, Family, and Community
Nursery School Theory and Practice
Methods and Materials in Early Childhood
Early Learning
Children's Speech Arts
Children's Literature
Educational Psychology
Observation of Preschool Children

Fundamentals of Testing
Personality Development
Supervision and Administration
Infant-Toddler Development
Practicum in Early Childhood
Education of the Exceptional Child

Two-year programs for training in nursery school or preschool teaching are offered by many community and junior colleges. Credit is given for courses that satisfy the requirements of an Associate of Arts degree. The course content of these programs overlaps to some extent with programs in four-year colleges and universities.

FIGURE 3.1
Personnel Training Levels in Early Childhood Education

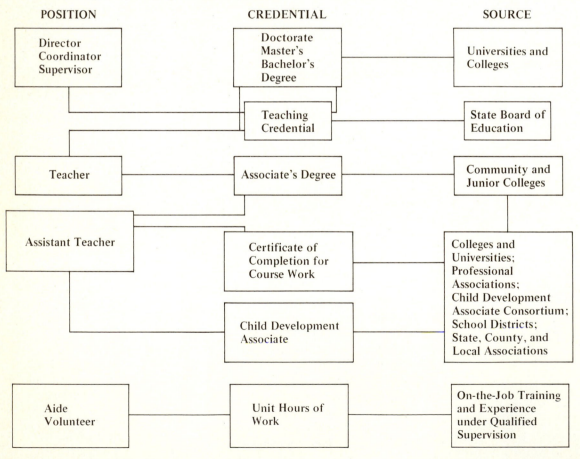

Colleges and extension divisions of many universities offer night school and home study courses leading to professional upgrading. Programs of early education designed with a prescribed number of units can, on completion, qualify a person for a children's center permit or some other certificate required by the licensing agency. Workshops and evening, weekend, and summer programs offered by professional associations and school districts also make continuing education possible. Such training usually includes a certificate of completion.

CERTIFICATION AND LICENSING REQUIREMENTS

Degrees or certificates do not automatically qualify one for employment as a teacher. Work in public school kindergartens and in many of the supervisory positions in preschool programs also requires credentials. Through separate boards of education, the various states issue teaching credentials based on a variety of requirements. Two of the prerequisites usually required are: (1) a degree from an accredited institution and (2) certain combinations of major and minor course work. Some states further require that without a fifth year in education at upper division or graduate level, plus practice teaching, only a provisional credential will be issued for a limited period of time.

The latest information for each state is available in "Certification Requirements and Administration" in *Early Childhood Education Programs: A State Survey*. Write to Education Commission of the States, 300 Lincoln Tower, 1860 Lincoln St., Denver, CO 80203.

Private and public nursery schools and other early education programs are often licensed to operate under the supervision of a state or other controlling agency. It is usually not necessary to hold teaching credentials to be hired as a teacher or assistant teacher in these programs. However, individuals seeking positions will have to meet educational and experience standards set by one or any combination of the following groups:

State licensing agency
County licensing agency
City licensing agency
Business licensing agency
School district
Individual owner
Administration of Children, Youth, and Families

"I have seen teachers with many years of experience who have not learned how to create positive environments for children. Training is *essential!*"

University Professor

Examples of some typical educational and experience requirements for teachers in early childhood education programs are given in Table 3.1. Nursery schools are not usually part of public educational systems. Kindergartens frequently are an integral part of the public school system, and teachers at this level must meet the same professional requirements as elementary school teachers.

TABLE 3.1
Requirements for Teachers in Early Childhood Education Programs

Directors and/or Head Teachers	Teachers and Assistant Teachers
At least 21 years of age	At least 18 years of age
University or college degree with emphasis on course work in early childhood education	At least 24 semester units of course work in early childhood education
From 1 to 4 years teaching experience in early education	At least 3 hours experience per day for 100 days in a calendar year under qualified supervision
Either 6 semester units or the equivalent in administration and/or staff relations	

"Experience should be emphasized as much as academic training. I've seen 'specialists' with master's degrees in early childhood education who didn't know the first thing about working with kids!"

Principal

For more information, write to: Child Development Associate Consortium, Division of Educational Services, Program Development Division, Administration of Children, Youth, and Families, P.O. Box 1182, Washington, DC 20013.

In many states, there is more than one way to qualify as an early childhood teacher or assistant teacher. In addition to approved university or college programs, recognition may be awarded for demonstrated on-the-job competence. Many states and licensing agencies are beginning to look at performance-based certification, which enables competent people to qualify for a teaching position through a variety of routes, such as special examinations or assessment of classroom performance.

The Child Development Associate (CDA) is a credential awarded to individuals who fulfill certain performance-based competencies and who may not have the traditional college training. There are many people who, through experience and attendance at noncredit workshops, seminars, and on-the-job training, are qualified to assume the responsibilities of working directly with three- to five-year-olds and their parents. As a result, a performance-based system of assessment was devised by representatives from early childhood education organizations, and the first twelve CDA credentials were awarded in 1975. By 1978, the number had grown to 3,470 (Hymes, 1979).

CAREER OPPORTUNITIES

Prospective teachers often ask, "How will I know if I can get a good job after I graduate?," "Will my training prepare me to work with young children?," and "What kinds of jobs are available?"

As the need for quality child care increases, so will the demand for better trained teachers. Those who are well prepared will be in a position to attract higher salaries. Even now, many jobs are open only to those who qualify for children's center permits, or who have at least an associate's degree in early education.

As requirements are raised, licensing or funding agencies will no longer allow employers to hire a teacher without minimum training. Parent groups also press for trained teachers who understand the needs of their children

"I was recently laid off my job as a third grade teacher, so I decided to start my own nursery school. I was surprised to learn I would have to take 30 units of course work in early education before I could qualify."

Unemployed Teacher

and who know how to plan for physical, emotional, social, and mental development.

Knowing there are jobs available is not enough. There are many different kinds of jobs for teachers of young children. In order to avoid disappointment and failure, it is important to learn about the possibilities that the field offers. Awareness of the different kinds of jobs, the responsibilities involved, and the training needed will help you establish more realistic goals in seeking employment.

Types of Schools

"I can't stress enough the importance of getting students to go out to visit schools and centers. Everyone should be required to work in a variety of settings during the training period."

Instructor

"I knew nothing about orthopedically handicapped children until I was assigned to work with Robbie. The day he finally stood up and walked across the mat to me had to be the most rewarding experience of my training. I shall cherish that moment forever."

Student Teacher

Questions about job opportunities do not have simple answers. Perhaps the best way to become acquainted with opportunities, benefits, and salaries is to consider the various types of child care arrangements available. A visit to centers and schools can be very enlightening. Training institutions often make arrangements for students to visit and work in a variety of community-based schools and centers.

Many people who are interested in working with young children are uncertain about the specific kind of work they want to do and know little about the opportunities available. But knowledge can lead to more realistic expectations. For example, working in a center with children of migrant families is quite different from being on the staff of a parent co-op: working conditions, hours, training requirements, and pay vary greatly.

One way to learn about the wide variety of existing child care programs is to look through the listings in the telephone directory and local newspapers. Programs operate under many different names. A sample of titles is given in Table 3.2.

TABLE 3.2
Types of Early Childhood Education Programs

Nursery	Day Nursery	Adult Education Preschool
Nursery Home	Cooperative Nursery School	Parish School
Nursery Kindergarten	Real Life Nursery School	Preschool Learning Center
Nursery and Kindergarten	Infant Nursery	Neighborhood Center
Nursery and Preschool	School	Children's Center
Nursery School	Day School	Education Center
Church Nursery School	Community Center School	Child Care Center
Church Co-op Nursery School	Play School	U.S. Govt. Navy Dept. Child Care Center
Temple Nursery	Preschool and Kindergarten	Parent-Child Group
Archdiocesan Opportunity Program	Church Preschool	Head Start Program
Parent's Community Co-op Nursery School	Preschool Training	Infants Day Care Home
Community Association Nursery School	Christian School	Day Home for Infants

Advertisements accompanying the listings frequently emphasize the "courteous" trained and/or certified staff; the provision of snacks and hot meals; availability of private transportation; half-day or full-day sessions both summer and winter; academic, social, artistic, physical, and character development as well as expert supervision and guidance; "structured programs" and "nonpermissive progressive programs." A few of the schools promise language training (usually French, German, or Spanish). Also mentioned are phonics and field trips. When the facilities themselves are described, it is in terms such as *separate buildings, shaded,* and *well-equipped play yard*. Groups that have full-day programs frequently make a special appeal to working mothers. The names and even the descriptions often supply insufficient information about the school and what the teachers actually do.

Schools do not fall neatly into specific categories according to their philosophies or purposes. It is more helpful to consider the following features of schools:

1. length of the program (number of hours in operation)
2. service offered (full-day care so parents can work, etc.)
3. number and ages of children
4. background of families
5. training requirements for staff
6. staff-to-children ratio

Sources of funds also give clues about opportunities for salary advancement.

Even if you know very little about program philosophies, you can learn a great deal by observing and asking a few questions. Let's suppose you visit the Maplewood Place Nursery and Preschool. Their ad in the yellow pages of the telephone directory promises "acquisition of social and artistic skills with an emphasis on school readiness." When you visit, you learn from the owner/director that they enroll twenty three- to four-year-olds in the morning program (from 9:00–11:30); the afternoon session (from 12:30–3:00) enrolls eighteen children ages four and one-half to six. You observe that each session has two teachers in addition to the owner. During the morning, the children engage in free-play activities—moving from art easels, play dough, books, blocks, and music to outdoor climbing, sand play, and carpentry. They are not required to participate in any particular activity and can choose to do whatever they want. During the afternoon, children are required to participate in teacher-directed group activities—learning numbers, colors, shapes, and other school-related skills.

How can you use this information to make some inferences about working conditions? What would it be like to teach in such a setting?

The Maplewood Place Nursery and Preschool is privately owned, so the major source of income must be from tuition. If you picked up their advertising brochure and list of tuition costs, you can get a good idea of gross

"If your college doesn't have arrangements to work in other centers, by all means, get on the phone and make your own!"

Student

"A group of us got together and researched other noncenter opportunities. We discovered a need for child care for stewardesses, for hospital workers, and for others who are called on short notice. A group of electronics companies indicated an interest in sharing the costs of child care for their workers."

Graduate Student

income by multiplying the monthly tuition by number of children enrolled in each program. Although you will not know the exact monthly costs for rent, supplies, and so forth, you can make some fairly accurate estimates to help determine what amounts are available for staff salaries.

Since the school offers half-day programs rather than full-day sessions, you can assume most of the children come from families who can afford to have at least one parent or caregiver at home. The location of the school and the types of homes in the neighborhood tell you something about the socio-economic level of its clients. The primary function of the program is probably geared toward middle-class families who want to enrich the lives of their children through a socially and educationally oriented curriculum. Teaching in such a program could mean working part-time hours, teaching children from fairly homogeneous backgrounds, and starting at a level close to minimum hourly wage. Assuming the owner/director is available to help with teaching and clean-up chores, the ratio is fairly comfortable and would allow a teacher to plan and carry out a workable curriculum.

Figure 3.2 illustrates how a funded child care center might provide information in its brochure. How would working in this facility differ from the Maplewood Place school? What should you ask about or watch for in a

FIGURE 3.2
Sample Brochure for Funded Child Care Center

> **Supervision • Instruction • Care**
>
> **for**
>
> **Two- to Five-Year-Old Children**
>
> **WHO?**   Families who qualify under the requirements of the state legislature. Fees are based on family income and number of children in the family.
>
> **WHAT?**   1. Experiences for children that will stimulate exploration, discovery, and learning.
> 2. Nutritionally balanced noon meal and two snacks per day.
> 3. Rest period after the noon meal.
>
> **WHEN?**   The Center is open from 7 a.m. to 6 p.m.
>
> **HOW?**   A staff of teachers, aides, and volunteers working in close contact with small groups of children.

JOB INFORMATION HELPFUL TO YOU

Primary function of the school
Number of hours school is in session
Ratio of teachers to children
Ages of children
Background of families served
Philosophy of the program
Program content
Sponsorship (source of funds)
Salary/fringe benefits
Opportunities for advancement
Inservice training available or required
Average length of service of present employees
Reputation of the school in the community

---

visit to help make a more accurate judgment about job opportunities and work satisfaction?

Working Conditions

The reason a school is in business and the functions it serves affect salaries and working conditions. Full-day child care facilities, for example, usually exist to provide a substitute home for children whose parents must work. Their curricula may be designed to help children acquire social and academic skills, but the hours of operation tell you that their schedules are oriented toward the needs of the parents they serve. A teacher in such a situation will probably be working longer hours than in a private half-day school.

"You have to learn to pace yourself to survive the long day. You can't 'shoot your wad' all at once without risking boredom and burn-out."

Child Care Worker

The children's ages and energy levels will have an important effect on the curriculum. Timing and pacing of activities must be adjusted to the abilities of the children and length of the program. Cognitively oriented activities are often presented in the morning; naps and quieter activities are scheduled in the afternoon.

No matter what the setting, the function, or sources of income of a child care program, it is possible to use available information to plan a comfortably paced program suited to the needs of the children, their parents, and the teaching skills of the staff. Knowing the primary reason for the existence of a school helps the prospective teacher assess probable working conditions.

Sponsorship: Sources of Funds

In descriptions of preschool programs, the term *sponsorship* usually refers to fiscal control—who provides the money, pays the bills, and sets policy about how funds are used. This is important information for a teacher, not only because it affects salary and benefits, but also because the policies of the school are tied to the philosophy and regulations of the sponsor.

The terms *sponsor* and *owner* are easily confused. A sponsor may also be the owner as in the case of a parent co-op or private school. But a sponsoring agency may provide funds for a program to help operate a school it does not own. For example, a school owned by a local district may obtain funds from the state for a special program in bilingual education.

Table 3.3 summarizes a number of ways early education facilities differ in sponsorship. Income sources and funding requirements provide clues about opportunities for raises and job duration. Funds that come through public school districts offer positions that are protected by tenure and that get automatic salary increases. Experimental programs may be subject to review on a yearly basis and may be discontinued with short notice.

The programs listed in Table 3.3 have public or private sponsorship.

TABLE 3.3
Different Forms of Sponsorship

Sponsor (Owner)	Distinguishing Features
Public	
Federal or state agency such as Office of Economic Opportunity; Department of Health and Human Services; State Department of Welfare; or State Department of Education	Funds allocated by Congress or state legislatures Program developers and supervisors may be quite remote from schools themselves May be experimental programs on a year-to-year basis Programs exceedingly varied, including those of compensatory education
Local agency such as a neighborhood council, community service organization, or welfare agency	Primarily day care centers in low-income areas May also include schools providing services to special groups such as retarded, handicapped, etc.
Private	
Individual or group	A small school operated by a single owner or a large enterprise with absentee owners who leave running of the school to a professional director and a staff
Religious group	May use church personnel for staffing and have secular emphasis, or may simply permit use of church facilities
Parents' cooperative	Parents hire professional director and then serve as assistants on a rotating basis with regularly scheduled meetings for families

In 1979 a family of four was considered "poor" if they earned no more than $7370 per year.

Department of Commerce

Some states impose heavy restrictions on infant-toddler programs, requiring medical supervision and a much higher staff-child ratio. Operating costs for such programs are much higher than those for older preschool children.

In 1967, there were 34,700 licensed centers and homes; in 1975, there were 115,900.

Generally, publicly funded programs have policies that require limiting enrollment to qualified families—often those designated as "poor." Church-sponsored programs may require that member families receive preference. Private schools are selective by virtue of the fees they charge and the limited number of hours they operate. For co-ops, the requirement that parents actively participate on a regular basis is a limiting factor for some families.

There are also infant-toddler facilities used as training programs in high schools and colleges and in communities with a heavy concentration of parents who work. Sometimes these youngsters (age range about three months to two years) are housed in quarters that are separate from older children. There must also be a higher ratio of trained teachers to infants and toddlers. In some cases, infant-toddler facilities are sponsored by city, state, or federal agencies; in others, they are funded by industry, or they may be owned and operated in private homes.

In communities where tax-supported programs are on the decline, teachers will find an increasing demand for private child care services. Home day care is a good source of self-employment for those who want the satisfaction of providing a warm home environment for young children.

Salaries, Benefits, and Advancement

"Dear Mrs. W., Remember you used to tell us not to work for low wages? Well, I just got a job in a preschool at $2000 a month."

Teacher (Barrow, Alaska)

Wages for nursery school teachers and child care workers traditionally have been low. Often, pay is close to minimum hourly rates with limited opportunities for raises. With such constraints on teaching salaries, you might ask if working with young children is likely to promise some financial security.

Salary levels will differ in organizations of varying size and structure. Schools supported by public funds will probably be able to offer better salaries. In centers operating within public boards of education, the salary structure will be similar from center to center and may be higher than a private school can afford to pay. In addition, fringe benefits—insurance, retirement, sick leave, and vacations with pay—will sometimes be better in a larger organization. Some schools, both public and private, may also pay tuition for teachers who want to take courses or workshops that give both inservice training and course credit.

Larger systems may offer better opportunities for advancement. A teacher working for an owner/director in a small private school has no promotion possibilities. A related concern is the job protection offered by different schools. A teacher in a private school may be more vulnerable to dismissal, but a publicly funded program can be eliminated when funds run out. Personnel policies of larger systems may make it difficult for a teacher to be fired. However, it may also mean that less competent teachers are retained because of the relatively greater difficulty involved in establishing grounds for dismissal.

MAKING A JOB DECISION

Suppose you are applying for a teaching position and you acquire the following charts showing the administrative organization of three different schools. How can this information be helpful in your decision on a job? What are some of the implications of these organizational structures for your role and success as a teacher?

One of the things you may be interested in knowing is how much you will be able to influence policies of the school such as the curriculum plan, choice of equipment, admission criteria, teacher role and responsibilities, and procedures for interacting with parents.

Figure 3.3 shows that in owner-operated schools the teacher is in direct contact with the person who decides how the program will operate. In larger organizations the teacher is further removed from those who make policies. For example, in the organizational structure for the children's center in Figure 3.3, the teacher can assume that policies are likely to be established by distant groups. A number of people, such as the district board members, the superintendent, and others shown in the illustration, participate in decisions that affect the teacher. Such decisions, once made, may be particularly difficult to change.

In a parent participation program, the same parents who sit on the board of directors are likely to be working alongside the teacher in the classroom. Both teachers and parents formulate policies and share in cooperative decision making.

In small organizations, the tasks of each teacher tend to vary from day to day. He or she will be responsible for a wide range of activities and will have few colleagues to assist in teaching. In a more complex organization, the teacher's tasks are likely to be more specific. There will be more team planning, interdependence, and possibly less flexibility in scheduling. The team teacher will share responsibility for decisions, whereas the teacher in a small school will exercise more autonomy and be responsible for making more decisions alone.

How does a teacher make the best choice? Satisfaction in a job will depend to a great degree on two factors: The people with whom you work, and the structure and organization of the school. As you volunteer in or visit schools where you are likely to work, try to determine the kinds of satisfaction that the staff derive from the different aspects of their roles. To what extent are their feelings of discontent or of satisfaction derived from their work with their colleagues? In what ways do you see yourself fitting into such a role? Perhaps sharing responsibility and trying to please many "bosses," as in a parent participation program, feels less comfortable and efficient to you than making decisions on your own. You may prefer to work with a director who spells out exactly what is expected of you. Or, you may find that you are happiest when you can be flexible and operate in a loosely defined structure.

"I like to work in a school where I am able to participate in decision making. I don't like to be surprised with new policies and rules that are developed without input from the staff."

Assistant Teacher

"Cooperative decision making is more democratic, but, oh, so time consuming!"

Director

"The profession of Early Childhood Education isn't one problem after another. The field offers many deep satisfactions. One solid satisfaction is the chance to work in a still unsettled, expanding field where there is much work to be done. Early Childhood Education is a good field for activists. It offers everyone the real possibility of contributing to the solution of problems."

James L. Hymes, Jr.

FIGURE 3.3
Organizational Structure of Three Different Types of Early Education Units

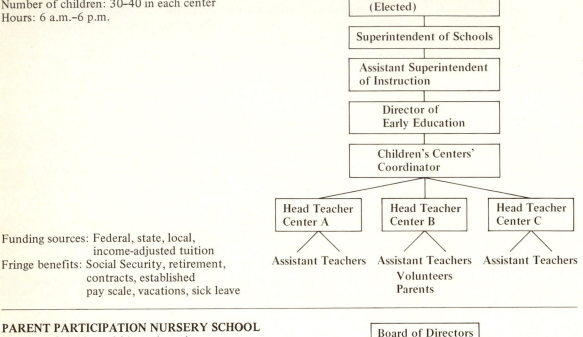

CHILDREN'S CENTER
Number of children: 30–40 in each center
Hours: 6 a.m.–6 p.m.

Funding sources: Federal, state, local,
           income-adjusted tuition
Fringe benefits: Social Security, retirement,
           contracts, established
           pay scale, vacations, sick leave

PARENT PARTICIPATION NURSERY SCHOOL
Number of children: 24 in each session
Hours: 9–12 a.m. morning session
      1–4 p.m. afternoon session

Funding sources: Tuition, state A.D.A.
           for adult education, donations
Fringe benefits: Social Security, sick leave

PRIVATE NURSERY SCHOOL
Number of children: 24 in each class
Hours: 9–11:30 a.m.

Funding sources: Tuition
Fringe benefits: Social Security

HOW TO GET THE MOST OUT OF
PRACTICE TEACHING

1. *Be clear about your expectations.* You are there to learn. Don't be shy about trying new techniques and making mistakes. Let your supervisor know through words and actions that you expect to be given responsibilities and feedback that will enable you to learn.

2. *Ask questions.* Don't be afraid of sounding ignorant. You are there to learn. When work schedules do not permit time for questions, you may need to arrange to arrive early, stay late, or write your questions and submit them to your supervisor.

3. *Use your best judgment.* When faced with uncertain situations, use your best judgment and ask for clarification of rules later.

4. *Be professional.* Arrive on time; be prepared to work. Let your supervisor know your schedule and the times you can be expected to be at school. Call if you are late or absent. Offer to make up the time.

5. *Respect the teacher's need to give first priority to the children and parents.* The teacher may not have time to take you on a guided tour. Use your time—observe, get to know the children, and study the environment. Familiarize yourself with locations of toilets and fire exits, and look to see where equipment is kept. Study the daily routine.

6. *Look for a need and fill it.* Make a mental note of the times a teacher might appreciate your assistance. Offer to redirect children, plan a project, hold a restless child on your lap, or simply step in to free the teacher for something else. Don't wait to be asked.

7. *Make yourself a welcome addition to the staff.* Schools are busy places. Don't wait for others to make you feel welcome. Learn the names of children, parents, and members of the staff. Smile; be friendly. Your job is to fit in quickly and be of help. Do your share—and more.

8. *Contribute something positive to the school.* Look for ways in which you can help improve the school: suggesting a new curriculum idea, repairing a piece of equipment, leaving something that will be appreciated.

9. *Model yourself after effective teachers.* Watch good teachers interact with parents and children. Listen to what they say and watch how they behave. Adapt their styles to your own.

10. *Avoid socializing with other adults.* Supervising teachers sometimes complain that students just "stand around and talk to each other" even when they have been assigned to specific areas to observe or supervise. Even when children are playing happily, stay alert for potential problems.

11. *Avoid staff politics.* Do not get involved in the problems of staff members. Taking sides may close off opportunities for you to learn.

12. *Withhold judgment about the school and staff.* Don't jump to conclusions about "good" or "bad" teaching. A few short visits can be misleading. Keep an open mind. The techniques you have learned in lab school or have read about in a book may not work in every situation.

13. *Learn from your experiences.* Replay in your mind the things you did that were effective. Ask for evaluations and suggestions for how you can improve.

Whatever your preference, think about different roles in relation to yourself when you talk with teachers and work in different settings. What didn't you like and why? If you become more aware of the separate sources of satisfaction, you will not only be better able to decide where you would like to work, but you will also be more effective in dealing with problems on the job and increasing your feelings of competence and satisfaction. A decision based on such knowledge will reduce the risks that are inherent in committing yourself to a job.

REFERENCES

Croft, D. J. 1976. *Be Honest with Yourself*. Belmont, Calif.: Wadsworth Publishing Company.

Hymes, J. L., Jr. 1968. *Early Childhood Education: An Introduction to the Profession*. Washington, D.C.: National Association for the Education of Young Children.

————. 1979. *Early Childhood Education, the Year in Review: A Look at 1978*. Carmel, Calif.: Hacienda Press.

Lorber, M. 1978. "Regulation—A Challenge to All NAEYC Members." *Young Children*, 33 (March), 13–14.

Sciarra, D. J., and A. G. Dorsey. 1979. *Developing and Administering a Child Care Center*. Boston: Houghton Mifflin Company.

Stevens, J. H., Jr., and E. W. King. 1976. *Administering Early Childhood Education Programs*. Boston: Little, Brown and Company.

Tarnay, E. D. 1965. *What Does the Nursery School Teacher Teach?* Washington, D.C.: National Association for the Education of Young Children.

Ward, E. H. 1976. "The Child Development Associate Consortium's Assessment System." *Young Children*, 31 (May), 244–254.

PART TWO

PREPARING TO TEACH
IN THE CLASSROOM

A PROLOGUE   "Start where the child is!" You will hear that command many times. What does it mean?

First, where the child "is" can mean the level of skill, ability, and information that each brings to a particular task. There is no need to teach things the child already knows, and concepts that are too advanced will only cause confusion.

There is another meaning to this first commandment of early education: children come to the preschool from very diverse backgrounds. Each child brings a unique culture—a history of personal experience that may include fun, stress, abuse, or warmth. Some parents have time and resources to select the best school they can find; others choose a program because it is the center nearest to home. Some parents pick up their children after a full day's work; others are unemployed. One child is from a family that owns the bank; another lives on welfare.

The inner world of the child reflects the social reality of the home. To begin where the child is, we must understand something of his or her life outside the center.

Children differ from each other in many ways. Sit in on a "show and tell" session to see the different levels of information and skill they display. A precocious two-year-old relates in detail how she and her family went on a trip. Another child, the same age, may be uttering only a few unclear phrases. Learning is an individual act; no teacher can learn for a child. It is not a matter of imprinting words on the blank spaces of the child's mind, nor a technique by which the teacher tucks away in the child's memory little bits and pieces of information to be taken off the shelf when needed. When children learn, they construct and reconstruct their internal worlds. The new things they feel, hear, and see are fitted into patterns that are already in place. This inner framework of experience is shaped, in part, through play, but almost all activity is a source of learning for the young child. The distinction between play and work is something imposed on children by the adult world.

The teacher's role is to prepare appropriate experiences—a curriculum—to match the child's internal patterns. Actually, we might think of not one but several curricula. One is the *prepared curriculum*—the materials, activities, and ideas that the teacher organizes in advance for the class. Another is the *hidden curriculum*—the subtle attitudes and values that we teach, perhaps unintentionally. There is also an *absent curriculum*—the things that we decide *not* to teach have an effect by their absence.

Teaching and learning are not inseparable. Children learn without being taught; teaching activities can go on when no learning is taking place. But effective teaching must match the internal processes in the child's mind.

This section introduces you to the children you will meet in preschools. It describes some of the exciting processes through which children learn and the ways that teachers can facilitate a child's growth.

CHAPTER 4

THE CHILDREN YOU WILL MEET

SOURCES OF INDIVIDUAL DIFFERENCE

Teaching is a skill and an art based on a mutual exchange between the teacher and the child. It is not a unilateral act in which the teacher impresses an idea or fact on the mind of a learner. The concept that teaching and learning is a mutual process means that teachers will function more effectively if they know something about the children with whom they will work. This knowledge will enable teachers to adapt to the needs and resources of each child.

The children who come to the preschool or day care center at the beginning of a year differ vastly from one another. Some of these differences are obvious to any observer. There are girls who are tall, boys who are short; children with brown skin and children with light skin; some heads are topped with red, some with blond, and others with black hair; there are freckled noses and chubby faces. Other differences are less obvious; they appear as a teacher gets to know the children in the class. There are quiet ones who seldom approach other children in the room; a few are assertive and always seem to be talking. Some are much stronger than others and can easily win a tussle over a bike or a race to the slide or swing. Some children learn the rhythm of a song the first time around while their friends may not get the beat for days.

Individual differences, found in any group of children, come from genetic heritage, sex role training, and the special influence of each child's unique personal history. Children come from families with different values, disparities of income, and distinct cultural traditions and customs. These differences in family experience have powerful effects. Two children who may look alike as they come to school may behave very differently in interaction with others.

FAMILY VALUES AND STYLES

In a sense, each family creates its own miniculture. This develops around the rituals of holidays and weekends, birthdays, and visits to the park, beach, and theater. It has its own standards of what is disapproved and praised, of responsibility for household routines—making the bed and helping with kitchen cleanup. These styles of dealing with others and with the community around them are part of what children bring to the preschool.

Families are enormously different from one another even within the same neighborhood. In a middle-class community, for example, the children of one family may stay up watching TV until they fall asleep; the family across the street allows very little TV viewing and then only after a program has been approved by the parents—and children must be in bed by 7 p.m. One mother watches ''Sesame Street'' with her child; another leaves program selection up to her youngster.

Attitudes toward sex and nudity also vary tremendously from one family to the next. In some homes, naked bodies are commonplace; the family may bathe or swim nude together. Some parents feel that children should get experience with such things early and that home is the best place to start sex education. Others insist on modesty; doors to bedrooms and bathrooms are locked; and sex doesn't come up in family conversations.

In one house, children take out the garbage, feed the dog, make their beds, and wash the dishes. In the house next door, the parents believe that housework is not the responsibility of children—little participation is expected. Some families use mealtime as a social event—the dinner table is a family forum to compare stories about the adventures of the day and build a sense of family spirit. Other families believe that people should eat when they are hungry and that there are better places for families to talk since they can't understand each other with their mouths full anyway.

Few things differ among families as much as the way they handle discipline. In some homes, bribes and spankings are used to keep children in line; in others, disobedience is ignored or simply evokes a scolding. Some parents run a tight ship; in other homes, almost anything goes. The amount of physical and verbal affection is astonishingly different. Touching, kissing, sitting on laps is common in one family; in others, people seem to be encased in plastic bubbles that keep them from physical contact with each other.

Virtually all families have two major features in common: they include adults and children and they have both males and females. But families vary greatly in the way they define the roles of men and women and they may be very dissimilar in the way adults share decisions and power with children. At all income levels you will find families who believe that woman's place

"I believe that you show children how to take care of little things, like pick up your shoes and don't throw your jacket on the floor. If not, those little things will start distracting from their ability to work in school."

Father

is in the home, that men should be the sole wage earners, that boys are not supposed to cry, and that only girls should learn to cook. But there will also be a family down the street who believes that tasks should be shared equally, including housework and child care, and that the only significant difference between men and women is anatomical.

VARIETIES OF FAMILY STRUCTURE

The nuclear family may still be an ideal in the mass media, but the traditional pattern—father at work, mother in the home caring for the children—is declining. It is now, numerically speaking, a minority.

The most dramatic change in the nuclear family is the entry of mothers into the labor force. Between 1950 and 1976, the proportion of mothers working outside the home increased sixfold (Department of Labor, 1977). Families have also decreased in size, and many more are living in urban areas.

Four types of families have emerged in the past two decades:

1. *Single parent households* have increased in number. Many children live primarily with one parent but spend part of the year with the other; some divide their time between two parents and there is recent pressure for courts to award joint custody to the parents after divorce.
2. The rising divorce rate has brought a corresponding increase in *blended families* of adults with custody who bring their children to a new marriage. Children have to adjust to new brothers and sisters. Stepparents in such families have an especially sensitive role in relating to their partner's children.
3. *Live-together arrangements* consist of an unmarried partner living with a divorced parent who has custody of the children. The live-in's status is often temporary and his or her relationship with the family may be ambivalent. Children are often tentative and cautious in such arrangements, uncertain about what it means for them.
4. There is also an increase in the number of families made up of *unmarried women with children*. In some instances, these arrangements may be the result of unplanned pregnancies, but an increasing number of women are making a deliberate decision to have a family without marriage. There are also cases in which unmarried individuals, male or female, adopt a child.

These new family experiences affect many children in this country. They represent models of adult relationships and interaction that differ from the traditional family. In a single parent household, for example, the parent does not need to negotiate with another adult on equal terms. The child does not have the opportunity to see how such interaction is handled and how differences are resolved. The consequences of such family circumstances carry over into the day care center classroom.

CRISES IN THE FAMILY

Children and Divorce

The focus of many investigations of family relationships has been the effects of marital dissolution on a child's sex role development, social behavior, and school performance (Hetherington, Cox, and Cox, 1978). As those who have witnessed divorce or experienced it themselves know, the breakup of a family is often traumatic. There is anger, sometimes violence; verbal battles between parents flare up in the children's presence. Children may get involved in these conflicts, sometimes by trying to soothe the parents or sometimes when they become targets for a parent's anger during or after quarrels. Physical abuse is a danger to both parents and children. The turmoil and the anger of these encounters disturbs and frightens young children. It comes at a time when they are trying to understand and control their own feelings. To see adults in extreme states of anger may arouse strong anxiety in a child.

In other instances of divorce or separation, the child never sees or hears the conflict leading to the final breakup. One of the parents leaves and the reasons given are incomprehensible or irrelevant to the young child. This, too, arouses anxiety and, possibly, guilt. Maybe the other parent will also move away unexpectedly. Some children fear they must have done something to cause the parent to leave.

The emotions of the parents are often so strong that they do not—perhaps cannot—take time to talk with their children about what is happening. We can only guess at the perceptions that young children have of such an event. Studies of young children indicate that they feel abandoned, seeing themselves as the ones who are rejected (Wallerstein and Kelly, 1975). It is difficult for them to understand their involvement in the marital dispute, and it is not uncommon for young children to blame themselves. This may be because they are disciplined during or before a marital quarrel and the argument may be sparked by one parent's criticism of the other about something that involves the children. Their level of conceptual development makes it difficult for young children to recognize that they are not necessarily involved in the dispute. If the conflict between the parents persists and becomes more evident to the children, they will have a more difficult time adjusting to the divorce (Hess and Camara, 1979). In some instances, the intensity of conflict between parents does not fade for many years after separation.

The dissolution of a marriage is a puzzle to a small child. It is an event that is beyond their comprehension; the reasons for a parent's leaving are not

(Did you know your Mom and Dad weren't going to live together anymore?) "No. When we woke up she was gone. And we went hysterical . . . you know, just screaming, crying. I don't think we gave Dad a chance to explain; we didn't want to listen."

Ten-Year-Old Child

(Why did your Mom and Dad split up?) "That's one thing they never really got straight. They just said they weren't made for each other. I guess they just thought it was better."

Nine-Year-Old Child

within their mental experience. They do not know the events that led up to the divorce or the evolution of feelings and thinking that the parents have gone through. The surprise, the lack of information, and the inability to comprehend—simply because of their limited experience—combine to make divorce a baffling, frightening experience.

During a divorce, children show the familiar symptoms of internal stress—anxiety, sadness, hyperactivity, low tolerance for frustration, aggression, dependency, difficulty sharing with other children. These characteristics are likely to reveal the sense of insecurity, loss, and guilt that a child feels (Hetherington, Cox, and Cox, 1978). The teacher is an especially important person at this point in the child's life. The parents, often under great stress, may not be able to give the support and nurturance the child needs. The teacher cannot replace the parent, of course, but if the source of the child's distress is understood, the teacher can give support through steady, sensitive understanding and care. Children find it difficult to talk about their feelings. Attempts to talk with the child are probably not as helpful as the nurturance and warmth the teacher can give when the child is going through a painful and frightening experience.

High-Stress/High-Risk Families

Divorce is only one of the crises that family life can bring to young children. Other circumstances that cause intense stress and risk in the normal pattern of emotional and social development include family violence—battered wives and children and, occasionally, husbands; drug abuse and alcoholism; death and chronic or terminal illnesses; and emotional instability. These conditions affect the child in various ways and may interfere with the usual pattern of interaction between the school and the parents.

As unreal as it may seem, some parents physically abuse young children. Many thousands of abuse cases are reported each year; many others are not known outside the family. Child abuse is not new but there have been more concerted attempts to deal with it in the past twenty years. Many abusing parents were themselves abused as children. They are ashamed and humiliated by their violent treatment of their children but they are often unable to stop. Federal legislation, entitled Child Abuse and Treatment Act (1974), and increased support for rehabilitation programs are bringing more attention to this sad aspect of family life.

Other sources of personal stress previously mentioned have their own consequences for the family and the child. Drug abuse or addiction can easily lead to emotional and physical neglect. Death or illness can cause depression and dependency. In all instances, the threat to the child is that he or she must deal with strong feelings—anger, anxiety, sense of abandonment, and con-

"More children under the age of five die at the hands of their own parents than are killed by tuberculosis, whooping cough, polio, measles, diabetes, rheumatic fever and hepatitis combined."

Sage (1975)

fusion—that interfere with the child's ability to focus attention on the developmental tasks of the early years. In some cases, of course, there may be threats to the child's health and the quality of basic care.

The problems that high-stress families present are not easily solved. The teacher usually cannot intervene in the family's problems but he or she has a responsibility to try to protect the child. If a teacher has knowledge or reason to suspect that a child is being abused, it is mandatory in all states to report the case to the authorities (see Chapter 9). If other conditions threaten the health or safety of a child, such as emotional problems or learning disabilities, the teacher may not be required to report the situation to the authorities; however, there are possibilities of referral to agencies that may be able to offer help and support to the family. In such circumstances, the teacher should consult with the head teacher or director of the preschool before speaking with the family.

Another crucial role of the teacher in high-stress situations is to give the child warmth, support, and special attention. These are essential even when programs of assistance for the child and the family have been developed with the aid of specialists (Schmitt, 1975).

SOCIOECONOMIC BACKGROUND AND CHILDREN'S EXPERIENCES

One of the most powerful elements of the child's world outside the classroom is the family's socioeconomic status. Our society has many very rich and many more very poor families. In 1978, there were 24,720,000 people living in poverty in the United States. The number of poor in this country equals or exceeds the population of many countries of the world. The poverty level in 1978 was $6,662. This official standard in the United States is measured by real income based on the cost of a minimal human diet. Any household is officially defined as "poor" by the Social Security Administration if its annual money income is less than three times the cost (in current prices) of a minimal diet for the persons in that household.

"Poor children are less likely to have had hearing test, vision test, or have seen a doctor for ear problems."

Diana Dutton

The differences in income in this country are part of a larger portrait of the opportunities of families in desperate socioeconomic circumstances. Differences among families reflect more than the amount of the paycheck or size of the bank account. Home mortgages are available in some areas of a city but not in others, a practice now being fought by federal legislation. Insurance rates on automobiles and homes may vary with the socioeconomic background of the owner. There is unequal access to quality medical care in communities with different social backgrounds. Even when the income of a family in a poor neighborhood is adequate, the health delivery systems that serve such areas do not provide care at a level comparable to middle-class regions of the city. Differences are especially marked in emergency room service and outpatient departments (Dutton, 1978).

Children from affluent homes often go to schools that have better equipment, more diversified programs, and higher paid teachers. Children from middle- and upper-class backgrounds, on the average, receive better scores and grades in school and are more likely to go to college and graduate school for advanced training. The number of students from low-income areas who drop out before high school graduation is disproportionately high. Young people who have the ability to go on to college tend to do so less often if they come from poor backgrounds or from families in which the education level of the parents is low. (See Table 4.1.)

The daily lives of persons from minority and low-income communities differ in other ways from those of middle-class families. The differences are most obvious in the immediate environment: availability of space, number of bedrooms for children, equipment, books and magazines, records, work areas, and the yard surrounding the house or apartment.

Other differences come from the effect that poverty and affluence have on the outlook of the people themselves. The feeling of having access to resources gives middle-class families a degree of control over their lives that people in low-income areas do not have. Families whose income depends in part on welfare, medicare, unemployment insurance, and food stamps are particularly affected by the policies of governmental agencies. Many decisions that affect their lives are made without their participation. Poverty and lack of influence restrict their choices. Families who live in poverty are more dependent on services controlled by offices distant from their homes. The poor are subject to arrest and detention more often than middle-class persons.

Families in poverty are especially vulnerable to disaster. They have only a thin margin of resources to fall back on if a crisis develops. Low-income families have difficulty getting credit or borrowing money to deal with the normal crises of everyday life. An accident or a prolonged illness may exhaust their reserves.

"My dad used to get up every morning, put on his suit and tie, and leave the house. It wasn't until years later that I learned he just wanted to maintain the impression that he was working."

Formerly Poor Parent

In 1978, 33% of black but only 9% of white families were below the poverty point.

TABLE 4.1
College Enrollment and Family Income

Income	Families with One or More Children in College (%)
Under $5,000	17.2
$5,000–$9,999	26.7
$10,000–$14,999	34.1
$15,000–$19,999	44.8
$20,000–$24,999	46.5
Over $25,000	63.7

Source: U.S. Department of Commerce, Bureau of the Census, *School Enrollment—Social and Economic Characteristics of Students: October 1975*, Current Population Reports, Series P-20, No. 303 (Washington, D.C.: Government Printing Office, 1976).

CHILDREN COME FROM MANY SUBCULTURES

The history of American society represents ethnic and racial groups from many parts of the world who came to this country with the values, habits, customs, and languages of their home countries. There is still significant migration, reflecting social, economic, and political events of the time. During the 1960s, many Cuban refugees settled in Florida and other eastern states. California, Texas, and other border states have large numbers of migrants from Mexico. Thousands of refugees from Indochina came to the United States in the late 1970s settling principally in the western areas of the country.

The image of the United States as a melting pot of different peoples and their cultures originally came from the assimilation of many ethnic groups into a single nation. American culture became the product of these groups. Each new group and new arrivals of any ethnic group often encountered discrimination and had to find a place at the lower end of the economic ladder. Public schools and social centers offered opportunities for newcomers to learn enough English to manage in school and on the job; schools offered training and experience with the new culture. In turn, steady employment furnished the means to move to more attractive neighborhoods, and marriage made social mobility possible. In addition, some ethnic origins could be disguised by changing surnames and adopting the values and styles of the dominant culture.

The melting pot assimilation process hasn't worked for everyone. Groups whose skin color or features make them easily identifiable—blacks, Mexi-

"I see many old people living alone in America. I worry about my children growing up here and leaving their family too early."

Chinese Father

cans, Puerto Ricans, Chinese, Japanese, Filipinos, Native Americans—continue to meet prejudice and discrimination and find it more difficult to become integrated into the mainstream of American culture. The families of some of these groups have been a part of the society for generations but they are still the targets of ethnic and racial bias (McAdoo, 1978).

RESPECTING CULTURAL VARIATIONS

"I was taught to respect my teachers when I was young; I insist that my children do the same."

Black Parent

Many families want to keep significant elements of their own cultures. They want their children to respect their native language, to enjoy a *pow wow*, to celebrate the Chinese New Year, *Cinco de Mayo*, and black history week. They realize, of course, that their children need to learn English and to acquire skills for economic and social success in the United States. They want their children to be bicultural, but not at the expense of losing their ethnic heritage, the courtesies in social interaction, food preferences, and religious beliefs and practices. In this situation, of course, it is easy for children to be caught in the middle and to find it difficult to see themselves as members of both cultures. They may feel they have to choose.

Cultural values and practices come with the child to the classroom. If the differences are not recognized and respected, they can become sources of embarrassment. A child who comes from a distinctive cultural or racial background may encounter two entirely different responses: curiosity or discrimination. Other children or the staff may display an interest in the language, holidays, dress, food, toys, humor, and children's stories of another culture because they have a novelty that is attractive. Some cultural events may become a part of the preschool program. *Cinco de Mayo,* a national holiday in Mexico, is celebrated in many schools in the Southwest; Hanukkah is often observed along with Christmas; Martin Luther King's birthday speaks of black culture and pride; and a few schools celebrate the Chinese New Year with brave attempts to say, *"Gung hay fat choy!"*

Children from other cultures and ethnic groups may also meet open or subtle discrimination. The notions we have learned of other cultures are often based on stereotypes and simplifications of complex cultural customs. Unless we are familiar with the nuances and subtleties of another culture, it is easy to call attention to differences in a way that makes them stand out as peculiar, quaint, or unusual. The aim of the teacher should be to recognize and accept cultural differences in the same way that individual differences are accepted as a natural part of group experience.

"We tell our children to follow the advice of the teacher if we think it is good. But if we think a custom is not good, we tell them not to follow it."

European Parents

Stereotypes may be derogatory and discriminatory. Although the more blatant forms of prejudice—refusing to serve food in restaurants, to hire, to sell or rent, to permit children to attend schools—are now illegal and carry severe penalties, less obvious forms of discrimination exist. Attitudes of racial or cultural bias are sometimes formed in the early years. One of the

"In Vietnam we always had someone around to help care for the children. Here in America, I know nothing about your medicines and I don't know how to get to a doctor. The teachers are too casual about colds. They don't have the same problems I do."

Vietnamese Mother

"I wish Tommy wouldn't bring that sweet, fruit-flavored drink to school. I know he doesn't like it when I pour it out but no child is going to drink 'junk-juice' in my class."

Teacher

purposes of preschool experience can be to offer a place where children see and interact with one another as individuals, rather than on the basis of ethnic, cultural, or racial stereotypes.

Teachers also bring to their work their own cultural habits and values, which can be the source of conflict and disagreement between the home and school. In one instance, a group of teachers complained that some of the minority parents overdressed their children for the preschool. The teachers thought children should wear casual, easy-to-clean outfits that would give them more freedom. The parents complained that the teachers allowed the children to get too messy and were not sufficiently concerned about reminding children to dress warmly out of doors. Another case in point is the teacher who had strong feelings about healthful foods and objected to the "nonnutritious" foods and sweet juices the parents sent with their children to the center.

Culture contributes to our sense of identity and esteem. The teacher can help children keep a sense of pride in their own cultures, even if they are in the process of learning a new one.

REFERENCES

Coles, R. 1964. *Children of Crisis: A Study of Courage and Fear*. New York: Dell Publishing Company.

Dutton, D. B. 1978. "Explaining the Low Use of Health Services by the Poor: Costs, Attitudes, or Delivery Systems?" *American Sociological Review,* 43, 348–368.

Hess, R. D., and K. A. Camara. 1979. "Post-Divorce Family Relationships as Mediating Factors in the Consequences of Divorce for Children." *Journal of Social Issues,* 35, No. 4, 79–96.

Hetherington, E. M., M. Cox, and R. Cox. 1978. "The Aftermath of Divorce." In *Mother-Child, Father-Child Relationships*. Ed. J. H. Stevens, Jr., and M. Mathews. Washington, D.C.: National Association for the Education of Young Children.

McAdoo, H. 1978. "Minority Families." In *Mother-Child, Father-Child Relationships*. Ed. J. H. Stevens, Jr., and M. Mathews. Washington, D.C.: National Association for the Education of Young Children.

Sage, W. 1975. "Violence in the Children's Room." *Human Behavior,* 4 (July), 40–47.

Schmitt, B. D. 1975. "What Teachers Need to Know about Child Abuse and Neglect." *Childhood Education,* 52 (November/December), 58–62.

U.S. Department of Commerce, Bureau of the Census. 1978. *Characteristics of the Population below the Poverty Level: 1977*. Current Population Reports, Series P-60, No. 119. Washington, D.C.: Government Printing Office.

U.S. Department of Labor, Women's Bureau. 1977. *Working Mothers and Their Children*. Washington, D.C.: Government Printing Office.

Wallerstein, J. S., and J. B. Kelly. 1975. "The Effects of Parental Divorce: Experiences of the Preschool Child." *Journal of the American Academy of Child Psychiatry,* 14, 600–616.

CHAPTER 5

SETTING GOALS FOR CHILDREN

INITIAL IMPRESSIONS

The first time you observe children carefully, the activity in the classroom may look like adults playing with small children. It is not easy to detect purpose and order in what is happening. You decide to watch for a while to see how one teacher responds to the children's behavior and how they are prompted to move from one activity to another. You see the teacher intervene immediately when George picks up a block and threatens to hit Eric, but completely ignore Mark who has just threatened Jeff. Your first reaction is to think that the teacher is inconsistent. But then you see that it is necessary to intervene with George a second time and you realize that there may be one kind of response for George and another for Mark. Maybe the teacher has a plan that you, as a short-time observer, can't easily recognize.

At first, the pattern and order in the teacher's behavior are not easy to spot. Until you have some experience, the things the teacher is doing may seem random: talking with one child, patting another on the head, warning a third, dashing off to take care of some detail of the program, chatting with a parent, and redirecting a group of children. There is no systematic plan that is obvious. What is done seems to be in response to what the children are doing and where the teacher happens to be at the moment.

That's partly true, but mostly misleading. Working with young children is never static; many things cannot be anticipated. Putting young children in an attractive environment designed to entice them to interact with one another creates many possibilities and most anything can happen. The teacher must be alert and responsive to what is going on. But, on the whole, there is an underlying order; preplanning is important to the successful operation of a classroom for children.

"I don't understand why a person has to have so much training to work with kids. Seems to me it just takes some common sense!"

Observer

THE PROFESSIONAL HAS A PLAN

Imagine, for example, a group of children building with blocks. A child knocks the structure down and runs away; the children who are building it start to cry and protest loudly.

The teacher grabs the offender, faces him directly, and says, "Johnny, I can't let you do that. These children don't like it when you knock their building down. I don't like it. Let's all help build it up again. This time you can be an engineer with Mary and Bobby. Look! That big block would make a good platform and it needs two children to carry. Johnny and Bobby, bring it over here. Good! You're playing with each other. I like the way you help each other and work together."

The next day you see the same teacher in the same situation, except that this time it is Erin who kicks the blocks and runs away. The teacher chases her, grabs her, and says, "I can't let you do that, Erin. You know the children get unhappy with you when you do that." Erin squirms, turns away,

and says, "Go away. I hate you. You're not the boss of me!" Erin spits, kicks at the teacher, and tries to break loose. The teacher struggles with Erin, holds her firmly so she can't kick and says, "I know you're unhappy with me, Erin, but I don't like you to kick or spit at me. I'm not going to let you go."

The two continue to struggle, but the teacher remains firm. Erin bursts into tears. The teacher's voice is more gentle now, "Let's talk, O.K.? I'm not going to scold you. Let's just talk about what happened."

"I don't want to talk about it," says Erin.

"O.K. We won't talk. We'll just sit here and hug. How about that?"

Erin relaxes; the two sit quietly. The teacher resists any urge to "lecture" Erin or to talk about "acceptable" behavior. This is not the time to talk. After a few moments of silence, the teacher says, "I'm not angry anymore.

"Understanding what is going on is a good start, but you still have to decide what to do about it."

Student Teacher

Are you?'' Erin shakes her head ''no,'' smiles, hugs the teacher, and says, ''Teacher, sit by me at juice time, O.K.?''

In both instances, the teacher confronted the child. Johnny was successfully redirected, but Erin needed more firm and direct handling. In both cases, the teacher had a long-term plan for each child. Both Johnny and Erin needed to learn how to be more cooperative and sharing. Erin also needed to learn to trust others and to get more of a sense of acceptance. The teacher's behavior and techniques for handling each child were not arbitrary.

In spite of the difference in technique, there is a great deal of consistency in what the responses of the teacher conveyed. Both children knew that their teacher's intentions were to keep them from hurting others or destroying their block play. Both children got firm handling. There's a sense of security for each child in knowing what he or she can expect as a response from the teacher. The children can predict how the teacher will respond every time they knock the blocks over. The teacher is consistent, clear, firm, supportive, and loving. There is little doubt about what makes him or her angry, what is not allowed—yet both children get the clear feeling that they are liked; the teacher is not punishing, scolding, or vindictive. He or she does not like their behavior, but still likes them. The teacher is in touch with the underlying causes of their behavior. They like their teacher because they know they can count on him or her.

Encounters of this kind lead to deeper understanding between teacher and child, and such shared experiences provide a basis for relationships. Children learn that the teacher really cares and, in turn, the children care how the teacher feels about their behavior. Children want to please the people they care about: an effective teacher is able to elicit appropriate behavior from children through consistency, fairness, and a caring relationship, rather than through threats and punishment.

Focusing on Significant Events

By watching the interactions with Erin and Johnny, you realize that the teacher interprets a particular act in very different ways, depending on its meaning to the children involved. This is not playing favorites; the same event is important for one child but not for the other. Learning to evaluate the significance of things you see in the classroom comes from both training and experience.

Some things are obviously and immediately important—illness, destruction of property, physical needs, anything that threatens to injure or create emotional trauma for a child. But other things are not so obvious. Most of the small crises of the classroom can be thought of along two dimensions: are they *intrusive* (interfering or potentially harmful) and *how often* do they happen? Some acts are so intrusive that they cannot be ignored because of the possible effects. Some behavior may not pose a threat to the child or to others but occur so often that it indicates something that needs attention. Thinking about a child's actions along these two dimensions—intrusiveness and frequency—may help the teacher to decide what things take priority when there isn't time to deal with everything at once.

Consider some examples. Actions that would be *intrusive* but *infrequent* might be a child who is about to tip over a fishbowl or crush a baby chick or bite another child. These actions need immediate intervention but may not be serious because their causes or motivations are probably natural—curiosity about the fish, fascination with the feel of the chick, a flash of anger in fighting for a toy. They should be taken in stride, but cannot be ignored because the *consequences* are serious—danger to the animals, the chance of injury to another child. Most of these behaviors are compelling because they are accompanied by noise (crying, demanding, screaming, general disruptiveness); they virtually require you to do something.

Some intrusive behaviors can also be chronic. For example, as an observer you might see a child bite another child. This might be an isolated incident, but it could also be a habitual, recurring event. Examples of *nonintrusive* behaviors are shyness, sadness or depression, or verbal rejections, and may be infrequent *or* recurring. They may not demand immediate reaction and can be handled in a less urgent manner. For the child, however, they can reveal problems more serious than the kinds of situations that bring the teacher running.

The experienced teacher may learn to think about the behaviors of indi-

vidual children along the following lines. When Annie, a usually placid and well-behaved child, squeezes the chick, it calls for quick intervention, but the teacher knows it is probably not as serious as Barbara's recurring need to bite others. It takes experience to decide quickly that certain behaviors should have priority for your attention, but thinking about them in advance will help prepare you for the first time you have to make a decision.

How to Develop Your Own Plan

As a new teacher, you will not be expected to know all the appropriate things to do. You cannot be as effective as the experienced teacher. You will gain skill gradually. You will also learn that in many situations there is more than one way to handle things.

Probably one of the most important tasks a new teacher can do is to learn the names of the children and other adults in the classroom. Your effectiveness is increased immeasurably by your ability to call each individual by name. Familiarity with your environment also helps to build confidence. You feel more adequate as a teacher when you can tell a child where to find the extra paintbrushes, when you can successfully redirect a parent volunteer to another area, or when you can explain something about the program to a visitor. Your interest in becoming an effective, experienced, respected teacher begins with the effort you make from the very beginning to learn all you can about the people with whom you work and the place with which you are associated.

Although behaviors cannot be placed into neat categories, you will find it helpful to think about individual children and events in light of their short- and long-term consequences. Your decision to reprimand one child, redirect another, and ignore still another will be the result of systematic considerations rather than uncertainty and spur-of-the-moment decisions.

Your growth in competence will depend greatly on your willingness to try new techniques. Watch expert teachers; make mental notes of what they do; copy them; try their techniques for yourself; discuss your mistakes and successes; make revisions. Unless you are willing to make mistakes and risk feeling foolish from time to time, it is difficult to become a skilled teacher. Your ability to use the appropriate technique depends on your intimate knowledge about each child and on your repertoire of tested methods.

Finally, your expertness as a teacher will be determined in large part by the plan you develop for your children and yourself. Your underlying agenda, whether it is dealing with the child who tips over the fishbowl out of curiosity or the withdrawn, despondent child, will be based on long-term goals. Within this context you will be developing techniques to regulate and redirect children, but you will also incorporate methods to encourage and to bring out desirable behaviors to help children develop to their fullest potential.

SOME QUESTIONS STUDENTS ASK

What should I do if a child is hurt?

What if a child asks me to go inside with him or her and I'm stationed outside?

Do all the children have to wear aprons at the paint easel? What if they should refuse?

What happens if children wet their pants? Do I change them? What do we do with the wet clothing? Is there a change of clothing for each child?

Is it all right to release children to adults who come to pick them up?

What should I always refer to the director, and what am I responsible for?

What is the policy about children going barefoot? Going nude?

What should I do if a child takes too many crackers at snack time?

What should I say if a child cusses at me?

Should I play with the children, or do I just watch them?

How far should I go in disciplining children? (Restrain them? Remove them from the group? Take them to the office? Scold them? Spank?)

SOME COMMON STRATEGIES FOR DEALING WITH CHILDREN

Watch any good teacher in a classroom of young children and you will begin to recognize some strategies and techniques that are commonly used. These techniques are based on the teacher's understanding of how young children grow and learn. Teachers respect the curiosity and inquisitiveness of children—their uninhibited, natural behavior that incline them at times toward disruptiveness and the need for intervention.

Effective teachers rarely need restrictive or negative phrases (''Don't do that!'' ''Stop it!'' ''You're a bad boy/girl!''). Instead, much of their success with children comes from the use of positive techniques that are oriented toward things children *can* do, not what they cannot do.

Redirection is a common technique and one that a new teacher will recognize easily. Instead of telling a child to stop doing something the teacher will redirect the child's attention by suggesting an alternative: ''Here's another toy like the one you want,'' or ''Ronnie's using the pie cutter. Why

''Give children plenty of opportunities to make choices and decisions. That kind of experience is an important step toward self-confidence and self-control.''

Kindergarten Teacher

don't you use the rolling pin to flatten the dough?'' Such redirection may be interspersed with *interpretive comments* such as ''It hurts when you hit. He doesn't like it. Here, use this instead while you wait your turn.''

Young children are active and much of what they feel and want is expressed in action. Their attention span is short, so redirection coupled with interpretation is a very effective technique the new teacher learns to pick up early in training.

Another commonly used strategy that is helpful in creating a positive climate in the classroom is *reassignment of space*. ''Margy, the children don't like it when you push them. I have an idea. Why don't you go to my office and get some train tickets out of my desk drawer and then you can be a conductor.'' Many altercations can be resolved and prevented simply by getting a child to move off to a different space. The child experiences an alternative to direct confrontation.

Cooperative help is another positive strategy successfully used with young children. They like to have the teacher offer to work alongside. Children may balk at having to clean up, but they often respond positively to a suggestion or an offer: ''We have to put the blocks away before story time. Here, let me help you,'' or ''Greg and Mary, let's help Jimmy put the blocks away. You carry the big ones and I'll take the small ones.'' This is an indirect and very effective way to teach children to cooperate. They are more likely to comply when your suggestion is put in positive terms and when your actions support their behavior.

Children need to be reminded frequently about the expectations of the teacher. In the excitement of their activity, they can easily forget the rules of the school. Good teachers recognize this and will use *reminding comment*

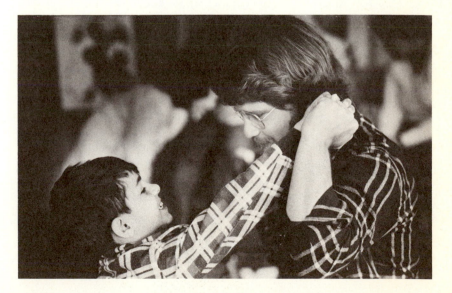

MODELS INFLUENCE BEHAVIOR
OF YOUNG CHILDREN

Using adults in staged situations, two Stanford University psychologists established that children will imitate the behavior they have seen in others they respect, admire, or whose behavior is particularly impressive (Bandura and Walters, 1963). In these studies, children imitated aggressive verbal and motor behavior, especially when they thought the actor they observed was rewarded for his or her behavior. These studies give weight to the old dictum that "actions speak louder than words."

rather than reprimands to encourage a child to behave appropriately. "Donnie, remember you are responsible for cleaning up when you finish," or "Margy, you forgot to clean your juice tray"—these and similar reminders help a child maintain self-respect and provide the opportunity for a child to follow through on expected behaviors without feeling scolded or guilty.

"Learning to use positive phrases takes practice and some self-monitoring. It's a good idea to tape yourself and listen to the way you talk with children. Then practice more positive ways to say the same things."

Student Teacher

These techniques for stressing the positive rather than negative aspects of a child's behavior are used frequently and successfully by skillful teachers. As a beginning teacher, you, too, will adopt and adapt these strategies for redirecting and rechanneling negative behaviors.

You may find, however, that you have used all these techniques and sometimes they work, but other times they don't. Is it because you are doing something wrong? Are the children abnormal? Or do you simply need more practice? Teachers who rely only on the use of these tactics are often accused of being "too nice" or "ineffective" with children who need firm handling. It is true that the positive strategies—redirecting, reassigning space, cooperative help and reminders of rules—are usually sufficient to regulate a child's behavior. The teacher soon discovers, however, that children also have strategies that they have learned to use with adults. You will find that children's behavior is far more complex than you first assumed, and although you have developed some effective strategies, you still have much to learn and a long way to go.

SOME GAMES CHILDREN PLAY

"I've had it with Mark!" complained Ms. T. "I've tried redirecting him, appealing to him to cooperate, and just about everything else in the book, and he still hurts the other children. I feel like I'm a failure as a teacher."

SOME TECHNIQUES FOR REGULATING BEHAVIOR

1. Be clear. Be certain in your own mind what it is you want. Then make your message clear through tone of voice, body language, and words.
2. Act immediately. Be certain the child has no doubt about what it was he or she did that pleased or displeased you.
3. Be consistent. Let the same message and determination come through on each and every occasion.
4. Offer the child acceptable substitutes to rechannel behavior.
5. Praise the child for acceptable behavior.
6. Accept feelings even when you disapprove of the behavior. "You must be very angry, but I can't let you do that," helps reduce the child's feelings and gives him or her a sense that you understand, even though you can't permit the specific behavior involved.
7. Develop a caring relationship that makes the child want to please you. This makes your approval and disapproval more effective.

What Ms. T. needs is some help in looking, not at her failing techniques, but at the ways different children, including Mark, refuse to do what is expected of them—in short, the games children play.

Just as the teacher has a repertoire of strategies to reach her goals, children, too, have learned to behave and react in a variety of ways. These behaviors are learned (sometimes by mimicking others, sometimes accidentally) and reinforced (rewarded by adult approval, encouragement by peers). Watch any group of youngsters in a preschool and you will see different ways of responding to similar situations. When the teacher tries to stop Mark from hitting, he may react to her strategy by ignoring her. She can explain and cajole, but he will continue with his actions just as though she were not there. This is frustrating to the teacher, to say the least, but Mark has learned that *ignoring* is or has been effective for him.

Laurie, on the other hand, always resists when the teacher tries to redirect her negative behaviors. *Refusing loudly* and deliberately to comply with the teacher's suggestions—"No, I won't, and you can't make me!"—is her characteristic way of responding to direction. Unlike Mark, Laurie may be doing this for the adult's attention. Whatever the reason, she is successful in forcing the teacher to confront her. This kind of behavior can be threatening to a teacher who feels that his or her skills are being tested and found lacking.

Another effective strategy used by some children is *passive resistance*. When the teacher intervenes by pulling Jonathan away from disrupting others, he simply goes limp. Few things can be more frustrating; you may not want to admit what you feel like doing at that moment. The child won't look at you, listen to you, or attend to anything you have to say. How do you talk sense or explain proper behavior to a child who by all appearances may as well be dead? Somewhere this child has learned how to turn an adult off.

Children who fight back, kick, spit, and resist in other such ways are using *active resistance* to respond to attempts to regulate their behavior. Teachers sometimes find it difficult to confront these children, knowing there will be a battle. Some adults find this testing of their authority uncomfortable and confusing. Should they give in, should they ignore the child, or should they fight to the end? Whatever the outcome, teachers usually feel less than satisfied with their effectiveness in the use of techniques.

Whenever Marty sees the teacher approaching to remind him of something he shouldn't do, he immediately thinks of something to distract the teacher.

"Marty, the records stay up here on the rack."

"Teacher," says Marty, "do you know what I did last night? I went to a show with my Daddy."

"O.K., Marty, but let's pick those records up off the floor and put them up here on the rack."

"Teacher, do you know what we did after the show?"

"Marty, we'll talk about that after we talk about the records. Now listen to me, do you know where the records go?"

"Teacher," says Marty, hugging and kissing his teacher, "I sure love you."

Children learn to use *distracting techniques* because they work—just as teachers have found distraction to work successfully with children.

As you continue your work in teaching, you will be able to see other games children play. These tactics will become apparent to you and you will recognize many variations on the basic themes. Clearly, these games call for specific techniques on the part of the teacher.

"When Roberto first started nursery school he began to use physical aggression at home. I was really upset, but I just let him know his tactics weren't acceptable. I guess all children have to test their limits."

Parent

PRINCIPLES IN ACTION:
SOME SPECIFIC TECHNIQUES

When children engage in unacceptable behavior and your usual strategies don't work, what do you do? Experienced teachers tend to classify methods for influencing behavior in two general categories: (1) techniques to regulate ongoing behavior and (2) techniques to regulate future behavior.

Some of the techniques for dealing with ongoing behaviors also have consequences for the future. Intervening when a child is disruptive and then explaining or invoking a rule are tactics that serve to affect future behavior. These are not distinct categories, but thinking about behavior in this way can help the teacher be clearer about goals.

Techniques to Regulate Ongoing Behavior

Invoking rules is probably one of the most commonly used techniques to manage and regulate the behavior of young children. "You do your running outside." "Use both hands to climb." "Wash hands before juice." Each school has its own rules. Children tend to do better as a group if the rules they are expected to follow are the same for everyone and if everyone knows the rules. Therefore, rules need to be specific, concrete, simple, inclusive, and part of everyday conversation—rather than a list posted on a bulletin board.

Rules also need to be reinforced, not only with children to whom they are directed but all within hearing. Conversations that reinforce rule learning provide alternatives to "don't do's." Children respond well to approval for doing the "right" thing.

Explaining why a child cannot do something should accompany intervention tactics. "I can't let you pour the water out of the bowl because the fish

---

CONVERSATION THAT REINFORCES
RULE LEARNING

"Good for you, Lennie. You remembered to keep your trike on the pavement, didn't you?"

"Sally, I think you're forgetting you're not supposed to climb on the fence. How about climbing to the top of the jungle gym instead?"

"Marcy, I like the way you used both hands going up the ladder this time."

"I noticed you all finished juice and crackers without getting up from your seats today."

"It's okay to run, boys, but not inside. There's plenty of space for you outside."

"Vincent, I'm really proud of the way you let Jenny work with your group in the block area today."

will die without water.'' ''When you hit Jimmy, it hurts. He doesn't like to be hurt.'' Comments and explanations contribute to the cognitive structuring of the young child. He or she learns and begins to understand that there is a good reason for certain regulations. Explanations help children internalize rules and are important because they provide the language needed for thinking about unacceptable behavior. This is a first step in developing self-control.

Appealing to feelings helps a young child begin to develop empathy. Although most preschoolers are not fully capable of seeing or feeling something from another person's perspective, it is still helpful to ask, ''How do you think Mary feels when you bite her?'' Interpret the other child's reactions and discuss feelings to help increase a child's sensitivity to other people's feelings.

Experienced teachers develop skillful ways to use *response expectation* as a means of regulating behavior. Watch a teacher reading a book to a large group of children. If there is no aide to help during the activity, the teacher will be especially sensitive to children who are likely to be disruptive or easily distracted. When Martha begins to look around and start squirming or talking with the person next to her, the teacher may say, ''Martha, can you see this picture? What are the people in this picture doing?'' Children can be drawn back from unwanted behavior by such techniques requiring that they attend in order to respond to the teacher's questions.

Diversionary tactics, such as redirection, rechanneling, and so on, were mentioned earlier. Teachers need to be resourceful and familiar with the child's interests. When a teacher intervenes because of undesirable behavior, he or she may need to use other strategies, such as first explaining why the actions are unacceptable and then suggesting that the child direct his or her energy and attention to something else. The tactic works most successfully if the suggested alternatives are equally or more appealing to the child than the original activity. As teachers get to know children individually, they will build up a history of experiences to help recall activities that have special enticement for each child.

Sometimes the most effective technique for eliminating unwanted behavior is to *ignore* it. This is especially true of behavior that is nonthreatening and nondestructive. Whining is a good example. The teacher may tell the child, ''You can use your normal voice. I'm not going to answer you if you whine.'' Each time the child whines for attention, the adult ignores the pleas. Disruptive behavior and other efforts to get attention usually stop when ignored.

A different strategy for dealing with unwanted behavior is to *withhold approval* or *take away a privilege.* Children who want the teacher to approve of their behavior and to compliment them for their achievements will respond well to this kind of treatment. Taking away a privilege (''I can't let you go outside until you put the blocks away.'') is also an effective tactic. Many

Using punishment to eliminate unwanted behaviors is most useful when quick training is necessary—for example, matters of safety. In such cases, punishment should be administered immediately after the behavior occurs and accompanied with an explanation.

experienced teachers use this approach with a more positive statement: "When you put your shoes and socks on, we'll go for a walk."

Getting help from others is used frequently by teachers who work in teams or who use aides and volunteers. This kind of technique is useful when the teacher is not able to reach a child or is attending to other demands: "Mr. W., Cheryl is having a hard time keeping her feet still. Maybe she can sit on your lap while I read to the children." Or the teacher might ask some of the child's peer group to assist: "Greg, will you show Marty where to hang his jacket?" Teachers learn to use the resources available and these include the help of other adults and children.

At times, rare to be sure, *power assertion* and sheer strength are called for. Your authority as a teacher is a powerful tool. Don't use it often; it is a last resort. Sometimes a child must be restrained, held, picked up, isolated, or taken to another part of the school. Don't feel guilty if this happens. Children may be more confused if you *can't* carry through than if you resort to authority. Authority is not necessarily punitive or vindictive; it is the ability to take charge of the situation and to assume the responsibility for setting and enforcing limits. Power is not invoked to win a battle; it is done to help the child regain self-control when he or she is unable to respond to less forceful methods.

Techniques to Regulate Future Behavior

Student teachers who first observe a well-run classroom may notice many of the strategies teachers use to regulate obvious and ongoing behaviors. But within the context of any effective curriculum, much preplanning has gone into dealing with future behaviors. The configuration of areas, equipment placement, and activities determine in great part how the children will interact. A well-planned room contributes to more orderly "traffic" and helps determine the kinds of activities that can go on simultaneously. Teachers can also exercise control by the variety and amount of materials they put out. The organization of activities reflects the teacher's knowledge about young children and the way they develop. Length of activity periods will be flexible enough to accommodate varying degrees of interest. There is a balance between active and quiet times so children will not become overstimulated or bored. There is a sense of order, but the routine will not be so highly regulated as to ignore the natural needs and rhythms of each child. Reasonable times are allowed for transition from one activity to another. Plenty of paper, scissors, and paste can mean fewer arguments.

Control and introduction of materials and activities help determine the mood of a class. Removal of a trike or other piece of equipment that inspires competition eliminates a cause of fighting. Drums need not be put out every day, all records don't have to be loud and fast, and the number of parties

---

"The first time I had to restrain a child I got upset because I was afraid he wouldn't like me anymore. Now I can focus on the child's needs and feelings. I think you have to go through a period of self-consciousness at the beginning."

Teacher

"I keep the lights dim and put on my most soothing quiet-time records the day after Hallowe'en."

Teacher

SYSTEMATIC REINFORCEMENT

Since behavior is learned, it can be strengthened, extinguished, or maintained by its consequences. If a child is systematically reinforced (rewarded) for hanging up her sweater when she comes to school, the behavior will likely become habitual.

To succeed, reinforcement must be seen as rewarding by the child, and it must be timed correctly. Young children initially respond well to external material rewards such as toys, special treats, and tokens; they also respond to external social rewards like praise, affection, or special privileges. In time, through development of interest and skill, certain behaviors supply effective internal rewards, and the child's pleasure and pride are self-reinforcing.

Internal rewards are especially effective in strengthening behavior when they are occasionally reinforced with external approval of some kind. The young child who waits cheerfully for his turn on the swing should at first be rewarded each time he does this, and then intermittently until the behavior becomes strong enough to be a habit. It should also be rewarded as the child does the waiting and not as a casual afterthought when he is ready to go home. In this way, the child sees the reward as a consequence of his behavior.

Many teachers are faced with the combination of a "mess" and children who have no idea they are expected to clean up or how to begin. A teacher will be more successful in teaching them a new behavior if he or she begins by thinking of the separate tasks involved in restoring order. Then by first rewarding children for whatever effort they make, even if it is only to screw a lid back on a paste jar, the teacher will be gradually preparing the children to pick up the paper, put away paste, scissors, crayons, and so on, and wash off the table top. Rewarding each level of effort eventually leads a child to keep trying until he or she masters the total behavior desired. The child also achieves inner satisfactions from having mastered this kind of skill and contributed to the efficient running of the school.

and holiday occasions can be limited. Introducing quiet activities to offset the aftermath of a holiday or an exciting field trip helps maintain an orderly classroom. By such means, teachers regulate the arrangement of stimuli and so control behavior in their classrooms.

Teachers know behavior problems often reflect a lack of order in classroom planning. Children do best when they know what is expected of them. A curriculum based on a *consistent routine with definite rules* that are reasonable contributes to predictable behavior. This does not mean inflexibility within any given structure; it does mean planning, organizing, and anticipating the needs of the children in setting up a classroom.

DIFFERENT CHILDREN, SIMILAR GOALS

"Sometimes we forget that what appears to be antisocial behavior to adults is perfectly natural to a child. He or she doesn't know that the behavior is unacceptable or that there may be negative consequences unless we take time to explain to them."

Parent

The children in your class will come from different backgrounds, with different kinds of problems and individual needs. There is no one method or technique that works best with them all. The strategies that are effective with each child will depend on many factors. You recognize that each child is different, but in one sense they are all alike. Whether it is George, whose aggressive behavior is causing a disruption in your classroom, or Angie, who does not speak English and is withdrawn and shy, your goal for both these children is to help them become more sociable and useful members of society.

Setting Goals for All Children

The day-to-day goals for your children will require intervention, explaining, rechanneling, and other techniques for regulating behavior. You will be dealing frequently with aggression, shyness, and other forms of antisocial behavior. Obviously, young children need your guidance. But the strategies to regulate daily behavior are directed not only toward stopping unacceptable behavior but also toward the long-term goal of helping children relate present experiences to future events.

"I can't let you hit. People don't like it when you hurt them." You may sound like a broken record repeating these phrases over and over again, but the message on your part is twofold: (1) you understand and accept the fact that children need you to act as their "consciences" by not letting them hurt others. They have not yet learned to be responsible for or to empathize with the pain others feel; and (2) you interpret society for the children by reminding them that others will not like them if they behave in this way. That is why it is not enough simply to stop or redirect a child who is behaving aggressively. You take the opportunity to use each situation to extend children's learning.

"Sometimes the best way to learn is through actual experience. I don't always prevent a fight. I'll intervene when I see that someone might get hurt, but explanations carry more meaning after a child has had an opportunity to bump up against some adversity."

Teacher

"Tell George what it feels like when he hits you, Jeff." "How do you think it feels, George?" "If you want the ball, how do you think you can get it?" "Let's talk about different ways you can get the ball." Jeff may learn about the use of aggression (and the results) from many such experiences during his preschool years. He may indeed learn that the best way to get the ball is to hit. Another day he may learn that if he hits someone, he is likely to get hit back. That shock, coupled with the teacher's interpretation and guidance, may lead Jeff to try a different tactic—perhaps cry, or ask an adult for help, or wait his turn, or even leave the scene. All of these responses are legitimate for Jeff at that given moment of his growth.

The teacher deals with each incident to resolve an immediate problem, but the long-term goal is the development of a healthy, well-adjusted adult

---

SOME LONG-TERM GOALS

1. Cooperation, sharing, and empathy—behavior that facilitates interpersonal and intergroup contacts
2. Self-esteem, strong self-concept, and self-confidence—behavior that helps a child develop a positive self-image
3. Initiative, persuasion, verbal interaction—behavior that shows competence in social interaction
4. Self-control, responsibility—behavior that shows competence in dealing with physical needs, emotions, and impulses
5. Self-care—skills in dealing with personal needs
6. Concepts, language ability, mental operations—competence in cognitive abilities

---

who can rely on many alternatives and resources to resolve his or her problems. A society that deals with conflicts using a variety of peaceable alternatives is preferable to a world resorting to violence as the means of settling disputes.

Make Goals Practical—Setting Behavioral Objectives

Setting long-term goals, such as protecting the environment or raising your children to be healthy, well-adjusted citizens, are well and good. But abstract goals are a bit like making resolutions on New Year's Day. They are too vague and distant to be attainable. This means they are usually ignored; we don't bother to evaluate how close we come to reaching them. Long-term goals for children should be an important part of a teacher's plan, but there are many intermediate goals between a specific incident and preparing a child for full participation as a member of society.

For example, you want Maggie to learn to share. This goal may become attainable only after many weeks and months of interaction with Maggie. In order not to lose sight of your goal, you need to state it in terms of behavioral objectives. The objective is not only that Maggie will share, but will do so in ways that you can actually see—that is, in terms of observable behavior. Thus, your objective for Maggie might be stated: "By the end of June, Maggie will be sharing by doing such things as (1) taking turns on the swings, (2) taking only two crackers at juice time, (3) helping to pass out art materials to other children, and (4) waiting willingly to take her place in line."

Short-term goals expressed in behavioral objectives provide the teacher

---

SOME SHORT-TERM GOALS

1. Recognizing own clothing/possessions
2. Ability to indicate the need for toileting
3. Willingness to stay at school without parent
4. Ability to attend to two stories
5. Willingness to sit at the lunch table

---

with guideposts toward progress. A child's behavior is partly the responsibility of the teacher. Unless you have a clear idea of the social behavior you want a child to display, you aren't likely to know if your efforts have been successful. Even though a teacher has certain goals in mind, such as those listed in Table 5.1, he or she must have some way of measuring the results in order to know whether a child's behavior is being modified in the desired direction.

Rather than calling for an abstract goal, such as being happy, the teacher will state the objectives in more realistic, attainable, measurable, observable terms, such as ''Jenny will smile more.'' If the teacher wants to be even more rigid about the standards, he or she can count the number of times Jenny actually smiles. This may be carrying the setting of behavioral objectives to an extreme and to the detriment of spontaneity; the point here is that the teacher can measure progress in more systematic ways than relying on memory.

Your methods for organizing the children's activities and your techniques for dealing with specific events thus forms a kind of unseen structure that can be used to achieve your goals for the class as a whole. The way you deal with an individual child in a particular situation not only responds to the event itself, but also helps orient the child toward the behavior you have in mind.

When a teacher deals with a child's behavior it is with both short- and long-term goals in mind. The rules and expectations you have for a child

TABLE 5.1

Examples of Goals and Behavior Indicating Their Achievement

Goal	Behavior Indicating Achievement of Goal
Learning that something can be achieved in more than one way	Child chooses an alternative action if he or she is unable to solve a problem through original means
Learning to defend interests and possessions	Child defends self or possessions verbally or by force if words are ineffective

from day to day are carried out with consideration for the child's immediate needs and future behavior. You intervene when Cheryl hits another child because you want her to learn to get along with others. You suggest Jimmy help pass the crackers because you want him to learn to share. You explain to Mary that Larry feels bad when she rejects him because you want her to be empathetic and sensitive to other people's feelings. It is not enough simply to stop an unwanted behavior. You want children to learn from each situation and eventually to apply what they have learned to similar events in the future.

REFERENCES

Bandura, A., and R. H. Walters. 1963. *Social Learning and Personality Development*. New York: Holt, Rinehart and Winston.

Chan, I. 1978. "Observing Young Children, a Science: Working with Them, an Art." *Young Children,* 33, No. 2, 55–63.

Cohen, D., and V. Stern. 1978. *Observing and Recording the Behavior of Young Children*. 2nd ed. New York: Teachers College Press.

Fowler, W. 1978. *Guides to Early Day Care and Teaching*. Toronto: The Ontario Institute for Studies in Education.

Galambos, J. W. 1969. *A Guide to Discipline*. Washington, D.C.: National Association for the Education of Young Children.

Kagan, J. 1971. *Understanding Children: Behavior, Motives, and Thought*. New York: Harcourt Brace Jovanovich.

Krantz, P. L., and R. Ostler. 1974. "Adult Expectations of Children—Do as I Say, Not as I Do." *Young Children,* 29, 277–279.

Krumboltz, J. D., and H. B. Krumboltz. 1972. *Changing Children's Behavior*. Englewood Cliffs, N.J.: Prentice-Hall.

Mager, R. F. 1962. *Preparing Instructional Objectives*. Belmont, Calif.: Fearon Publishers.

Osborn, D. K., and J. D. Osborn. 1977. *Discipline and Classroom Management*. Athens, Ga.: Education Associates.

Rowen, B. 1973. *The Children We See: An Observational Approach to Child Study*. New York: Holt, Rinehart and Winston.

Schulman, A. S. 1966. *Absorbed in Living, Children Learn*. Washington, D.C.: National Association for the Education of Young Children.

CHAPTER 6

HOW CHILDREN LEARN

THE ROLE OF PLAY IN LEARNING

Playful activities form a bridge between the developing mind of the child and the external world. For an adult, play is often a digression—a shift away from the principal tasks of the day. For children, play is the main event; it is center stage, where the child acquires skills, knowledge, and attitudes. In the experience of young children, learning cannot be separated from play.

"Do you have an educational program here? I never see my child learning anything; all he does is play!"

Parent

The adult idea of play as the opposite of work suggests that play is frivolous and, perhaps, a waste of time. Yet adults also value play, recreation, and sports. This ambivalence about whether play is productive activity or indulgence is soon picked up by the children themselves. When asked whether tasks such as carpentry, cooking, painting, riding wheel toys, rolling out play dough, and so on, are work or play, children tend to label carpentry, cooking, and sweeping as "work" and to categorize riding a trike, dancing, and tossing a ball as "play."

The notion that play is a central component of early development goes back as far as Froebel, who described play as one of the highest expressions of the child's behavioral growth. The familiar adage, "Play is the child's work," captures the sense that play is indispensable to the young child's experience with the physical and social world.

What Is Play?

The Concise Oxford Dictionary lists thirty-four definitions of play.

We all believe that we know what play is and would recognize it, but play is remarkably difficult to define. There is some agreement among specialists, however, that play has two features: (1) it is an activity without a particular goal, undertaken for its own sake, and (2) it often involves actions that are spontaneous. One writer offers five criteria that she believes to be widely accepted for defining play in young children (see box).

Some writers make a distinction between *object play* and *social play*.

THE CHARACTERISTICS OF PLAY

1. Play is enjoyable and is an activity that is valued by participants.
2. Motivation for play is intrinsic; it has no extrinsic goals; it is not intended to produce anything useful.
3. Play is chosen freely; it is spontaneous and voluntary.
4. Play involves active engagement of the player.
5. Play is related to development of other activities—language, social roles, and creativity. (Garvey, 1977, pp. 4–5)

Teachers often hear two complaints from parents: first, that their child is alone too much and should play more with a group, and second, that their child plays too much and should be learning.

"During the gas crisis I noticed long lines of wheel toys queued up in front of the 'gas pump' and children carrying on extended conversations about having to wait in line."

Teacher

Object play is an activity in which a child plays alone with an object; social play involves interaction between two or more children.

Object play is very common in infancy. It is an extension of exploratory activity in which the child examines unfamiliar things in the environment. This early stage of play appears to have a great deal in common with the object play of chimps, kittens, and puppies. At a very young age, about eighteen months, children at play begin to use symbols—a block becomes a train, a bite out of a cracker turns it into a gun, a stick becomes a horse (Piaget, 1952).

There are signals when play begins. "Let's play!" is a sign that what is about to happen should be interpreted in a unique way, defined by the participants, and should not be taken seriously. Chimpanzees make a "play face" indicating that play is about to begin (Bateson, 1955) and comparable gestures appear in children's play (McGrew, 1972). In both child's and adult's play, there are ways to signal that the meaning of interaction is about to change.

Although play is a central component of children's activity, young chil-

ROUGH-AND-TUMBLE PLAY

Rough and tumble is more than play; it is most likely to occur out of doors and represents a combination of social and motor activities that may engage the class. It often breaks out after children have been released from a classroom or activity where they have been confined. Boys engage in more vigorous play of this sort, with more noise and shouting and physical contact than do girls. Boys tend to move toward the outer edges of groups; girls more often play in more restricted areas, staying close to the staff and playground equipment. (N. Blurton–Jones, 1972)

"When new children join a group, rough and tumble is about the last activity in which they engage when getting acquainted."

Garvey (1977, p. 37)

dren do much more together than play. They also talk, solve problems, and interact in nonplayful ways. Conversational exchanges begin as young as age three. Play takes place, of course, in solitary situations, pairs, or groups; it can involve materials or go on with no objects or props. It takes many forms.

Piaget's description of play follows his view of major changes in the child's growth. Sensorimotor play is most typical during the first two years of life. The child gets obvious pleasure from repeating motions, mastering motor skills, manipulating objects to do what he or she wants them to do. In the second stage of play, the child utilizes symbols and images in activities. Using objects, the child pretends that a table is a ship or that a rope is a snake. At a later stage, rules become a part of play. Although not quite as formal as the rules of a game, the child's elementary rules help guide play and define the roles of some of the actors. Play becomes increasingly complex as children grow older, but the basic elements of manipulation/contact, use of symbols, and use of rules are present in preschoolers.

There are sex differences in play behavior. In chimps, for example, males play more aggressively than females; this is true of many species (Dolhinow and Bishop, 1970). Play behavior of female monkeys is made more aggressive by injections of male hormones (Young, Goy, and Phoenix, 1964). Also, aggressive play increases with age. In monkeys, aggressive play leads to a status and dominance structure (Harlow and Harlow, 1966) as the young males develop. Play sets patterns of adult behavior.

Play has important effects on development in monkeys. Play with peers develops affectional ties, social attitudes, and sexual behavior (Harlow and Harlow, 1962). Monkeys reared without the opportunity for peer play were deficient in sexual activity and group behavior as adults. Maladaptive behavior of young monkeys raised in isolation, on the other hand, was corrected

The Harlows (1962) raised monkeys in isolation until they reached physical maturity. Then they were placed with other monkeys. The experimental monkeys were so maladjusted they had to be removed for their own safety.

in large part by the opportunity to play with peers (Harlow and Suomi, 1971). Such studies do not necessarily apply to humans, but the role of play in the social development of relatively advanced species suggests that the significance of play in early childhood may not yet be fully realized.

How Play Influences Development

The contributions that play can make to development can be grouped into several categories.

Play Is a Source of Information about the Environment   The young child uses playful manipulation of objects in the environment to acquire information about the physical world. This view comes largely from the theories of Piaget and fits most readily with his description of the sensori-motor stage of development. Play is a rich source of information. From this information the child abstracts concepts about the external world and about others.

Play Is Practice for Future Behavior   Play is used by young children to imitate behavior of others, to "try on" roles, to practice with relatively little risk. This helps them gain perspective of others by taking on their manner, voice, and actions. Children who grow up in poverty may not have ample opportunities to engage in role playing, according to Smilansky (1968). This may be one way in which impoverished backgrounds affect cognitive and social development. Dramatic play gives the child cognitive challenge, new affective experience, and, for a short time, changes interpersonal relationships. Play is preparation for adult roles.

Kids quickly acquiesce to each other in accepting roles in a game—Jason won't listen to his mother's suggestion, but when Carla (a child his own age) tells him he is to be the daddy, he accepts his role.

Play Is Social Rule Learning   Social play often involves rules, some of which are made up on the spot for the group and occasion. This type of social learning helps the child internalize a sense of responsiveness to group norms, to practice adjusting behavior to that of others, and gives the child a chance to participate in the process of forming rules. Recognizing that rules can govern one's own as well as the group's actions is an important step in social development.

Play Is Catharsis   Dramatic play offers children opportunities to express emotions they are encouraged to suppress in many other situations. This is not only an emotional release of sorts, but it also gives children experience with their emotions in situations that are not threatening.

Play Develops Cognitive Operations   The symbolic function of play was described earlier. The child recognizes that play is not real—it has a quality that is distant from the serious, demanding parts of daily life. The ability to gain distance, to pretend, and to step back and look at oneself is an important cognitive step (Sigel, 1972). The ability to use symbols, to see things as representing something different from what they are, is the beginning of the more abstract ability to use symbols in problem solving and other forms of thought. It is also a way of practicing for future roles.

In common tasks, such as block play, spatial abilities and coordination emerge dramatically between the ages of two and five (Hubner, 1979). A two-year-old will use blocks either by piling them on top of one another or by laying them in a row or side by side. The next phase in block construction is to make walls and floors of blocks. This type of play begins at about two and one-half years. Sometime later (the age varies a good deal) two dimensional forms begin to appear. Just under three years, children can build a single arch (Figure 6.1a). The next form is the arch built in multiples, either in rows or piles of arch upon arch (Figure 6.1b). At about age four, a primitive sort of hierarchy begins. The child can build a structure like that shown in Figure 6.1c. At about five years, the arch patterns become even more complex.

These abilities are age linked. Three-year-olds cannot reproduce a structure like that in Figure 6.1c, although more than half of them can recognize it in a photograph—that is, they perceive it correctly. They have the physical coordination to manipulate the blocks but the connection between perceiving and planning the structure and placing the block is somehow not sufficiently developed.

Play as Development of Self-Control   Some forms of play involve physical contact and arouse emotions. The rough-and-tumble play of children,

FIGURE 6.1
Stages of Block Construction

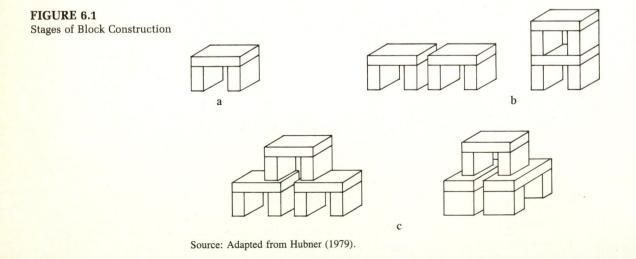

Source: Adapted from Hubner (1979).

for example, requires them to behave aggressively while keeping within the rules of play. The hits and bruises are not to be taken seriously; the temptation to hit back harder is to be controlled. Taking turns on the slide also requires a degree of self-control; the temptation to push ahead into the line has to be resisted. Play helps develop a sense of social rules and fair play. It is training for adult social behavior.

The Outcomes of Play

''For a young child, play and learning are not separate entities; they are inseparable.''

Child Development Instructor

There is a sequence in the development of play that illustrates its significance in learning. This is the ''exploration-leads-to-play-leads-to-application'' chain of experience. When confronted with a new event or toy, young children often are cautious until they have examined it to see if it is safe and worthy of further exploration (Hutt, 1966). This is the first phase in the sequence. Through exploration and play, children become acquainted with novel parts of their environment. The second phase involves using the object in a more obviously playful situation, thus giving experience with the object or activity and helping develop competence in its use. The third phase in the sequence is to use the object or activity in some other situation. A hammer, for example, may first be examined in an exploratory way. The child may then play with it, hitting for the fun of hitting, using it in games. The application phase comes when the child uses the newly developed skill to

EXPLORATION—PLAY—APPLICATION

Most teachers accept the idea that a child must be given plenty of opportunity to explore. But this is only the first of three stages. For example, a child may be tentative at first in approaching finger paints. This is the time to encourage exploration—touching, tasting, smelling. During this first stage, the teacher might offer the finger paints on a washable plate or table top, not caring whether the child creates a finished product.

In the next stage, the child needs time to practice by rubbing, smearing, and using the paints to make random designs. Paper might be introduced, but the expe-

rience of painting and playing with the new medium is still the primary purpose of the activity.

In the third phase, the teacher can help the child develop competence by demonstrating how to make more deliberate designs by using finger tips or holding hands in different positions. The child can then use these skills to create an intentional design or communicate an idea.

Curriculum activities should be planned and presented to meet the needs of individual children at varying stages of development.

construct a simple form. This sequence—explore it, play with it, then use it—is seen often in preschools. A similar pattern probably continues through later years. Learning adult skills may well begin in the play of the preschool.

SOME PRINCIPLES OF LEARNING

Play is a versatile, complex pattern of activities through which children learn about the physical world, personal feelings and fantasies, and ways of interacting with others. Much of the child's play is shaped by the surrounding adults: they provide toys and equipment; they often guide and supervise dramatic play; and they regulate games and playful interaction.

What the child learns through play depends on how well the teacher recognizes the principles that govern learning. The child brings unique experience and capabilities to the preschool. The teacher organizes a curriculum with specific goals and content. How the two are blended is determined by processes of learning. A curriculum of activities, even a good one, is not absorbed automatically by the child. Learning is not random; it happens in systematic and predictable ways.

In this discussion, the word *learning* is used in a broad sense to refer to several things:

1. acquiring specific information (names of colors, knowledge that seeds take time to sprout)
2. acquiring patterns of motor behavior (skipping, hopping)
3. developing attitudes and emotional responses to objects and events
4. developing social skills

Two Views of Learning

To learn is to comprehend. To comprehend is to grasp, to understand, to know.

Cognition is the mental process by which knowledge is acquired; from Latin *cognoscere,* meaning to learn, to know.

There are two major and somewhat different views of the learning process. One theory holds that people adopt behavior that has been rewarded in some way. The external reward encourages similar responses in the future. Patterns of behavior are developed over time as the rewards and punishments encourage or discourage behavior. According to this theory, the environment is the controlling influence.

A very different conception of learning is the *cognitive-developmental approach* proposed by Piaget and his followers. Proponents of this view believe that learning is governed by internal, mental structures. Experience has no meaning without someone to do the "experiencing"; how a child experiences any event depends on the internal state and resources. The structures of the mind will "grasp" new stimuli and interpret them according to information already stored. For instance, a sudden sound outside the house in early morning is understood by what the occupants already know and expect. Perhaps the newspaper hit the screendoor instead of the porch steps, or the milkman may be making his deliveries, or the garbage collectors may be banging trash cans. If the sound doesn't make sense, the listener may be puzzled or even frightened. New information is sorted out to see where it best fits with the knowledge already stored in the pigeon holes of the brain. Is there a slot where it clearly belongs? No matter what the new stimuli are, we interpret, ignore, or categorize them according to available information.

During a cooking project, a student teacher asked one of the boys to "break the egg." He responded by slamming his fist down on top of it, splattering it over the table.

Young children will use their own techniques to find out about new things. A teacher may prepare finger paints, expecting children to smear them on paper in some creative way. A very young child, however, is likely to try first to "understand" the paints by touching or tasting them—that is, through ways of perceiving that he or she has used in the past.

"The stimuli contribute some of the raw meat for human learning, but the learner is the chef who creates the meal."

Howe (1975, p. 88)

The notion that there are internal structures of the mind has special significance for preschool teachers. In planning the curriculum and the way in which it is presented, the teacher must consider whether the young child is ready to receive and organize new information. Otherwise, the teaching situation will be ineffective.

We do not have to choose between the two descriptions of learning. The child obviously does respond to the external environment; behavior is altered by rewards. But it is also true that the young child cannot accept and assimilate certain types of stimuli that have meaning for children who are older. All experiences are not equally valuable for encouraging cognitive growth. The preschool teacher can use both perspectives to arrange an effective environment and design a useful curriculum for learning.

How Behavior Is Acquired

Learning happens in an orderly way and a good bit is known about the conditions that affect it. Some processes have special importance for preschool situations. They are drawn from learning theories and suggest strategies or methods that teachers may use to achieve a particular goal.

"Every time I said a bad word, my mother would wash my mouth out with soap. I learned not to say bad words—at least around her!"

Adult

Reinforcement   Behavior is likely to be repeated if it is reinforced (rewarded) and is likely to be suppressed or inhibited if it is punished. This is common knowledge, but the process is more complex than ordinary experience suggests.

What appears to the teacher or other adults to be punishment may be rewarding in some way to the child. The "sit down, stand up" study is an example (Madsen et al., 1968). A kindergarten teacher complained that she had several children who would not stay in their seats even though she told them repeatedly to "Sit down!" whenever they stood up. The researchers suggested that she ignore the children who stood up and pay special attention to those still in their seats. Over a period of several days, the frequency of standing up decreased markedly. They suggested that she switch back to her traditional habit of telling the youngsters to sit down when they got out of their seats. The frequency of standing up increased to its previous level. The children were being reinforced by the attention they received from the teacher, even though she believed she was punishing them.

A study by Greene and Lepper (1974) indicates that sometimes the reward itself takes the child's attention away from the behavior that is being reinforced. The researchers asked teachers to bring felt-tipped markers for children to draw with during free play periods. The children's interest in this new activity was recorded. The children were divided into three groups. Some were shown a "Good Player Award" and told they would receive it if they drew with the marker. A second group received no reward for drawing. Members of a third group were rewarded unexpectedly but were not led to believe that they might be rewarded. About three weeks later, the children in the three groups were observed again. Those who had been promised and given rewards showed less intrinsic interest in drawing than children in the no-reward or unexpected-reward groups. Apparently, the reward became so attractive that the children focused on it and disregarded the activity it was meant to encourage. Teachers can use rewards excessively. Sometimes the activity itself is the best reward.

An excessive reward or a reward that is earned too easily loses its effectiveness. The child's desire for a reward may be satiated. The teacher who tells a child that his or her every effort is "good" or "excellent" dilutes the value of praise. Rewards are effective only if they are valued. The easy conquest is often not highly prized!

Observation   Behavior is also acquired by imitation or by seeing the consequences of the actions of others.

Even when the teacher does not offer an external reward, the child may learn from a model. The model may be another child, the teacher, or another adult. Models may be imitated if they are not real but are displayed on videotape or television. Children are more likely to imitate those they like, individuals with authority, status, or power to do things for them.

"The children watched intently while I helped Susan, our handicapped child, feed herself. Within one week, every child at the table was able to assume the responsibility without any direct instruction from me. They even used the same phrases and helping movements I did."

Teacher

Modeling and reinforcement are often combined. The teacher who is liked and whose praise or affection is eagerly sought is doubly effective. He or she is a good model and is in a position to use approval as a reward. Imitating the teacher may also be intrinsically rewarding.

Imitation may occur incidentally and unconsciously. The child may take on the behavior of a teacher that is incidental to the things the teacher was attempting to model.

Discovery   Direct experience with the environment gives children information and allows them to form concepts or come to conclusions themselves.

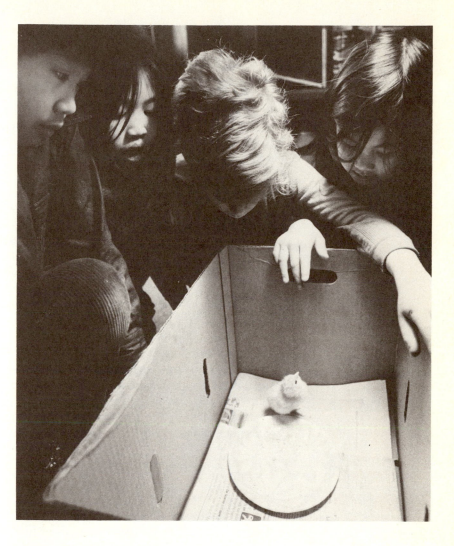

The notion of "same" or "different" cannot be taught without immediate contact with objects in the environment. A child may discover where chicks come from by watching eggs hatch in an incubator or may learn about evaporation by leaving a saucer of water out in the sun. There are those who believe that learning by discovery is more effective and long lasting for the child. It is a type of learning that fits well with the child's own level of readiness and mental development.

Direct Instruction   Some things are learned most efficiently by providing explicit information. When children need to use the toilet, for example, they are helped more by verbal instruction than by modeling or by using a discovery method! Much learning comes from access to information that is provided just when it is needed—supplying a word for an object, informing a child about what is going to happen, and giving directions. However, instruction may not be effective in changing established patterns of behavior.

Explanation and Reasoning   A reward or punishment lets children know by their own experience the implications of their actions. They may also learn by being told what the consequences *will be* and *why*. They can use this knowledge to control their own behavior. Explaining helps a child understand and thus establish control over the reward or punishment that will result.

Repetition   Repetition is a familiar technique used to help children (and adults) learn. It has received much criticism for being a ''mindless'' tactic that doesn't ask the learner to think, but it is, nonetheless, an effective strategy for teaching and learning. Learning a multiplication table or a phone number is often accomplished most efficiently by repetition. Repetition can be presented more attractively as a song or rhythm or pictures, but the learning technique is the same.

Dividing the Task   A task is often easier to master or to memorize if it is divided into small segments that are each mastered separately. If children realize that they can learn the *first* line of a song or the name of *one* shape, they will gain confidence that the second line or second shape can also be learned. Narrowing the task to concentrate on a specific part of the whole is a useful technique that can be incorporated in a learning situation.

Matching Teaching to the Learner

The previously mentioned techniques are the tools and resources that the teacher can use to help arrange an environment in which the child can learn most naturally. For all of us, there is sometimes a teachable moment when we are ready to see relationships we have not seen before. When it appears that the child is ready to deal with a new concept, to learn a different social skill, or to solve a problem, these techniques offer ways to make learning possible. The teacher has the twofold responsibility to recognize the teachable moment and to have a strategy at hand that will facilitate and encourage learning.

REFERENCES

Bateson, G. 1955. ''A Theory of Play and Fantasy.'' *Psychiatric Research Reports,* 2, 39–51.

Blurton–Jones, N. 1972. ''Categories of Child-Child Interaction.'' In *Ethological*

Studies of Child Behavior. Ed. N. Blurton–Jones. Cambridge: Cambridge University Press.

Dolhinow, P. J., and N. Bishop. 1970. The Development of Motor Skills and Social Relations among Primates Through Play.'' In *Minnesota Symposium on Child Psychology,* Vol. 4. Ed. J. P. Hill. Pp. 141–198.

Garvey, C. 1977. *Play.* Cambridge, Mass.: Harvard University Press.

Greene, D., and M. Lepper. 1974. Effects of Extrinsic Rewards on Children's Subsequent Intrinsic Interest.'' *Child Development,* 45, 1141–1145.

Harlow, H. F., and M. K. Harlow. 1962. ''Social Deprivation in Monkeys.'' *Scientific American,* 207, 137–146.

Harlow, H. F., and M. K. Harlow. 1966. ''Learning to Love.'' *American Scientist,* 54, 244–272.

Harlow, H. F., and S. J. Suomi. 1971. ''Social Recovery by Isolation-Reared Monkeys.'' *Proceedings of the National Academy of Science,* 68, No. 7, 1534–1538.

Howe, M. 1975. *Learning in Infants and Young Children.* Stanford, Calif.: Stanford University Press.

Hubner, J. J. 1979. *Block Building: Instruction and Development.* Unpublished doctoral dissertation. Stanford University.

Hutt, C. 1966. ''Exploration and Play in Children.'' *Symposia of the Zoological Society of London*, 18, 61–81.

Madsen, C. H., Jr., W. C. Becker, D. R. Thomas, L. Koser, and E. Plager. 1968. ''An Analysis of the Reinforcing Function of 'Sit-Down' Commands.'' In *Readings in Educational Psychology.* Ed. R. K. Parker. Boston: Allyn and Bacon.

McGrew, W. C. 1972. *An Ethological Study of Children's Behavior.* New York: Academic Press.

Meyer, M., ed. 1972. *Cognitive Learning.* Bellingham, Wash.: Western Washington State College Press.

Piaget, J. 1952. *The Origins of Intelligence.* New York: W. W. Norton.

Rubin, K. H. 1977. ''Play Behaviors of Young Children.'' *Young Children,* 32, No. 6, 16–24.

Sigel, I. 1972. ''The Distancing Hypothesis Revisited: An Elaboration of a Neo–Piagetian View of the Development of Representational Thought.'' In *Cognitive Learning.* Ed. M. Meyer. Bellingham, Wash.: Western Washington State College Press.

Smilansky, S. 1968. *The Effects of Sociodramatic Play on Disadvantaged Preschool Children.* New York: John Wiley & Sons.

Vandenberg, B. 1978. ''Play and Development from an Ethological Perspective.'' *American Psychologist,* 33, No. 8, 724–739.

Young, W., R. Goy, and C. Phoenix. 1964. ''Hormones and Sexual Behavior.'' *Science,* 143, 212–218.

CHAPTER 7

HOW TEACHERS TEACH

WHAT TECHNIQUE SHOULD YOU USE?

Each learning mode discussed in the previous chapter corresponds to a distinctive teaching strategy or technique. Some of these are fairly obvious. For example, direct instruction should be given in specific, clear messages. Explanation is given in terms that the child can understand and that show how a given behavior has predictable consequences. ("If you ride your trike into that corner, the space is so small, you won't be able to turn around.") Others involve less obvious principles. For example, reinforcement is most effective if given immediately. Rewards are also likely to be more effective if they are not excessive. Children model or imitate behavior more if it is assertive and confident than if it wavers or is inconsistent from one time to the next. They are also more likely to learn if the experience is presented in several ways—modeling, verbal explanation, and reinforcement.

Feedback is an important aspect of learning. Young children need to know how they have done on specific tasks so that they can acquire standards against which to judge their behavior (Gagnè, 1977). The feedback need not be critical—indeed, should not be. But the teacher can help children perfect their performance on tasks by giving them information about what they have done.

The technique appropriate for a given behavior depends on the type of learning and the unique circumstances of the moment. The following examples of various strategies that a teacher might use in the preschool illustrate how techniques may be selected to fit the material to be taught.

The Learning Situation	The Teacher's Technique
Four-year-old Mark rushes into the classroom, flushed from outdoor play. He flops on a cushion on the floor of the quiet area, notices his shoe laces dangling, and tries to tie his shoe. "Need some help, Mark?" asks the teacher. "Nope!" replies Mark. A few minutes later, Mark is still struggling with his shoe laces, only now they are hopelessly knotted.	1. The teacher monitors Mark's individual progress and decides it is time to set a learning goal.
"It takes a lot of practice to learn to tie shoes," comforts the teacher. "Here, let me help you unknot the laces and you can start again." Mark sticks his	2. The teacher reinforces Mark's effort by providing comforting attention.

The Learning Situation

The Teacher's Technique

foot out for the teacher to undo his handiwork.

Aware that Mark is clearly motivated to learn this skill, the teacher leans over to help.

3. The teacher selects a teachable moment.

The Learning Situation	The Teacher's Technique
First, getting behind Mark, the teacher reaches over his shoulders, takes his hands, and has him hold the laces while making his hands go through the motions of crossing the laces, pulling them tight, making the loop with the other lace, and finally pulling the laces into a bow. The teacher explains as the task is demonstrated.	4. The teacher recognizes that the task must be taught from Mark's perspective; he cannot see what's happening if the task is done from a different angle.
"O.K., O.K., I can do it," says Mark. This time, he successfully makes the first step of crossing the laces and pulling them tight. "That's right," encourages the teacher. But after making the loop, he cannot complete the bow. No amount of verbal instruction can help Mark succeed.	5. The teacher realizes that Mark will learn more quickly if the task is demonstrated (models), if a tactile mode is used (has his hands go through the motions), and if direct instruction is given at the same time. 6. Teacher reinforces the correct performance, gives feedback.
"O.K.," reassures the teacher. "Today, we learned one part of tying your shoe. Just keep practicing that part. Tomorrow we'll work on it some more."	7. Teacher divides the task into parts. Helps Mark see that he has made progress. 8. Teacher reinforces Mark's attempt at the task.
Ms. N. is sitting in a low chair supervising children in the block-building area. Half-a-dozen children are engaged in a cooperative project. Billy approaches the scene and starts to force his way into the group.	
"Get out of here, Billy," shout the children. "We don't want you!"	
Ms. N. suggests that the children might need a helper but they disagree. She then explains to Billy that his aggres-	1. The teacher suggests an approach technique that Billy might use in the future. 2. The teacher gives direct in-

The Learning Situation

The Teacher's Technique

sive behavior is not welcome and suggests that he might try being helpful and cooperative. Billy puts his hands over his ears and refuses to listen. He sulks in the corner, kicks at a block, and calls the children and Ms. N. "stupid," "dumb-dumbs," and other such names.

"He's calling us names!"

"Just ignore him," says Ms. N. She makes it a point to give special praise to the coopera-tion and helpfulness of the children.

"Jamie, I really like the way you helped Margie put that big block up on top. That was very good. Janie you and Robbie can get more done if you both hold one big block together and help carry it over here. *Very good!* Now see, you can do a lot if you work together. I like to see co-operation. It's good to help each other, isn't it?"

Billy is no longer calling names or kicking the block. Ms. N. pretends not to be aware of him. The children are too busy to pay attention.

"I can build, too," says Billy. No one responds.

Alice watches Mr. W. make marks on the paper with his black felt-tip pen.

"What are you doing, Mr. W.?"

"I'm writing addresses for the parents," replies Mr. W. "Here, this line tells where you live."

struction; social rules and norms are described explic-itly.

3. The teacher uses nonrein-forcement to let Billy know that his behavior will not pay off.

4. Rewarding cooperative chil-dren shows Billy what kind of behavior will get the teacher's attention and praise.
5. The teacher reinforces the cooperative behavior of the other children.
6. The teacher is explicit about her expectations.

7. The teacher keeps track of Billy, ready to respond when or if he shows the behavior she wants.

8. This isn't quite it—she waits.

1. The teacher provides infor-mation; gives explicit feed-back to Alice's question.

The Learning Situation	The Teacher's Technique
Alice's interest is piqued. "What does it say?"	
"Well, this says 'Alice Robertson, 5842 Harper Street,' " explains Mr. W., pointing to the letters and numbers. "Would you like to learn your address?"	2. The teacher responds to her interest with attention and information, reinforcing Alice's questioning.
"Sure!"	3. The teacher senses that this is a teachable moment; Alice is motivated and seems to understand the task.
"All right," says Mr. W. "Let's get a special piece of paper just for you, and I'll print your name and address very carefully on it."	4. The teacher personalizes the task and rewards Alice by this sort of attention.
As he prints, Alice watches intently. Mr. W. names the numbers and letters as he writes. Alice recites along with him while he prints the letters of her name. Mr. W. has her repeat them several times. Then he folds the paper, hands it to Alice, and tells her it is hers to keep and study. He suggests that Alice show it to her parents and have them help her learn her address.	5. The teacher uses repetition and direct instruction. 6. The teacher uses the visual as well as auditory and verbal modes. 7. The teacher enlists cooperation of parents as another source of reinforcement.
The next day during sharing time, Mr. W. holds up some cards with names and addresses of children written on them.	
"What street do *you* live on, Alice?"	8. The teacher knows that practice is required for this sort of learning. This is a memory task; repetition is important.
She looks uncertain.	
"You live at 5-8-4-2 . . ."	
"HARPER STREET!" she shouts.	
"Great! You know your street! Now all you have to do is remember 5-8-4-2."	9. The teacher rewards performance.
"5-8-4-2. 5842," repeats Alice.	10. The teacher divides the task into components and helps Alice see that it is easier to learn in parts.

The foregoing examples show that different techniques are called for in different learning situations. They also show that many different techniques are used in learning even simple tasks and skills.

Weaving together the various elements of a learning situation—watching for the teachable moment; arousing curiosity; building confidence; teaching through reinforcement, direct instruction, or other techniques; providing feedback and helping the child consolidate learning through practice—is an art that takes skill and practice. Knowing what the elements are, however, makes it easier to acquire these skills.

Preparing the Environment for Learning

The previous discussion concentrated on the circumstances that facilitate learning for young children and indicated some of the methods teachers may use in the center or preschool classroom. The notion that children learn only if they are taught is, of course, absurd. We could not keep children from learning, even if we tried. They learn something from their experiences, if only that some things are dull and boring. Learning is a natural, inescapable part of human experience. The role of teachers is to plan a learning environment; in doing so, they influence *what* is learned and how *quickly* it is learned. The preschool offers a special place in which children are encouraged to learn certain things more efficiently than they would have otherwise.

The teacher influences the learning environment by applying his or her teaching skills, by preparing a curriculum of activities, and by developing a program philosophy that guides day-to-day activities and sets both short- and long-term goals.

The Place of the Prepared Curriculum

A *curriculum* is a schedule of planned activities for the classroom. By "planned," we mean that activities are selected in advance, the necessary materials are obtained, the sequence in which activities will be presented is worked out (though it may be changed if necessary), and the planning is accomplished with the characteristics and needs of the children in mind.

The activities are offered to the children for their enjoyment and learning; they also provide a context and routine in which teachers and children interact from day to day. In an ideal sense, the curriculum includes the schedule of activities for the day *and* serves as an integrated plan that incorporates long-term goals and objectives in all areas of the child's development.

In some schools, most of the day's activities are included in the curriculum plan. In others, the curriculum may require a minimum of formal organization in which the activities exist mostly in the heads of the teachers and are carried out in a relatively spontaneous manner. Most curricula probably

reflect a compromise between a highly detailed schedule and a completely random list of activities.

A well-planned curriculum supplies the structure and direction necessary for an effective program (Croft and Hess, 1980). It requires cooperative planning, discussion and consultation among staff, clarification of the manner in which concepts are to be presented and taught, and methods for evaluating and revising the curriculum.

A planned curriculum provides clear direction but is not necessarily rigid. It offers flexibility and spontaneity and opportunities to capitalize on teachable moments. The plan leads to specific goals and includes ways to chart each child's progress toward mastery of specific skills.

A curriculum helps teachers clarify the purpose of activities, decide what it is they want to achieve, and measure their success. The teacher selects materials, asks questions, and determines the direction of a project with a clear purpose in mind.

Matching the Curriculum to the Child

A child of three may be able to identify a square but not be able to copy it.

Children have their own internal schedules for learning. Each child has a level of maturation that limits his or her ability to coordinate what is seen and what can be done. He or she has a pace of learning, ways of perceiving, and a particular store of knowledge, which will govern the way he or she accepts, selects, or refuses the experiences the teacher and the environment offer. Children have their own outlines and schedules for learning. The teacher's curriculum is modified and shaped by the way each child perceives it.

Planning the curriculum implies that the teacher knows what children need, how they learn, and a great deal about each individual child. The teacher matches preplanned tasks to the children's interests and abilities. What is offered will not be too difficult for children to manage physically, beyond their ability to comprehend, or unsuited to the goals the teacher has in mind.

Once activities have been selected, the success and effectiveness of the plan depends heavily on the individual teacher's skill in using the techniques to teach the children. The activities are tools to help the teacher achieve specified goals. He or she will use personal expertise to match teaching strategies to the learning styles of individual children.

Education Begins at the Level of the Child's Ability   What children learn depends largely on what they already know (Gagnè, 1977). This is not a new idea. Maria Montessori, with her focus on individual learning, established procedures for evaluating the ability level of children in her classes so that instruction could be appropriate to the child's ability. This principle appears in many forms, especially in individualized pupil instructional programs and in diagnostic testing that is used to assess levels of mastery.

Teaching Should Adapt to the Needs of the Individual Child
Although children within a group may have similar experiences or abilities, they will differ greatly as individuals. Each child will have unique skills, special interests and talents, and particular worries about personal achievement. Therefore, in order to be effective, teaching must be geared to the individual characteristics of each child in the group (Kagan, 1971).

A Child Learns Best When Motivated   Exposing children to numerous experiences and providing them with a wide variety of materials does not mean they will absorb what the teacher wants them to learn. No matter how attractive the environment may seem from the teacher's viewpoint, each child has a unique response to various stimuli. Some children respond to rewards such as stars on a chart, a cookie or sweet, or a special privilege. For others, social approval is sufficient. The method may differ but, for the most part, children will respond to the interest and enthusiasm of their teacher.

DEVELOP YOUR OWN PHILOSOPHY

Many professionals in early education and day care agree on the usefulness of the teaching principles previously discussed. There are other matters on which professionals are not so united. Although as a team they have the same goal in mind, not all players agree on the best signals to call in order to make progress. As you gain experience, you will recognize some differences in teaching style and approach among your colleagues and you will probably develop your own ideas about the kind of curriculum and program you think are best. Your philosophy will be composed of many specific items—preferences for how things are done, ideas about materials and discipline, and many other components of a program. Many of your thoughts will focus on several questions, or issues, concerning how to prepare a learning environment and how to deal with children.

Some Major Questions

Let's consider some of the major issues that will concern you. We will present extremes of each issue to highlight the questions involved. Most teachers take a position in between; no one must stand firm on either pole! The question is not "Which end do I favor?" but "Where between these extremes do I stand?"

"Plan everything in advance" vs. "Let them learn on their own"

Prepare a Structured or Unstructured Curriculum?   Much controversy has arisen over the terms *structured* and *unstructured*. To some, a structured curriculum means having teacher-directed activities during which children are expected to "sit down and learn" and are more likely to participate in groups. Generally, adults expect structured curricula to be academically oriented. Supporters of the structured programs believe that, in order to learn school-related skills, children should be instructed in an orderly way.

Unstructured, to some, connotes a free play program in which children learn at their own pace and move freely from one preplanned activity to another. Advocates of unstructured programs believe children learn best when they are ready. Activities are offered and planned to arouse children's curiosity and to encourage exploration. Teaching is spontaneous and geared to each child's individual ability.

The negative connotation of structure suggests the image of mechanical, insensitive rigidity. The negative aspects of an unstructured curriculum, on the other hand, suggest a laissez-faire environment with little or no instructional program. These definitions are misleading and divisive. It is more likely that both programs offer academically oriented activities as well as free play. The terms become confusing when they are used to describe a philosophy rather than the actual arrangement of a learning environment.

When applied to the way a program is carried out, structure exists in two forms: (1) a constant awareness in the teacher's mind of a clear purpose underlying a total curriculum or (2) a prearranged sequence of materials for presentation to the child.

In the first form, the teacher keeps in mind overall goals that he or she uses to help organize and provide learning experiences for the child. The sequence of presentation of this underlying curriculum has not been arranged, and a casual observer might think it is unstructured. The teacher makes constant use of incidental experiences to provide teaching situations. For example, when a child comments about his or her shirt the teacher may help the youngster label colors, count buttons, and so on.

In the second form, the structure lies in the arrangement and presentation of information. This kind of structure may be highly similar from school to school and can easily be programmed and used somewhat like a script. (The process of instruction is more apparent to the observer.) The most highly structured programs of this form use definite lesson plans in which one lesson is presented and mastered before the next is introduced.

A truly unstructured program is one that has neither an implicit curriculum in the teacher's mind nor an organized and thought-out presentation. There is no statement of objectives in behavioral terms. Neither the physical nor the human environment has a design. The program lacks specified objectives. Given these definitions, it is imporant for teachers and parents to clarify what they mean when discussing structured versus unstructured curricula.

Teach Cognitive Skills or Affective Skills?   A philosophy that emphasizes development of academic skills is likely to stress teaching of language, shapes, colors, concepts, and prereading skills. The staff will see that children work with numbers and number concepts. Children's speech habits will be closely monitored. Teaching will focus on a curriculum that makes it possible for children to move more easily into the primary grades (Weikart et al., 1971).

At the other end of this dimension is emphasis on affective skills. Teachers who espouse this philosophy spend a major portion of their time helping children build positive self-esteem. Their primary concern is to develop humanistic skills, to heighten children's awareness of their feelings, and to focus on the individual's contributions to the group.

"Help them feel and be" vs. "Teach them to think"

Emphasize Content or Process?   Should teachers stress content by teaching specific information and academic skills or should they be concerned with learning processes?

Those who favor content focus on what is learned. They try to make certain that children acquire skills and concepts as well as a store of specific knowledge.

Those who focus on process think of teaching *how to learn*. They attempt to make the young child self-sufficient and autonomous in the school setting. In a program that emphasizes process, it is more important to know how to solve problems or to obtain information than to store specific knowledge.

"Teach them facts and concepts" vs. "Teach them how to learn"

Use Planned Instruction or Self-Discovery?   Another dimension of philosophies concerns how learning can best take place. Do children learn best from discovery or from specific instruction? Is it better to give children information deliberately or encourage them to find out what they are expected to know?

"Give them instruction" vs. "Let them learn on their own"

One philosophy holds that the goal of teaching is to produce specific behavioral changes. School programs based on this theory begin by determining which behaviors are desired and proceed by building up the child's repertoire of responses one at a time. For example, in learning to write his or her name, a child would first need to know something about writing materials and their uses as well as the shape and sequence of certain letters. A child's responses are regulated by stimuli that the teacher introduces in a planned sequence. The process by which a child thinks is immaterial, according to this view; this teaching strategy deals only with what can be observed and controlled.

An alternate, Piagetian view is that early learning builds cognitive structures in the child's mind (Furth, 1970). Rather than being governed by external stimuli, the child exerts control over stimuli. Through personal experience (discovery), structures emerge in the child's mind that guide further perception and the acquisition of concepts. The child can learn only if he or she has already built up the store of structures needed to master a new task. According to Piaget, children make their own contributions to the learning process. Therefore, teachers need to provide materials that serve the child's desire to see how new information compares to his or her present knowledge and concepts and that permit revision of ideas through examination and questioning. Only by changing internal structures does the child progress from one state to the next.

Because this theory emphasizes maturation in development, critics of Piaget's theory claim it does not permit teaching. One must wait for the child to reach a particular stage in order for learning to take place. Those who favor the cognitive-developmental view tend to feel that the emphasis on "acquiring responses" is merely rote learning without understanding. To their way of thinking, if children do not understand (that is, do not relate new materials to what is already known), then they have not really learned.

Use Extrinsic or Intrinsic Motivation?   One side of this argument emphasizes the value of extrinsic (external) motivation. Those who emphasize its use do not deny that children are normally curious and ready to learn. They simply feel that children's interests should be aroused deliberately rather than waiting for natural desire to initiate learning.

Using extrinsic motivation often includes a tangible reward for the child other than satisfaction for completing the task. Although social reinforcement, such as words of praise and approval, or physical contact of some kind (pat, hug, handshake) is usually sufficient to keep a child working, in many instances a more tangible symbol of approval is given in the form of candy, raisins, a toy, or other object desired by the child.

At the other end of the continuum are programs that emphasize the value of intrinsic motivation. Advocates of this approach believe that learning and mastery of a new skill are satisfying and rewarding in themselves.

Work Out Your Own Ideas

As a start, the teacher combines experience, training, thought, and discussion. However, there are ways to be more active. Role-play a situation in which a parent or another teacher asks about your reasons for handling a child in a certain way. Consider your response. Ask other teachers about some of the issues in this chapter that concern you. Compare and think about the views your family and friends have. Be aware of your responses and reactions and watch other teachers in the classroom. How does behavior reflect personal beliefs? Listen to other teachers and the director discuss their ideas. Then begin deciding what you think is best for children.

Don't be afraid to try out your own philosophy—your beliefs about your work and about children. Be aware of why you do what you do. You will change your ideas with experience, discussion, and new information. You may want to add some ideas to those discussed here.

The issue of widespread availability of publicly supported child care in the United States is of great interest to many people. Perhaps you think that special priority for child care should be given to children from low-income backgrounds or from one-parent households in which the parent has to work. Or you may believe that parents should be involved in and informed about the care and education their children receive. Perhaps the effect of violence and advertising on television appall you and you favor strong community control of broadcasting.

Don't be afraid to take stands. This will make it easier for you to exchange views with others, to learn about new findings on a given issue, and to learn from your own experience. In any case, as part of your philosophy, keep an open mind!

REFERENCES

Ault, R. L. 1977. *Children's Cognitive Development*. New York: Oxford University Press.

Croft, D. J., and R. D. Hess. 1980. *An Activities Handbook for Teachers of Young Children*. 3rd ed. Boston: Houghton Mifflin.

Donaldson, M. 1978. *Children's Minds*. New York: W. W. Norton.

Furth, H. G. 1970. *Piaget for Teachers*. Englewood Cliffs, N.J.: Prentice-Hall.

Gagnè, R. M. 1977. *The Conditions of Learning*. 3rd ed. New York: Holt, Rinehart and Winston.

Kagan, J. 1971. *Understanding Children: Behavior, Motives, and Thought*. New York: Harcourt Brace Jovanovich.

Sharp, E. 1970. *Thinking Is Child's Play*. New York: E. P. Dutton.

Weikart, D. P., L. Rogers, C. Adcock, and D. McClelland. 1971. *The Cognitively Oriented Curriculum*. Urbana, Ill.: University of Illinois Press.

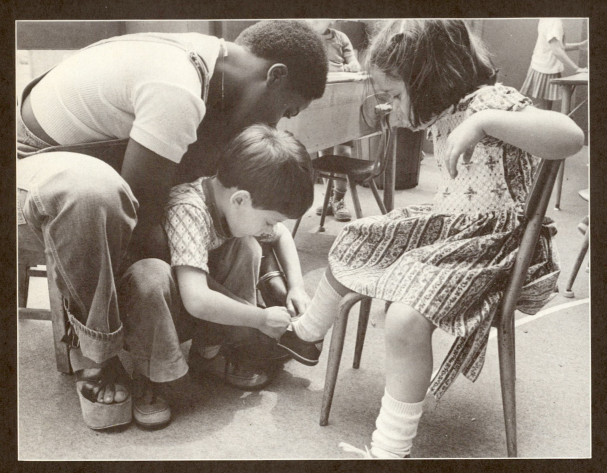

PART THREE

HEALTH AND SAFETY
IN THE PRESCHOOL

A PROLOGUE "Combine one active kid with some climbing equipment and what have you got? The potential for a broken bone and a lawsuit!" This comment was made laughingly by a co-op father who also happened to be an insurance salesman. But such a statement evokes no laughter from teachers who are responsible for the safety and care of youngsters in their school. Considering the large number of preschoolers attending child care centers and other play groups, the relative infrequency of serious accidents is surprising. As a teacher, what can you do to prevent mishaps and to what degree are you liable if something serious were to happen?

In this section you will read about legal liability and what the courts have to say about your responsibility to the children in your care. The information is not intended to frighten you out of teaching. The chances are unlikely—given safe equipment, adequate teacher-child ratios, and properly trained staff—that you will have any major crises to handle. It is much more likely that you will be dealing with the day-to-day minor "crises" that come up with young children: scraped knees, splinters, sand in the eyes, and childhood illnesses.

Chapter 8, "Keeping Children Healthy," though not a first aid course, will acquaint you with some of the more common health and medical problems and will provide suggestions for handling and preventing crises.

Views of crisis as expressed by preschoolers, their parents, and teachers are included in Chapter 9, "Keeping Children Safe." You might want to jot down your notion of what constitutes a crisis before reading this chapter.

Although some of the topics discussed are technically not crises, teachers agree that minor problems, if handled improperly, can often become more serious. Proper handling means redirecting a destructive child, intervening when fights erupt, suggesting an alternative when a youngster feels like hitting someone, soothing an unhappy child, and anticipating potential crises by being alert and sensitive to the children in the classroom.

Fights are more likely to erupt when youngsters are tired or excited. Children are more likely to get hurt if they are poorly coordinated or improperly dressed for active play. Teachers who have worked with children for any length of time can predict that a particular child will be hyperactive if allowed to run around with the older children or that another child will be moody and prone to accidents after a weekend with daddy. A youngster with allergies may be cranky and irritable during certain times of the year. Children may be more aggressive after an exciting Halloween or birthday celebration.

Your experience with young children, together with your training, good judgment, and common sense, will see you through most of the daily crises that will arise in the classroom. Your knowledge about legal liability and health and safety precautions will help you avoid major crises. The important thing to remember is that your attitude and confidence in the way you deal with daily problems help prevent more serious crises.

CHAPTER 8

KEEPING CHILDREN HEALTHY

MEDICAL CRISES[1]

Administrators and teachers must learn to deal with children's physical problems—ranging from minor bruises to traumatic injury. The demands that these make on the teacher and the possible dangers to the child vary enormously. Every wound, sniffle, exposure to measles or mumps does not constitute a crisis. There are, of course, potentially severe consequences, and part of the teacher's role involves judging the severity of the situation and knowing when to soothe and when to call for professional aid. The familiar medical situations are described in the following pages.

Eye, Ear, Nose, and Throat Infections

"My son caught one cold after another when he started nursery school. I still had to pay full tuition even though he was absent most of the time. I finally took him out."

Parent

To some parents preschools are breeding grounds for colds, coughs, sore throats, and all the familiar childhood diseases. Parents are probably right in thinking that young children do get more colds and illnesses when they first go to school. The reason for this is exposure to so many children in a confined area. Also, whether or not parents realize it, the child isn't getting the *same* cold over and over. Each time children are infected by a new virus, they get a new illness. As children build up antibodies, they also build up immunity to certain viruses. Eventually, the number of illnesses a child contracts begins to diminish.

Most colds are not communicable after the first three days. After that, the child may have a runny nose, sore throat, low spirits, and may be more susceptible to other illness, but he or she is not likely to infect another person. (See Table 8.1.)

Colds are a problem in the classroom only if sniffling and sneezing interfere with the child's activities or make the teacher uneasy about parents' reactions to allowing children with cold symptoms to be in school. Response to the concerns of parents often guides school procedure. Some schools have a nurse on duty each morning, even though nurses are not required by state or local health regulations. The presence of a nurse means that the parent is more likely to keep a child home during the first few days of a cold rather than risk having the child sent home. The nurse can also give professional answers to parents' questions about health and encourage good habits on the part of the children.

Tonsillitis (inflammation of the tonsil) may be caused by bacteria or viruses. A viral tonsillitis must run its course but the period of communicability is usually short. A child may return to school when his or her temperature has been normal for twenty-four hours. Bacterial tonsillitis is

---

[1]Information in this section is based largely on lectures by Dr. Birt Harvey, assistant clinical professor of pediatrics, Stanford University School of Medicine, Stanford, California.

TABLE 8.1
The Common Cold

Cause	Average Occurrence	Incubation	Symptoms	Contagion	Duration
Various viruses	In young children, 4 to 6 per year—usually in winter	From several hours to 2 or 3 days	Sneezing, runny nose, eyes tearing, fever, sluggish feeling	Spread through droplets from nose and throat to those nearby; uncovered cough or sneeze extends radius of infection to 12 feet	Few days to several weeks

most commonly caused by the beta hemolytic streptococcus, which responds to antibiotics. (See Strep Throat and Scarlet Fever, Table 8.2.) A child with bacteria tonsillitis may return to school a day after treatment has been started if he or she feels well and has a normal temperature.

The most common types of eye infection in young children are *conjunctivitis* (pink eye) and *sties*. Pink eye is highly contagious and is almost always accompanied by discharge and crusty matter around the eyes. In general, as long as there is a discharge the parent should be requested to keep the child at home while the infection is being treated by a doctor. With antibiotics conjunctivitis can usually be cleared up very rapidly. Sties are not communicable.

Allergies may also cause children's eyes to tear and redden and itch, but they are not transmittable. Even though they are noncontagious, allergies do have a potential for crisis: some children develop acute allergic reactions to insect (especially bee) stings, certain foods (including chocolate), animal dander, and inhalants (sprays and so on). These problems should be noted on the child's records together with whatever emergency treatment is prescribed. Naturally, every effort should be made to avoid exposing the child to potentially dangerous situations, but if it occurs, the parent should be notified and the instructions on the child's record followed. Obviously, the school staff should not administer medicine, either prescription or nonprescription, without *written* authorization from parents or legal guardians and a doctor.

Earaches occur frequently in young children. They are almost always secondary to a common cold. A child may not be able to locate the point of distress but can be observed tipping his or her head to the side that hurts, rubbing the area, and exhibiting general fussiness. Ear infections are not contagious, but the child is generally more comfortable at home. The common belief that the infection will be prevented by having children wear hats

"Post a big notice in the food preparation area with a list of allergies for each child. Parents get mad when the staff is careless about such things."

Teacher

TABLE 8.2

Communicable Diseases Common among Preschool Children

	Chicken Pox	German Measles	Measles	Mumps	Strep Throat and Scarlet Fever	Tuberculosis	Whooping Cough
Cause	Virus	Virus	Virus	Virus	Bacterium beta hemolytic streptococcus	Tubercle bacillus	Pertussis bacterium
How Spread	Droplets in air from sneezing, coughing, or from rash	Droplets from nose and throat of infected person	Droplets from talking, breathing, sneezing, coughing	Droplets from infected person's throat	Droplets and direct contact with contaminated food and milk	Cough	Droplets and direct contact with discharge
Incubation Period	Usually 14–16 days; maximum 21 days	Usually 17–18 days; can be 13–21 days	Usually 11 days; can be 7–14 days	Usually 18 days; can be 11–26 days	Usually 2–4 days; can be 1–7 days	Usually 6–8 weeks; can be 2–10 weeks	Usually 5–7 days; can be 5–14 days
Symptoms	Fever, rash, itching; bitelike eruptions starting on face and trunk	Usually mild; swollen lymph nodes, low-grade fever, rash, cold, or merely a stiff neck	Red eyes, runny nose, cough, and high fever for 3–4 days, then rash	Swollen, tender glands in front of and below ear; fever, general discomfort	Fever, headache, vomiting, sore throat (rash, flaking skin in scarlet fever)	Persistent cough, low-grade fever, weight loss or no symptoms	Mild hacking cough or cold followed by spells of heavy coughing; maybe vomiting
Possible Complications	Skin infection	If pregnant, injury to fetus	Many, including pneumonia and encephalitis	Injury to testes and ovaries and (rarely) encephalitis or deafness	Inflamed glands, sinuses, pneumonia, kidney disease, rheumatic fever	Damage to brain, liver, kidney, intestines	Pneumonia, bronchitis
Communicability	1 day before rash until last lesion crusted	Usually 3–7 days	Especially during first few days of "cold" symptoms; 7–8 days total	2 days before swelling starts until swelling gone; 5–7 days	7 days unless penicillin given; then 1 day thereafter	At any time by active case, especially during coughing	5–6 weeks

or turn up their collars to cover the ears is incorrect. The cause of ear infection is obstruction of the Eustachian tube that blocks the normal drainage from the middle ear.

Reportable Diseases

When a child in preschool contracts one of the communicable diseases described in Table 8.2, the school should report that child's illness to county health authorities and notify parents of exposed children immediately. Parent awareness of exposure is particularly important in the following cases:

German measles   Mothers should be notified because those who contract German measles during the early months of a pregnancy may give birth to babies who have defects of the brain, eyes, ears, heart, or other body systems.

Measles   This is a dangerous disease in childhood and the death rate can be high. Complications can be drastically reduced if gamma globulin is given early after known exposure.

Strep infections including scarlet fever   When suitable drugs are administered at the onset of illness, kidney involvement and rheumatic fever are usually avoided.

Tuberculosis   This illness deserves special attention in the preschool because it is easily spread to children and the disease often manifests itself in particularly severe form in children. Adults with the disease who may not feel or act ill are the chief threat to children. Yearly chest x-rays or tuberculin tests should be required for all adults who interact with children at school, including volunteers serving on any regular basis.

The incidence of many of these diseases in a school can be reduced by requiring immunization before admission (see Table 8.3). Many states require immunizations before a child is accepted into a day care or preschool program. In addition to the diphtheria, pertussis (whooping cough), and

TABLE 8.3
Immunization Guide

Immunization	Ages	Initial Series	Booster(s)
Diphtheria	Persons 6 weeks to 7 years of age get DPT vaccine	3 immunizations one month apart; 4th immunization one year after 3rd	5th immunization on entering school
Tetanus	Persons 6 weeks to 7 years of age get DPT vaccine	3 immunizations one month apart; 4th immunization one year after 3rd	5th immunization on entering school
Pertussis (Whooping Cough) (There is a 3-in-1 type vaccine called DPT and a 2-in-1 called Td.)	Persons 7 years of age and older get Td vaccine	2 immunizations one month apart; 3rd immunization one year after 2nd	Td booster every 10 years
Polio (Live Sabin trivalent oral vaccine)	Persons 6 weeks to 19 years of age	2 doses two months apart; 3rd dose 8 months after 2nd	Booster on entering school
Measles (Rubeola) (Live vaccine)	Persons 12 months or older	One immunization	No booster needed

tetanus immunizations (commonly referred to as DPT), many schools now require polio and measles vaccine.

Broken Bones and Head Injuries

Those who work with young children must be cognizant of the constant threat of serious injury to youngsters. Because motor control, balance, and physical strength are undergoing rapid change, falls are common. Children have little understanding of safety for themselves or others and are therefore careless about leaving equipment in hazardous places or throwing toys and tools without thought of the consequences. The wonder is that there are so few accidents in school resulting in serious injury to children. Proper precautions and knowledge of procedural steps can alleviate many of the anxieties of both child and teacher in the event of an accident.

Broken Bones Fractures are not always readily detectable, unless there is a compound fracture, that is, a breaking of the skin. When children fall, it is best not to be too eager to pick them up. If there is no danger, let the child lie still until he or she attempts to rise. Serious injury to an ankle, a knee, or a leg means the child will be unable to stand up. Breaking a collar bone, rib, arm, or wrist usually causes too much pain for the child to want to move this part of the body.

Directing a child to point to where it hurts gives some idea of what may have happened. If after a few minutes everything seems to be all right, it is probably safe to let the child get up and continue whatever he or she was doing when the interruption occurred. The teacher should watch carefully to make sure that the child's activity seems normal. Whatever type of accident report is required by the school should be filled in (Figure 8.1) and a copy given to the parent when the child is dismissed for the day. Time should also be taken to tell the parent what happened.

When the consequences are more serious—a bone broken or a child obviously in pain or distress—the child should be made as comfortable as possible and the instructions on the child's emergency card followed immediately. No matter how well trained in first aid or experienced in similar emergencies, the teacher should not try to diagnose or minister to the child beyond doing whatever is necessary to preserve life (as in the case of serious bleeding or asphyxiation).

Head Injuries Inexperienced teachers often misinterpret the seriousness of head injuries. Because the scalp has more blood vessels than any other part of the body of similar size, even a minor blow to the head may easily form a large bump. Where the child is hit and the amount of swelling have relatively little bearing on the degree of injury. What needs to be determined

FIGURE 8.1
Example of an Accident
Report Form

GREENMEADOW NURSERY SCHOOL

ACCIDENT REPORT

Date: _____ Approx. Time of Accident: _____

Name of Child: _____

Address: _____ Phone: _____

Accident Reported by: _____

Nature of Injury: _____

  Location: _____

  Type: Bump _____ Bruise _____ Scratch _____ Blister _____

    Abrasion _____ Cut _____ Laceration _____ Suspected

    strain or sprain _____ Suspected fracture _____ Burn _____

    Bite _____ Other _____

  Extent of bleeding _____

  Estimate of extent and severity _____

Description of Child's Overt Reaction to Injury: _____

Description of First-Aid Measures: _____

  First-aid given by _____

Description of Accident: _____

Disposition of Case:

  Parent or doctor not notified _____ Reason _____

  Parent notified _____ Parent's instructions _____

  Family physician notified _____ Name _____

  Other physician notified _____ Name _____

    Reason _____

  Physician's instructions _____

  Child remained at school _____; was taken home _____;

  was taken to _____

  for medical attention by _____

  (Name of person transporting child)

  Other disposition _____

               Head Teacher _____

               Director _____

**Use reverse side for additional information pertinent to case and
disposition.**

DO'S AND DON'T'S IN CASES OF SEVERE INJURY

1. DO keep the child quiet and accompanied until his or her parent or a doctor takes over.
2. DON'T try to diagnose or repair damages.
3. DO follow the procedure given on the child's emergency card.
4. DON'T neglect the other children in the class.
5. DO make a complete report to the parent and for the school records.

---

is whether internal bleeding is taking place. After any head blow, three significant signs should be watched for:

1. Initial unconsciousness
2. Progressive lethargy
3. Recurrent vomiting

Even if a child is unconscious for only ten or fifteen seconds after a fall or a blow to the head, this fact needs to be reported. Normally the family should be notified immediately and their instructions followed. If the child must be kept for a time, however, and becomes very lethargic or starts to vomit recurrently, call the doctor and follow his or her suggestions. The teacher should keep an exact record of what is done and when. This should be given to the parent or the person taking over the treatment of the child.

Vomiting immediately following a head (or any other) injury is frequently an emotional reaction and may have little significance, but it should be recorded. Vomiting that occurs one-half hour or more after an injury is considered significant.

What seemed to a teacher to be an inconsequential head injury brought serious consequences to a three-and-one-half-year-old girl, her family, and the owners of a nursery school. The details of this event are described fully in Chapter 9.

Minor Injuries

Many common emergencies in preschools present little threat to experienced teachers, even though they know the consequences could be serious for the child and themselves depending on how each situation is handled. Wherever there are children, there will be a certain number of cuts, scrapes, bruises, eyes with sand in them, nosebleeds, abdominal pains, and so on. Every school provides first aid supplies and has them readily available. However, the head teacher, or the teacher most likely to see the parent after school, should have knowledge of even the most minor bumps or bruises so he or she can enter them in the school record and inform the parent. It is advisable to inform the parents of every accident lest they discover even a small injury later and be disturbed both by the accident and by the teacher's failure to notify them. Of course, in the case of serious injury, the parent or indicated guardian should be called immediately.

Following are descriptions of common minor injuries and remedies with which the teacher should be familiar:

Cuts (*knife, glass, paper*)   If there is any possibility that stitches are needed (to avoid scarring when healed), the child's parent should be notified. Otherwise, clean the wound with soap and water and protect it with bandage.

Scrapes   If gravel, sand, or any foreign substance is deeply imbedded, call the child's parent. (The injury may need a doctor's attention in order to avoid infection or scarring.) Otherwise, clean *thoroughly* with soap and water. It is important to remove all foreign matter. Cover lightly.

Burns   If a burn blisters, call the child's parent. While waiting, keep the affected area under cold water or wrapped in clean cloth. Do not apply any ointments. If the burn is minor and small in area, soothe with cool water. The area is already bacteria-free from the burn itself.

Sand in eye   This injury is not harmful but quite irritating to child. Wash eye(s) with plenty of cool water.

Nosebleed   Keep the child quiet and squeeze the nostrils together for a few minutes. If bleeding persists or recurs, call the child's parent.

Abdominal pain   Pains in the abdominal area are often related to infectious diseases, in which case there will be other symptoms present. If the pain is connected with appendicitis, the child won't want to move and he or she will probably be feverish and vomiting. The abdomen will remain rigid and painful when touched, particularly low on the right side. The child's parent should be called in either of the aforementioned circumstances. Common "tummy ache," which often accompanies anxiety, comes and goes but while present is very real to a child. This can be alleviated with a judicious amount of reassurance. Report these aches to the child's parent.

Choking   Choking can be very serious if foreign matter gets into lungs or if the air passage is completely blocked. Enforce simple rules in the nursery school: (1) sit to eat and (2) avoid giving foods such as raw carrots, peanuts, bacon, and popcorn (exceedingly difficult to remove once in the windpipe). When choking occurs and there is no sign of breathing, clutch the child from behind, clasp your hands together where the rib cage forms a V in front (just above the stomach). Give a sudden upward squeeze under the ribs. This procedure is known as the Heimlich Maneuver (see Figure

FIGURE 8.2
The Heimlich Maneuver

8.2). If this is ineffective, place the child face down and give a sharp "whack" across the shoulder blades. If still gagging, get medical help immediately and notify the child's parent.

MISCELLANEOUS MEDICAL PROBLEMS

Teachers hear about the following group of medical problems far more than they encounter them. Yet because these conditions sometimes represent serious problems for young children, teachers understandably want to know how they can identify them and in what way they should attempt to help.

Skin Problems

Children suffer from a wide variety of skin diseases. Those caused by fungi are probably the most widespread, including athlete's foot (tiny, itchy blisters between the toes) and ringworm (circular, scaly lesions on the body and in the scalp). They are difficult to cure and a physician's advice is needed in

---

SUGGESTIONS FOR ENSURING CARE IN EMERGENCIES

1. There is a written and posted plan for evacuation of children in case of fire or other disaster. Caregivers are aware of the plan and have evacuation drills at least once a year.
2. A telephone is on the premises and immediately accessible. Emergency phone numbers are conspicuously posted on or adjacent to the phone.
3. A readily understandable chart describing first aid and emergency medical treatment techniques is conspicuously posted in the preschool or day care center. At least one staff member understands these techniques and is able to carry them out.
4. There is a planned source of emergency medical care—a hospital emergency room clinic or other staffed facility—known to caregivers and acceptable to parents.
5. A place is provided for an ill or injured child to rest or play quietly away from other children yet under adult supervision.

determining whether an infected child should be in school. Impetigo, a bacteria-caused infection, is characterized by yellowish crusted sores anywhere on the body, but especially at nostril openings. It is highly contagious and if not cured may occasionally lead to erysipelas or kidney diseases. Until all infected areas are healing, children should probably remain at home, although a day or two after proper treatment the disease is not communicable. Boils, an infection at the root of a hair, may be caused by the same bacteria responsible for impetigo. They start as a red swelling, fill with pus, and are quite painful. Their treatment should be left up to the child's family and agreement reached with them as to whether the child should be in school.

Infestation with lice is not uncommon whenever there is a shortage of soap and laundering. Unwashed hair, unwashed bodies, and unwashed clothes furnish perfect breeding places for head and body lice. They usually are found in a child's hair or the seams of clothing, where they cause severe itching and irritation. Although lice rarely carry disease, they need to be removed. This can best be done by disinfection—a task not usually handled by the school.

The bite of any sharp-toothed animal can be quite painful, may become infected, and generally brings discomfort to the person bitten. When the skin is broken, whether by guinea pigs, rats, or any other animal, including a human being, tetanus or other infections may result and make the victim ill. Wash the area thoroughly with soap and water. A physician should determine if a tetanus injection is appropriate.

Convulsions

Convulsions are spasmodic muscular contractions that come without warning and cannot be stopped. When having a convulsion, the child falls unconscious, muscles stiffen and then relax and start a series of somewhat rhythmical contractions. When the attack is over, the child sleeps from a few

---

SAFETY TIPS FOR CHILDREN

1. Sit down to eat or drink.
2. Keep sticks, balls, and all foreign objects out of your mouth.
3. Keep wheeled equipment on the paved areas or in the sheds.
4. Walk around swings.
5. Use both hands when climbing.
6. Use tools properly and keep them where they belong.

moments up to an hour or more. The duration of a seizure may be brief or prolonged. During an attack, the child needs to be protected so that breathing is not impaired (from choking on vomit or from swallowing the tongue) and so that he or she is not bruised from movement caused by muscle spasms. Until help comes, the child should be placed face down on a soft surface with the head to one side and rolled-up cloth between the teeth. Seizures of this kind accompany certain sudden high fevers and are also associated with epilepsy.

Child Abuse

Occasionally, a teacher suspects that a child is the victim of brutal treatment. The teacher may notice welts and bruises, find the child crying for no apparent reason, or hear the youngster innocently remark, ''They hit me all the time.'' If tactful questioning and further observation confirm the teacher's suspicion, the proper authorities should be notified immediately.[2] Usually this means a call to the Department of Dependent Children of the local welfare office. Many of these groups are now in a position to take over with no further involvement on the part of the teacher. Some states have laws that protect the teacher from lawsuit.

Seeking help from an outside agency is considerably facilitated if the school and agency personnel have already met and are familiar with one another's work and jurisdiction. Prior introduction of this kind, whether formal or informal, makes it possible to give maximum help to children if and when it is needed.[3] Additional references on this important topic are listed at the end of the chapter.

TEACHER RESPONSIBILITY

Prevention is perhaps a teacher's best strategy as far as medical crisis is concerned. The teacher probably can do little beforehand about the illnesses children bring to school, but he or she is in a position to do a great deal about injuries at school. Careful maintenance of equipment, strict enforcement of safety rules (such as those previously listed), and consideration for the rights and comfort of others are effective ways to eliminate many of the accidents that all too often precipitate crisis.

When teachers must deal with illness or injury, they need first of all to remember that they are neither parent nor doctor. Other than providing simple

''Although it is not standard practice, it is probably a good idea to have written medical releases from custodians authorizing the director to give consent for medical treatment in an emergency when parents can't be reached.''

Doctor

[2]Failure to notify proper authorities is a misdemeanor in many states.
[3]A good source for materials on this subject is Children's Division, The American Humane Association, 5351 S. Roslyn St., Englewood, Colorado 80111.

first aid and large quantities of reassurance, the teacher's primary responsibility to the child is to notify the parent and follow the instructions on the emergency card. He or she should also make the child as comfortable as possible until someone who is responsible arrives and can take over.

Neither during the time of crisis nor in the normal routine of the day should the teacher administer medication (including aspirin) without written permission and instructions from a parent. Some children, such as those with certain allergies, are on a schedule that requires dosage during the time the child is in school. When this is the case, the teacher should act only on explicit, written procedures worked out with the parent and kept on file at the school. Teachers should not make medical decisions regarding the kind of care a child is to receive when illness or injury occurs. Both the child and the school are best served by following instructions exactly as they are given in the child's records.

Fortunately, real medical crises are rare in a preschool, considering the number of hours and the number of children involved in routine procedures. When a child is hurt or ill, the critical factors are not likely to be the time required to decide what to do and the way in which the decision should be implemented. The crisis is far more likely to rest in the psychological effect on the staff, the child, and the parent.

REFERENCES

Austin, G., J. S. Oliver, and J. C. Richards. 1978. *The Parents' Medical Manual.* Englewood Cliffs, N.J.: Prentice-Hall.

Green, M. I. 1977. *A Sigh of Relief: The First Aid Handbook for Childhood Emergencies.* New York: Bantam Books.

Pantell, R. H., J. Fries, and D. Vickery. 1978. *Taking Care of Your Child: A Parents' Guide to Medical Care.* Reading, Mass.: Addison-Wesley.

Reinisch, E. H., and R. E. Minear, Jr. 1978. *Health of the Preschool Child.* New York: Wiley & Sons.

U.S. Department of Health, Education, and Welfare, Office of Child Development. 1973. *Health Services: A Guide for Project Directors and Health Personnel.* Day Care Series, 6, DHEW Publication No. (OCD) 73-12. Washington, D.C.: Government Printing Office.

Vaughan, G. 1970. *Mummy, I Don't Feel Well: A Pictorial Guide to Common Childhood Illnesses.* London: Arcade Publishing.

Vigare, V. 1978. "Signals of Child Abuse." In *Readings in Early Childhood Education 79/80.* Guilford, Conn.: Dushkin Publishing.

CHAPTER 9

KEEPING CHILDREN SAFE

LIABILITY IN THE PRESCHOOL[1]

Suppose that in the day care center or preschool where you work a child is injured

1. by a child who has previously been cooperative, pleasant, and quiet.
2. by a child whom you know is destructive and physically aggressive.
3. because of a defective piece of equipment (a slide that has a sharp edge, a jungle gym that collapses, and so on).
4. through his or her own carelessness and in violation of school rules that have been explained.
5. because of your carelessness or that of another teacher.

Who is liable for the child's injury?

When the owners of a preschool occupy a facility and enroll students, they establish a relationship recognized by law. The owners automatically assume certain responsibilities, whether or not these are written into the school records. The same is true for a person who agrees to teach in a preschool. By law, in many instances, a teacher may also share in the responsibility for what takes place during school hours even if he or she is not directly involved. In essence, the administration and staff become liable for the health and safety of the students and, if legally challenged, must provide suitable explanation for the way they met this responsibility.

General Principles of the Law

For facilities that deal with young children, liability is essentially different from that of other schools. When young children are injured, there is deemed to be no contributory negligence on their part. If older children are injured, lost, kidnaped, or in some way harmed while at school, the courts hold that they may conceivably have contributed to their condition. In cases involving preschools, however, the law is clear that young children are not expected to be able to take care of themselves. Because caretaking, not education, is interpreted to be the primary purpose of a preschool, a special burden is placed on the school and its teachers. Although a given situation may not in any sense be an emergency, the threat of a lawsuit constitutes a crisis for many teachers. The anxiety resulting from the prospect of court proceedings is very real not only for the teacher but for the child, the parents, and the school as well.

The case of *Fowler* v. *Seaton,* involving action against a nursery school, brings out the broad range of responsibility that lies with the school. The

[1]Information in this section is based on lectures by Richard G. Mansfield, attorney at law, Palo Alto, California.

plaintiff, Jenny Gene Fowler, at the age of three years and ten months, was a student in a private school that provided day care for children of working mothers. Mrs. Seaton, the defendant, was the owner of the school.

When picking Jenny Gene up one evening, the mother was told there had been an accident—Jenny Gene had wet her pants. This was unusual but not alarming as far as the mother was concerned. What was alarming was the fact that at supper an hour later the parents noticed that Jenny Gene's eyes were crossed and that there was a large lump on her forehead. The mother immediately called Mrs. Seaton, asking what had happened. The owner then explained that another child "who had nothing in his hands" had struck Jenny Gene in the forehead.

Jenny Gene eventually had three operations to correct the crossing of her eyes, and the parents sued the school, alleging negligence resulting in personal injuries to their child. At the time of the proceedings the child's eyes were still crossing. After a judgment by a lower court, in favor of the owner of the school, a higher court reversed the verdict in an opinion that included these points:

> Thus, it appears that the school was a preschool nursery operated for profit. We know, as a matter of common knowledge, that such schools are primarily intended to give the children an opportunity to engage in supervised group play and other supervised activities. Such schools hold themselves out as furnishing supervision for the children. *Furnishing supervision is the basic service for which these schools charge. It is their main function.*[2] The duty owed by the operator of such a school to the students in attendance is substantially different in degree from that owed by schools whose primary function is education, where the children are much older, and where supervision is incidental. *The supervision required must be commensurate with the age of the children and with their activities.* Thus the several cases cited by respondent relating to the duties owed to grammar and high school students are not in point. (61 C. 2d 681; 39 Cal. Rpts. 881, 394 P. 2d 697, p. 688)

> Certainly it is true that this was an unusual occurrence. *While it may be common knowledge, as contended by defendant, that in the normal course of play children suffer bumps, bruises, and scratches, it certainly is not a matter of common knowledge that children normally come home from a nursery school with concussion of the brain and crossed eyes. If that were "normal" or "usual," nursery schools would not stay in business very long. Such a school, as already pointed out, by its very nature, holds itself out as a place where children can be safely left and carefully supervised.*

"Unlike elementary-school-age children, in the eyes of the law preschoolers are too young to be responsible for themselves. This means preschool teachers are especially vulnerable to lawsuits."

Attorney

[2]Italics have been added for emphasis throughout the opinion.

Of course, in most *res ipsa* cases, it is incumbent on the plaintiff to show that the actions of the plaintiff did not contribute to the injuries. Here it was shown that plaintiff is of an age that, as a matter of law, she could not be guilty of contributory negligence, and also that, as a result of shock caused by the accident she cannot remember or communicate the cause of the accident. Under such circumstances, of course, she is entitled to the presumption that she exercised due care for her own safety. (61 C. 2d 681; 39 Cal. Rpts. 881, 394 P. 2d 697, p. 690)

In *Fowler* v. *Seaton* the California Supreme Court found that the facts justified application of the doctrine of *res ipsa loquitur* to require the Happy Day Nursery School to produce evidence that it was not careless. This doctrine includes three central conditions:

1. That the plaintiff for some good reason really does not know or cannot say how the injury occurred and cannot produce witnesses of his or her own to tell what happened
2. That the plaintiff's injuries are of the sort which are usually caused by carelessness or negligence
3. That if anyone was careless, it was probably the defendant

The teacher or school director or owner should understand that if a situation analogous to *Fowler* v. *Seaton* should occur, and the three elements of the doctrine of *res ipsa loquitur* apply, the school will have to prove its innocence. If, on the other hand, the doctrine does not apply, the burden will remain on the child and his or her parents to demonstrate that the school staff was careless.

In general, the following principles of law apply to centers and preschools:

1. Children in the nursery-school-age group are too young to be required to take care of themselves, therefore no doctrine for contributory negligence exists because very young children cannot be negligent.
2. Care is the predominant principle. The law views the nursery school as a place that cares for children primarily and only secondarily educates them.
3. The employer is liable for the acts of his or her employee. If a teacher or other employee is involved in harming a child, either negligently or intentionally, the owner is usually also liable if the employee was in the scope of his or her employment. It does not, however, release the employee from liability.
4. The standard of care that must be exercised in providing for the safety of a child increases as the child's capacity for self-care decreases.
5. Waivers signed by parents or guardians do not release the teacher or preschool operator from liability. The child is considered a ward of so-

ciety through the courts and even the parents cannot waive a child's rights. However, from a psychological standpoint, it is always a good idea to require signed permission slips or detailed releases for field trips and emergency treatment. A release prepared by the school with details of every field trip should be signed each time; a general release for all trips is not adequate.

The Teacher's Responsibility

"I can't stress enough the importance of being able to document that you have shown reasonable care to avoid accidents."

Attorney

Since the courts have established that owners and teachers are responsible (and therefore liable under the law) for the health and safety of their students during school hours, the staff of a school must be able to show they have consistently done all that is reasonably required to maintain the health and safety of the children in their school. Teachers should not wait until something happens before meeting their responsibility. Practical steps can be taken to protect those in charge should they become involved in legal action—steps that often discourage the initiation of such action. Even though the final decision of the courts may be favorable to the school, the inconvenience, expense, and emotional strain of a suit can be very great.

In order to lessen the dimensions of a potential legal crisis, a school should constantly observe the following measures:

1. Adequate and consistent recording and reporting
2. Comprehensive safety measures
3. Realistic insurance coverage

Many errors can be avoided if records for every child are complete and up to date. A teacher needs to have information available regarding whom to call in case of an emergency, who is responsible for each child when he or she is not in school, and who is authorized to pick up the child. The school should also have on file any limitations on the child's diet or physical activity and a record of any family beliefs that take precedence over usual school procedures.

Written reports made at the time of illness or injury at school and filed as a matter of record can be an important resource if a teacher's actions are questioned later on. Regularly reporting to parents any unusual occurrence or any emergency action taken and involving them as much as possible in the affairs of the school build support rather than suspicion and show good faith on the part of the school and the teachers.

A school's safety program indicates as much as anything the extent to which it meets its responsibility for the children in its care. In addition to establishing simple rules which are easy to remember, enforcement should

"Parents don't like to bring lawsuits against teachers. You are less likely to be charged with negligence if you invoke safety rules and are careful to take all necessary precautions."

Attorney

WHO IS LIABLE?

1. If a child whose temperament is generally pleasant injures another child, and the teacher is exercising proper supervision, the teacher is not liable because the event is completely unforeseen.
2. If the teacher knows that a child has a tendency to hurt others, the teacher is liable for not protecting other children from that child.
3. A school (and/or teacher) is liable for accidents caused by defective equipment.
4. The teacher is probably not liable for the child's carelessness if reasonable precautions have been taken, such as providing soft surface under climbing equipment, having play equipment suited to age of children, and so on.
5. The teacher is liable for injury to another due to the teacher's own carelessness. The owner or administrator of a school is also liable for the negligence of an employee.

be carried out in such a way as to make the staff and children mindful of safety.

Whatever equipment is provided should be sturdy and bought or built with consideration for safety features as well as economy. Because of the danger of children being hit in the mouth or face, swing seats should be made of canvas or soft material, never of wood or metal. Teeter-totters are a poor choice of equipment for similar reasons. Raised sandboxes are more likely to cause tripping than sunken ones. All permanent supplies and equipment should undergo regular inspection and constant upkeep and should not be allowed to break or wear out.

A realistic insurance program must cover teachers as well as the owners of a school in a variety of ways and for many contingencies. It lessens the fear of the consequences of unavoidable accidents such as loss by fire or injury in a car accident while on a field trip. When hired to work in a preschool or day care center, you should determine what insurance coverage a school has and in what way, if any, it protects you.

The consequences of critical situations, of course, can be tragic for all involved, including the teacher. You need not be apprehensive; with good training, reasonable precautions, and sensible reactions, you will be able to deal effectively with crisis.

CRISIS COMES IN MANY FORMS

Crisis intrudes into the routine of a preschool or center as surely as it is part of the life of a family with young children. No matter how experienced teachers may be or how carefully they plan, crises will arise. Experienced teachers see crisis as a natural part of the job and prepare to deal with it. They know, too, that it almost always crops up unexpectedly and in different kinds of situations.

Problems of Custody

It is almost the end of nap time in a small, private nursery school. The owner has not returned from a series of errands and the assistant teacher is busy helping children put on shoes and sweaters so they can go out to play. The older children are already at the far end of the yard on a nature walk with Brad, who comes in two afternoons a week. The teacher looks up to see a well-dressed man walk in and hears him say, "How do you do. I'm Jennifer Hamilton's father. I realize it's a bit early, but I've come to take her home."

Hearing his voice, Jenny runs to him crying, "Oh, Daddy, come look. I did a painting today." At her urging, Mr. Hamilton accompanies Jenny to see her work and all the areas of special interest to Jenny. The teacher hastens to get Jennifer's coat and mittens and to speed the girl and her father on their way.

"Use standard strategies to check out phone calls before releasing a child. For example, if someone calls to authorize release of a child, call the custodial person back to verify."

Attorney

If parents of a child make conflicting claims about custody, the director may have to check the court order.

Within moments of their departure Jennifer's mother arrives. She is horrified when told that Jenny's father has already taken the child. She becomes upset, cries, and then threatens to sue the teacher and the school for releasing the child to her former husband. They are embroiled in a dispute over custody and her attorney has requested a temporary order by the court that would assign the child to her. All of this had been explained to the owner. By the way, where *was* the owner?

Situations involving custody and release of children are among the most sensitive the preschool has to consider. In families where remarriage has occurred or in living-together situations, persons other than the parents may occasionally call for a child. If the school records do not show authorization for friends or stepparents to take the child, awkward and difficult situations can arise.

Combined Crises

Some critical situations seem to combine all the elements of crisis—physical injury, psychological stress, and possibility of legal action. Consider one such incident and how it was handled. This involved a young college student hired as an aide.

Ted lived in the neighborhood of the nursery school where he worked and knew many of the children and their families personally. He enjoyed the children's affection for him and willingly joined in playground supervision, pleased that so many of the children seemed to like being with him.

He initiated games, rough-housed with the children, organized "races," and was the center of one project after another. The head teacher suggested he do more guiding and less directing, but Ted felt he wouldn't be doing his job if he "just stood around and watched." Besides, when he tried to follow her advice, the kids spent a lot more time arguing and fighting, and he couldn't stand that. Kids should have fun together.

One day, while pushing Lester and Ellie on the swings, he noticed how much hitting and shoving went on as the other children waited their turns. He felt he had a good solution to the problem when he thought of putting one of the climbing boards across the swings so that as many kids as could hang on to the board or each other could have a turn.

The children responded enthusiastically, eight of them finding places for the first turn. "Higher! Higher!" they shrieked, their excitement matching the request. Amidst the screaming and shouting

"The teacher as a professional should know how to use better judgment than someone without training—including parents."

Director

Ted suddenly heard another sound, a thud. Susie had somehow been hit by the end of the board. A moment ago she had been walking around the swing; now she lay motionless.

"Stop! Stop pumping!" Ted shouted. "Susie's hurt!" His fright communicated more quickly than the command. As the board slowed, the children slid off to cluster around the limp form. Rufus spoke Ted's question. "Is she dead?" he asked.

In answer, Ted stooped and took Susie in his arms. Too confused to think what was best, too frightened to remember what to do, oblivious to the others, he knew only his own fault, his own guilt. Her parents would never forgive him; he would never forgive himself.

The two children closest to him began to cry. Several of the boys shoved forward demanding to see. Attracted by the noise and confusion, the director came quickly to see what was wrong. As she took in the situation she spoke quietly.

"Ted, put Susie down carefully. Everyone else, inside, and Miss Lewis will read you a story."

Dutifully the children moved toward the classroom, only to turn back as they heard Ted remonstrating with the director. "Susie needs help bad . . . her parents won't ever . . . to the hospital. I'll drive her myself. I'll take care of her. I'll . . ."

Noticing that Susie had begun to stir, the director again gave instructions. "Ted, stay with her. I'll be back in a moment." Then calling Miss Lewis to take the children in for a story, she went to summon both doctor and parent.

The calm, positive action of the director had restored order, but other things must be done to resolve the confusion. The children involved should have a chance to talk about and learn from the accident. The concern and attitude of the parents must be considered; they will need to be reassured that safety standards are being observed by the staff.

WHAT IS *CRISIS* TO A CHILD?

1. Separation from parents
2. Loss of bladder or bowel control
3. Arbitrary attack by other children
4. Being called "names"
5. Parents forgetting to pick them up at going-home time
6. Deviation from usual routine

Ted is also a victim of the incident. His poor judgment invited the crisis and his difficulty in dealing with his own feelings contributed to the turmoil. The director needs to talk with him about his reaction and about the safety procedures to be observed at the center.

A single event thus can mingle stress, threat of injury, possibility of lawsuit, and a challenge to the reputation of the preschool.

HOW TO DEAL WITH CRISIS

Emergencies are an unscheduled part of a preschool program but the alert teacher can be prepared with strategies for dealing with threatening situations. Usually, the staff has some degree of control over the consequences of a crisis.

Avoiding and Minimizing Crisis

Even though some stress and an occasional emergency will be inevitable, this does not mean that they are to be awaited with a passive philosophy of "accidents will happen." Crisis is not only accidental, it may come from carelessness, neglect, and lack of foresight or experience. An apparently smooth, safe, well-run school is never accidental.

The basic rules of safe equipment and procedures were discussed earlier.

WHAT IS *CRISIS* TO A TEACHER?

1. Inability to reach parents when a child is ill or hurt
2. A bleeding or badly injured child
3. Sand or soap in a child's eye; choking, nosebleeds
4. Children running out of the room and refusing to return
5. Child who loses self-control
6. Wrong person taking child home
7. Volunteers who don't show up when expected
8. Child's work discarded by mistake
9. Children arguing adamantly over toys or equipment
10. Parent upset about a classroom situation as reported by his or her child
11. Supplies and materials not available when needed
12. Collapse of play equipment
13. Small child bullied by larger child

> ### WHAT IS *CRISIS* TO PARENTS?
>
> 1. Severe illness or injury
> 2. Children fighting, hitting, biting one another
> 3. Child striking a teacher or parent
> 4. Readjustment due to teacher change during the school year
> 5. Temper tantrums
> 6. Child released to unauthorized person
> 7. Not enough supervisory staff due to absence of teacher
> 8. Other parents not doing their part in co-op program

''Every time the phone rings during the time my child is in school, I have this fear that something has happened to him.''

Parent

In addition to the elementary principles covering physical injury or illness and liability, the teacher can avoid crisis and stress by creating an environment in which accumulated frustration is minimized. The teacher can provide many safe places for play, many acceptable outlets for aggression. Trees to climb, dirt to dig in, clay to thump, nails to pound, drums to beat, balls to kick, dolls to spank, mattresses to jump on, paint and paste to smear, and water for washing, splashing and bubbling provide opportunity to work off a great many aggressions without extra help.

The teacher who praises and spends time with children when they are engaged in approved behaviors is likely to minimize stress in the classroom. This may be especially important for those children who come to school with fears and frustrations. These children often need more help than those who have been allowed to explore and share a variety of experiences with other children their age.

In a program of early education there are many experiences that are naturally frustrating to children. Someone else wants what they want; the teacher expects them to pick up after themselves, to wait until later, to take turns; they aren't strong enough or skilled enough to pursue many of their interests; they ask questions that no one answers; they want to read but the book they're looking for isn't on the shelf where it belongs; when they need a red crayon, the only ones left are black, blue, or green; just when it's their turn on the slide, it's time to go home. Even an environment that is designed to meet the needs of children seems to induce frustration. Anything that can be done to help reduce frustration can help deal with crisis.

Some Principles for Dealing with Crisis

When a genuine crisis cannot be avoided, the teacher's response to it may be more effective if he or she acts on the basis of two general principles.

"I've learned to preface my phone calls to parents by saying, 'This is not an emergency. I only called to talk about some business.' "

Director

The first of these is that a crisis has a number of consequences that follow the event itself—the ripple effect described earlier. In dealing with a stressful event, the attention should be paid to other persons who may not be the central focus but who are affected in various ways. The incident involving Ted, for example, illustrated how the director or head teacher needed to attend to his reaction and those of the other children as well as the injury to the girl. Children who hit others may also need help in dealing with their own reactions as they see the response of other children and adults to what they have done. Parents whose children have been involved in a crisis may need reassurance and information.

Another general principle in dealing with social and psychological stress is to follow up in a day or two—and perhaps again later—by contacting persons outside the immediate staff with information about how a crisis turned out. Word of how an injured child is doing, comments about whether safeguards have been taken to avoid future accidents, or sharing the resolution of a problem can give people a much needed opportunity to express their concerns, which they may not otherwise have had occasion to voice.

The teacher's skill in coping with crisis may in itself be useful in dealing with the effects of stress. Studies of disaster, for example, show that adults who remain calm instill similar behavior in children; when they become openly frightened, children also react in frightened ways. In the classroom, children obviously imitate their teachers. In times of stress they are especially in need of models as to how to respond.

Dealing with crisis is partly a matter of experience, and you will find it useful to take time to reflect on what has happened once the situation has passed. You need to review the circumstances that led to the event and your own response to it. You may then consider alternatives and decide whether you handled your feelings and those of the others involved as effectively as possible. Every crisis should become a learning situation and provide a background for sound action in the future.

REFERENCES

Child Welfare League of America. 1960. *Child Welfare League of America, Standards for Child Protective Service*. New York: Child Welfare League of America.

Fowler v. *Seaton*. 1964. (61 C. 2d 681; 39 Cal. Rpts. 881, 394 P. 2d 697). San Francisco: Bancroft-Whitney, August.

PART FOUR

HELPING CHILDREN

LEARN

A PROLOGUE   Children will learn from contact with the world around them. What they learn, however, and how quickly depends on what the environment offers. They may learn that the environment is forbidding and unresponsive or they may learn to manage their surroundings so that their efforts are rewarded. The task of the teacher is to arrange the physical and social setting so that children can learn the things that will help them in later life experiences—school, interaction with peers, their views about themselves and the world in which they live.

The settings that best facilitate learning are not created by accident. Mental and social growth follow an established order. Understanding this order can be a tremendous resource to teachers in planning a program and in dealing with individual children.

This doesn't mean that you should become a specialist in all the areas of growth—language, social behavior, moral development, cognitive behavior, and physical maturation. This would be impossible and unnecessary. What you can do, as a teacher, is gain the basic knowledge in each area that is most relevant for the preschool. The most useful knowledge is that which gives you cues about things that you might do to assist development—information that can be translated into action in the preschool.

The chapters in this part describe several areas of development and some of the implications that knowledge about growth has for teachers. We offer two types of information. One is a sense of the major concepts that may be applied in many different situations and for many children. The other is specific information about a particular behavior. Both the general principles and the specific information are needed to understand development and to plan the preschool environment.

In going through this section, you may find it helpful to identify points that have particular meaning for you. The two questions to keep in mind are: "Does this help me understand general principles of growth?" and "Can I use this information in the preschool?"

The competence you now have and will gain during your training is only a beginning, not a finished product. Research in child development is going on at a lively pace; new information is described every month in professional journals. You must keep in touch with the field to maintain your competence. New studies bring new insights.

Publications dealing with child development provide ways to keep in touch with the results of relevant studies. The Society for Research in Child Development publishes a series on research that reviews the findings and state of knowledge of various fields. The series began in 1964; new volumes have appeared since, others are now in preparation. Look them up and read some chapters that are especially relevant for young children, keeping in mind whether the studies described and the conclusions the authors made can be applied in the preschool.

There are also journals that present results of recent studies—*Child Development, Developmental Psychology, Merrill Palmer Quarterly* are among the best known. *Young Children* reviews and describes certain studies for professionals in early education. *Day Care and Early Education* offers articles on curriculum and other aspects of the preschool, including results of research. The National Association for the Education of Young Children provides publications on a wide range of topics. The federal and state agencies that deal with education and child care also have several types of publications—bulletins, newsletters, and reports. You may find it useful to develop a file of the addresses of such agencies and the publications they offer (see the "Appendix of Resources" at the end of the text). A letter of inquiry from time to time may bring you a list of materials that are available. Conventions, conferences, workshops, and conversations with other people in the field also serve to keep you informed.

We have included a chapter on children as consumers in response to the growing complexity of the marketplace in our society and because young children now have much more direct contact with messages from manufacturers of commercial products, primarily through television. We believe, also, that young children can be made aware of the need to protect the physical environment in which they live. This will be an even more crucial issue for them when they are adults. It is not too soon to encourage them to think about ecology and conservation.

Simply acquiring knowledge about development isn't enough; this information must be translated for children through the warmth and concern of a sensitive teacher. Warm, sensitive interaction can be even more effective when it is based on an understanding of children.

CHAPTER 10

THE DEVELOPMENT OF LINGUISTIC COMPETENCE

LANGUAGE AND COMMUNICATION

Language is a remarkable capability. It is versatile, flexible, complex, capable of an infinite range of nuance and meaning. For example, take a few simple words—*Sally, Susan, likes*—plus some auxiliary words and explore the different meanings that can be created by rearranging them: Sally likes Susan; Susan likes Sally; Does Susan like Sally? Is Susan like Sally? Susan, like Sally! Susan is like Sally. All of these meanings (and more) can be modified by tone of voice, facial expression, tempo of comment, and other nonverbal cues. Children communicate with nonverbal cues at an early age. A whine, a frown, temper tantrums, tears, an engaging smile—all are part of the repertoire of communication skills accessible to young children.

Language itself may be used to communicate in indirect ways when combined with nonverbal cues. The message conveyed by the phrase ''I understand,'' varies enormously, depending on the context in which it is used and the tone of voice. It may mean, for example, ''I heard what you said but I don't agree,'' or ''I get what you are implying,'' or that a problem has been successfully solved. Language is used to express many meanings other than the literal translation of the words spoken.

In this chapter, our interest is in the growth of ability to speak and to comprehend speech. Children probably learn to use nonverbal modes of communication from observing others and as a result of their own experience. If whining is successful, it will become a technique for persuading a parent or other adults. If physical touching is effective in getting a desired response, it is likely to become part of the array of communication skills.

SEQUENCES IN THE DEVELOPMENT
OF LANGUAGE

There are four distinct aspects of language development—speaking, listening (in the sense of comprehending speech), writing, and reading. Each has its own pattern of development. Competence in one aspect is not always closely related to competence in another in either degree of skill or timing. Speaking and comprehending speech are the skills of greatest interest during the preschool years.

The ability to speak does not necessarily indicate the ability to comprehend. A young child can repeat the words of a song, nursery rhyme, commercial, or pledge of allegiance to the flag without knowing what the words mean. Some sounds that infants make represent an ability to vocalize and probably do not mean what the eager adults like to read into them. The ability to recognize sounds of speech and to repeat them does not always mean that the child connects these sounds to actions or objects in the surrounding world.

TABLE 10.1
Children's Progress in
Language Ability

Age	Ability
2 years	Should be able to follow simple commands without visual clues: *Johnny, get your hat and give it to Daddy.* *Debby, bring me your ball.* Uses a variety of everyday words heard in home and neighborhood: *Mommy, milk, ball, hat* Shows developing sentence sense by the way words are put together: *Go bye bye car* *Milk all gone*
3 years	Understands and uses words other than for naming; is able to fit simple verbs, pronouns, prepositions, and adjectives such as *go, me, in,* and *big* more and more into sentences
4 years	Should be able to give a connected account of some recent experience Should be able to carry out a sequence of two simple directions: *Bobby, find Susie and tell her dinner's ready.*
5 years	Speech should be intelligible although some sounds may still be mispronounced Can carry on a conversation if vocabulary is within his or her range

Adapted from *Learning to Talk,* prepared by the U.S. National Institute of Neurological Disease and Stroke, National Institutes of Health, U.S. Department of Health, Education, and Welfare (Washington, D.C.: Government Printing Office, 1969), pp. 22–24.

There are great differences among children in the age at which they begin to acquire language and the rapidity with which they reach adult levels of competence. The sequence in which language is acquired, however, seems to be very similar for most children. General patterns are roughly related to age (see Table 10.1).

From the appearance of the ability to make speechlike sounds, the utterances of the child continue to grow more complex. One of the first major phases is the use of single words, called *holophrases,* that *may* (there is some dispute about this) express a more extended message. "Doggie," may mean "I see the dog," or "I'm afraid of the dog." "No," may mean that the child objects to whatever is happening. There is not complete agreement among students of language about the meaning of holophrases (Gardner, 1978). If these one-word messages convey an extended meaning, one might expect the child to string together words to express their meaning. Children are capable of doing this during their second year, either by repeating the same word or by saying two different words with an intervening pause. The single-word utterance may be simply an echoing of a word or an expression of a label for an object. In any case, holophrases represent the beginning of speech.

The second major phase is marked by the appearance of the *duo* and usually begins late in the second year. A *duo* is a pair of words that convey

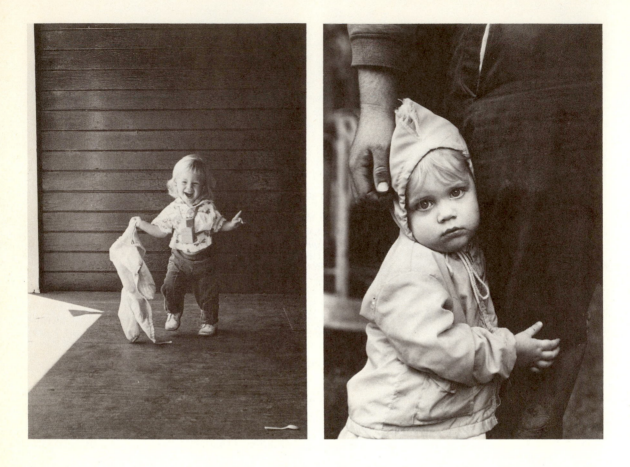

a comprehensive message. "Fall down," "All gone," "More milk," are examples. Duos can be used in many ways: to name or label an object, to show possession, or to indicate action.

At about two-and-one-half years of age, child speech becomes increasingly complete and complex. There are great individual differences at this age. Some children sound like miniature adults; others scarcely speak. Sentences are usually still primitive, often simple, declarative comments ("The truck is red."). Negatives are used awkwardly ("No go bed."). Sentences are short and limited to one topic or idea ("Car go away. Daddy go away," rather than "Daddy went away in the car."). This is the age, also, that the rules for making plurals, past tense, and possessives are not yet clear. The child may consistently produce incorrect forms ("I goed," "He holded the kitty," "mouses").

The next phase is one that the preschool teacher often encounters. Children begin to use words in a more precise way. Bits of speech, *ed, ing, est,* articles such as *the*, plurals, and possessives begin to be used correctly.

Observations (Brown, 1973) suggest that children acquire these skills in a roughly similar sequence, even though some youngsters use them much earlier than others. That children follow a developmental sequence whether the skill is learned relatively early or late is an important idea. The teacher who is observing language patterns in young children will realize that mastery of these specific forms will occur in a given order. Constructions such as "*on* table" or "*in* box" occur before "James walk*ed*" or the use of articles as in "on *the* table." Individual differences in use of such forms probably can't be eliminated easily by training.

The average child has an expressive vocabulary at age three and one-half of over 1,000 words.

More complex forms begin to appear by age three. Sentences are longer, more precise. As children approach age four, they begin to use questions in more adult forms. They can usually handle auxiliary verbs ("I *don*'t want to."). By age five, the speech of most children resembles adult language in several ways: sentences are longer and more complex than before; more than one idea is expressed in a single sentence; double negatives ("I won't never. . . .") have usually dropped out of speech, unless they are part of a dialect and are retained as an appropriate form of adult speech. By the age of six, a child has learned most of the adult pattern of speech and has accomplished an impressive feat in acquiring such a tremendously complex skill, considering the fact that most adult skills are not acquired until much later.

HOW LANGUAGE IS ACQUIRED

Children seem not to be taught a language so much as they acquire it on their own. The child is not a passive learner, absorbing words, imitating phrases, and gradually accumulating the words and phrases he or she will use as an adult. The child takes an active role in developing patterns of speech. Language acquisition develops through interaction of the child's comprehension of speech and the speech he or she hears in the surrounding world.

Imitation and Reinforcement

Knowledge about how language is learned has expanded rapidly in the past twenty years. A traditional view held that learning in this area proceeded through imitation and reinforcement of adult speech. It was assumed that children would imitate models around them, that they would learn patterns of speech that parents praised or otherwise reinforced, and that they would learn more quickly if adults around them corrected their errors or gave them feedback about their language use.

Children obviously do learn by imitation and reward or they would not speak the language of the adults around them and use the same dialect as their parents. But imitation and reinforcement do not explain what is known about the growth of children's speech. A close examination of the role of imitation in language acquisition uncovers weaknesses in the theory.

One weakness in the imitation theory is the fact that much of our speech is original. We do not use identical sentences over and over again. Sentences are not constructed of phrases that we fit together like tinker toys. Children make up their own phrases and sentences to communicate in a unique way about the situation of the moment or to respond to something said or done. Children's sentences are not selected from a list that they heard from adults around them and stored in a memory bank to use at the appropriate time. A child could not become linguistically competent by imitation alone.

As part of the compensatory education movement of the 1960s, attempts were made to facilitate language learning by providing models of adult speech. Courtney Cazden (1965), for example, worked daily for three months with two groups of young children. In one group, the staff member talked with the children but was careful not to repeat the child's words or phrases. In the other group, the experimenter completed sentences and phrases and repeated them in proper grammatical form. Cazden reasoned that children who heard the adult version of the sentences they were trying to construct would develop linguistic skills more rapidly. As it turned out, the opposite was true! Children who had only talked with the experimenter made as much progress as those who heard their own words rephrased and expanded in adult terms. Providing models seems to be an ineffective way, by itself, to bring about changes in children's speech. Modeling does result in changes, however, if it is combined with opportunities for children to use the types of speech they hear (Gleason, 1972).

Other studies show that imitation and instruction are not the only explanations for language acquisition. Parents usually do not correct their children's grammatical errors—children learn grammar without instruction (Brown and Hanlon, 1970). Also, there is little correlation between the frequency with which parents use words and the order in which the child begins to use them. The fact that a child hears a word or phrase often does not mean that he or she will begin to use the word earlier than other words heard less frequently.

Another bit of evidence that raises doubts about the role of imitation comes from children's use of double negatives. Most children use double negatives for a short time during their language-learning stages, despite the fact that they may never hear their parents or other adults use this form of speech.

Imitation and reinforcement obviously do play a role in language development. Expanding vocabulary, labeling, and clarifying the exact meaning of words are among the skills that probably respond to reinforcement and imitation. The puzzling and fascinating research finding, however, is that these familiar learning processes do not account for much of children's speech or for the phrases through which it develops.

Children Develop Their Own Rules

A striking outcome of research on children's speech is that it seems to follow similar developmental sequences even for children raised in quite different linguistic environments. Some constructions, for example, almost always appear before others, as described earlier. Questions typically do not appear until about age three, despite the frequency of questions in the child's experience.

Children make up words in a way that seems to be an application of a principle they have learned to use in solving a problem in phrasing or tense. The familiar errors in past participle ("He goed," "I holded") are not imitations; they are words that seem to be applications of the rule that actions which took place in the past are indicated by adding *ed* on the end of a verb. No one teaches children this rule and they certainly could not describe it, but somehow they come to sense and apply it. Usually it works, but occasionally it is an error. Children make up and form their own language by the application of such rules. It is in this sense that language grows through the interaction between the child's capabilities, understanding, and initiative and the language of his or her surroundings. This is a dramatic example of the role of the child's own inner curriculum in the preschool classroom.

"Richard's mother understood what he wanted when he said, 'sookegg.' It meant, 'I want a soft-cooked egg.' "

Teacher

Biological Factors

Biological factors affect acquisition of speech. The exact nature of genetic influence on language ability is not clear. If there are genes for language, they have not been identified, although research studies on twins indicate genetic influences. Lenneberg (1969) shows that the onset of speech occurs more nearly at the same time for identical twins than for fraternal twins. Also, if there is a delay in learning, it will be the same for both twins of an identical pair. Fraternal twins may sometimes experience the same delay, but frequently one twin will start later and learn more slowly than the other.

Because of biological heritage, children respond to speech directed toward them, but how much they continue to respond seems to be highly dependent on environmental factors. During the first three months of their lives, normal babies born to deaf parents obviously do not hear the same kind or amount of verbal discourse as children in families where the mother and father are not deaf. Nor are their normal vocalizations responded to as immediately. Yet it has been shown that their initial cooing and sound production are almost identical to those of babies born to mothers who can hear them and whose sounds the babies hear. As long as children of deaf parents hear language from others, their learning proceeds normally. Communication with their parents takes place through gestures and a repertoire of other nonverbal responses.

Most children who are born deaf may go through the cooing stage but since they do not hear speech, even their own, this behavior is soon extinguished. Their introduction to language as a system does not take place until they reach school age, unless they have attended a special preschool. Blind children's learning to speak is closely related to physical maturation and follows that of children who have sight.

Observation of a wide variety of children shows that the acquisition of speech is a natural process that cannot be deterred. Even when children have only minimum resources to aid them, they can and do learn to speak the language they hear. Some researchers argue that the ability to speak is biologically "programmed"; it is already part of the biological capability, only waiting for an opportunity to be activated (Chomsky, 1975).

Children have ideas for which they have no words; they also have words for which they have no ideas. An example of the latter is when children use "bad" language, not knowing what it really means.

Another theory is advanced by a Russian psychologist Vygotsky (1962), who argues that language and thought grow in somewhat independent ways, at least in early stages of development. As both language and thought emerge, they serve one another. This view is consistent with the fact that children learn words and phrases that have no meaning for them. They also act as if they have developed concepts at some level that they cannot express in words. Rules that govern early language usage, for example, are developed before the linguistic competence is available to talk about them. The implications for teaching in the preschool are clear. If speech and thought (through experience) can grow separately, the teacher can help children connect the two by providing words that represent their experiences.

LANGUAGE AND THINKING

Does facility in speech help a child to think more clearly? What is the relation between linguistic competence (language) and cognitive strategies (thinking)? These are old questions that have led to many debates.

One view proposes that language sets limits, regulates, and defines thought processes (Sapir, 1921; Whorf, 1956). The concepts and labels that children learn are the channels that guide their thoughts. A young child can use words and instructions to help establish control of attention and action. A child painting at an easel may be heard to say to himself, "Keep the paint on the paper." Or, carrying water to the rabbit cage, a young girl may repeat, "Walk slowly so I won't spill." These are the teacher's words; children use them to focus attention and control their actions. Words also help children organize information for storage in their memories so that they may recall things they have learned. A child is more likely to remember a list of names of objects if given categories in which to organize them. For example, the word *animals* may prompt children to make a list of apparently unrelated nouns—lion, fish, robin, horse. This type of verbal mediation is less useful, however, for preschoolers than for children in the early grades (Gardner,

1978). The word *family* immediately brings to mind a group, evoking mental images and organizing them. According to the theory that language channels thought, early language training may have a great effect on potential mental development: teach the words and they will help regulate thought processes.

The theory that language *follows* thought, that is, language is a reflection or expression of mental processes, is represented by Piaget and reflected in more recent writings (Blank, Rose, and Berlin, 1978). The child's experience is the raw material from which thought develops; language is another manifestation of underlying cognitive operations. The child experiences events and recognizes sensations before having the words to use in talking about them. The feeling of an object that is hard may come before the word is learned; the feeling of being alone may be familiar before the child has a term to use in describing it. A child may realize that flicking a switch on the wall causes the light to come on long before the language to talk about causality is part of his or her vocabulary.

HELPING CHILDREN COMPREHEND SPEECH

The focus of this chapter is on children's language, but communication in the preschool involves both children and adults. Teachers are obviously more effective if the children understand what is being said.

A study of children's comprehension of adult speech was carried out by Blank, Rose, and Berlin (1978). They identified three elements of *discourse* in the preschool: (1) a speaker-listener pair, (2) a topic about which they are talking, and (3) the level of the discussion (Moffett, 1968). In the preschool, two *speaker-listener pairs* consist of child-to-adult and adult-to-child. The *topics of conversation* are the child's own experiences and are usually based on his or her perceptions; the *level of discussion,* however, can range from direct and simple language to relatively abstract questions and statements.

Analysis of discourse identifies the distance or disparity between the direct perception of the child and the language used by the adult. For example, verbs and nouns are prominent in the speech of young children; this may reflect the fact that objects (nouns) and actions (verbs) are easy to observe and the labels are thus more easily learned. The language of the teacher is most readily understood if it "maps" directly onto the child's experience— that is, a direct and obvious connection is made between things the child sees and the words that represent them (Blank, Rose, and Berlin, 1978).

Children have difficulty following adult language that is abstract. The teacher who is not aware of this can easily lose the listener, especially the very young child. Children understand a phrase more easily if the *actor* is mentioned first, then the *action,* then the *object.* "The dog chased the rabbit," is much easier to grasp than, "The rabbit was chased by the dog." Luria (1961) describes the problems that a young child has when a negative

It is more effective to say, "Keep the sand in the sandbox," rather than, "Don't spill the sand"; or to say, "Speak quietly," rather than, "Don't shout."

TABLE 10.2
Levels of Abstraction for
Preschool Discourse

Have you ever spoken at Level
III to a child whose
comprehension is at Level I?

Level	Questions/Statements
Level I: Matching perception and language; this is the simplest level—the child must be able to apply language to what he or she sees (identifying, naming, imitating, etc.)	What is this? What did you see? Show me the circle.
Level II: Selecting from perception; similar to Level I except child must focus more selectively (describing, completing a sentence, giving an example, selecting an object by two characteristics, etc.)	What is happening? Name something that is. . . . Finish this sentence. . . .
Level III: Reordering what is seen; the child must restructure his or her perceptions (excluding, assuming role of another, following directions in correct sequence, etc.)	Find the things that are not. . . . What will happen next? What would she say?
Level IV: Reasoning about what is not seen; this category is the most complex, requiring the child to go beyond immediate perception (predicting, explaining, finding a logical solution, etc.)	What will happen if . . . ? Why should we use that? What could you do?

M. Blank, S. Rose, and L. J. Berlin, *The Language of Learning: The Preschool Years*. (New York: Grune & Stratton, 1978), pp. 18–33. Adapted by permission of Grune & Stratton.

is inserted in a command. Children who were asked to press a rubber bulb when the adult said, "Press," and to refrain from pressing when the adult said the words, "Do not press," often pressed on *both* commands. The request to press is directly translated into action. The request to avoid pressing the bulb is more abstract; the listeners must recognize that *not* is a signal to refrain from pressing. The negative command does not represent an action they can see or an object they can recognize.

Some questions and statements involve even more abstraction and are thus further from the child's immediate experience. "What do you think will happen if we put this piece of ice out in the sun?" is a question that asks the child to imagine a situation that he or she is not observing. The words cannot be directly linked to the event; the child must imagine the event and base it on past experiences. Table 10.2 describes four levels of abstraction in preschool discourse.

Young children also pass through a phase when they easily confuse the opposite dimensions of pairs of words (*tall* and *short, more* and *less, high* and *low,* and so on). Even after children have grasped the central meaning of the pair and realize that the terms refer to height, length, or magnitude, they may still confuse the end points. Two researchers in Scotland observed an example of this sort of confusion (Donaldson and Wales, 1970). They devised two cardboard trees with hooks to which apples could be attached. Young children were shown two trees with different numbers of apples and

Teacher: "Before you put the juice on the table, put the cups and napkins out."
Child: (Looking confused, puts juice on the table.)
Teacher: (Realizing lack of clarity) "No, let me show you. *First,* you put the cups out, *then* you put the napkins here, and *last* of all, you put the juice on the table."
Note: Children understand *first* and *last* before they understand *before* and *after.*

Amidon and Carey (1972)

were asked, "Does one tree have more (apples) on it than the other?" or "Does one tree have less (apples) on it than the other?" If the child answered, "Yes," he or she was asked to indicate which one. The procedure was varied to examine different patterns (some presentations had two trees with the same number of apples). The children in this study could not consistently identify *more* and *less.* They were likely to recognize either that one tree had more or that the trees did not hold the same number of apples, but they confused the meaning of *more* and *less.* They responded to *less* as if it meant *more.* Other researchers have followed up these results with similar studies and found that children confuse other pairs of words—*before* and *after, little* and *big* (Clark, 1973; Maratos, 1973).

Thus, a young child's ability to comprehend seems to follow somewhat different patterns than does the ability to speak. For example, a child will understand the mother's comment, "I went to the store," at the same stage that he or she is saying, "I goed to the store." Children can put together pieces of meaning in a sentence they hear and make sense of them, ignoring the fact that the syntax doesn't match their own. It may be that hearing and speaking are organized and controlled by different parts of the brain.

The transitional phases in the development of language in young children follow discernible patterns. Children talk as if they have come up with their own rules of speech to fit a particular level of mastery. They eventually make the adjustments needed to accommodate irregular verbs and bits of speech that add precision and to conform to the usage of language they hear around them. The rules children develop stubbornly resist change; the adult who understands this will let the child advance at his or her own pace.

THE IMPORTANCE OF LANGUAGE IN THE PRESCHOOL

If modeling and reinforcement seem to have limited influence on children's language use, is the importance of language in the preschool overestimated?

Future studies of language learning will clarify the process by which language is acquired, but one principle of great significance to early education already seems well established: children learn to speak by speaking. Opportunities to practice throughout conversation with adults are especially important.

A number of basic principles can be summarized from writings that describe things adults can do to facilitate children's speech (Cazden, 1972):

Get children to talk.
Children talk more if there is something of importance (to them) to talk about.

Children talk more about things that they care about. Continuity in the adult-child relationship makes for richer content in conversation.

Provide activities that lend themselves easily to verbal interaction and relate verbal exchange to the real world when possible.

Connect words or phrases to actions or demonstrations rather than offering linguistic exercises.

Use language that is more precise and more complex than that which the child is now using.

Informative comments evoke responses from children more often than commands or directives. Give children something to talk about.

For children who do not talk easily, structured situations may make them more comfortable.

Monitor teacher-child talk for a period of time and certain patterns will become clear. With some adults, the tendency is to lean toward the "interview" technique—"What is your name?" "How old are you?" "Where do you live?" "How many brothers and sisters do you have?" and so forth. These questions usually prompt simple one- or two-word replies. The teacher who consciously picks up on topics and activities that are of interest to children will get many more elaborate verbal responses. When the topic is of importance to the youngster, he or she is much more likely to become engaged in conversation.

Teachers should be sensitive to any tendencies to carry on a monologue. Giving directions ("Put the brush in the paint can."), making comments ("I like what you're doing."), and warning children ("Be careful not to spill."), constitute much of a teacher's verbalization during a workday. Such utterances do not encourage extended conversations; equal interaction between adult and child do not happen accidentally. Teachers have to monitor themselves and plan an environment where such interaction can take place naturally.

When snacks and other meals are set up for small groups, or when stories and sharing allow plenty of time and space for individual children to express themselves verbally, conversation is natural and enjoyable. When adults ask open-ended questions ("What do you suppose Mary wanted to do?") and make comments that encourage thinking responses ("I wonder why that happened. . . ."), children are more likely to respond and be motivated to carry on extended conversations.

The teacher who is most likely to succeed in motivating children to talk is the one who listens very carefully to the child and watches for clues that tell more about the child's interests and concerns. Attending totally to children means not finishing their sentences for them or assuming that you already know what they want to say. Ask children to elaborate and explain what it is they mean when they make comments. For example, a child might complain that another "won't share." Ask the youngster to tell you what he

or she means and to verbalize in greater detail how such a conclusion was reached. When children expand on their ideas, they gain practice in verbalizing and they also clarify their thought processes for themselves and the listener.

We all appreciate a good listener—a person who genuinely wants to understand what it is we are trying to communicate. Children, likewise, respond favorably to the adult who attends to and appreciates what they are saying. Children like to be praised and rewarded for using language and expressing themselves verbally. The best reward and reinforcement is an appreciative and attentive listener.

Sometimes teachers are guilty of using comfortable phrases—"That's very nice, honey," "I like that," "You're doing a good job," "How are we doing here?"—without really expecting any response from children. Such phrases do not encourage a child to think. They become hollow and soon the children learn to turn them off. When questions and comments are geared to children's level of understanding, however, and are intended to engage them in thought and conversation, the adult-child interaction is greatly enriched.

Teaching language does not require a formal teacher-directed setting where the child sits and listens passively and then responds to the teacher's questions. Young children learn to speak best when they are actively engaged in doing something of real interest to them and relating their physical activities to appropriate speech. They are motivated to practice language in natural settings. Language competencies are enhanced by activities that encourage cooperation and interaction, such as cooking, building, dramatic play, and similar group projects.

Teachers can help stretch a child's verbal abilities by using a wide variety of expressions. Instead of saying, "Marty, think of another way to do that," the teacher might say, "Marty, have you considered other possibilities?" Marty may not be able to define all the teacher's words, but will be challenged in a nonthreatening way to think about the meanings of those words within a given context. The teacher must be careful to see that the child doesn't have to stretch too much. Since children have difficulty following language that is abstract, they are more likely to learn, use, and understand the words they hear when verbal interactions are directly related to their activities.

Teachers tend to address their remarks to children who respond. Unless the adult is sensitive to this tendency, he or she is likely to overlook the shy or quiet child who is reluctant to talk. Sometimes there may be a language deficiency or handicap of some sort. It is important that the teacher initiate conversations with reluctant youngsters and persist in talking and encouraging discussion. Quiet children appear to respond most favorably to the friendly, warm, and chatty teacher who makes no demands for verbal response. The "interview" technique would be least successful with these

CAREGIVER SPEECH

In an article in *Scientific American*, Moskowitz (1978) describes how adults working with young children modify their speech to make language learning easier. Following are some examples:

Simplifying vocabulary
Using higher voice pitch
Exaggerating intonation
Using short, simple sentences
Asking many questions
Duplicating syllables ("wawa" for *water*; "choo-choo" for *train*)
Talking about things in the present—what is happening here and now
Minimizing discussion of feelings

Moskowitz reports that adults modify their speech not when the child is babbling and cooing, but as soon as he or she begins to talk.

children. Young children whose primary language is something other than English may have difficulty in making the transition to a second language, even when they understand what they hear. A sensitive and loving teacher—one who does not give up on these children or treat them as though they were less intelligent than the rest of the class—can do much to help them risk speaking in a less familiar tongue.

The teacher should not assume that the highly verbal child always understands what others are saying. For example, the teacher may point to an object and say, "There it is under the table"; the child may appear to understand *under* when the teacher's pointing actually provided a cue. Children may also repeat phrases they have heard without understanding their meaning. They are often impressed with phrases they hear within a dramatic context—television commercials and cuss words are such examples.

Although the exact nature of how a child learns a language may not be clear to researchers, it is safe to assume that children are likely to learn best in a setting that is warm, friendly, safe, and designed to engage them actively in verbal participation. Children learn language by practice; teachers develop competence in motivating language by practice. A setting rich in language-motivating experiences makes talking enjoyable. When teachers and children are enjoying themselves and each other, language competence will grow and flourish. (For additional curriculum ideas, see the section on "Language" in the companion handbook, *An Activities Handbook for Teachers of Young Children,* Third Edition.)

REFERENCES

Amidon, A., and P. Carey. 1972. "Why Five-Year-Olds Cannot Understand *Before* and *After.*" *Journal of Verbal Learning and Verbal Behavior,* 11, 417–423.

Blank, M., S. Rose, and L. J. Berlin. 1978. *The Language of Learning: The Pre-school Years.* New York: Grune & Stratton.

Brown, R. 1973. *A First Language: The Early Stages.* Cambridge, Mass.: Harvard University Press.

Brown, R., C. Cazden, and U. Bellugi-Klima. 1969. "The Child's Grammar from I to III." In *Minnesota Symposium on Child Psychology,* Vol. 2. Ed. J. P. Hill. Minneapolis: University of Minnesota Press.

Brown, R., and C. Hanlon. 1970. "Derivational Complexity and Order of Acquisition in Child Speech." In *Cognition and Development of Language.* Ed. J. R. Hayes. New York: John Wiley & Sons.

Cazden, C. 1965. *Environmental Assistance to the Child's Acquisition of Grammar.* Unpublished doctoral dissertation, Harvard University.

Cazden, C. 1972. *Language in Early Childhood Education.* Washington, D.C.: National Association for the Education of Young Children.

Chomsky, N. 1975. *Reflections on Language.* New York: Pantheon.

Clark, E. V. 1973. "What's in a Word? On the Child's Acquisition of Semantics in His First Language." In *Cognitive Development and the Acquisition of Language.* Ed. T. E. Moore. New York: Academic Press.

Donaldson, M., and R. Wales. 1970. "On the Acquisition of Some Relational Terms." In *Cognition and the Development of Language.* Ed. J. R. Hayes. New York: John Wiley & Sons.

Gardner, H. 1978. *Developmental Psychology.* Boston: Little, Brown.

Gleason, J. B. 1972. "An Experimental Approach to Improving Children's Communicative Ability." In *Language in Early Childhood Education.* Ed. C. B. Cazden. Washington, D.C.: National Association for the Education of Young Children.

Lenneberg, E. H. 1969. "On Explaining Language." *Science,* 164, No. 3880, 635–643.

Luria, A. R. 1961. *The Role of Speech in the Regulation of Normal and Abnormal Behavior.* New York: Pergamon.

Maratos, M. 1973. "Decrease in the Understanding of the Word *Big* in Preschool Children." *Child Development,* 44, 747–752.

Mattick, I. 1972. "The Teacher's Role in Helping Young Children Develop Language Competence." *Young Children,* 27, No. 3, 133–142.

Menyuk, P. 1963. "Syntactic Structures in the Language of Children." *Child Development,* 34, 407–422.

Moffett, J. 1968. *Teaching the Universe of Discourse.* Boston: Houghton Mifflin.

Monaghan, A. C. 1971. *Children's Contacts: Some Preliminary Findings*. Unpublished term paper, Harvard Graduate School of Education.

Moskowitz, B. A. 1978. "The Acquisition of Language." *Scientific American,* 239, No. 5, 92–108.

Pflaum, S. W. 1974. *The Development of Language and Reading in the Young Child*. Columbus, Ohio: Charles E. Merrill.

Sapir, E. 1921. *Language*. New York: Harcourt Brace Jovanovich.

Vygotsky, L. 1962. *Thought and Language*. Cambridge, Mass.: The M.I.T. Press.

Whorf, B. 1956. *Language, Thought, and Reality*. New York: John Wiley & Sons.

Williams, F., R. Hopper, and D. Natalicio. 1977. *The Sounds of Children*. Englewood Cliffs, N.J.: Prentice-Hall.

CHAPTER 11

COGNITIVE BEHAVIOR: SOME DEVELOPMENTAL PERSPECTIVES

THE OPERATIONS OF THE MIND

The activities of the mind can be grouped into three general processes: (1) what we take in to the mental system, (2) how we organize and store this information, and (3) how we use it in everyday life. What we take in involves attention, curiosity, selectivity, and other aspects of perception. How we organize and store information raises questions about the structure of the mind—how things are remembered, how they are organized in our memory, and how mental activities are themselves changed by new information. How we use information involves problem solving, carrying out activities that we do by habit, making decisions, and applying what we know to guide and regulate our behavior.

In this chapter, we summarize some of the concepts and current knowledge about the mental activity of young children during the early years. The preschool curriculum deals with activities that draw on this knowledge.

PIAGET'S VIEWS OF MENTAL DEVELOPMENT

Jean Piaget is probably the most influential scholar in the field of children's thought. He was so fascinated by the mental processes of children that he devoted his life to the study of cognitive development. His theories are based on observations and experiments, many of which he carried out initially with his own children. He developed ways of thinking about thinking—terms, concepts, and categories that have greatly influenced research and have been the basis for developing curricula for teaching young children.

"We have to be especially careful in selecting toys and equipment for our infants and toddlers because they learn about things by putting them into their mouths. The first time our 14-month-old got next to some finger paint, she smeared it all over herself and tasted it."

Teacher

Schemes

There are several core ideas in Piaget's theories. One of these is the concept of *scheme*. A scheme is a group of activities that are organized and related to one another usually to accomplish some purpose.

In its earliest form, a scheme is simply a pattern of behavior. An infant's nursing, for example, involves sucking movements directed to a nipple and swallowing. Early schemes are predominantly sensorimotor; they involve several sense modalities. Mental activity—developing information about objects in the world—begins from the early schemes that bring the infant into direct contact with the physical world. The child learns about the rattle from touching, hearing, and seeing it; mental activity depends on such sources of information. Because a child relies on direct experience with objects, his or her mental processes use concrete ways of thinking about the world. The child must touch, see, and perhaps taste a ball before developing an idea of what a *ball* is. The sound "ball" has no meaning until experience gives the child something to attach to the world. The printed word *ball* lacks meaning until the child has an internal image of the object and a sound to go with it.

The principle of scheme as a pattern of acts leads to another principle used by Piaget: simple patterns, like schemes, are later organized into more complex patterns. A child may learn to sound the letters of the alphabet, to sing the music to a song, and to perform certain movements that go with the words and music. When these activities are put together into a coordinated, integrated combination of words, music, and movement, the child has organized the information into a higher order pattern. That human beings combine and organize patterns of behavior seems to be a natural, inherent tendency.

Adaptation: Assimilation and Accommodation

Another process described by Piaget is *adaptation,* which refers to the ways that new information is handled. There are two parts to adaptation: *assimilation* and *accommodation.* Assimilation refers to the processes of taking in new information. We do not gather information like a sponge takes water, accepting everything that comes along. The space around us is filled with an incredible number of stimuli. Young children learn very quickly that some stimuli are more important than others. They learn to select, to attend, and to fit these stimuli into existing schemes. If a child begins by nursing at the mother's breast and is then given a bottle, he or she will approach it applying the pattern of behavior already known from previous experience with the mother. The child then discovers that the bottle is different from the mother's breast. In Piaget's terms, there is accommodation. The new information is blended with the old to organize new schemes. The infant's behavior is changed. He or she develops new patterns of dealing with the bottle: the child may be able to control it more, to move it, discard it, and reach for it at will. This new experience has changed the child by providing new ways of dealing with the world. He or she will approach a new object in a different way.

Accommodation is not confined to children. Adapting from roller skating to ice skating or from tennis to racquetball may be familiar forms of accommodation to adults.

"If you want to see a good example of accommodation, watch a preschooler trying to skate for the first time."

Teacher

PIAGET'S STAGES OF COGNITIVE DEVELOPMENT

In Piaget's view, mental operations progress through several *stages* (Table 11.1), a concept that is much debated. We will discuss later in this chapter why the concept of developmental stages is important for professionals who

TABLE 11.1
Piaget's Stages of Cognitive
Development

Period	General Age Range	Operations
Sensorimotor	Birth to 1½–2	Makes contact with external world through senses; develops coordination between motor activity and sensory information
Preoperational	2 to 6–7	(The preoperational stage is sometimes divided into two periods, which can be a useful distinction for staff working with preschool youngsters.) *Early* (2–4): Begins to develop concepts about patterns that have begun to be discriminated *Later* (4–7): Makes good perceptual comparisons; deals with immediate and observable events; cannot hold abstract ideas in mind to compare with unseen objects
Concrete operations	6–7 to 11–12	Can conserve and hold information in mind; can articulate consequences; can handle two dimensions of object more easily
Formal operations	11 to adulthood	Can use abstract symbols to solve problems in mind; can consider alternatives by using symbols, less dependent on visual or tactile information; can see logical possibilities

work with young children. In this chapter, we discuss the two stages that apply to the preschool period of development: sensorimotor and preoperational.

Sensorimotor

In the first stage, the child begins to organize into patterns the mass of sensations that come from the environment. One jumble of sensations becomes a face; another becomes a bottle; a moving cluster of stimuli becomes a hand. The world begins to take on patterns; it becomes objects, color, repeated movement. The stimuli come through the various sensory modalities—vision, touch, taste, hearing, smell. The child's own abilities and coordination grow to engage this emerging pattern. Infants grasp the jumble of stimuli by organizing it into meaningful and repeated patterns; they are able to touch and manipulate it on their own initiative.

During this period, children begin to accumulate ideas about the world

"Early mental development is no less than conquest by perception and movement of the entire practical universe that surrounds the small child."

Jean Piaget

Two-year-old Anthony heads for the pots and pans in grandma's kitchen. Finding his way blocked, he takes another route. When one cabinet door won't respond to his tugging, he tries another and another until he finally succeeds.

"Baby loves to play hide and seek, but he keeps looking in the same place for me—even after I have moved."

Mother

and represent these ideas with simple words. They also can begin to plan and to think in advance about what they are about to do. When faced with a problem he or she is trying to solve, a two-year-old may try a new strategy if the first attempt does not work. The child is thinking before acting— thought is beginning to be independent of action, separated into an activity of its own.

These planned acts are used only with objects children can keep in direct contact. They do not plan an action with a toy that is in the other room out of sight, nor do they plan something that they will carry out in half an hour or some other time in the future. Thinking is still tied to things that are immediately before them in space and are in the present, not the past or future.

A fascinating process, the development of *object permanence,* takes place in the sensorimotor period. Object permanence refers to the knowledge that objects, including people, continue to exist even when they are not visible.

Very young infants will look at an object in their visual field but will cease looking if the object is removed from sight. In the next phase, infants may continue looking at the spot where the object was last seen, almost as if they expected it to reappear. They don't assert themselves to recover the object. A child who drops a rattle from his or her hand onto the floor may continue to move the hand but won't look at the floor to see where the rattle

has gone. In the next phase, the infant may show a sense of the direction and may look at the floor where he or she thinks the rattle may have landed.

Toward the end of the first year, children can uncover objects that have been covered (with a lid, pillow, hat, and so on) but they can easily be fooled. If a ball is put under a pillow, the child will move the pillow and get the ball. If this sequence is repeated several times and then, while the child watches, the ball is placed under a coat or some such item, the child will often remove the pillow to seek the ball where it was found in the past. The child uses a previously learned scheme to deal with the new information but that scheme is no longer effective.

In the second year, children may make more active efforts to find the object, but they cannot follow sequences where two stages of hiding the object are used. If a ball is placed under a hat and then both the ball and hat are hidden under a pillow, the child will move the pillow expecting to find the ball. These involved arrangements can often be solved by children late in their second year.

Studies by Bower (1971) indicate that memory plays a crucial role in object permanence. Infants who have an object obscured from their view by a screen for a very short time (one and one-half seconds) seem to expect to see the object when the screen is removed. If the screen hides the object for several seconds, they appear to be surprised to see it again. Permanence thus seems to be a matter of memory; if mommy continues to exist as an image in memory, it is easy to accept the notion that she hasn't disappeared but still exists in some place out of sight.

Preoperational

The staff of preschools and child care centers deal with children who are in Piaget's second stage—preoperational. This is the age at which symbols, concepts, imagery, and other internal representations become a familiar part of the child's mental systems.

To develop cognitive ability young children need multiple kinds of experiences and the chance to repeat these over and over. Such activities should not be hurried and it is important to make certain that the simpler levels are neither overlooked nor skipped. Constant observation and diagnosis by teachers will help them set the needed pace and make effective choices.

Children should have many experiences pouring liquids, stacking blocks, bouncing balls from different heights, shoving, pushing, pulling, fastening. In this way, notions of cause and effect can begin to take form. From their own involvement, children learn to predict the responses of their teachers, their classmates, and the world around them.

The early preoperational stage (roughly ages two to four) is when children begin to develop concepts about the patterns that they have begun to identify. They must do this on their own. The notion that some things are alike or different comes from repeated contact. Awareness that the stove is hot, that the chair is hard, that he or she will fall from the edge of a chair—these notions and many more are formed from the child's own experience.

Children will also gain impressions about the social world but these concepts are developed at a later stage. They are more difficult for a child to understand because they are less tangible and less accessible to observation. The concept of *mother* as distinct from the child's own mother and as an individual person with specific attributes is something not easily grasped.

The sensorimotor stage involves getting acquainted with objects and separating the perceptual field into specific, discrete things, whereas the preoperational stage deals with concepts and judgments. Children begin to be aware of consistent patterns in their environment. They know that windows afford a view of the outside even though abstract labels like "visual access" are not part of their experience.

Children in the preoperational stage are still easily misled by their perceptions. If shown six egg cups placed at a short distance from one another in a line with the six eggs grouped close together, children in this stage will probably believe that there are more egg cups than eggs. Several pieces of candy may look like "more" than one large one even if the amount is

Young children can begin to develop concepts related to cause and effect. Their daily experiences can be used as examples to help them understand causal relationships as consequences of their own actions. When a child is using a crayon and it breaks, the teacher can ask, "What happens when you press too hard?" Likewise with chalk: "What happens when you drop a piece of chalk?"

Children tend to quantify items by the amount of space an array occupies. Consequently, for a situation like the one illustrated, preschool children will probably say there are more buttons in the top row than in the bottom row since they judge from the amount of space occupied rather than by number. Linear ordering and one-to-one matching help build a logical rather than spatial basis for judging amount. With mastery of numerical equivalence, children are ready for simple addition and subtraction games.

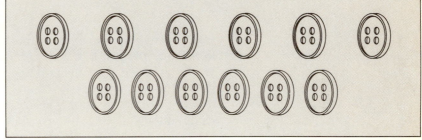

If a cookie is broken into three or four pieces, a child may think he has "more" than the child with an entire cookie. (He may, of course, be unhappy that you broke his cookie!)

"When my children were young, they loved to play a game of trying to find the matching sock when they helped me fold the laundry. Parents can do all kinds of learning games around the house. Matching teacups to saucers and getting enough spoons, forks, napkins for each person at the table are other ways children get experience in sorting and making one-to-one correspondence."

Teacher

actually the same. Children are misled by one characteristic of the objects. If they can compare things directly, they read the perceptual cues very well. They have difficulty, however, holding perceptual information in their minds and applying it to new problems. It is difficult for them to get "distance" from their own thoughts or to see the world as others see it.

At this age children struggle with concepts of change and sameness in objects. They begin to realize that some properties remain constant despite the fact that they change in other ways. This concept is known as *conservation*.

The classic experiment showing children's difficulty in conserving is to take two glasses and fill them with equal amounts of water. Take a third glass, thinner and taller than the other two and place it nearby. Help children recognize that the two glasses have equal amounts of water. Now pour water from one of the glasses into the tall, thin glass. If asked, children will say that the taller glass has more water, even though they have seen you pour the water from one glass to another. To very young children, the amounts seem to change. Later in the preoperational stage—from about age five to seven years—children begin to acquire the notion that the same quantity of water is involved. Younger children are able to attend to only one characteristic at a time. They have difficulty taking into account both dimensions of height and width at once.

Problems of conservation also apply to numbers, to length, and to various materials. And while most of us learn the essential skills involved in con-

In order to understand number concepts, the child must first establish numerical equivalence by one-to-one correspondence. Use sets of identical small items that can be easily manipulated (bottle caps, checkers, game pieces, slugs, and so on) and include five or six different items in each set. Teach the child that two sets are equivalent by one-to-one correspondence if each element of one set is exactly duplicated in the other set, and vice versa. Following is a procedure for practicing linear ordering to make equivalent sets:

1. Make a row of items such as those shown and ask child to make a row just like it underneath.
2. When the child has finished, ask, "Do we each have the same number of pieces?" Then, "How do you know?" (Even if child can count, he or she should be asked to show understanding by matching one-to-one.) Repeat this many times with different arrangement of items and also having child arrange a line and check teacher's "wrong" matching.

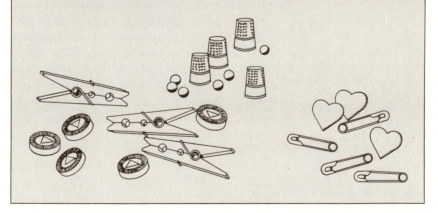

serving, we are still often misled by clever packaging of materials in ways that make the quantity appear to be larger than it really is.

The preoperational period is the time for children to "organize" their experiences. They do this in roughly the same way you would organize things in a cluttered room—by sorting, arranging things in compartments, hanging things on hooks, and stacking these on shelves. Children begin to classify, to see that some things are alike, and to think of them as belonging in the same category. Things are put into sequence—recognizing that there

Preschool children do not yet realize that when the shape or location of objects is changed, quantity is conserved because the original condition can be re-established. Although they are unable to consider destruction and re-establishment at the same time (reversibility), they can be started toward this kind of cognitive ability by practicing arrangement, disarrangement, and then rearrangement of objects. Thus, by proceeding successively in only one direction at a time, children begin to understand that objects can be returned to the same spatial relationship and will also retain their original amount. The following exercise helps develop this ability:

1. Provide the child with sixteen counters, identical in all ways but color; half white and half green.
2. Ask the child to make a row using all the green counters. Then have the child make a row of white counters underneath the green without mentioning number. Ask, "Are there the same number of green pieces and white pieces?" "How do you know?" Tell the child to make the rows so they have the same number.

3. Remove one counter and ask, "Now are there the same number of green pieces and white pieces?" "How do you know?" Proceed with the exercise by arranging and rearranging the rows (adding two, taking two, taking one from each row, and so on) and asking, "Now are they the same number?" "How do you know?" Continue to rearrange them until the child has the notion of "same number."
4. Have the child continue to arrange and rearrange the counters in various ways, asking him or her to tell if the number of counters is more, less, or the same.

Good practice can also be gained by pouring liquid into different size and shape containers and back, stacking blocks one place or another and then back, or making play dough "balls" into "sausages" and back. From such activities (some of which Piaget used in his classic experiments), children develop experience that enables them to predict results. The most fundamental requirement is the child's active participation. At no time should the teacher perform all the action and have the child merely observe.

can be a progression of blocks from short to tall to taller. When you sort and arrange things in your room, you are using the mental operations that were developed in the preschool years.

Children may give labels (symbols, words) to items in the way that individual children have their own unique names. Each object, at first, is one of a kind. Later children use a word to stand for an entire group of objects. If they have the idea that several different objects are *all* chairs, even though they differ in some ways, they have developed the concept of chair and the label for the concept. Concepts and labels help children organize the raw material of their experiences. They can grasp several items into a single idea and name. A child can say "my family" rather than name each member

Seriation is a concept based on a system of relative dimensions. For example, you might ask a child to arrange three toy cars in order of size. Then produce a fourth car that is either larger or smaller than the first three and ask, "Where should this go so it will be in the right place?" Comparisons should first be made on the basis of gross differences and then gradually more subtle differences should be introduced.

Concepts of relative size can be developed by having children learn they are taller than some of their friends but also shorter than others. Examples can be used with chairs, books, desks, cups, and so on. The ability to place items correctly along some dimension is closely tied to the demands of many school subjects.

individually. Children can talk of their "toys" or their "clothes" and so refer to many things with a single word.

Organizing the world with conceptual knowledge and finding labels for these concepts is a basic task during the preoperational period, yet it is not easy to accomplish. Even sorting simple objects, like blocks, poses problems. Blocks differ from one another by *shape, color, length, width,* and so on. If you ask children to sort items into piles that are "alike," interesting things happen. One child may begin by grouping a few things that are the same color—say yellow—and then may make a second pile of things that are all circles but includes a yellow circle in this group without being aware of the inconsistency.

As they mature, children will be able to stay with a single dimension in their sorting (colors *or* size *or* shape, but not all simultaneously). They will, at a later time, be able to group these basic dimensions into a larger idea ("These are all made of wood," and so on).

The many motor experiences of young children help build space concepts: putting objects *in* and taking them *out;* crawling *over, through, around,* and *under;* looking *high* and *low.* From these experiences, children learn that a cup may be *in* or *on* the sink, a cookie *behind* or *in front of* a glass of juice.

Elementary number concepts such as "just enough," "the same number," "more," and "less" are an important part of logical thinking. Their beginnings are a natural part of preschool activities. The boy who holds up four fingers and says, "I'm four," when asked his age, or who can correctly count from 1 through 5, may or may not have number concepts. Unless he can also select 4 of something or know that by adding 1 more to 4 he will have 5, he lacks the elementary concepts of "the same number" and "more."

Before children can solve problems involving number—that is, quantity and measurement—they must be able to do more than count. They must be able to comprehend differences between big/little, full/empty, long/short, same/different, and so on. Unless children perceive these contrasts, they will not realize there is a problem to solve.

Another interesting feature of the preoperational stage is the way children differ in their mental plans. For example, when children age two and one-half to five are shown a model of a structure made of wooden blocks glued together, asked to think of how they would build one like it, and then told to "touch the block you would use first; now, the one you would use next . . . ," the younger children's responses were unsystematic and illogical (Figure 11.1). They often planned to begin building at the *top* of the structure, ignoring blocks in the back of the model or forgetting that the top blocks would need other blocks for support (Hubner, 1979).

THE CONCEPT OF STAGES

Piaget believed that mental development progresses through stages, some of which have substages within them. The idea of stages in human development has several distinct characteristics. One is that the child goes through stages in an unchanging order, that is, the third stage always comes before the fourth and after the second. These stages do not involve isolated types of behavior that can appear at any time. This theory suggests that mental growth has a predetermined quality that cannot be changed by training.

A second characteristic is that the achievements of one period are necessary in order to move to the next stage. A stage cannot be skipped.

A third aspect of stage theory is that the stages, once attained, cannot be reversed. This idea is consistent with the claim that skills build on one another and that progress is made as a result of a great number of direct

experiences with the physical world. If so, the knowledge involved is acquired slowly and with such repeated experience that forgetting is unlikely. Once a child has learned to classify or group objects by color or arrange them in order by height, he or she cannot return to the level of growth where such classification or ordering is impossible. When children become aware that things continue to exist even when not in view, they cannot honestly adopt a belief that, when they look away, objects disappear.

Can growth through these stages be accelerated? Efforts to do so have

FIGURE 11.1
Examples of Sequences
Children Would Use to
Build Block Structure

PLAN OF
SUCCESSFUL BUILDER

PLAN OF
UNSUCCESSFUL BUILDER

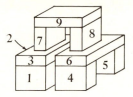

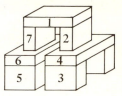

(Numbers refer to sequences in which blocks would presumably be placed.)

Adapted from Hubner (1979).

TEACHING YOUNG CHILDREN ABOUT TIME

In general, *time concepts* involve (1) temporal order: first, next, last; before, after; sooner, later; if . . . then (cause and effect); and (2) Intervals: minute, hour, day, week, year; some time ago; in a little while.

Studies by Piaget and his associates indicate that children's ability to structure uniform intervals comes much later than their ability to deal with temporal order. Therefore, at the preschool level it is desirable to help children develop time concepts based on temporal order. Following are some typical questions that young children ask about time:

Is today a long time?
Is a year big? Is my birthday a year?
When will it be tomorrow?
When is it today?
How old will I be when I'm forty?
How much time is 10 o'clock?
What does 4:30 mean?

Many opportunities for children to learn relationships about time come through the teacher's emphasis on what is going on now, what has already been done, and what happens next. Telling a child, "We'll do that in an hour" carries little meaning. Explaining, "That's something we will do after juice time," relates a forthcoming event to the child's own experience.

Reminders about the regular events of the preschool schedule is one way of making children more aware of time. In addition, teachers convey ideas about time whenever they use expressions such as the following:

As soon as everyone's quiet . . .
When you go home at noon . . .
This morning we'll . . .
Tonight I'm going to . . .
Right now let's . . . then later on we . . .
Before you go out, be sure to . . .
When you come in . . .
First let's finish this and then . . .
Next time, why not . . .
It's Danny's turn first, Maurine is next,
	and Gerry can be last.

"Look for the 'teachable moment' when children are ready to learn."

Teacher

been only partially successful. Where acceleration does appear to succeed, the child sometimes learns to apply a rule (conservation, for example) if the problem is stated in another way. It would probably be safe to conclude at this time that only modest progress can be made in accelerating the development of a child through the Piagetian stages. More progress can be achieved if the child is beginning to deal directly with the operation that is being taught. Berison (1969) successfully taught conservation of quantity to kindergarten children and they showed superior performance seven months later. But conservation is usually acquired between ages five and seven anyway. So, practice at this age might help children master this concept more quickly.

REFERENCES

Ault, R. L. 1977. *Children's Cognitive Development*. New York: Oxford University Press.

Berison, D. J. 1969. "Role of Measurement Operations in the Acquisition of Conservation." *Developmental Psychology,* 1, 653–660.

Bower, T. G. R. 1971. "The Object in the World of the Infant." *Scientific American,* 225, No. 4, 30–38.

Flavell, J. H. 1963. *The Developmental Psychology of Jean Piaget*. Princeton: Van Nostrand.

———. 1971. "Stage-Related Properties of Cognitive Development." *Cognitive Psychology,* 2, 421–453.

Hubner, J. 1979. "Block Building: Instruction and Development." Unpublished doctoral dissertation. Stanford: Stanford University.

Piaget, J. 1929. *The Child's Conception of the World*. New York: Harcourt Brace Jovanovich.

———. 1930. *The Child's Conception of Physical Causality*. London: Kegan Paul.

CHAPTER 12

HELPING CHILDREN USE THEIR MINDS

THREE TYPES OF MENTAL ACTIVITY

Although Piaget's view of mental development is impressive, there is a large body of research based on perspectives that do not use his formulations. Much of this sprang up during the time when interest in Piaget's work was greatest. Sometimes called *information processing,* it is the work of many people who examine the specific ways that the mind works. This knowledge is essential for teachers of young children. Knowing where the child is means also knowing how his or her mind deals with the activities of the curriculum and other experiences in the early years.

Mental operations most relevant for early education can be grouped into three major areas: *perception, memory,* and *problem solving.*

Perception

Perception refers to the various ways that the nervous system takes in information from both the internal and external world. Sensory modalities—vision, hearing, touch, taste and smell—are the basis for perceptual functions.

Perception is not merely the transmission to the brain of the stimuli that reach the sensory organs. It includes the ways that sensory organs read and interpret the information they receive. Unless the stimuli are translated and given meaning, they are virtually useless. The meaning of the stimuli is derived from their connection to past experiences that are important in some way.

Perception is thus selective. We pick out from the mass of incoming material those stimuli that have significance. A mother sleeps through the sound of an airplane flying overhead and wakes up to the much quieter sound of an infant fretting in the crib. We are scarcely conscious of the automobiles that we pass, but a familiar make or model draws our attention. At a party, we may ignore much of the conversation and concentrate on only one, even though we could, if we chose, hear a dozen others.

What children perceive is governed in part by what they already have acquired by way of labels and schemas. Perception is also affected by the child's size. If you haven't done so, try seeing the world from the level of a three-year-old. Walk on your knees for a few minutes and, aside from the discomfort, you will notice the undersides of tables, chairs, and people; objects look very different from this perspective in contrast to your view of them from above.

Children learn to discriminate perceptually among the various things they see. To discriminate is simply a matter of seeing similarities and differences. If I am outside in my yard, can I tell if it is my phone or my neighbor's that is ringing? Is the weather cool enough for a jacket? Is that my car in the dimly lit parking lot or a model very much like it? These discriminations all carry information; they help us sort and classify events and objects. In some areas—for example, plant identification and bird watching—small patterns give meaning. A certain visual configuration may indicate whether the plant or bird we see is common, unusual, or so rare as to be a specimen that should be reported to the local naturalist.

As children learn, they make more and more distinctions among the objects and events in their world. They learn a vocabulary that expresses differentiations in their language. The dog is not just a dog; it is a poodle, collie, or terrier. This process goes on indefinitely. At the same time, children also learn to group different things under single labels, as described in Chapter 11. These two processes—making increasingly finer distinctions and learning more general concepts that cover many separate events—go on at the same time.

Memory

When you call directory assistance for a phone number that you want to dial immediately, do you write it down or try to remember it long enough to complete the call? If you try to remember the number, you will find that any interruption will cause it to fade from your memory. Yet you can recall phone numbers that you have not used for weeks, months, or, sometimes, years. The different ways the mind handles these two very similar bits of information illustrates a crucial mental process—the storage and retrieval of information.

The brain is a storehouse, containing an incredible number of bits of information that are filed away. The process by which they are recorded is chemical, perhaps analogous to the recording of sound on a tape. The tape is changed slightly by an electric impulse; the molecules of the tape are rearranged and the sound, in effect, is stored for later use. The storage and retrieval of information causes the brain to change in some fashion and these changes can be permanent. We all have images and memories of events that happened in childhood that can be immediately and vividly recalled. Even though we can't recall some things we once knew, this information may still be recorded in the brain. Stimulating the brain electronically can evoke images from the distant past, as if the traces were there but not easily accessible. They may also be recalled under hypnosis (Hilgard, 1977).

We now know that the brain handles information in two or three different ways. The telephone number obtained from directory assistance is stored briefly in what is called *short-term memory*. One of the leading researchers, Gordon Bower, calls this a sort of "mental scratch pad" that jots things down briefly then discards them. Indeed, items are easily crowded from short-term memory. If you look up a phone number, start to dial, and someone interrupts to ask you a question, chances are that you will have to look

"The first time two-year-old Jonathan saw a dog, he called it 'big kitty-cat.' "

Parent

"My four-and-one-half-year-old can dial our seven-digit phone number, but he still has trouble reciting the number. Every time I ask him our phone number, he takes me to the phone to show me."

Father

up the number again. Short-term memory is tentative and is also very limited. We can remember only about seven items—numbers or letters, for example. There is a seven-plus-or-minus-two rule about short-term memory: most adults and children can recall at least five numbers but not more than nine. The license plates of automobiles are designed with that feature in mind. It would be very difficult to recall a license number of ten or twelve letters and digits long enough to write it down. Under usual circumstances, the mind doesn't have that capability (Simon, 1974).

Long-term memory is the permanent file. It stores information either directly or transfers it from short-term memory. This is done in several ways—repeating information over and over again, using a mnemonic trick, or concentrating very carefully. Some things have more impact than others. Scenes that have special importance or are vivid, frightening, or surprising appear to be recorded directly and permanently.

"My daughter could recite the whole alphabet long before she could spell her name."

Mother

Memory develops rapidly during the preschool years. By age five, children can usually keep in their short-term memory five numbers or letters spoken in random fashion. (Counting numbers or reciting the alphabet is a different matter since the entire sequence may already be familiar.) The development of both short- and long-term memory is part of early cognitive growth. You may recall from your reading of Chapter 11 that studies of object permanence—the ability to realize that an object continues to exist when it can no longer be seen—indicate that a major factor in the development of this concept is the child's ability to hold the object in memory. If an object disappears for a very brief time, the child expects to see it again; if an object is hidden for several seconds, the child "forgets" that it was there, as though it had faded like the face of the Cheshire cat in *Alice in Wonderland*.

By five years of age or thereabouts, children's capability for short-term memory is equal to that of adults (Belmont and Butterfield, 1969). Adults may *appear* at times to do better on tasks involving short-term memory, but this is probably because they have learned to use tricks to aid the basic memory skills.

Problem Solving

Perception is the process of selecting and bringing information into the mental library. Memory is the process by which information is arranged, retained, and made available. The third general phase involves the use of such information in everyday life and in solving problems.

What is *problem solving*? It is a term that refers to the way information is used to accomplish something. It might more accurately be called *taking action*—using information and taking steps needed to accomplish a goal, whether it is brushing your teeth or deciding what automobile to buy. In one usage, *problem* suggests a task that is particularly difficult, one that has no obvious or immediate solution. Such "problems" are merely situations that call for more complex action and require more time and thought than others. What may be considered a "problem" for a child may be no problem for an adult.

In this sense, a problem is something you want to do that you find difficult. Children solve problems continually. Developing a general concept of *mother,* apart from the one person who is the child's own mother, is problem solving; writing one's name is problem solving.

Techniques for solving problems are really elementary forms of what we know as research or science. Problem solving requires

1. a question to be answered
2. a store of information
3. a hypothesis or idea about what a solution might be
4. a technique or method for trying out these ideas
5. a way to see if the ideas work

In a sense, the "try-it-out-and-see-if-it-works" approach embodies a true scientific spirit. Experiments for preschool children in a science corner use this strategy.

The growth of the ability to solve problems—that is, applying knowledge and thought processes to new situations—parallels the development of cognitive operations and linguistic abilities. The child who grasps a concept of a shape or color for the first time has solved a problem. Recognizing that one event leads to another—if the carrot plants are not watered they wilt—solves a problem of a relationship between two events. A child who develops a rule of grammar and applies it to new situations even when it may not be appropriate is engaged in problem solving.

Much of problem solving for young children seems to adults like an accumulation of information. The problems being solved involve learning how the physical world operates, the function of language in interaction, and the principles of social interaction. The child senses principles before they can be described in words; the problem solving is mediated through concrete objects and observable actions. Abstract problem solving, such as mathematics, comes later when the child can manipulate symbols and ideas separate from the concrete reality of things that can be observed, felt, or heard.

Science and math are actually distilled, condensed versions of the kinds of processes we have been describing—classifying, grouping, developing rules, seeing associations between events, and trying out ideas to see if they work. When used more systematically, we call these ideas *hypotheses*. They have one thing in common: they state a belief that things will happen in a certain way, that two events will be connected.

In applying rules of grammar, the child's thought may go something like this: "I know a word (*go*); it is an action word. I want to use it to refer to something that has already happened. I know that other action words refer to things in the past if I add *ed*. So I will add *ed* to this word, too." The result, "I goed," sounds like an error, but it is also the child's solution to a problem. Children's solutions will get "better" (by adult standards) as they learn more. However, the underlying process—(1) to recognize the problem, (2) to recall the relevant information, and (3) to apply this information to the new situation—is the beginning of scientific operations.

THE TEACHER'S ROLE

Children are continually perceiving, remembering, and using knowledge to solve problems of one sort or another. Development of the efficiency of mental activities and the power of the adult mind is affected significantly by the resources of a child's social environment. Raw experience with the physical and social world is not sufficient to develop effective use of mental capabilities. The preschool staff and other adults contribute to the growth of these mental abilities.

The three general mental activities previously mentioned—perception, memory, and problem solving—may seem to occur simultaneously, but they can be considered as individual abilities that are fostered in different ways. Perhaps more important than the efficient operation of a child's mind are the kind of information stored in the child's brain and the type of problems he or she tries to solve.

Guiding Perception

Perception combines several operations: attention, awareness of visual or other stimuli, recognition of pattern, and interpretation. This is not as complex as it sounds. While walking down the street, you may not attend to the cars passing by, but they cross your visual field or you hear them. You may attend to them for one reason or another—a siren, a screech of brakes, or idle curiosity. If you see one that looks like the car of a close friend, the perceptive process is greatly intensified. You attend more closely and try to recognize patterns of color or shape that tell you if it is, indeed, your friend's car.

As a teacher, you may want a child in your class to learn a skill or respond to what you are saying. The first principle is to get the child's attention. At times of concentrated attention, the mind focuses and closes in on information quickly. Things are acquired and stored in memory more easily under conditions of high stimulation or arousal (Lassen, Ingvar, and Skinhøj,

1978). *Engagement* is a key element in helping children learn. ''Sesame Street'' was designed with this idea in mind. The cognitive content of the show is useless if the show does not compete successfully with other television programs for the child's attention. There are countless techniques for getting the attention of young children. These are a matter of both familiar

strategies and individual style. Whatever your methods are, use them. They will help children store the information you want them to have available.

Attention alone is not enough. Children also need to learn how to look. You can help children see things they would not otherwise notice by encouraging them to compare two objects and describe the differences. They can look at some things from two different angles or imagine what an object looks like from someone else's view. The object can be touched, tasted, handled, and explored. Children can be encouraged to describe objects and events through show and tell, guessing games, and similar activities. The teacher is a model for concentrated perceptual activities. Observing and talking about what is seen becomes an effective part of the child's experience.

Determining the kinds of information that children store inevitably involves value judgments made by the adults responsible for a child's early development. Until taught by experience, the brain is impartial; it takes in almost everything. In the preschool, the staff plays a major role in selecting the type of information to which children will be exposed.

All types of research on learning and mental development emphasize that future learning is influenced by what is already learned. Information that teachers help children store today will affect what they will learn and what they will want to learn in the future. We remember new items, in part, because they are hooked up to things we already have in store. If you follow tennis, you are likely to recall the semifinal scores of the U.S. Open that you heard on the car radio driving to work; a teenager who knows the titles of the top records will remember a new title as soon as it appears. The professional scout and the casual fan see quite different things at a football game even if they are sitting next to one another in the stands. This channeling of attention and selective learning begins early. What children learn in preschool and what they are taught to believe is important will give related information more vividness in their minds.

"Five-year-old Timothy often wears his favorite football sweatshirt bearing the number 12. If you ask him to identify the number, his reply is 'number 12 Roger Staubach.' "

Teacher

Helping Children Remember

The brain is able to store vast quantities of information. It might be thought of as a library with almost unlimited space. Some of the items are short and contained entirely on one small card; others are more like chapters in which the idea and pictures are connected by themes or a particular experience or time. In operations involving memory, the difference between one person and another involves three issues:

What type and how much information has been stored?
How is it organized (catalogued)?
What techniques does the individual have for getting access to it?

"A good children's book always has illustrations on the same page as the words that describe the illustration. Teachers should watch for this in making book selections."

Librarian

You remember your address not letter by letter or word by word but as a single unit. This is called *chunking*. Children remember nursery rhymes by this method of grouping. When they sing the ABC song they are chunking.

Although the brain is continually working and recording at least some of what is happening, there are ways to make remembering more efficient.

If a child is asked to remember something that is not familiar, such as a new letter or word, he or she will not be able to keep the word or visual pattern in mind for more than a few seconds. If you want a child to associate a word with a picture, be sure both are adjacent to one another. He or she may lose the image of the word from short-term memory when turning the page or looking away from the task to find a matching picture or shape. Repeat things; keep them in easy view; avoid distracting objects.

Rehearsal is a useful technique for committing things to long-term memory. Sometimes called *rote learning,* rehearsal is a common practice for adults as well as children. The example of the phone number offered by directory assistance comes to mind again. If you have no paper on which to write the number but want to keep it available, you may repeat it over and over again until you can get a pencil to record it. Repeating the number apparently has the effect of putting it into short-term memory over and over so that it is re-entered before it fades. A similar process is used to put things into the mental library. Repetition, whether group or individual, is effective.

Do not be reluctant to use rote learning in the preschool. There is nothing wrong with this technique. Its bad reputation came from accusations that rote memory work was rigid and lacking in meaning. Rehearsal or repetition is an essential teaching tool; it is sometimes the most effective way to learn a given bit of information, such as multiplication tables or the alphabet. This technique is especially effective when used in a way that is agreeable or entertaining to the child (or adult). Learning the alphabet by putting the letters to music is one example; children learn television commercials by rote and recall them years later. Rote learning is one way to help children store information that they will need about themselves and the world around them. It is a proven tool that is too good to be ignored.

Young children do not use either spontaneous rehearsal or chunking (Moely et al., 1969). They can be taught to do both, however. Rehearsal helps young children improve their recall (Flavell, Beach, and Chinsky, 1966; Kingsley and Hagen, 1969). Chunking can be used with very young children by combining words with a rhythm to make a phrase, by setting words to a familiar song ("Mary Had a Little Lamb"), by rhyming so that one word helps lead the child to another (*cat, rat, hat, mat*). These associations help link the ideas or sounds in the child's memory.

Mnemonic devices are tricks to make recall easier. "Thirty days hath September, April, June, and November . . ." is easier to recall than to learn the exact number of days in each month. So is the rhyme, "*I* before *e*, except after *c*; exceptions . . ." Such devices are little crutches or, perhaps, hooks for us to use in reaching up into the shelves of our mental libraries for a specific bit of information.

Helping Children Solve Problems

Helping children solve problems and use the knowledge they store in memory is a challenging task. For the young child problems come in many forms and at unexpected times. They include simple tasks such as putting puzzles together, building a tower of blocks, learning how to manage the wash basin, or persuading another child to relinquish a swing.

Solving problems takes two types of competence. One is motivational: interest, a sense of confidence, willingness to attempt new tasks, and the ability to persist if the task is not easily learned. The other type of competence includes strategies for solving a problem or accomplishing a task. We suggest here some things teachers can do to help the child acquire both types of competence. They overlap one another in practice, but the distinctions are useful as a way of thinking about children's behavior and recognizing which aspect of problem solving the child is dealing with at a given time.

Capture the child's interest   Teachers have many successful strategies for motivating children. A word or phrase of challenge, enticement with an interesting task, or simply a well-placed toy or piece of equipment—all these and others help arouse the child's curiosity. Whatever the strategy, if it works, use it. Of course, the child's natural interest and eagerness to approach a task are the teacher's best indications of what the child is ready to learn.

Assure that the child will succeed   During the early stages of learning a new task or dealing with an unfamiliar situation, the teacher should try to help the child avoid failure and defeat. This is not to suggest that a child should never experience frustration, but chronic failure is likely to impair the child's sense of confidence and adventure. Confidence that a problem can be solved comes from successful attempts in the past. A series of small successes can help a child reach his or her goal more readily. "Maria, today you learned how to make an *M*. That was very good! Tomorrow I'll help you learn how to make an *a*. Before long, you'll be writing your name all by yourself!"

Keep the level of frustration low   Once the child has begun a task, help keep the level of frustration low so that emotional responses do not interfere with the child's concentration on the problem. This may be done through support, verbal encouragement, touching, and the like. "Sometimes it takes a long time to learn how to skip. Here, hold my hand and we'll try skipping together."

Select problems that are within the child's ability range   If a child has tackled a problem that is obviously beyond his or her ability and failure is inevitable, the child may need to be diverted or distracted. "This is a hard puzzle, isn't it? Here's an easier one. Let's do this together." Also, a task may be simplified by breaking it up into manageable parts. "Let's find all the pieces with straight edges and put them over here. We can work with these first and do the others later."

Praise frequently   Praise is most useful if it follows a specific accomplishment. Praise must be used carefully, given sincerely and at the appropriate times. Indiscriminate praise loses its value.

Use concrete materials and situations, not abstract ideas   Children usually solve problems and learn tasks by doing them. Even when the task is learning words or letters, it is helpful for children to use materials that can be perceived through more than one sensory mode. Manipulating letters on a magnetic board, sounding out words, listening to stories, placing words on a flannel board, tracing letters with a felt-tipped pen all help the child experience words and letters.

Asking *why* questions may only puzzle young children ("Why does the ice melt?"); asking *what* questions encourages the child to think about reasons ("What do you think will happen if we leave the ice out? What are some of the things we can do to find out?").

See what the child's strategy is and give useful feedback Each child attempts to solve problems in his or her own way. Discover which strategies a child is using and make suggestions that will help him or her learn from mistakes. "The pieces won't fit when you force them together. Let's try it another way."

Encourage the child to try alternative methods Children are less likely to become discouraged if they learn that there can be more than one way to solve a problem. The teacher can help by asking, "Can you think of another way to try that?" or by encouraging, "That doesn't quite do it, but I know you can get it if you try other ways."

Explain, label, and identify the task Talk to children as you watch them work on tasks. Describe what is happening; help them see a situation as you see it. Label things, put feelings into words, and provide the vocabulary that fits what a child is doing.

Provide repeated experiences with similar problems Competence in problem solving comes with practice. A child learns to erect a high block structure from having many opportunities to construct with different kinds and shapes of materials. A child learns to get along with others from repeated interactions with different people. A rich variety of experiences helps children acquire skills to approach problems in different ways.

Encourage the child to use a plan Children learn from trial and error, but they may also be encouraged to use a plan and think about a task in advance. Encourage children to anticipate what will happen; ask them to recall what happened the last time and to recognize that they may be able to predict the outcome based on past experiences. Help the child verbalize his or her plan and talk about it after it has been carried out. Review and repeat the steps of the plan. Help the child remember and verbalize his or her actions. Eventually, the child will be able to use memory to help develop a plan for another task or problem.

Finally, teachers offer another resource: serving as models for children by showing how adults solve problems. You can talk about your frustration and disappointment when you fail to solve a problem; you can show the children how you choose another alternative, explaining what you are doing and why. Children learn a great deal about problem-solving strategies by imitating those they admire.

What we have just described are the processes of the mind and how they are developed to handle the tasks of learning math, science, social studies, and other topics that the child will meet in school. During the early years, children develop cognitive operations and store knowledge in their rapidly growing mental libraries. In preparing children for school, you, as the teacher, can help them learn to remember, to organize information, to sort it according to personal experience, and to apply their knowledge and mental operations to new situations.

REFERENCES

Ault, R. L. 1977. *Children's Cognitive Development*. New York: Oxford University Press.

Belmont, J. M., and E. C. Butterfield. 1969. "The Relations of Short-Term Memory to Development and Intelligence." In *Advances in Child Development and Behavior,* vol. 4. Ed. L. P. Lipsett and H. W. Reese. New York: Academic Press.

Flavell, J. H., D. R. Beach, and J. M. Chinsky. 1966. "Spontaneous Verbal Rehearsal in a Memory Task as a Function of Age." *Child Development,* 37, 283–299.

Hilgard, E. 1977. *Divided Consciousness*. New York: John Wiley & Sons.

Kingsley, P. R., and J. W. Hagen. 1969. "Induced versus Spontaneous Rehearsal in Short-Term Memory in Nursery School Children." *Developmental Psychology,* 1, 40–46.

Lassen, N. A., D. H. Ingvar, and E. Skinhøj. 1978. "Brain Function and Blood Flow." *Scientific American,* 239 (October), 62–71.

Lichtenberg, P., and D. G. Norton. 1971. *Cognitive and Mental Development in the First Five Years of Life: A Review of Recent Research*. National Institute of Mental Health. Washington, D.C.: Government Printing Office.

Moely, B., P. A. Olson, T. G. Halwes, and J. H. Flavell. 1969. "Production Deficiency in Young Children's Clustered Recall." *Developmental Psychology,* 1, 26–34.

Simon, H. A. 1969. *The Sciences of the Artificial*. Cambridge, Mass.: The M.I.T. Press.

———. 1974. "How Big Is a Chunk?" *Science,* 183, 482–488.

Smedslund, J. 1963. "The Effect of Observation on Children's Representation of the Spatial Orientation of a Water Surface." *Journal of Genetic Psychology,* 102, 195–202.

CHAPTER 13

THE DEVELOPMENT OF
SOCIAL KNOWLEDGE

SELF-CONCEPT AND SELF-ESTEEM

Beginnings of Self-Knowledge

The first play activities of infants center around things within reach—moving body parts, poking themselves, putting their fingers in their mouths. Watch a baby at "play" while he or she is being held by the mother. Often the infant will be bouncing up and down on her lap, pulling at her hair, feeling and poking her face and eyes, and exploring whatever and whomever happens to be within reach.

This kind of exploration is essential to the infant's learning to differentiate self from others and to become aware of the limits or boundaries of his or her own body. Sucking his or her own fingers, for example, creates a sensation both in the infant's mouth and in the fingers. But in grasping the mother's fingers and sucking, the infant gets a sensation in his or her mouth only. If the mother were to suck the baby's fingers, the baby would feel it only in his or her own fingers and not in the mouth. Through such seemingly random play, children learn where their bodies leave off and where the external world begins. A child care environment that encourages exploration and gives children freedom to poke, push, and pull helps them acquire concepts about themselves.

When the room has a large (unbreakable) mirror at a child's eye level, young children can discover what they look like. They need labels for things, of course, but they can see for themselves the color of their hair, whether they are big or little, how they look when they smile, frown, or cry.

"If he wills his fingers to move or his toes to wiggle, they do; if he wills his mother's fingers to wiggle, or his teddy bear's, they don't. His thoughts control his body. No one else's."

Piers and Wallach (1977),
p. 142

The Self

In developing curricula to facilitate the growth of self-awareness in young children, it is important to distinguish among self-concept, identity, and self-esteem.

Self-concept is knowledge about oneself. It is a mental activity that involves children's awareness of their own characteristics and of the differences and likenesses between themselves and others. A little girl learns to think of herself as "tall," "talkative," "red-haired," "strong," "right-handed," and the like. Even though she may not be able to verbalize the differences, she sees herself as separate from the adult members of her family and distinct from other children. By age three, children know whether they are boys or girls; their vocabulary includes the words *me, mine, I, you, yours,* and sometimes *we* and *ours.*

Identity has a social meaning. While self-concept gives the child an image of self as an individual, identity brings awareness of group membership. A child learns that having certain physical characteristics means he is a boy. This precedes knowledge that there is a group called *boys* and that member-

"Johnny, are you a little girl?"
"NO!"
"What are you?"
"I'm a boy!"
"How do you know?"
"My mommy told me."

"Who are you?" As identity is formed, children will answer this question in ways that express sexual identity, citizenship, family ties, and ethnic membership.

ship in this group carries with it certain expectations, privileges, and re-straints. Social identity includes the knowledge that one belongs to a family, an ethnic group, a church, and is a citizen of a particular country.

Self-esteem reflects how we feel about ourselves. As children become aware of themselves and their individual features and attributes, they may begin to think of themselves in positive or negative terms.

These self-evaluations are usually influenced by the judgments of others. The tone of evaluation in comments—"My, aren't you a big boy!" "Isn't she cute?" "You look like you're going to be a football player when you grow up!"—gives the child the knowledge that physical features or behavior have social value. Self-concept and self-esteem are thus related but are different aspects of self-knowledge.

Origins of Self-Concept and Self-Esteem

Children form ideas about themselves in much the same way that they acquire knowledge of the physical world: through direct observation and experience. There is, however, a fundamental difference. Knowledge of the physical world comes primarily from the attributes of the objects themselves—things are soft, rough, cold, or sharp. Social knowledge comes in part from experience but a major source is the judgment, attitudes, and values of others. Children acquire knowledge about physical characteristics—blue eyes, red hair, dark or pink skin—through direct observation, but the social value they attach to these attributes comes from others.

Self-concept and self-esteem grow from four major sources:

1. The child's own accumulated experiences
2. The impressions the child receives from others
3. The capacity to internalize goals set for the child and to evaluate his or her own behavior
4. The child's ability to live up to his or her own standards (Coopersmith, 1967, p. 37)

The memory of success and failure, of acceptance and rejection, is a source of self-concept and self-esteem. The child whose face and charm bring comments and attention from adults comes to see herself as a person different from the child who meets with indifference or rejection. She has not only the awareness of her attractiveness but also has the experience of acceptance by others.

Success in school-related tasks also plays an important role in the development of self-esteem and self-concept. Indeed, one experience may be powerful enough to form an impression that lasts for years. A student teacher reports:

I didn't realize I was showing so much favoritism until I read an obser-

---

Sidebar notes:

Mikie's mother asked him why he was crying. "Because the teacher said I looked sharp today!"

Self-esteem may be positive or negative; self-concept may be clear and specific or incomplete and vague.

"I do not know if I am withdrawn by nature or as a consequence of how I was treated by my classmates. Even now I am terribly shy. . . ."

Sophia Loren

"Maria used to put her fingers in her mouth, look dejected, and say, 'I can't,' whenever I asked her to do something. I made it a point to put my arms around her, praise her when she tried, and called attention to her abilities. She really didn't know she was as capable as the other children—or that she is pretty. One day, after I told her she had beautiful dark eyes and long eyelashes, I saw her studying herself in the mirror."

Teacher

vation of my work in the lab school. At first I was really upset to think that I would be unfair to some of the children. Then I felt angry at the observer for exposing me. After some discussion with my supervisor, I decided to consciously monitor my own behavior.

I noticed that I held and touched little Edy several times while I worked at the puzzle table, and I even reached out to her when she made no gestures toward me. I asked her questions in an effort to get her to look at me and each time we had eye contact, I would smile at her. When Lisa sat down next to me, I practically ignored her. I answered when she asked me a question, but I didn't give her the sustained attention, the warmth, and personal care that I gave to Edy. I guess I'm attracted to Edy because she's so cute, so well coordinated, and speaks so clearly. Lisa is clumsy, kind of messy, and doesn't talk very much.

Children experience success or failure very early in life. After they begin formal schooling, their self-esteem is further enhanced or diminished by the competitive system of rewards and grading prevalent in many school systems. They continually compare themselves with others.

In some countries, competition in school is between groups of students, not between individual children.

Some professionals are reluctant to introduce an academic curriculum at the prekindergarten level. They fear it may establish premature notions of competence or inadequacy before a child has had a reasonable chance to tackle solid academic tasks. Formal instruction in the preschool makes it clear to the child how much he or she has (or hasn't) learned. More informal teaching integrates school-related tasks into the other activities of the day and doesn't put the child on the spot with an obvious success or failure on a specific lesson.

There is some disagreement as to whether self-esteem leads to successful performance or follows from it. One view is that children need to feel good about themselves and their abilities and that a sense of confidence will enable them to achieve. Another view is that self-confidence comes from mastery of a task and a clear demonstration of skill. Children who have learned to read or count or name the common colors have a firmer sense of competence because they have shown themselves and others that they can perform tasks that are valued.

"The route to self-esteem is skill; we mislead children if we tell them they are doing fine when they aren't."

Teacher

It is difficult to take sides on this argument; both are appealing. Perhaps the solution is to let children know they are valued as individuals, and, at the same time, to help them acquire the skills they need to maintain self-esteem. The confidence that a teacher displays in a child is a key element in developing self-esteem. Children who believe they can learn will try harder; children whose teacher believes they can learn begin to believe in themselves. The mastery of the task thus confirms the child's expectations. The child gets a double reward—feeling more competent and realizing that self-confidence is justified.

Impressions that children receive from parents, teachers, and others who

"You can't simply decide you are going to teach a child self-esteem. It is not a skill or a concept; it is the child's sense of what other people think about him."

Teacher

are important to them are particularly powerful. From them, children come to know whether they are shy, aggressive, funny, neat, stubborn, or appealing. These are not judgments children can make about themselves; they come from remarks made to or about children. Sometimes adults seem to forget that children are listening to their conversations:

Mother: (*while Cindy listens*) I just don't know what I'm going to do about Cindy.
Neighbor: Why, what's wrong?
Mother: Well, she takes forever to eat. And messy! You just can't imagine. By the time she's finished half of what I give her, it's either on the table or on the floor. You know, her father's just the same way. That's why I always use those washable table cloths. Have you ever tried them?

Children hear more than the words and ideas of adults' conversations; they also realize that some adults don't care whether they hear the criticism.

Another source that affects self-concept and self-esteem is the child's ability to live up to the goals that he or she has internalized. If a child must be near perfect in order to be satisfied with his or her performance, self-esteem is likely to be very low. Consider the following example:

Five-year-old Marshall came from a family that insisted on excellent performance at all times. So strongly had the notion of doing something perfectly or not doing it at all been impressed on Marshall that he saw himself as a failure in much he attempted on his own. He often went to the art table at school but could not bring himself to draw the dinosaur he really wanted because "I can't make them good enough." Instead he contented himself with scribbling as he had when he was much younger.

Very young children can be helped to decide for themselves what success and good performance mean in things they do. They can learn to recognize when they have accomplished a task satisfactorily. Self-concept and self-esteem are continually developing through the accumulation of experience. These fundamental perceptions of oneself cannot be taught or altered in brief sessions of a few minutes each day.

THE CHILD IN THE SOCIAL SYSTEM

Two Aspects of Social Development

There are two aspects to young children's social development: One is their behavior—how they act toward others—and the other is what they know and understand about the social world around them.

Jimmy grabs the basket of crackers from Miss S., knocking over Julie's juice in his eagerness to help during snack time.

"Jimmy, it isn't nice to grab things. Say 'please' when you want something," reminds Miss S.

Jimmy looks embarrassed.

"Now tell Julie you're sorry that you spilled her juice. Here's a sponge. You can help her wipe it up."

Jimmy is silent as he wipes the juice.

Meanwhile, the other children are saying, "I want more juice," "let me pass the crackers, Miss S.," and generally asking for recognition of some sort.

"What do you say?" asks Miss S. to the whole group.

"PLEASE!" they all chorus.

Miss S. is teaching a social technique that many parents and teachers want children to learn: the social skills that help in interaction with others and that make others feel that they are being treated with consideration. In the exchange at the snack table, Jimmy and the others have learned from Miss S. that certain kinds of behavior (saying "please" and "thank you") will get rewards—permission to pass the crackers. The teacher has taught the children a behavior that will be useful to them. But Miss S. doesn't know how much Jimmy or the others understand *why* such phrases as "please" or "thank you" are effective, or *how* their politeness makes the teacher feel. Miss S. is losing an opportunity to help children see a connection between these verbal techniques and how they affect others.

Jimmy learns to say "please" and is rewarded with a basket of crackers. He has learned to say such things through reinforcement. Children learn many social techniques in this way. Games like "Mother, may I?" are examples.

If Miss S. were to say, "Jimmy, I don't like it when you grab the crackers out of my hands. It makes me feel like you don't care about me. I like it when you're nice to me," Jimmy might begin to learn that his teacher has feelings separate from his and that his behavior can affect how one feels.

> "What do you say when you want something?"
> "Please."
> "Why do you say 'please'?"
> "I don't know. Just 'cause!"

> "I sometimes sound like a broken record when I explain again and again about feelings."
>
> *Teacher*

Taking Another's Point of View

Learning to understand how others see the world is a major developmental task for young children. This task is achieved in at least four phases:

1. Recognition of physical boundaries between the body and other objects
2. Understanding that others have a perspective different from one's own
3. Understanding how others feel
4. Recognizing the reasons for others' feelings or behavior

This process probably continues throughout much of life, but it is especially crucial in the early years as young children gain their first impressions of the reasons for the behavior of those around them.

In talking about others, the child under seven uses observable, concrete, external behavioral cues. If asked to identify a child, he or she will say, "The one who threw sand at me," or "The one who sings with me," or "The one who rides in the red wagon." Young children do not typically use words that have internal references—"The child who is happy," or "The child who is sad a lot." More likely, they refer to behaviors they can see— "The child who was crying." They do not yet attend to the feelings and internal states of others.

This behavior is often easy to misunderstand. When two-year-old Amy steps on three children as she tries to get closer to the book the teacher is holding up for story time, she is not disregarding the other children's feelings. She doesn't feel the discomfort and has not yet learned to pick up the clues that tell her that she is affecting someone else.

Children learn about how others feel through a number of routes. A child may see or hear the behavior of another person (an angry face or voice) and remember that in the past this brought punishment. A smile may be perceived as a sign that something pleasant is about to happen because the child knows how he or she feels when smiled at. A child experiences certain feelings when scolded, and therefore thinks others feel the same way. Children begin to recognize feelings in others because they realize that they would have those feelings in the same situation.

Young children, before age six, often do not realize that others have views (feelings, preferences) different from their own. But if they are aware that another person has a different point of view, they may not know what it is. Often, children assume that another's viewpoint is very much like their own. Young children may be wary around others because they do realize that others have feelings and thoughts that are different from their own, but they do not know what these views are or how to find out.

The teacher can facilitate development of social cognition by asking children to try to imagine how someone else feels. Children may be encouraged to remember how they feel when a classmate treats them in the same way they have behaved toward someone else. Children will thus learn to connect their own feelings with cues about feelings that they see in others.

Adults who are successful in working with children often have an unusual ability to let their feelings and intentions be known in explicit ways.

Awareness of Group Membership and Identity

Once they recognize themselves and members of their immediate families as separate entities, children become aware that there are other kinds of people with whom they may share things in common. For instance, other people also have mothers and fathers. To the notions of "my mother" and "my father," the child adds the new realization that there are *other* parents, and

"The children refer to my husband as my 'daddy.' "

Preschool Teacher.

> **FACILITATING DEVELOPMENT OF
> SOCIAL CONSCIENCE**
>
> While fighting over a toy, Jody pokes Donna in the face and
> makes her cry. The teacher intervenes and says, "Jody, that
> hurts Donna when you poke her." Jody watches the teacher
> comfort Donna but says nothing.
> The next day Donna hurts another child and the teacher
> says, "Donna, do you remember yesterday when Jody hurt
> you? Remember how you cried? That's how Bobby feels
> when you hurt him."

arrives at the more general concepts of "mother" and "father." Gradually,
children begin to see that families are composed of fathers, mothers, sons,
and daughters and that a school consists of teachers and children. This kind
of concept development is like other conceptual growth; it proceeds from
awareness of repeated events and objects to a sense of their common characteristics.

Developing Attitudes Toward Groups

As children become conscious of themselves as individuals, members of a
family, and part of society, they develop awareness of racial and social-class
differences between themselves and others. Children as young as age three
notice skin color, facial features, and hair texture. They look at, touch, and
make comparisons to one another in much the same way that they explore
the physical characteristics of any aspect of the world around them.

One of the ways in which young children explore these differences in
racial characteristics is illustrated by the following observation.

During story time, Janey, a blonde, blue-eyed three-year-old, sits
and stares at the four-year-old black girl, Denise, sitting beside her.
Janey seems to have discovered Denise for the first time and obviously is unaware of the story being read by the teacher. Suddenly
Janey remarks loudly enough to disrupt the teacher, "You should
wash your hands. They're dirty." The teacher stops reading, but
before she can say anything, Denise replies, "It doesn't come off."
"Why not?" asks Janey curiously. By now the other children as well
as the teacher watch and listen intently. " 'Cause I'm black." "She's
born that way and her skin is naturally dark," adds the teacher.

"Let's go see," says Janey, as she takes Denise by the hand and leads her to the bathroom wash basin. The teacher decides the whole group can go along to watch while the two girls wash their hands. After thoroughly washing their hands, Janey turns to Denise, looks at her again, then looks at her face, arms, hands, legs, and feet and then remarks, "I believe you."

Recognition of racial differences has little effect on children's behavior toward one another. Working with a group of three-year-old black and white children, Stevenson (1962, p. 118) found that "the interaction between children appeared to depend, as it does in most types of social interaction, upon the degree to which the relationship between individuals satisfied each other's needs." Various studies show that by age five labels such as "He's black," or "She's Chinese," or "They're Mexican," have discriminatory meanings and children of other groups begin to take on negative attitudes and behaviors toward those so labeled. Their prejudice is based for the most part on attitudes they have picked up from adults.

Awareness of differences in socioeconomic resources begins to emerge in the preschool years. Young children are aware that some people are "poor" and others are "rich," even though they are only vaguely aware of what the terms mean. The young child's realization that being rich is better than being poor marks the beginning of an ability to evaluate others and self in these terms. The indicators, however, may be specific and misleading: awareness that others have more (or fewer) toys is perhaps more significant than the actual socioeconomic status of the child's own family.

AUTHORITY, RULES, AND MORAL JUDGMENT

The Child's Perception of Authority

The young child lives in a world dominated by adults and their rules and expectations. A child's dependence on adults makes it impossible to ignore their authority. In time, the rules of adults become internalized as the child's rules. Indeed, the child begins to try to enforce these rules with younger brothers and sisters and other children in the preschool or day care center.

Young children's perception of authority is determined by their stage of cognitive development and by the limitations of their own experience with authority figures. Much of the complex social system of which children and their families are a part is outside the child's awareness. Children have little knowledge, if any, of how decisions are made and by whom, even within their own families and the preschool. They are aware of only a few figures who affect their lives directly, including parents, close relatives, friends, and teachers. Later, awareness is expanded to include community workers such as the doctor, the dentist, the police officer, the fire fighter, and more distant figures (the president of the United States). However, the preschooler's understanding of the roles these people play in the community is superficial and incomplete. Young children tend to have idealized notions of authority figures. The president is wise, works hard, and attends to individual citizens. Police officers and fire fighters are seen in a similar light. Usually, young children have confidence in the police and look to them for help and protection because this is the image presented in children's books and in many preschool curricula.

The world of adult authority and its institutions are disconnected fragments. Although children may know of the fire fighter and the police officer, they are not aware that these individuals are part of a political system connected through the local government. Although incomplete, these early realizations are important because they later combine to form more complex perceptions.

Young children have vague concepts of what poverty means. Some think that the way to get rid of poverty is to get rid of people who are poor.

Five-year-old: "The teacher says you have to put those blocks away."
Four-year-old: "He's not the boss of me!"

"The president would read the letter himself if I wrote to him."

Six-year-old

Children's sense of nationalism and patriotism is one of their first political experiences.

Development of Concepts about Rules

Closely related to the child's perception of authority is the development of reasoning about rules. For young children, rules are associated with authority, and authority is linked with the possibility of punishment if rules are broken. Whereas older children distinguish between conventional rules—manners, proper dress—and moral rules—justice, harming another person (Turiel, 1977), preschool children often are not aware of this distinction. Getting clothes dirty (breaking a conventional rule) and hitting one's brother (breaking a moral rule) both evoke similar responses from adults and the child has difficulty detecting the difference between the two. Most prohibitions that are associated with punishment or reward tend to fall into a single category in the child's thinking (Damon, 1977).

A child's sense of rule is limited; often he or she does not see it as something that applies to different situations. Waiting his or her turn, for example, is a specific restraint, not a general rule to govern the child's behavior in the future.

A child entering nursery school encounters new rules. They are made by adults whose standards may be quite different from those of the child's parents. Some of these standards are, of course, important—where to go to the bathroom, how to dress, rules of safety, and so forth. However, even more important is the fact that there are rules and standards by which others will evaluate the child. Children acquire concepts about rules in a more or less predictable sequence but not in well-defined stages. Initially, children see themselves as subject to adult authority. Acts that are in accord with rules made by adults are right. The rule may not be a formal one in the usual sense; "helping mother" or "doing what daddy tells me to" is being "good" and doing "right" things. If punished, it follows that whatever the child did must have been "wrong."

"As a child, I was punished so often and so severely for wetting my bed that I came to the conclusion I could be bad even when I had no control over what I did."

Adult

Rules made by parents guide behavior until the child accumulates the experience needed to formulate more sophisticated concepts of right and wrong. Adult authority in the form of rules continues to dominate the child's conception of morality until approximately age eight. This is the first general phase of moral development. After this time, the child becomes aware of rules based on group agreement and cooperative action. Rules are less absolute; they can be changed by the group.

Moral Development

Morality is the outcome of three aspects of behavior: moral knowledge, feelings of guilt, and moral behavior. These are not independent of one another; they are parts of a whole.

For example, suppose a child is told, "Do not steal." Before this ideal of conduct becomes part of his or her moral code, the child must know what stealing means. Is a young girl stealing when she takes a toy from her shelf or only when she takes the same toy from a shelf at a store? Is a young boy stealing when he shuts Mrs. Johnson's cat in his garage? What is stealing?

DIMENSIONS OF MORALITY

Moral knowledge: Information about right and wrong behavior—specific rather than general

Moral feelings: Inner reactions of guilt or innocence regarding one's behavior

Moral conduct: Acting according to group standards of behavior

---

What isn't? Even though a child knows what it means to steal, if stealing does not evoke a sense of wrongdoing, morality is only partially developed. The moral rule must also serve as a guide to conduct. If children know they are stealing, feel guilty, but go right ahead and steal, they have not developed morality. Knowledge, feeling, and conduct must all be present before morality is acquired.

Moral development in the sense of understanding, rather than acting, begins during the preschool years and continues long after. Understanding is limited at first. Perhaps the first principle children learn is that there *are* rules. Children judge "rightness" and "wrongness" according to how much harm has been done; older children take into consideration the intent of the actor (Piaget, 1932). Piaget asked two different age groups of children to tell him which of the boys in the situations summarized below had been naughtier. The younger children (all under seven years of age) agreed that John was naughtier than Henry because he had broken more cups. On the other

---

HYPOTHETICAL SITUATIONS USED TO TEST MORAL JUDGMENT OF CHILDREN

When John is called to dinner, on entering the dining room he inadvertently overturns a tray of fifteen cups and breaks them all.

While his mother is out, Henry goes to a cupboard and helps himself to forbidden jam. In reaching to the shelf where the jam is kept, he knocks over and breaks a cup.

Adapted from J. Piaget. *The Moral Judgment of the Child* (Glencoe, Ill.: The Free Press, 1965), p. 118.

hand, children ages nine and ten were just as certain Henry's disobedience made him the naughtier child. The tendency to attend to the *external* aspects of moral situations (rules, amount of damage, consequences) persists for many children into the early grades. After that phase, more attention is given to *internal* criteria (motives, intentions, feelings) for making moral judgments.

Children develop moral knowledge and behavior in part through their own efforts to understand the social world around them. In a sense, they have their own moral ''rules'' that change as they grow in cognitive competence. Developing moral judgment is not merely a matter of internalizing the rules of the adult world. Moral knowledge does not necessarily lead to moral behavior; studies of reasoning and conduct seldom show a close connection (Damon, 1977). One *behaves* in a moral fashion more often if it is rewarded, if someone provides an example, and if there are feelings of guilt about misbehavior. Guilt is instilled by punishment, praise, approval, and, especially, by the withdrawal of love.

The teacher's example of what is ''fair,'' ''good,'' ''honest,'' and ''right'' is the most effective tool for developing moral behavior in young children.

> Conditions of a specific event, especially the likelihood of punishment or detection, are involved in the arousal of guilt feelings.

Young children are impressed by seeing what happens to others when they disobey adults. A study of young children (kindergarteners and first graders) examined their response to a videotape that showed a girl (model) who was punished for touching toys (Zimmerman and Kinsler, 1979).

The children were divided into groups. Some were given strong prohibitions before they saw the videotape: "In this room, there are some toys. You are not to touch or play with them." Other groups were given mild or no prohibitions in advance. Another group of children was also given the three types of prohibitions but was not shown the videotape.

A week later, one of the researchers returned, took each child into the same room but gave no instructions. She then made an excuse to exit, leaving the child alone with the toys for fifteen minutes.

The experience of seeing the videotape of the child who was punished for playing with the toys was more effective for the younger children; verbal prohibitions were not as effective with kindergarteners but were with first graders. The greatest impact was noted for those children who received the strong prohibition *and* saw another child punished.

REFERENCES

Brown, R. W. 1965. *Social Psychology*. New York: The Free Press.

Coopersmith, S. 1967. *The Antecedents of Self-Esteem*. San Francisco: W. H. Freeman.

Damon, W. *The Social World of the Child*. 1977. San Francisco: Jossey-Bass.

Flavell, J. H. 1966. "Role Taking and Communication Skills in Children." *Young Children,* 21, No. 3, 164–177.

Kohlberg, L. 1963. "The Development of Children's Orientations Toward a Moral Order: I. Sequence in the Development of Moral Thought." *Vita Humanae,* 6, 11–33.

Piaget, J. 1926. *The Language and Thought of the Child*. New York: Harcourt Brace Jovanovich.

———. 1965. *The Moral Judgment of the Child*. (Originally published London: Kegan Paul, 1932). Glencoe, Ill.: The Free Press.

Piers, M. W., and L. B. Wallach. 1977. "Playways to Learning." In *Readings in Early Childhood Education 77/78*. Guilford, Conn.: Dushkin Publishing.

Shantz, C. U. 1975. "The Development of Social Cognition." In *Review of Child Development Research*. Ed. E. M. Hetherington. Chicago: University of Chicago Press.

Stevenson, H. W. 1962. "Studies of Racial Awareness in Young Children." *Journal of Nursery Education,* 17, 118–122.

Turiel, E. 1977. "The Development of Concepts of Social Structure." In *Personality and Social Development,* Vol. 1. Ed. J. Glick and A. Clarke-Stewart. New York: Gardner Press.

Zimmerman, B. J., and K. Kinsler. 1979. "Effects of Exposure to a Punished Model and Verbal Prohibitions on Children's Toy Play." *Journal of Educational Psychology,* 71, No. 3, 388–395.

CHAPTER 14

THE EMERGENCE OF SOCIAL BEHAVIOR

WHAT IS SOCIAL ABOUT SOCIAL BEHAVIOR

As the sense of the self grows in early childhood, so does an awareness of others. With this separation of *self* and *other* comes the attempt to establish contact. This interaction is social behavior.

The purpose and nature of social interaction vary greatly from one situation to another. Bumper stickers are a form of social behavior; they send messages to those who want to read them. An angry quarrel is a form of social interaction; so are silent, shared feelings at a play or on the beach. The range extends from the casual greeting of a neighbor whose name one scarcely knows to continued contact with a coworker or a close friend. Social behavior includes affective ties, skills in impersonal social exchange, styles of interacting with friends, and preferences for some social activities.

THE PURPOSES OF SOCIAL BEHAVIOR

Social behavior usually has a purpose not always apparent to the observer. The child who approaches another may be curious, friendly, or have an eye on the trike that the classmate is guarding. The smile and hug that a child offers a teacher may represent a personal tie or an attempt to win a favor. Knowing the purpose of behavior helps put individual acts in perspective. Teachers who understand the reasons that children engage in different types of social behavior are better able to decide if a specific act calls for intervention, reinforcement, or serious concern.

It may be useful to think of social behavior in the following dimensions:

1. Protecting (territoriality or establishing and maintaining social space and boundaries)
2. Influencing (attempts to obtain something from others or change the environment or situation)
3. Joining (aligning with others for individual benefit or group goals)

Social behaviors are often so subtle, so interrelated, or so transitory as to challenge specific identification. Thinking of them as manifestations of protecting, influencing, or joining, however, gives the teacher a basis for understanding children's attempts to relate to one another.

Protecting

Territoriality is the term given to the attitudes and actions humans and other animals use to establish and maintain geographic and psychological boundaries (Ardrey, 1966). As though posting a "private property" sign, young children take possession of and defend the physical space that they consider their own. The area child chooses may be a corner of a sandbox marked by a finger-swept line, a bit of floor space outlined by blocks, a particular chair or place at a table, even a favorite branch in a tree. The child does not always occupy a chosen space alone; others play there with or without the "owner," but they are there only with his or her consent.

Territoriality is not selfishness; rather, it is a means by which children learn to defend their activities, interests, and property. In this sense, it is natural behavior. Although territoriality may lead to conflict if others intrude, it is not in itself antisocial. One can expect a child to feel wronged if his or her territory is invaded, even if for the benefit of the teacher or a larger group.

In addition to geographical boundaries, children also seek to establish and maintain psychological space. A youngster claims "my teacher" and "my friend" as if these individuals were part of the child's exclusive property.

Influencing

The ability to persuade or influence others in order to get a desired response is an essential part of social competence. In turn, the ability to deal with the

---

CHILDREN DISPUTE BOTH PSYCHOLOGICAL AND PHYSICAL SPACE

It is juice time and Sheila says, "Miss Cramer, I get to sit next to you today, don't I? It's my turn."

It is Rudy who answers, "No, it's my turn."

Sheila insists, saying, "No, it isn't. You sat by her yesterday."

Now Opal joins the conflict. "I never get to sit by her. It's my turn."

Rudy and Sheila join forces. "Yes, you do, Opal. You sit by her more than anyone else."

"No, I don't."

"Yes, you do!"

"No, I don't."

The teacher may elect to resolve the conflict in any number of ways, but her solution will invoke a rule the children can understand, such as "We have to take turns," or "Opal can sit next to me because she is new in school," or "I am going to choose a child who never asks to sit by me."

demands or overtures of others is equally essential. This particular aspect of social development involves feelings of assertiveness, guilt, disappointment, and gratification.

Some youngsters are able to influence others with ease, convincing peers and adults alike that their overtures and ideas are reasonable. In contrast, there are other children who are much less comfortable in trying to persuade others to see things their way.

The teacher plays an important role in the growth of this area of social competence. First, he or she is an important model for the children; the way the teacher asks the children to do things and the manner in which he or she responds to their requests and demands show children how to behave effectively. Second, the teacher can reinforce and support behavior that shows effective styles of approach and influence.

Joining

A familiar scene in any preschool is the joining or alignment of two or more children against an individual or group. It can be seen in the derision of boys by a group of girls, taking of sides in a quarrel, or identification with an ethnic group. Alignment begins in the later stages of the three-to-five period, although temporary loyalties develop in the classroom and on the playground for specific purposes. Joining includes acts of friendship and companionship, encompassing the sharing displayed when a child breaks off a piece of clay and gives it to the one who has none, or offers to squeeze over so that a friend can occupy the same mat or chair.

When a group of children play store or house together, build an elaborate block structure, or engage in dramatizing a story, alignment takes the forms of cooperation and collaboration. Yet children interacting in this way are also involved in approach-influence behavior whenever one of them attempts to persuade another.

THE BEGINNINGS OF SOCIAL INTERACTION

The young child moves into social contact with others gradually. At first, play is *solitary*. Later, children engage in *parallel play,* which means they are playing alongside others with little or no intentional interaction. During this stage, children will play with whomever happens to be in the vicinity without any conscious effort to choose or show preferences.

Associative play links the child to others in some way. The interaction is loose—for example, one child following another on a trike—and does not involve group cooperation. Children do pretty much their own thing, yielding little to the demands of others involved.

Cooperative play is usually seen with older preschool children. Building a block structure together, doing a dramatic skit, taking turns on the slide, competing as groups are all examples of cooperative play. For the first time, these activities require the child to comprehend and to comply with rules of the game, which are established by the group or by the teacher. This type of social interaction marks the beginning of rule-governed behavior, which requires the child to restrain personal preferences or impulses and subordinate his or her wishes to the norms of the group. The child will have the opportunity to engage in cooperative social interaction throughout life.

Friendship preferences appear during the late preschool years. They may not indicate any deep sense of loyalty; they are often simply preferences. They do, however, regulate the child's social interaction to some extent. They indicate that the social world of the day care center is not merely a random assortment of contacts between children.

Children also begin to establish patterns of *dominance* in interaction with

Two- and three-year-olds engage in solitary play more often than older children.

The price of joining a group may be the willingness to agree to its rules.

one another, which may be displayed by assertiveness and aggression or by friendliness and personal attractiveness.

When you observe in a preschool, notice how some children receive much more attention from the teacher and peers than do others.

These early forms of social interaction appear to set the stage for patterns of behavior that will often persist into elementary school and beyond. They make their distinctive contribution to the child's concept of self and offer opportunity for acquiring social skills that will enable the child to relate to peers and to adults. The expanding field of research in social behavior suggests that we are only beginning to understand its role in the development of adults within society.

SEXUAL IDENTITY AND ROLES

During the preschool years, the child becomes aware of sexual identity, and corresponding changes begin to take place in behavior. As in many other aspects of development, the initial step is a recognition of difference. It is as if the child thinks, "There are two sexes; I belong to *this* one and not to *that* one."

At this point, there is little knowledge about the meaning of sexual identity. Initially, it is much more like a label. The specific information about what boys are and do and what girls are and do is accumulated gradually over the next few years. Indeed, this conception of sex roles is, for many people, revised from time to time during the rest of their lives.

There are two continuing debates about sex roles. One is about the influence that biological sources have on sexual behavior. The other debate concerns the process through which sex roles are acquired.

One view of the involvement of biological factors holds that virtually all behavior not specifically required by physiological equipment (giving birth, for example) is learned. Sex differences are the product of cultural training; they can be unlearned. Within limits of physical size and strength, girls and boys can do the same things and enjoy them equally. There are no patterns of behavior that are "naturally" feminine or masculine; such ideas are culturally based. Those who hold this view often advocate elimination of sex-typed toys or behavior in education and child rearing. Boys should be given both dolls and trucks to play with; girls should be encouraged to play with toys traditionally thought to be appropriate for boys. This view has obvious implications for curriculum and for teaching behavior in preschools.

"Boys play outside more and use more physical space than girls."

Teacher

Another view of the biology-versus-cultural-training debate argues that sexual differences are rooted in physical characteristics and, to a degree, are natural. The particular form that sex-related behavior takes, however, is shaped by cultural conditioning. The differences are biologically based even though the style of expression is not fixed.

A comprehensive discussion of sex differences is found in Maccoby and Jacklin (1974). In their review, they identify differences they believe are

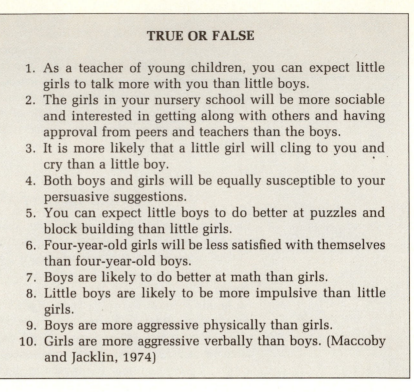

TRUE OR FALSE

1. As a teacher of young children, you can expect little girls to talk more with you than little boys.
2. The girls in your nursery school will be more sociable and interested in getting along with others and having approval from peers and teachers than the boys.
3. It is more likely that a little girl will cling to you and cry than a little boy.
4. Both boys and girls will be equally susceptible to your persuasive suggestions.
5. You can expect little boys to do better at puzzles and block building than little girls.
6. Four-year-old girls will be less satisfied with themselves than four-year-old boys.
7. Boys are likely to do better at math than girls.
8. Little boys are likely to be more impulsive than little girls.
9. Boys are more aggressive physically than girls.
10. Girls are more aggressive verbally than boys. (Maccoby and Jacklin, 1974)

supported by sound research. They also discuss some common beliefs that have no research basis which are included in the boxed insert. Check your knowledge of differences in behavior of boys and girls.

How are these behaviors acquired? Are they learned or are they biologically based? Our information is incomplete, but there are several possible theories, two of which are especially relevant for planning a preschool curriculum.

Parents give little boys different toys than those they give little girls.

One view is that children observe the behavior of others, both males and females, and imitate it. They are reinforced for imitating behavior thought to be appropriate for their sex. Boys get no reward for "feminine" behavior; girls get none for "masculine" behavior. They gradually acquire sex-typed behavior through the observe-imitation-reward sequence. This pattern is reinforced further by their sense of having something in common with other boys or girls, and the sex role identity is consolidated.

Another view is that a child first learns he or she is a boy or girl. Aware of this differentiation, they begin to model their behavior after older children and to show behavior that displays that they are like boys or girls. They thus begin to feel a sense of similarity to father or mother and identify with them. In this view, the sequence is different: recognizing their own sex identity,

ANSWERS TO TRUE OR FALSE QUESTIONS

1. *False*. During the preschool years, there appears to be little difference between the sexes in verbal abilities. However, from about age eleven and on, girls begin to score higher on verbal tasks than boys.
2. *False*. Both boys and girls are equally susceptible and responsive to social stimuli and reinforcement.
3. *False*. Girls are no more dependent than boys; boys are no more willing to leave their parents than girls.
4. *True*. Both boys and girls are equally likely to respond to your suggestions.
5. *False*. Both boys and girls do equally well on visual-spatial tasks, but boys are often superior to girls as they approach adolescence and adulthood.
6. *False*. Both boys and girls are similar in self-satisfaction, self-confidence, and self-esteem.
7. *False*. Both are similar at the preschool level, but beginning at about ages twelve to thirteen, boys' mathematical skills increase faster than girls'.
8. *True*. Little boys appear to be less inhibited than girls during the preschool years, but the sexes do not differ thereafter.
9. *True*. Even as early as age two, males in all cultures are more aggressive physically than females.
10. *False*. Boys are more aggressive physically *and* verbally than girls. (Maccoby and Jacklin, 1974)

observing others to see how boys (girls) behave, and then identifying with the parent of the same sex. This view emphasizes the initiative of the child in sex role learning.

"Some of the parents suggested that I was 'lecturing' the children too much about sexual equality. I never dreamed some of them might not agree with me!"

Teacher

The role of the teacher in dealing with sex role development is not always easy. There are great differences among parents in the extent to which they wish to have sex-typed behavior encouraged in their children. Many teachers feel strongly that equality between females and males means that differences in training and socialization should be eliminated from the curriculum. Where their beliefs collide with those of parents, an accommodation may have to be worked out.

Whatever the *content* of the behavior, it is learned by observation of others and by awareness of sexual identity. Teachers play a special part in these early stages of the child's awareness of sex-linked behavior and in helping children form concepts of themselves in which sexual differences have appropriate meaning.

AGGRESSIVE BEHAVIOR

The occasional outburst of quarrels, hitting, biting, and even fighting in the classroom or on the playground is a persistent concern of parents and teachers. The noise may signal danger that someone may get hurt; in any case, it disrupts the daily schedule and program of activities. Aggression is also embarrassing to the teacher when visitors are present; he or she may fear that it reflects on his or her ability to keep a group of children happy and constructively occupied.

Aggression Is Natural

From the children's standpoint, frustration and irritation are a natural part of their lives. Observations of young children at home and in school show that they meet, on the average, almost one hundred barriers a day to things they want or activities they would like to pursue. Such conflicts, though common, are short lived, and the youngsters appear to react rather calmly, taking apparent frustrations in stride (Fawl, 1963). Conflicts between very young children (age three and under) also tend to be brief. Aggressive exchanges are usually over in about thirty seconds, rarely lasting more than a minute (Dawe, 1934). Children often can resolve their own problems without adult intervention.

Using TV tapes, Houseman (1972) found interpersonal conflicts appearing on the average of once every 5 minutes per child. Most were of short duration and of little consequence.

Children learn through aggressive behavior that they can control the behavior of others. Aggression is usually successful; the aggressive child is rewarded. Patterson, Littman, and Bricker (1967) report observations of children in two nursery schools. They recorded every act of aggression and noted whether the response was rewarding—the victim yielded, ran away, cried, gave up a toy, and so on—or aversive—the victim hit back, snatched the toy back, complained to the teacher, and so on. In the groups they observed, there were about seventeen aggressive acts per hour for each child. They recorded over two thousand separate actions. More than three-fourths of these acts were successful. Also, if the aggressor was rewarded, a greater probability existed that he or she would behave aggressively toward that child again. If the response was aversive, the probability decreased. Children who were passive at the beginning of the year appeared to learn to be more aggressive as the year progressed. Perhaps the aggression of their peers forced them to be aggressive in turn, and they discovered that such acts were effective in controlling the behavior of others.

As children interact in groups, aggression and the response to it begin to form a social pattern. A hierarchy of dominance emerges. If child A is successful in aggression with child B, the reverse is seldom true: B is not aggressive toward A. If child B can dominate child C, then A can also dominate C (Patterson, Littman, and Bricker, 1967). These patterns are similar to social structures that emerge among nonhuman species. They tend to persist; an individual's place in the group is rarely changed once the hierarchy is established.

Hierarchies of dominance, once established, may actually reduce the level of aggression. Children who are low in the status system are unlikely to challenge the dominant members. Those who are dominant do not confront those much lower on the ladder, but use their aggression to maintain their position with those nearer to them in the hierarchy and who are thus more likely to challenge their position (Strayer and Strayer, 1976).

The major source of aggression in the preschool is the frustration of immediate circumstances—not having enough space or equipment, fighting with someone who happens to be in the way or who interferes with what is going on. Such natural conflicts can be reduced with careful planning of environment. However, children who are chronically aggressive or who deliberately hurt others may be showing signs of anger that are indicative of more serious problems.

The limitations of cognitive development play a role in aggression. Very young children often seem not to understand what brought on a fight or quarrel. They will accidentally get into or create a conflict situation because of their limited ability to anticipate the consequences. They lack the ability to see a situation from the other person's view. Children often inadvertently create frustrations for themselves and others. Not all aggression is inadvert-

"Increase of group size increases hitting behavior."

McGrew (1972)

Martha rushes to the basin to wash her hands. In her exuberance, she turns the water on full force, anxious to return to play. Jennifer, who is standing at the next basin, gets wet from the splattering water. Jennifer says, "Stop it!" pushing Martha. Martha looks puzzled and hits Jennifer back.

DID YOU KNOW THAT . . . ?

Amount of equipment has greater impact on social behavior than amount of space. When there are fewer toys and less playground equipment, children show more social interaction *and* more conflict.

The block area is most frequently inhabited by boys, the art area by girls.

Active social interchange is highest in the doll area, moderately high in the block area, and relatively low in the art area.

Children remain longer at the art area than the block area.

Limiting the number of toys increases sociodramatic play.

Teacher attention to an activity sustains child interest more than mere teacher presence.

Vigorous activities lengthen transition times and increase disruptive behaviors in subsequent activities.

Children sleep as well in large spaces as in closed or partitioned areas.

Large mixed-sex groups are more raucous than small single-sex groups.

Changes in space affect the frequency of running behavior, but running behavior is not affected when space is held constant and group size is changed.

Boys resort to hitting more than girls; girls are more apt to scold and insult.

The peak age for aggression in the preschooler is around five years.

From summaries of research by Gump (1975); Bryan (1975); Mussen and Eisenberg-Berg (1977); and Campbell (1964).

ent, however; older preschoolers (ages four and five) are quite capable of deliberate teasing, intruding, and aggressing. Intentional aggression is apparently more often the exception, and does not typify preschool behavior.

Environments and Aggression

"My daughter is much more aggressive since she has been at the children's center," comments a parent. How should a teacher respond? Is it possible for young children to become more aggressive when they attend preschool?

Increased aggressiveness is possible, but it depends on the curriculum, the environment, the adults, and the other children. Children are responsive to the physical conditions in which they play. Quarreling increases in areas where space is limited. The probability for frustration is greater as density of children increases (Yarrow, 1948). This information may seem self-evident, but keep it in mind as you monitor areas of the school. One teacher reports, "Fights erupted consistently in the dress-up area. Teachers thought at first it was due to the quarrelsome nature of certain children. Then they thought it might be the need for more clothes. Finally, the problem was solved when the area was expanded."

Aggressive behavior is also influenced by modeling and reinforcement. When children see others behaving aggressively, they are more likely to copy what they see. Studies of children who view aggressive models on television or videotape report that observing aggression tends to increase incidents of such behavior.

When teachers praise cooperation and withhold attention from children who act aggressively, aggression drops and cooperation increases. Much time and attention is given daily to dealing with aggression—intervening, discussing, redirecting, explaining. It is easy to overlook interactions that are going smoothly. The attention given to aggressive behavior is likely to maintain or increase it. Take time to reward cooperative behavior.

"The incidence of biting increased dramatically when Sam, a new boy who was a biter, entered our center. The teachers quietly but firmly removed him from the group each time he bit. We praised nonbiters for their cooperation. Soon all biting stopped."

Teacher

Adults Affect Aggression

The behavior of the teacher also regulates aggression. For example, suppose a group of children are playing with blocks and fighting breaks out. The teacher who is supervising the situation does nothing—he or she does not praise positive behavior and cooperation, nor does the teacher state personal feelings about aggression. Suppose, also, that later the same children are playing with blocks *without* any teacher supervision. Observations show that children are less aggressive when no adult is present than they are when supervised by an adult who accepts their aggressive behavior (Siegel and Kohn, 1959). Children's behavior seems to indicate that an adult who sees aggressive behavior and does not intervene apparently does not object to or may even approve of aggression. There may be times when having a teacher who does nothing is worse than having no teacher at all!

When parents complain that the school is too permissive and that their children are learning to be irritable, they may have a point; children tend to react to frustration with aggression, especially in situations where supervising adults are permissive (Yarrow, 1948). Therefore, for some children, the preschool may not offer the constraints that they need to learn to control their aggressive behavior. Children may be rewarded for aggression if the teacher does not intervene or gives in and lets dominant children have what they want.

"It is unlikely that the nursery school setting will provide a basis for the *extinction* of aggressive behaviors for children who enter the school with these behaviors already at high strength."

Patterson, Littman, and Bricker (1967), p. 20.

TIMIDITY AND SHYNESS

Much less is known about the opposite aspect of aggression—timidity and shyness in children. Because it creates fewer problems for parents and teachers, timidity is more easily overlooked and regarded as a nonbehavior. Teachers in preschools, however, will often see shyness. Like aggression, it is a form of relating to others; it is rewarded and reinforced in much the same way.

In working with timid youngsters, remember that children differ in their natural tendency to be outgoing and assertive. Children who let others take the lead or who spend time by themselves may simply prefer a less active level of social interaction. If so, parents and teachers can help by accepting the child's own preference.

"Cautious preschoolers like to sit at the playdough table or stand behind an easel where they can look busy and still watch what is going on around them."

Teacher

If there is reason to believe that the child is uncomfortable in social situations and holds back because of fear, the first thing that a staff member might do is to let the child find some space where he or she feels least uncomfortable. The teacher can help by gradually establishing a relationship of trust and communication with the child. There is rarely little reason to rush or hurry a shy child. As the sense of security with the staff grows, the child will begin to venture out, sometimes with encouragement from the teacher. Each step toward participation and initiative should be rewarded immediately. Confidence in one's social skills and acceptance by others grows slowly.

THE PROSOCIAL BEHAVIORS: ALTRUISM, SHARING, AND COOPERATION

Prosocial behavior includes cooperation, helping, empathy, sympathy, generosity, and unselfishness (altruism). We will discuss these as a cluster of positive, socially supportive acts.

DEVELOPING COOPERATIVE BEHAVIOR
IN CHINESE PRESCHOOLS

Culture shapes the development of altruistic behaviors. The age at which they appear among young children may depend greatly on the expectations of their teachers. Cooperation, caring, and helping behaviors are actively and deliberately encouraged in preschool settings in China. In these settings, curriculum activities are designed to encourage the peer group to control and socialize. Recitations, games, songs, and skits stress sharing and unselfishness. Outdoor activities include group games like tug-of-war in which the winning side sends one or two of their members to the losing side while all players recite, "Friendship and cooperation before competition." Skits dramatize giving the larger apple or cookie to a friend and keeping the smaller portion for oneself (Croft, 1973).

Children are rewarded for their altruism, usually through recognition and applause, by teachers and peers. A spirit of cooperation builds on itself: the more cooperation is rewarded, the less likely that aggression and competition will persist or be encouraged. The principles that the staff use in a Chinese preschool are familiar to all teachers: reward the behavior you want; ignore or punish the behavior you wish to discourage.

Helping behaviors are generally related to the growth of empathy—the ability to understand the feelings of others. As discussed in an earlier chapter, young children have difficulty empathizing with others. It is not surprising that they often do not express sympathy or offer help. Some observers report, however, that such behavior does occur occasionally, even with two-year-olds.

Several studies show that helping behaviors appear to increase with age, but so does competitiveness. If given a choice (in a research game) to cooperate or to compete, the tendency to compete rises with age among preschool children. It may be that as children grow older, they acquire both competitive and prosocial skills and use both more often than younger children who may be more likely to hold back or to use more neutral types of interaction (Bryan, 1975).

Research on helping and other prosocial behaviors reflects remarkable agreement on one point: one of the best ways to influence children is by modeling. Cooperation and sharing are learned in part from peers, but learning is most likely to occur through the example of adults who enjoy being cooperative and who show children how to share, help, and cooperate in actual situations. Indeed, models who preach one thing and do another are not effective; they may even encourage hypocrisy in children (Rosenhan, 1972). Models who are in a position of control or power (this applies to other

Sammy stared wide-eyed as one of the visiting parents sat down to share lunch with the children. He watched her every move as she smiled, chatted, and ate with the youngsters. After lunch, Sammy approached the parent and exclaimed, "Lady, you sure do eat nice!"

children as well as adults) are especially effective and their influence is enhanced if they have established warm relationships with the children. Peers who are natural leaders and are dominant in the group are also imitated; they deserve special consideration by the teacher because of their influence on other children.

Modeling works both ways; that is, observing selfishness is likely to encourage nonsharing and reduce helping behavior. Once children begin to display generosity and cooperation, do not assume that these behaviors are in place indefinitely. Prosocial behaviors can be altered by observing other children—especially those who are rewarded for antisocial behavior—and by observing adults.

The ease with which prosocial behaviors can be changed does not mean that a teacher's efforts are in vain; it does mean that persistence and consistency are needed in order to reach long-term goals. The behavior that a child establishes eventually stabilizes and becomes an enduring pattern. Children who frequently display anger at age three are also more likely to do so at age five. The level of aggression that a child shows in preschool is a good predictor of the amount of aggression he or she is likely to exhibit in kindergarten. This may be because the child's behavior is consistently rewarded by surrounding adults. It takes time to establish behavior; it takes more time to change it.

SOCIAL PROBLEM SOLVING

Helping children solve their personal and emotional problems is a new area of the curriculum. *Affective education,* as it is called, is designed to foster

''While some of the children went to story time, I met with a few of the older children to discuss feelings and some of our daily problems. Sometimes when difficulties arose during the morning, some of the children would say, 'Let's talk about that at our meeting.' ''

Teacher

self-esteem and to give children a better understanding of their feelings and behavior as well as the feeling and behavior of others. Affective education has been developed as a response to the stress that many children face through divorce, separation, moving, and day-to-day mini-crises of their lives.

Affective education programs attempt to deal with children's awareness of their own experiences, especially their feelings about themselves, and their comprehension of the connection between their own behavior and the actions of others. They also attempt to teach methods of solving interpersonal problems (see boxed insert).

Through their many first-hand experiences at the preschool, along with guidance from the teacher, young children learn to be aware of feelings, to express and communicate feelings, and to think about solutions and alternatives for solving problems. The practice and skill they achieve help determine future success in dealing with the affective areas of their lives.

EXAMPLE OF SOCIAL PROBLEM-SOLVING TECHNIQUE

One familiar technique used to help children solve interpersonal problems is for a teacher or program leader to ask a child to describe a situation that was bothersome. The teacher then leads the child through a series of questions that help him or her analyze the problem and solve it:

"What happened when you hit Bobby?" (Child considers past consequences.)
"Hitting is one way. Can you think of another way to get Bobby to let you use the tricycle so (child's response to previous question) won't happen again?" (Child is guided to think of alternative courses of action.)

If the child proposes an alternative, relevant solution, the teacher proceeds with the following suggestions and questions:

"That's a different idea. Go ahead and try it." (Encourage child to translate thought into action.)
(If it is successful) "Very good! You thought of that all by yourself. How does that make you feel?" (Encourage consequential thinking: the child is helped to realize that his or her feelings may themselves be rewarding.)
"How do you think Bobby feels?" (The child is guided to evaluate the effect of his or her act on another and to see or feel the event from another's perspective.)
"Can you find out if he likes that idea?" (Child is encouraged to find out how others feel and that his or her behavior can be rewarding to others.)

Adapted from Spivack and Shure (1974), pp. 59–75.

REFERENCES

Ardrey, B. 1966. *The Territorial Imperative: A Personal Inquiry into the Animal Origins of Property and Nations*. New York: Atheneum.

Bandura, A., D. Ross, and S. A. Ross, 1961. "Transmission of Aggression Through Imitation of Aggressive Models." *Journal of Abnormal and Social Psychology, 63*, 575–582.

Barnes, K. E. 1971. "Preschool Play Norms: A Replication." *Developmental Psychology, 5*, 99–103.

Berenda, R. W. 1950. *The Influence of the Group on the Judgments of Children*. New York: King's Crown Press.

Bryan, J. H. 1975. "Children's Cooperation and Helping Behaviors." In *Review of Child Development Research,* Vol. 5. Ed. E. M. Hetherington. Chicago: University of Chicago Press.

Campbell, J. 1964. "Peer Relations in Childhood." In *Review of Child Development Research,* Vol. 1. Ed. M. L. Hoffman and L. W. Hoffman. New York: Russell Sage Foundation.

Croft, D. 1973. "Education in the Land of Mao." *Learning: The Magazine for Creative Teaching, 2*, 27.

Dawe, H. C. 1934. "An Analysis of Two Hundred Quarrels of Preschool Children." *Child Development, 5*, 139–157.

Fawl, C. L. 1963. "Disturbances Experienced by Children in Their Natural Habitats." In *The Stream of Behavior*. Ed. R. G. Barker. New York: Irvington.

Feldman, R. E. 1974. "Aggression and Timidity in Young Children." In *The Formative Years: Principles of Early Childhood Education*. Ed. S. Coopersmith and R. Feldman. San Francisco: Albion Publishing Company.

Feshbach, N., and S. Feshbach. 1972. "Children's Aggression." In *The Young Child: Reviews of Research,* Vol. 2. Ed. W. W. Hartup. Washington, D.C.: National Association for the Education of Young Children. Pp. 284–302.

Gellert, E. 1961. "Stability and Fluctuation in the Power Relationships of Young Children." *Journal of Abnormal and Social Psychology, 62*, 8–15.

Green, E. H. 1933. "Friendships and Quarrels among Preschool Children." *Child Development, 4*, 237–252.

Greenberg, P. J. 1932. "Competition in Children: An Experimental Study." *American Journal of Psychology, 44*, 221–249.

Gump, P. V. 1975. "Ecological Psychology and Children." In *Review of Child Development Research,* Vol. 5. Ed. E. M. Hetherington. Chicago: University of Chicago Press.

Houseman, J. 1972. *An Ecological Study of Interpersonal Conflict among Preschool Children*. Unpublished doctoral dissertation, Wayne State University.

Maccoby, E. E. 1980. *Social Development*. New York: Harcourt Brace Jovanovich.

Maccoby, E. E., and C. N. Jacklin. 1974. *The Psychology of Sex Differences*. Stanford, Calif.: Stanford University Press.

Marcus, R. F., and M. B. Leiserson. 1978. "Encouraging Helping Behavior." *Young Children, 33*, 24–34.

McGrew, W. C. 1977. *An Ethological Study of Children's Behavior*. New York: Academic Press.

Mussen, P., and N. Eisenberg-Berg. 1977. *Roots of Caring, Sharing, and Helping: The Development of Prosocial Behavior in Children*. San Francisco: W. H. Freeman and Company.

Patterson, G. R., R. A. Littman, and W. Bricker. 1967. "Assertive Behavior in Children: A Step Toward a Theory of Aggression." *Monographs of the Society for Research in Child Development*, 32, No. 5, 1–43.

Rosenhan, D. 1972. "Prosocial Behavior of Children." In *The Young Child: Reviews of Research*, Vol. 2. Ed. W. W. Hartup. Washington, D.C.: National Association for the Education of Young Children. Pp. 340–359.

Rubin, K. H., T. W. Jambor, and K. S. Watson. 1978. "Free-Play Behaviors in Preschool and Kindergarten Children." *Child Development*, 49, 534–536.

Rubin, K. H., and C. G. Seibel. 1979. "The Effects of Ecological Setting on the Cognitive and Social Play Behaviors of Preschoolers." Paper presented at the annual meeting of the American Educational Research Association, April, San Francisco.

Sherman, L. 1975. "An Ecological Study of Glee in Small Groups of Preschool Children." *Child Development*, 46, 53–61.

Shure, M. B. 1963. "Psychological Ecology of a Nursery School." *Child Development*, 34, 979–992.

Siegel, A., and L. Kohn. 1959. "Permissiveness, Permission, and Aggression: The Effect of Adult Presence or Absence on Children's Play." *Child Development*, 30, 131–141.

Spivack, G., and M. Shure. 1974. *Social Adjustment of Young Children*. San Francisco: Jossey-Bass.

Strayer, F. F., and J. Strayer. 1976. "An Ethological Analysis of Social Aggression and Dominance Relations Among Preschool Children." *Child Development*, 47, 980–999.

Yarrow, L. J. 1948. "The Effect of Antecedent Frustration on Projective Play." *Psychological Monographs*, 62, No. 6.

CHAPTER 15

YOUNG CHILDREN AS CONSUMERS AND CONSERVERS

THE GROWTH OF RESPONSIBILITY AND SELF-REGULATION

A central theme of early development is the growth of competence. The ability to deal with social and cognitive areas of behavior are familiar components of the preschool. Less familiar is behavior that helps children take responsibility for themselves and their environment.

In this chapter we deal with the broader aspects of development—the growth of consumer skills, responsibility for health, and protection of the natural environment.

Children's vulnerability and their lack of knowledge and sophistication make them especially dependent on adults for information and training. Parents and teachers are the filters through which messages of the advertising agencies are interpreted; they are also the most effective sources of information about health, conservation, and protecting the environment.

The effort to protect citizens from exploitation should begin in the preschool. The ultimate hope is to develop knowledge and competence to help children manage their own lives and make sensible choices among the alternatives in a free and complex society. Teaching self-management skills deserves an important place in the preschool.

"Many of us allow our children to eat junk, watch junk, listen to junk, play with junk, and then we're surprised when they come out to be social junkies."

Rev. Jesse Jackson

CHILDREN IN THE MARKETPLACE

When four-year-old Janey gets up on Saturday morning, she turns on the TV to watch cartoons. While waiting for breakfast, she munches on a sweetened crunchy bar she persuaded her mother to buy at the grocery check-out stand the day before. The cereal she eats for breakfast is poured from a brightly colored box she has seen many times on TV.

Although Janey herself does not pay for these products, she and other youngsters her age decide how millions of dollars are spent each year on cereals, snack foods, candy, soft drinks, toys, books, records, and clothing. The audience they represent has been deliberately cultivated. Agencies that prepare advertising for corporations know the powerful influence young children have on the marketplace. TV commercials are created to appeal to the preschool market; packaging is designated to attract; items are displayed at eye level to interest young children who, in turn, influence the purchasing choices made by parents. The children themselves are objects of promotional strategies intended to stimulate and influence their consumer behavior.

Training young children to make sensible choices and to become careful consumers prepares them for the time when they will have their own money to spend. But they also need to develop consumer competence as young children. They are the objects of advertising as soon as they can comprehend the messages of the TV screen. The appeals to them as consumers begin before they have their own money to spend. Parents and teachers can develop consumer competence in youngsters. We teach young children as soon as possible to avoid common dangers—running out into the street, electric plugs and outlets in the home, matches, and swimming pools. Why not begin at an early age to teach consumer skills that will protect them from exploitation?

Children's Vulnerability as Consumers

It is recognized, by custom and law, that young children need special protection because of their dependence and vulnerability. This principle is obvious in matters of health, care, and physical or sexual abuse. Young children are also vulnerable in the marketplace; they are naive, inexperienced, and unprepared to play the consumer role—choosing, evaluating, selecting on the basis of product quality.

The natural vulnerability of young children comes from at least three sources.

1. They tend to believe adults and other sources of information that appear to have authority. This trust in adults is reflected in their ideas that rules are absolute, their belief that adults have the right to reward and punish, and in their general dependence on the adult world.

2. They cannot easily take the role of others and imagine that someone may intend to deceive or mislead. They cannot role-play the possible motives of people who offer them advertising messages.

3. They lack the information on which to make choices. Young children do not have a consumer's skepticism; we purposely treat children in ways that will foster trust and confidence in the social world around them. Adults are cautious as consumers in part because they have been fooled in the past. The wariness that is needed for adequate consumer behavior thus comes from (a) knowledge that others *may* try to mislead consumers about a product, (b) opportunity to compare the quality and cost of alternatives, and (c) the ability to resist impulse buying. Experience is essential in the development of consumer competence.

The lack of certain cognitive and social skills, which are developed during preschool years, makes it difficult for young children to distinguish among four types of messages that form the bulk of the mass media, especially television: *information, instruction, entertainment,* and *persuasion.* Advertising on TV and radio often takes the guise of an informing message. Even adults may find themselves misled for a moment when an ad begins with the authoritative tone of a news item. Persuasion can also be disguised as entertainment or as an interesting bit of information.

When adults recognize and thus categorize media messages as informing,

Teacher: "So the fox said,
'Jump up on my nose!' Did
he really want to save the
Gingerbread Boy?"
Children: "No! He wanted to
eat him!"
Teacher: "That's right. The fox
was fooling the Gingerbread
Boy, wasn't he? Do you get
fooled sometimes?"

instructing, entertaining, or persuading, they adopt a suitable response; that is, they assign meaning to a message according to these categories. The sight and sound of a gun on a news program is interpreted very differently than the same picture in a fictionalized police-and-crime series. Adults use these cognitive filters to organize and interpret the world around them. Young children are developing this ability but they are still easily misled.

The attempt to teach young children to be consumers requires them to make difficult distinctions. It asks them to mistrust others and to be cautious which runs counter to principles of dealing with young children. Ideally, we want them to have confidence in adults, to trust the meanings of words, and to feel that they are effective in interaction with adults. Teaching children to be consumers thus requires that we teach them to be selective in the trust they place in different sources of messages that come to them.

Very young children have no way of knowing that the animated cartoon on the TV screen is an attempt to sell a product and is not necessarily offering a factual report. They do not recognize the distinction between program content and commercials unless they are taught.

Effects of TV Commercials on Children

The FTC has studies that show many preschool children believe there are little figures inside the TV set urging them to buy products.

In 1979, the Federal Trade Commission (FTC) began holding public hearings on the effects of TV commercials on children. These hearings were conducted in response to demands of child advocacy groups to limit or eliminate commercials aimed at young children. Parents, teachers, and social scientists

THE DEVELOPMENT OF ECONOMIC COMPETENCE

A young child does not automatically grow up to be a wise consumer. An understanding of the concepts of buying and selling are basic to the development of economic competence.

Concepts of money, of purchasing, and of ownership are unclear to preschoolers. The two-year-old "has a robust sense of *mine* but a very weak sense of *thine*" (Gesell and Ilg, 1946, p. 53). The young child may use the term *mine* as an attempt to lay claim to a toy, but he or she has only a faint idea of what it is that gives justification for ownership.

When asked, "What things belong to you?", four-year-olds can usually identify several things that are theirs. If asked how they know that something belongs to them, they will often call on authority ("My mommy told me"), offer explanations by naming or by circular reasoning ("Because my name is on it." "Because it is."), or claim ownership by default ("Because no one else plays with it.").

By age five, many children have been to the store and observed transactions involving the exchange of money and goods. Yet when asked who determines how much things will cost in a store, some children thought their parents decided the prices, others attributed the price to God, and some indicated "by a person . . . because he gots the thing to put the price on." When asked "How does the person at the store decide what things will cost?" explanations are usually literal or based on authority—"They decide," or "Because it's stamped on top." (Fox, 1978).

Young children sense that there are rules about such things as ownership and purchasing but they depend on someone else to know about them. This reliance on authority is one aspect of the child's vulnerability and naivete.

Teachers help young children develop concepts of ownership, buying, and selling by providing experiences in "playing store," by asking questions ("Why does this belong to you?" "How do you know this belongs to Johnny"), and through discussions about their actual experiences. Teachers can suggest situations for role-playing and help children create experiences in economics by having them make toys or bake cookies, then selling them at prices established by the maker and the storekeeper.

argued that young children were not capable of making sound judgments about the products they saw advertised.

The average child between the ages of two and eleven is exposed to more than twenty thousand commercials a year (Adler, 1977). Many of these commercials are designed for young children; appeals to preschoolers are deliberately incorporated into the advertising message. Their techniques succeed. Children are affected by TV advertising. They draw inferences about things they see; they prefer advertised over nonadvertised products and they implore their parents to buy advertised goods (Adler, 1977; Comstock et al.,

"We are not dealing with little robots, helplessly glued to the set, incapable of discerning between commercials and programs."

Vice President of General Mills

1978; Ward, Wackman, and Wartella, 1977). There are side effects. Children develop materialistic values (Goldberg and Gorn, 1977). Commercials carry an underlying message: to consume is to be happy (Roberts et al., 1978).

The food commercials that young children see usually display highly sugared foods (cereals, candy bars, fruit-flavored drinks, and so on). As many as two-thirds of commercials associated with children's television programs are for such sugared snacks (Barcus, 1975b). The mere repetitiveness of commercials may increase the attractiveness of advertised foods, thereby affecting food preferences.

Young children need to be educated about food—what it is for, how it is related to their health and well-being, how it is produced and consumed. Part of educating for responsible citizenship means recognizing waste and irresponsible consumption. According to Joan Gussow (1977b),

> Food ads on television surely fail to teach children that food comes not from plants in Battle Creek, but from plants that require clean air, clean water, and fertile topsoil to sustain them. Certainly blue, pink, orange, and yellow confections—urged upon children as essential components of a good breakfast—must confuse children about the reality of food: its sources, its nature, its role in human life. (p. 8)

In 1978, annual sugar consumption reached 128.1 pounds per person. That works out to 28 teaspoons of sugar per day for every man, woman, child, and infant in the United States.

Twenty million adults in the United States are missing all their teeth; there are one billion unfilled cavities in the mouths of Americans.

"It is probably not necessary to point out that the increasing emphasis on "nutrition" in food advertising seldom has anything to do with the products' real nutritional value to the folks who will be consuming them. In the United States and in Canada, vitamin and mineral deficiencies—at least deficiencies of what advertisers bill as the "important" vitamins and minerals—would appear to represent a very minor proportion of nutrition-related disorders.

". . . On the other hand, degenerative diseases associated with overconsumption—of calories, of saturated fats, of refined carbohydrates, and possibly of animal protein as well—are becoming epidemic. The addition of vitamins and minerals to products which are low in fiber and high in salt, sugar, saturated fat, modified starches and other fillers does not make them nutritious (though nutrient information carried on their labels may, unfortunately, help convince children—and their parents—that they are)." (Gussow, 1977a, p. 4)

Children are little consumers, exercising their preferences through their parents' wallets and shopping habits. Mothers usually yield to the persuasion of their young children in the selection of breakfast cereals and snack foods. In a study of families with five- to seven-year-old children, almost 90 percent of the mothers reported that they usually accepted their children's preferences in cereals, and more than half of the mothers reported that they usually yielded to children's choice of snack foods (Ward and Wackman, 1971).

"More and more parents tell me that they have put their small children on a weekly TV budget—there is a certain amount of time allocated for TV watching—and, together, the parents and child decide what programs the child will be allowed to watch."

Ralph Nader

EFFECTS OF TV ON CHILDREN'S BEHAVIOR

Although much attention is given to the debates about TV commercials and their effect on children's food preferences, what are some of the other effects of TV viewing in general? Some research evidence most relevant to parents and teachers of young children indicates the following:

1. Television program content can have a negative effect on children's behavior, and that effect is likely to endure. More superficially, watching aggressive and violent programs tends to increase aggressive behavior in young children.
2. What children bring to the televiewing experience (states of arousal, anger, excitement, and so on) can modify the effect that a given program has on their behavior.
3. Programs showing prosocial (helping, sharing, cooperative) behavior can increase such behavior in young children.
4. Educational content—"Sesame Street," for example—can facilitate children's concept and vocabulary development.

In short, children learn from television. There is no moratorium on learning when they sit in front of the TV set. While there is much that is not known about TV and its effects, we do know that it is a real part of the child's daily learning experience.

From reviews of TV research by Cater and Strickland, 1977; Comstock et al., 1978; Cook et al., 1975; Stein and Friedrich, 1971, 1975.

Studies show that preschool children comprehend only a part of TV program content, even when the programs are designed for them. Children aged four to six were shown a three-minute segment from the "Most Important Person" series that was broadcast nationally as part of the Captain Kangaroo program. They were then asked questions about three aspects of the segment: the ongoing action, the "facts" offered, and "asides" that were not a part of the central activity. Children in this age group understood about three-fourths of the ongoing action material but comprehended only one-third of the "facts" and asides. The items dealing with information were then grouped by the method of presentation: visual and verbal, verbal only, and visual only. The children understood about 70 percent of the information presented in *both* verbal and visual channels but only about 40 percent of material presented in either modality by itself (Friedlander and Wetstone, 1974).

Immunizing Children Against Advertising

Although children lack adult sophistication, some concepts are within their mental capacity. A preschooler may have difficulty grasping the ideas behind purchasing and using money, but he or she can be taught to identify commercials and learn that they are intended to sell something. The young child can develop an ability to regard commercials with skepticism.

Children watch a great deal of TV programming designed for adult audiences. Even if ads were banned or modified when used with children's programs, children would still be exposed to commercials. Several attempts have been made to develop training films and curricula that might prepare children to evaluate TV commercials critically (Goldberg, Gorn, and Gibson, 1978; Roberts et al., 1978). These are based on a concept that the child can be "immunized" against TV advertising.

It is both impossible and unwise to attempt to restrict TV programming to things appropriate for the preschool child. Parents can play an evaluative role, of course, but eventually the child needs to be given the conceptual and attitudinal tools to make his or her own judgments. The training programs are intended to provide the child with the analytic resources to recognize what TV commercials are and to evaluate them cautiously.

Simply providing information about commercials or about the quality of a product appears insufficient to alter children's behavior. Children can repeat, "Sugar is bad for my teeth," but still urge their parents to buy heavily sugared foods that they know are "not good for them." (Obviously, they are not different from adults who smoke even when they know of the hazards.) While concepts and knowledge are probably essential, they do not necessarily alter behavior.

In one study, a group of first grade children were shown ads designed to persuade them to eat less sugared snacks and breakfast foods. These ads showed attractive children eating fruits, vegetables, milk, and eggs. This modeling approach seemed to have some effect, but was much less useful than another approach. A program designed for children, "Fat Albert and the Cosby Kids," was used to arouse affective involvement in the message. The appeal was not so much to the nutritious quality of foods as to the social consequences. Eating junk food, mostly candy, leads to toothache and a visit to the dentist. In one segment, failure to eat nutritious foods led to defeat in a football game. These social and affective appeals of "Fat Albert" were the most convincing; they reduced the number of choices of heavily sugared cereal and candy.

Helping young children develop consumer resistance is not easy. Advertising appeals to the impulses of the child; the things offered are attractive. Red, pink, and purple animated confections are more enticing than ordinary natural foods; violence is more stimulating and demanding of attention than a symphony. How can teachers hope to counteract the compelling messages of TV commercials? The task demands the support and cooperation of other adults in the child's life. It is not enough to talk about the deceptiveness of advertising, nor even to limit the amount of viewing. The ultimate goal is to help children develop their thinking, reasoning, and problem-solving abilities so that they can be responsible for making choices.

In day care centers where children are allowed to watch certain programs, teachers can share in the viewing, comment on what is shown, identify the commercials, and talk about their intent. Teachers are among the most important adults in a young child's life. The teacher's skepticism and comments about commercials can be a strong influence on the child's thinking.

Parents often are not aware of the impact TV has on their children. A short newsletter with facts summarized from surveys and research studies such as those reported in this chapter can mobilize parents to reinforce the teaching of the school staff.

Exposure to TV commercials can be used to teach children to be selective, to be skeptical, to understand what they are seeing. Curriculum activities that provide experience in reasoning and thinking help build a strong base for immunizing children against advertising.

> "The educators have not differentiated food habits from any other type of habit. If children could be taught to write by the Palmer method . . . then they could be taught to eat foods which contained vitamins instead of foods that did not."
>
> *Margaret Mead*

> "My teacher let me pour water on the towel just like on TV, but it didn't work!"
>
> *Preschooler*

HEALTH AND SELF-CARE

Teacher: What happens when you are sick?
Child: My mommy takes me to the doctor.

Dear Parents:
DID YOU KNOW THAT . . .

1. almost 90 percent of the mothers in a survey reported that they let their five- to seven-year-old children select the breakfast cereal?
2. television program content can have a negative effect on children's behavior.
3. watching aggressive and violent programs tends to increase aggressive behavior in young children?
4. as many as two-thirds of the commercials associated with children's TV programs are for sugared snacks?

HOW CAN WE IMMUNIZE OUR CHILDREN AGAINST TV COMMERCIALS?

What we plan to do at school:

1. The teachers are going to help the children identify commercials on TV.

2. We are going to talk about commercials and why the cereal and snack food companies show them.
3. We are going to let children test the claims that some TV ads make about certain products.
4. We will present our own "commercials" for nutritious foods—fresh fruits, vegetable, dairy products.

What you can do at home:

1. Watch TV with your children. See if they can tell the difference between a commercial and the program.
2. Show them that what they see is not always what they get.
3. Teach them what is good for their teeth and what is bad for their teeth.
4. Reinforce what we are doing at school and *share your good ideas with us.*

The average adult male in the United States is twenty to thirty pounds overweight and the average female is fifteen to thirty pounds overweight.

"Parents and schools should teach children to take responsibility for their own health. I feel strongly that the childlike acquiesence and passivity some adults show with physicians is not what their children should learn. The cliché 'you're the doctor' has outlived its usefulness. The so-called good patients are probably not doing themselves or their children any good."

Doctor

Teacher: What happens there?
Child: The doctor gives me medicine and makes me well again.

Young children begin to believe at an early age that their health and well-being are dependent on someone other than themselves. Again, as in advertising, their trust of adults and dependence on them make this a natural response. It is an attitude found in adults. Many people believe that medical technology is the most effective route to health. Yet health does not come from drugs. Drugs may only alleviate the symptoms but not treat the causes.

The most common health problems in the United States are obesity, alcoholism, allergies, asthma, arthritis, heart disease, and cancer. The medical profession deals with the symptoms of these diseases but the contributing factors are found in individual patterns of living. Cigarette smoking, lack of exercise, bad food habits (especially overeating and poor nutrition), abuse of drugs, and emotional stress set the stage for, or directly influence, the quality of health. Responsibility for oneself includes behavior that affects the way our bodies function.

Unfortunately, like the child who is taken to the doctor for medicine to make him or her well, our attitudes about health generally encourage passivity. Visiting the doctor is sometimes viewed in the same way as dropping a car off at a repair service: it is easy to think of oneself as a machine with a broken or poorly functioning part and not be responsible for the condition it is in or for its repair.

Actually, the most important influences on a child's health are the family and teachers, not the physician. Attitudes about health and how to deal with illness are taught by the adults in a child's life. Learning to take responsibility for one's own well-being can begin in the early years.

Teaching Children Responsibility for Self-Care

Comments such as "Better put on a sweater. It's cold outside," teach children to rely on others to monitor their needs rather than to learn how to be responsible for self-care. "But," argues a parent, "my child would freeze before having the sense to come in and get a sweater!" Instead of telling children to put on more clothing, a teacher might help them learn to monitor their feelings of warmth and cold: "How do you feel?" "Is your skin warm or cold?" "What does your body tell you?" "What can you do about it?" These questions turn a youngster's attention to body temperature. Adults also model by remarking about how they feel when cold or warm, ill or well.

Science projects provide opportunities to experience different degrees of cold and warmth. Cooking, making ice cream, and using thermometers provide opportunities to learn about cold and warmth. Verbalizing and labeling are as important to learning about self-care as to acquiring other cognitive skilis.

Preschoolers are curious about their bodies; they enjoy activities that identify body parts requiring that they move their fingers, touch their toes, wiggle their noses, and so on. They are interested to learn what different parts of their bodies can do. The teacher can extend the child's natural curiosity to include learning to monitor and take responsibility for physical needs.

Teaching Children about Nutrition

Children can also learn to monitor their need for food. If preschoolers could eat when they are hungry, most would need less food than adults would have them consume. They would eat more frequently, but take smaller amounts. Obviously, it is not practical to prepare six or seven meals a day, but young children seem to respond best to small amounts of food served throughout the day.

Set up a juice corner where children can squeeze fresh orange juice, serve it to their friends, and clean up after their juice party.

Most children prefer bland foods and raw vegetables to highly seasoned foods and cooked vegetables. They also prefer lukewarm to hot foods.

"One parent brought her electric juice maker to school and made vegetable juice with tomatoes, carrots, celery, and onions. The children loved it!"

Teacher

Some publicly funded food programs require that certain amounts of food be served to each child, but the manner and timing of service is often flexible. If healthful foods such as raw vegetables, fresh fruits, nuts, seeds, and cheese are available for snacks, the children can eat when they are hungry. Children will also drink more if liquids are made readily available and they are allowed to pour what they need.

Because young children's capacity for food is limited, their nutritional needs are great. Everything they eat should have nutritional value. Snacks can be the most important part of a child's daily food intake. However, unplanned snacks often contain many empty calories, with little or no protein and few essential vitamins and minerals. Whether a youngster eats a piece of cheese or a candy bar, an apple or a doughnut, is very much a matter of careful adult planning.

The attractiveness of foods—color, texture, variety—makes eating more enjoyable and tempting to the young child. Preparing food in bite-size pieces and serving only small amounts encourage children to eat more readily. Small group seatings in pleasant surroundings are conducive to better eating experiences. Adults who enjoy food and maintain a calm attitude during meals set a good example for youngsters to model.

The growth rate slows down between the ages of two and three (Smart and Smart, 1977). Parents may become concerned about the child's decreased appetite. At the same time, the two-year-old is just beginning to exercise autonomy and wants to do things for him- or herself. This push for independence coupled with a decrease in appetite can cause many problems if adults press children to eat. Teachers can plan the classroom to recognize and support the child's sense of autonomy, providing activities that encourage self-help and allowing freedom to choose from among several alternatives. When children can select from among foods that are all good for them, and they can eat as little or as much as they want, they will acquire eating habits based on their bodies' needs for food.

Teaching Children about Physical Fitness

"At its best, nutrition serves as a basis for a healthy body, but regular exercise at virtually all ages is essential to keep the body functioning well."

Doctor

Health habits are acquired early. If adults make vigorous exercise something that is fun, young children will learn to appreciate the values of developing muscle skills that are rewarding—playing ball, riding bikes, swimming, jogging, and hiking. Teachers who are in poor physical condition are poor models for the youngsters they teach. Physically inactive adults are less likely to reward physical fitness. An enthusiastic teacher supports a child's running, climbing, and jumping activities. As a teacher, you are the model; the priorities you give to physical fitness go a long way toward the development of physical health in young children.

CONSERVING RESOURCES AND PROTECTING THE ENVIRONMENT

"Overseas there is rising fury with Americans who now consume close to 30 percent of the world's oil output."

Frank Vogel, U.S. Economics Correspondent for the London Times *(July 8, 1979)*

The citizens of the United States make up less than 6 percent of the world's population, yet we account for almost one-half of the annual world consumption of nonrenewable resources (metals and chemicals), about one-third of the world consumption of energy, and about one-third of the annual consumption of animal protein (Gussow, 1975). As individuals, we consume a disproportionate share of the resources of the planet.

Even if we could be persuaded to reduce our use of resources, the world is still faced with a growth in population that, according to many experts, will create shortages of food, energy, irreplaceable materials, forests, and water. The population of the world was relatively stable for many centuries. It has expanded dramatically in the past two hundred years and will almost double by the year 2000—less than twenty years away (Figure 15.1). It will double again before the middle of the twenty-first century. The United States had a population of 5 million in 1800, 76 million in 1900, 151 million in 1950, and will have approximately 280 million by the end of the century.

The demand that will be placed on the world's resources by world population growth makes conservation a matter of survival. The preschool is not too early to begin to teach children that natural resources are not unlimited.

"I saw . . . children dying of leukemia and cancer. I realized that these diseases would increase as the radiation in the environment increased."

Dr. Helen Caldicott, Pediatrician and President of Physicians for Social Responsibility

Place plastic bags and paper bags in a compost pile. Let children see how plastic will not decompose.

Children have a real part in conserving resources and protecting the natural environment. They are not insulated from the effects of water pollution, pesticides on the food they are served, smog in the air they breathe, chemicals in the water they drink, and excessive levels of noise and radiation from many sources. They can begin to learn that the choices they make have effects on them, on others, and on the environment.

Young children cannot easily grasp on their own the concepts of conservation of resources or protecting the environment to avoid crisis in the future. Although they gain knowledge about the physical world from direct experience, awareness of the problems must come from adults.

Recycling cans and newspapers is time consuming and rewards are not apparent or immediate. Litter and waste often go unnoticed. To be effective in teaching responsible consumerism, the teacher needs to use all the tactics

WORLD COMMUNITY

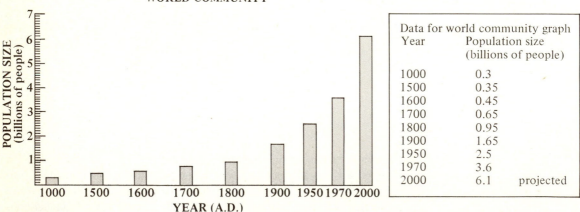

Year	Population size (billions of people)	
1000	0.3	
1500	0.35	
1600	0.45	
1700	0.65	
1800	0.95	
1900	1.65	
1950	2.5	
1970	3.6	
2000	6.1	projected

FIGURE 15.1

Population in the World Community (A.D. 1000–2000)

Reprinted with permission from Ann Smith, *Child Ecology*, Los Altos AAUW, 1974.

For information on conservation, write Sierra Club, 530 Bush Street, San Francisco, Calif. 94108

at his or her command—reinforcement, modeling, direct information, and correcting.

How can the habits of overconsumption be counteracted when young children are surrounded by messages that encourage waste? Can adults impress on youngsters the necessity to consume less and conserve what we have? Every society adapts its child-rearing practices to the physical and economic circumstances of daily life. Water is used with great·care where it is scarce; in drought areas, children are taught to become sensitive to the need to turn off faucets, to use less water, and to avoid waste. Pollution is a very real part of children's lives when, because of smog alerts, they cannot go outside to play.

In the People's Republic of China, a country populated by more than a billion people, young children are given the responsibility of raising some of their own food for the child care centers. Through stories and songs, they are taught to admire the work of the peasants and laborers. While traveling through China, Doreen Croft talked with teachers, who said, "Ninety percent

---

TEACHING ABOUT THE ENVIRONMENT

1. Show children newspaper and magazine pictures of birds affected by oil spills. Talk about the pollution and damage caused by carelessness.
2. Have children match pictures of animals with their natural habitats. Talk about incorrect matches and why animals would not be able to survive.
3. Collect or buy some ladybugs and demonstrate how they help to maintain a natural balance by eating aphids. Talk about the advantages of using natural methods rather than spraying with insecticides. A good book to use is *This Pesticide Has Polka Dots,* by E. Tanson (*National Wildlife Magazine* April–May, 1972), available from the National Wildlife Federation, Inc., 1412 16th St., N.W., Washington, D.C. 20036).
4. Select books and stories (such as "The Gingerbread Boy") to lead into discussions of "being fooled." Relate this skepticism to daily activities, such as TV commercials, adults smoking, using disposable products, and so on.

(Additional activities can be found in the section on "Conservation and the Environment" in *An Activities Handbook for Teachers of Young Children,* Third Edition.)

of our people must toil very hard to provide food for the country. In planting and caring for their vegetable gardens, our young children learn to appreciate how much work it takes to produce food. We remind each child to take only what he can eat. He can eat as much as he needs, but if he takes more than he can consume, we talk with him and tell him it is wasteful and remind him of how hard one must work to raise that food.''

REFERENCES

Adler, R. 1977. *Research on the Effects of Television Advertising on Children*. Washington, D.C.: National Science Foundation.

Armstrong, L. 1978. *How to Turn up into down into up: A Child's Guide to Inflation, Depression, and Economic Recovery*. New York: Harcourt Brace Jovanovich.

Barcus, R. E. 1975a. *Television in the Afternoon Hours*. Newton, Mass.: Action for Children's Television.

Barcus, R. E. 1975b. *Weekend Commercial Children's Television*. Newton, Mass.: Action for Children's Television.

Burris, V. L. 1976. ''The Child's Conception of Economic Relations: A Genetic Approach to the Sociology of Knowledge.'' Unpublished doctoral dissertation, Princeton University.

Cater, D., and S. Strickland. 1977. *TV Violence and the Child*. New York: Russell Sage Foundation.

Comstock, G. A., S. H. Chaffee, N. Datzman, M. McCombs, and D. F. Roberts. 1978. *Television and Human Behavior*. New York: Columbia University Press.

Cook, T. D., H. Appleton, R. F. Conner, A. Shaffer, G. Tamkin, and S. J. Weber. 1975. *''Sesame Street'' Revisited*. New York: Russell Sage Foundation.

Feingold, B. F. 1975. *Why Your Child Is Hyperactive*. New York: Random House.

Fox, K. F. A. 1978. ''What Children Bring to School: The Beginnings of Economic Education.'' *Social Education*, 42, No. 6, 478–481.

Friedlander, B. Z., and H. S. Wetstone. 1974. ''Suburban Preschool Children's Comprehension of an Age-Appropriate Informational Television Program.'' *Child Development*, 45, 561–565.

Gardner, H. 1978. *Developmental Psychology*. Boston: Little, Brown.

Gesell, A., and F. L. Ilg. 1946. *The Child from Five to Ten*. New York: Harper and Brothers.

Goldberg, M. E., G. J. Gorn, and W. A. Gibson. 1978. ''TV Messages for Snack and Breakfast Foods: Do They Influence Children's Preferences?'' *Journal of Consumer Research*, 5, No. 2, 73–81.

Goldberg, M. E., and G. J. Gorn. 1977. ''Material vs. Social Preferences, Parent-Child Relations and the Child's Emotional Responses: Three Dimensions of Responses to Children's TV Advertising.'' Paper presented at symposium on television advertising and children, Fifth Annual Telecommunications Policy Research Conference, Airlie House, Va. March 30–April 2.

Gussow, J. D. 1972. ''Counternutritional Messages of TV Ads Aimed at Children.'' *Journal of Nutritional Education*. 4, No. 2, 48–52.

Gussow, J. D. 1975. ''Consuming in the Year 2000.'' *Teachers College Record*. 76, No. 4, 665–673.

Gussow, J. D. 1977a. "Using and Abusing the Mass Media." *Journal of the Canadian Dietetic Association,* 38, No. 2, 89–108.

Gussow, J. D. 1977b. "Children vs. the Gross National Product." *Nutrition Action*, 4, No. 11, 7–9, 12.

Harrison, W. C. 1973. *Conservation: The Challenge of Reclaiming Our Plundered Land*. New York: Messner.

National Geographic Society. 1971. *As We Live and Breathe: The Challenge of Our Environment*. Washington, D.C.: National Geographic Society.

Pringle, L. 1971. *Ecology: Science of Survival*. New York: Macmillan.

Roberts, D. F., W. A. Gibson, P. Christenson, L. Mooser, and M. E. Goldberg. 1978. "Immunizing Children Against Commercial Appeals." Paper presented at the annual meeting of the American Psychological Association, Toronto, Canada, August 30.

Saltonstall, R., Jr. 1970. *Your Environment and What You Can Do about It*. New York: Walker.

Schwartz, G. E., and B. S. Schwartz. 1974. *Food Chains and Ecosystems: Ecology for Young Experimenters*. Garden City, N.Y.: Doubleday.

Smart, M. S., and R. C. Smart. 1977. *Children: Development and Relationships*. 3rd ed. New York: Macmillan.

Stein, A. H., and L. K. Friedrich. 1971. "Television Content and Young Children's Behavior." *Television and Social Behavior, Reports and Papers, Vol. II: Television and Social Learning*. Washington, D.C.: Government Printing Office.

Stein, A. H., and L. K. Friedrich. 1975. "Impact of Television on Children and Youth." In *Review of Child Development Research*. Vol. 5. Ed. E. M. Hetherington. Chicago: University of Chicago Press.

Strauss, A. L. 1954. "The Development of Conceptions of Rules in Children." *Child Development*, 25, No. 3, 193–208.

Ward, S., and D. B. Wackman. 1971. "Television Advertising and Intrafamily Influence: Children's Purchase Influence Attempts and Parental Yielding."

Ward, S., D. B. Wackman, and E. Wartella. 1977. *How Children Learn to Buy*. Beverly Hills, Calif.: Sage.

CHAPTER 16

THE ARTS IN THE PRESCHOOL PROGRAM

THE PLACE OF THE ARTS IN THE CURRICULUM

"His spirit, the spirit of man, should hover over the shapeless and move it that it may take shape and form, a distinct being and life of its own. This is the high meaning, the deep significance, the great purpose of work and industry, of productive and creative activity."

Frederick Froebel

Art activities have been part of early education for a long time. Frederick Froebel (1782–1852), founder of the *kindergarten,* created materials that he called *play songs, gifts,* and *occupations.* These were designed to challenge the children, stimulate mental activity, and produce inner organization and integration (Table 16.1). He saw coloring, drawing, tracing, and working with clay as activities that would develop concepts and facilitate cognitive growth.

In this chapter, the term *arts* includes activities that help children develop responses to artistic stimuli and express those responses in some perceptible or tangible form. Efforts to stimulate imagination, stir emotion, and enhance perceptual awareness lie within the arts. A teacher's comment about the color and design of a dress or jacket, the choice of a picture to help children come to recognize the work of a famous artist, or the request, "Show me how this kind of music makes you feel," contribute to the development of artistic experience. Anything that helps a child *recognize* artistic forms in the environment, *respond* to them, or *produce* them is part of the art curriculum.

This definition encompasses a wide variety of activities and materials in the preschool curriculum. They can be used in many ways and for many purposes. The staff members of a preschool do not always agree about the purposes that art activities are to serve, as illustrated by the following conversation among several teachers:

TABLE 16.1
Example of Picture Song Card and Description of Froebel's Materials

Play Songs	Gifts	Occupations
These were originally prepared for use by the mother but were later employed by teachers in the kindergarten when Froebel observed children spontaneously joining hands in a circle as they played and sang together.	These were a series of play materials that fitted into boxes as units.	Children engaged in each or all of the following activities freely, but the materials were presented in a somewhat sequential manner.
He placed chairs in a circle and engaged the children in singing games and stories using his picture song cards.	They were used for creative play but primarily to encourage certain kinds of learning (development of concepts and cognitive skills).	Clay modeling Dot patterns Pricking cards Bead stringing Sewing cards Paper weaving Paper folding Drawing Coloring Tracing Pasting Making gardens Nature study
	The concept of a ball was basic to the understanding of the relationship and form of a unified whole—this unity was basic to all of Froebel's work and philosophy.	

"Frankly, I'm confused," Miss F. announced. "Rich's mother visited today and saw him at the easel. He was painting those figures he's been doing so much of lately. You know, the kind with big heads and enormous eyes but no bodies and just long lines for arms and legs. I was clear across the room but I heard her say, 'Rich, you know better than that! That's not what people look like.' You should have seen his expression. Poor little guy—he was really crushed."

"What did you do?" Mr. S. asked.

"I went over and tried to explain that it's quite natural for children to draw people this way at a certain stage, but she wasn't at all impressed. She wanted to know what he was learning from this experience."

"What did you say?"

"Oh, something vague like 'He needs to have lots of opportunities to explore with the materials in order to express himself.' This obviously didn't satisfy her. She complained that we should at least point out to him that people have bodies."

"That's a fairly common complaint," Miss L. remarked. "I've been here five years and I remember how helpless I felt the first time one of the parents confronted me with 'Just what do you teach the children in this school?!' "

"I think Rich's mom is unhappy with us because she can't see the value of an exploratory kind of art activity. I know she is anxious to have him learn to read and write and doesn't want him to 'waste his time' here," commented Mr. S.

"I don't want him to waste his time here either," interjected Mrs. A., "but I happen to believe that painting and other art activities are not a waste of time."

"I agree," said Miss L., "but we haven't convinced Rich's mother, and I really think we're doing her a disservice if we ignore her concerns and treat her as if she didn't know anything."

"Look," Miss F. said. "I have to admit that I often wonder just what the kids are getting out of their experiences, especially when they're splattering paint around in the art area and jingling bells like crazy in the music room."

"What's all this got to do with teaching art?" Mr. S. insisted.

"We have to be more clear about our own goals and the ways in which we achieve them," said Mrs. A. "I think the reason we feel threatened by people like Rich's mother is because we aren't sure about what we are doing."

Some teachers think of the arts as isolated, specific activities. Painting is done at a particular time in the paint corner; the product is to be taken home

"Whenever a child shows an interest or creates a problem, you have to be able to know enough to lead him through that problem or even to provoke him to a higher one. You must have creativity in yourself to respect the creativity in the child."

Victor D'Amico

and prized. During the Christmas season, handprints in plaster of paris may be taken home as gifts. The dittoed turkey page is an activity used to teach about Thanksgiving. At music time, children may be given rhythm band instruments to beat in time with a record. To these teachers, art is bound to materials, constrained to predefined acts, areas, and times. The end of a specific activity is the end of the art lesson or experience.

To other teachers, an art experience is where one finds it. It may be in the design of frost on the window, the pattern of a foot or hand in the sand box, the rhythm of a swing. Many experiences may contribute to the child's awareness of feelings and stimulate inner responses to the external world. No part of the curriculum is excluded from the arts.

One group views the arts as *preselected* activities; the other sees the arts as *any* activity that accomplishes a particular goal of artistic response or expression. This allows a teacher to be more flexible in using the resources, both planned and spontaneous, at his or her command.

Imagine a visit to two different preschools, both of which use play dough as an art activity. If the teachers are asked why they have play dough, one may say that it is an easy activity to supervise; the children like it, and they play quietly with it for long periods of time. The other teacher agrees, but adds that the children learn about texture, consistency, color, and shape from play dough. This teacher creates artistic experiences by having the children help mix the play dough in different consistencies, textures, and colors, by asking questions as they are manipulating the dough, and by helping the children talk about what they see and feel.

These scenes in the two preschools may look alike to an observer, but the expected outcomes of such experiences will differ. One teacher has a clearer idea of a goal and how to achieve it. The fact that the teacher has a plan in mind does not detract from the pleasure or spontaneity of the children's play. It does mean that daily routines are used to create more possibilities to develop the children's capabilities. By preplanning and selecting activities, the teacher makes the outcome more predictable.

In this chapter we discuss some of the ways that teachers may use the arts to achieve goals. We do not describe the activities themselves. There are many sources of specific art tasks, including the handbook of curriculum activities prepared as a supplement to this text.

The staff of a preschool may use art activities in several different ways:

1. To develop artistic competence by encouraging responses to artistic objects and events and by providing experience and training for artistic expression and judgment
2. To develop competence in cognitive operations
3. To develop competence in social behavior
4. To encourage learning about cultural heritage

DEVELOPING COMPETENCE IN THE ARTS

"Words are an imperfect language for children. Their sensations and experiences find more exact and complete expression in another language, the language of art."

Arno Stern

There are several ideas about how preschool activities develop artistic competence. One view is that the child's ability develops best on its own in a free environment. Thus, innate ability in the early years is best allowed to develop naturally. The responsibility of the staff, according to this view, is to facilitate children's efforts. They should be allowed to express themselves freely without staff members imposing adult standards or using direct teaching.

"My definition, then, of the creative process is that it is the emergence in action of a novel relational product, growing out of the uniqueness of the individual on the one hand, and the materials, events, people, or circumstances of his life on the other."

Carl Rogers

Others believe that perceptual skills are more fully trained with instruction than without and that training can be effective even with quite young children. The staff provides specific experiences and teaches certain aspects of the arts. The children are helped to see relationships and patterns and how to use form, line, color, and texture. Some professionals claim that certain types of instruction are more helpful than others in encouraging artistic development. We have argued in preceding chapters that success in teaching in the preschool depends on planning. This principle probably applies as much to art activities as to any other part of the curriculum. The following interaction between a four-year-old and his teacher illustrates what can happen if the staff member has no specific objectives in mind or hasn't yet found ways to achieve those goals that he or she has formulated.

Interaction	**Teacher's Thoughts**
(*Robert stands at an easel, a paint brush in each hand, vigorously stroking heavy, vertical lines on his paper.*)	
Robert: Look, teacher, look what I'm doing!	
Teacher: Mmmmm—you're using both hands, aren't you?	*I wonder if it's all right to let him paint that way. Maybe he should have only one brush.*
Teacher: Robert, why don't you use just one brush?	*If I can't stop him he'll make an awful mess. How can I get him to stop?*
Robert: I don't want to. (*Robert keeps on dipping and slapping.*)	
Teacher: But you're making such a mess.	*That's not what I should say, but how can I get him to stop? Maybe I should just let him paint the way he wants to. He really isn't doing any harm. How can I make this a learning situation? Maybe I should talk about circles, or thick and thin lines.*
Robert: I like making a mess, it's fun.	
(*Robert switches to painting large, drippy circles accompanying each stroke with a loud ZOOM-ZOOM.*)	

Interaction	Teacher's Thoughts
Teacher: I see you're making circles. (*As though he hadn't heard, Robert continues to apply paint in rhythm to his ZOOM-ZOOM.*) **Teacher:** Are you finished now, Robert? (*Without answering, Robert drops his brushes and runs off to play.*)	*What do I do now?* *Thank goodness the paint's almost all gone.* *What a relief to have him stop. I don't think I handled this situation in the best way.*

From discussions with her supervisor, the teacher realized that her feeling of inadequacy came from the fact that she had no objectives in mind for Robert, only her desire to have him stop. She did not really understand his behavior and why she could not influence him. The supervisor asked her to formulate objectives that she might have in mind for Robert and to make a list of techniques she might have used to achieve them. The teacher prepared the following summary:

Possible Objectives	Possible Ways to Achieve Objectives
Robert should be allowed to paint without being made to feel guilty.	Encouragement "Sometimes it's fun to make a mess, isn't it?" "It's okay to do that but you'll need to keep the paint on the paper."
Robert should have opportunities for being "messy."	Presentation of attractive alternative "I'll bet you'd like using finger paints even better, Robert. Let's go see."
Robert should develop concepts about shapes.	Calling attention to and reinforcing specifics "That's great, Robert—you just made some circles. Now, make another circle for me." "Good work! Now I'd like you to make a square—two lines the same length side by side but with space between them—and two lines to join the ends."
Robert should be helped to acquire art techniques.	Using questions (*Pointing*) "First you drew a ——— ?"

Possible Objectives	Possible Ways to Achieve Objectives
	"And then you drew a ———?"
	"Now, tell me, which one is made with straight lines?"
	"What do we call the shape you drew using a curved line with the ends joined together?"
	Modeling
	"Robert, show me if you can hold your brush like this."
	"Let's see what a line looks like when you hold a brush this way. What do you think a line will look like if you turn your brush this way? Let's try it and see."
	Questioning
	"Can you think of another way you can make a line? Are both lines the same? Which one is thicker?"
	"Draw another thick line."
	"Draw another thin line."
	"What did you do to make one line thicker than the other?"

"Using play dough to keep children quiet is hardly a good reason to justify the use of art materials for young children. A person who does that is ill equipped to be a classroom teacher."

Director

Ideally, at any moment in the day teachers should be able to see a stop-action, instant replay of their work and be able to identify what they are doing and for what purpose. The purpose may be general or specific. A teacher could have in mind smoother, less noisy transitions from one activity to another or "getting Maria to use more than one color" as specific objectives. Also, knowing what children can learn through art experiences can help teachers be more conscious of their teaching strategies.

Developing Sensitivity and Discrimination

For all their curiosity, many children have never really looked up at the sky or down at the earth long enough to become aware of what they see. They have never run their hands over a stainless steel surface or touched the bristles of a brush. They haven't thought about the sensations they experience when they put their feet in cool mud or warm sand. Some have smelled their mother's perfume and their father's shaving lotion but may not know the odors of paper, paste, leather, wood, fruit, or flowers. They hear noise but have never listened to silence.

Such experience alone is not enough. Teachers help children recognize

WHAT CHILDREN CAN LEARN
THROUGH ART EXPERIENCES

1. They can create images with materials; they can make an imprint on the world around them.
2. The images they create can function as symbols.
3. Symbolic images can be used as vehicles for dramatic play.
4. The artistic process requires making choices about what to create and making judgments about the quality of the creation.
5. Images can be related to other images to form a whole.
6. They develop skills to create illusion and to form images that are visually persuasive.
7. Ideas and emotions that are not physically present can be symbolized by the images one can create.
8. There are ideas, images, and feelings that can only be expressed through visual form.
9. The world can be regarded as a source of aesthetic experience and as a pool of expressive form.

Adapted from Eisner (1978).

and talk about how these experiences make them feel, and become aware of their responses. Children are curious and eager to explore. To help them become aware of inner responses, the teacher can start simply but must be willing to take time. No script is necessary, but some general strategies are useful.

Make use of familiar experiences and events to get children to focus on one aspect of an experience they may not have noticed before. Ask them if they can see a face or an animal shape in a cloud, or tell them to put their heads back and look at the sky while they are swinging. The first step is to get the child to experience sensual stimuli aesthetically and in a new way. Ask children how events or experiences make them feel or whether they like something they have observed and why. The ''How-does-that-make-you-feel?'' approach has many variations and can be used in many different situations.

Miss P. watched three-year-old Opal tentatively run a pudgy finger along the edge of a hardwood block. The child picked up another and did the same thing. Then she spread her hand and rubbed it across the top surface of the block as one brushes crumbs from a

table. Leaving Opal for a moment, Miss P. went to get a piece of rough bark, slightly curved and not as thick as the block, but about the same size. She put it in the deep pocket of her smock.

When she returned she sat on the floor beside Opal and said, "I like the way you're playing, Opal. What does it feel like when you rub your hand across the top of a block?"

Opal smiled but did not answer.

Miss P. picked up a matching block and held it out. "Rub your hand across the top of this block, Opal."

Opal willingly followed her teacher's instruction.

"Do both of them make you feel the same way when you rub them?"

Opal smiled but did not answer.

Miss P. began swishing her hand like a metronome across the floor. Opal joined happily in this new game. Swish-swish.

"Does it feel the same when you rub your hand across the floor as it does when you rub your hand across the top of the block?"

Opal answered by rubbing first the block and then the floor but she said nothing. Instead she began stacking pairs of blocks. Every so often she took time to rub one with her hand.

Miss P. watched. Waited. Slowly she took the bark from her pocket and placed it on the floor between them. Opal reached over, picked up the bark, and rubbed her hand across the top. She frowned and rubbed it again. She gave her teacher the bark and picked up a block.

"Do they feel the same, Opal?"

Opal shook her head, her eyes puzzled. "No," she said.

"You're right, Opal. They feel different. The block is SMOOTH. The bark is ROUGH. I'm glad you noticed they were different. Here, feel them again. This block is smooth. The bark is rough."

Opal looked, but put her hands behind her back and said nothing. Miss P. smiled. Then she got up. As she rose she gave Opal an affectionate pat. "Good girl," she said, and walked away. A start had been made; it was all that was needed for now. There would be time enough to engage Opal's interest in the different properties and kinds of wood and bark, in having her find out where bark came from and in getting her to make other comparisons later on. But for now she felt she had made the right start by gaining Opal's confidence and waiting until she was willing to express her response to the way two different objects felt.

Helping children discriminate between tactile sensations of "smooth" and "rough" may seem far removed from the arts in the traditional sense. But a recognition of such differences leads to new experiences. Part of what children learn is that exploring and learning is rewarding. A sense of texture becomes one element of response they can use to explore other materials.

Learning to recognize differences in materials and stimuli is a first step. Teachers can help with a second—getting children to express their reactions to what they see, hear, and touch.

Jack, a sturdy five-year-old, sat listening to loud music with a pronounced beat. After the third playing of his record, Mrs. N. joined him.

Goal: To develop awareness of internal response to external stimuli

Objective: To get Jack to express freely his response to feelings engendered by music, either by body movement or in words, or both

"You like that record, don't you Jack?"

"Yeah," Jack answered, ready to drop the needle for a fourth time.

"How does the music make you feel?"

"I like it."

"Does it make you want to do anything?"

"I don't know."

"Does it make you want to get up and march or dance or anything?"

"I don't think so. I just like it."

During the conversation Mrs. N. had sorted through several other records and found one she knew had low tones and a slow rhythm. She handed it to Jack. "Here, play this one. I'd like to listen to it with you."

"Okay." But halfway through the music, Jack stopped the machine. "I like the other one better," he explained. "I'm going to play mine again."

"All right," Mrs. N. agreed. "But tell me, do the other two records make you feel the same?"

"I guess so. No, I don't know."

"Look, Jack, let's play the one you like and you show me how it makes you feel. Move around any way you want to."

''[Creative persons] seemed to be less afraid of what other people would say or demand or laugh at. Perhaps more important, however, was their lack of fear of their own insides, of their own impulses, emotions, thoughts.''

Abraham Maslow

''The perceptive nursery school or kindergarten teacher knows well how to make use of her children's desire to produce rhythms and to move to rhythms. Motion and music belong together while children are young and they should not be divorced as they grow older.''

Berthold Lowenfeld

Goal: To develop awareness of internal response to external stimuli

Objective: To have child use thought and feeling at the same time

Mrs. N. could tell from Jack's expression that he wasn't sure he wanted to follow the suggestion. She smiled and asked David to join them. ''David, we're going to play Jack's record and I'm hoping he'll show me how it makes him feel. Will you do that, too?''

David liked this idea. With the first note or two he began to shuffle his feet, wriggle his hips, and soon was slapping his thighs calling out, ''Man, man!'' Clearly David recognized his feelings and found them easy to express.

Jack watched David for a moment and then began to move about. His motions were awkward but the beat caught him up, too, and by the end of the record his response was almost as vigorous as David's. He grinned happily.

''That was fine, boys. Just fine. I could certainly see how happy this kind of music makes you feel. Now I want to play the other record and you show me how that makes you feel.'' Sensing Jack's hesitancy, she added, ''Here, Jack, you put it on for us.''

This time several measures went by before either boy responded. David was again first. His shoulders drooped, his head fell forward, and slowly he let himself down to the floor where he lay sprawled like a rag doll. Jack watched and imitated. But when both were lying down, it was Jack who got to his knees and began to rock back and forth in time to the slow music. The sounds stopped before he did.

Mrs. N. made no comment. She sat quietly waiting. Jack straightened up and came over to her. ''I liked the record better this time,'' he said.

Mrs. N. put her arm around him. ''How did it make you feel, Jack?''

The boy hesitated, uncertain not of his response but of the teacher's. ''It was like being in a rocking chair,'' he said.

Jack's interest in music enabled his teacher to make him aware of his inner response and to encourage him to express how he felt through body movement. In this instance, the arts also included David's response and the teacher's affective behavior. By having in mind what she wanted to do, the teacher was able to take advantage of a combination of resources in order to achieve her objective.

Inner responses to art need not be treated as though they were separate from thought. In fact, a teacher can often help children to feel and to think about an object at the same time. The following is an example:

Mr. B. was standing next to Jenny when he saw her stoop to pick up a leaf. ''What a beautiful leaf, Jenny,'' he commented.

Jenny held her leaf at arm's length, twisting and turning it as though it were a gigantic butterfly whose red and yellow wings flashed in the sun.

"How does it make you feel when you see a leaf like that?" he asked.

"I like to look at it. I think it's pretty."

"I do too, Jenny. What do you suppose makes it so pretty?"

Jenny looked at the leaf, turning it over and back again, but didn't say anything.

"It's the kind we call a maple leaf, Jenny. What do you notice that makes it different from leaves on that tree over there?"

"It's red and yellow."

"What's different about that?"

Jenny grinned. This was a game she'd played with the teacher before. He knew, but he wanted her to tell him. "You can see that the leaves on the tree are green," she said.

"That's right, Jenny. They have a different color." He stopped and picked up a dry leaf and held it next to Jenny's. "Which of the leaves has brighter colors? Yours or mine?"

"Mine."

"How do you think the outside edge of your leaf feels?"

Jenny's finger slowly explored the outline of the leaf. "It's bumpy," she said.

"I agree. It's bumpy," her teacher said. "Is the leaf round?"

"No."

"Is it square?"

"No. It has points."

"Hmmmm. Points. How many?"

"One-two-three-four-five."

"That's right, Jenny. We've noticed a good many things about your leaf, haven't we? It has bright colors. Its edges are ———; and there are five ———. Was it a big leaf compared to this one of mine?"

"Yep," Jenny said and ran off for a turn on the swing.

Learning Artistic Skills

For many children, preschool is an introduction to a wide variety of materials and equipment. This can be puzzling as well as pleasurable. Some may be hesitant, slow to explore; others are eager to experiment with paints, move to rhythms, and try out the hammer and saw.

Youngsters learn from a wise mingling of experience and guidance. If the goal is to teach children about consistency and to develop competence to make mixtures thick or thin, they must first have opportunities to explore qualities of thickness and thinness, mix dirt with water to make mud, stir a thick batter for muffins or a thin batter for crepes, mix water and flour and oil for thick play dough, or beat cream to make butter. Giving a child labeled cans of thin and thick paints is a much less effective tactic.

Teaching competence in artistic activities does not mean that children are given freedom to follow their own inclinations without guidance. Nor is it a formal, organized pattern of instruction. The members of the staff combine materials, guidance, and plenty of time for children to explore and satisfy curiosity.

Shapes of faces on a flannel board give children an opportunity to use lines to indicate feelings; a line curved downward for the mouth and eyes to express sadness, or curved upward for a smile. The soft, curved, dark lines and three-dimensional effect of Ruben's *Head of a Negro* can be used to show how lines and light help create a mood or feeling.

A simple skill, such as using a hand punch to make holes in paper, can be highly satisfying to a child. Learning how to use scissors adds to feelings of competence. A child who knows the names of the colors, which color he or she wants to use, and how to mix a new color with those that are available, gains a degree of competence. The teacher might suggest that children stir the primary colors at the easel, or the teacher might give children food colors and test tubes of water and eye droppers with which to experiment. Ability to mix colors and create new ones gives added skills.

Children can acquire perceptual ability when they are encouraged to look for components of an artistic creation such as color, line, texture, and form. Grossman (1970) reports on a 1967 study by Douglas and Schwartz in which professionally made ceramic pieces were used to illustrate some basic ideas to a group of four-year-olds. Four of the basic ideas were:

1. Art is a means of nonverbal communication.
2. The art product is the result of the artist's idea.
3. The artist uses what he or she sees, thinks, and feels to create art.
4. There is a great variety of materials available to the artist.

The children in the study were able to understand these ideas and use them to interpret their own as well as other works of art.

A teacher with five years of experience describes her first attempt to help children learn to use woodworking tools:

When I first started teaching nursery school, I remember being assigned to supervise the carpentry table. I had no idea what to expect. I got the children to help me push the wood box and tools out and before I knew what had happened, someone ran to the sandbox with a saw and a couple of other children had started hammering on the cement and trikes.

I was really frightened. I ran after everyone, grabbed the tools from them and put everything away. I went home that night and decided I couldn't avoid potentially dangerous situations like that. I thought a lot about just what the carpentry activity is for, how I can best help the children participate in this activity and how I can help them gain competence in the use of the carpentry materials.

I learned from experience that I had to start simply. The rules for safety had to be clear for the children and me. For example, I brought out the wood box and suggested that children select a piece of wood first, then I let them select a tool—(sometimes I left the saws in the shed until I was sure the children knew how to use a hammer first). I used to let them bang around on the wood and try to get the nail in as best they could (or I would just end up doing it for them).

I noticed many of the children, especially those who had never had any experience with carpentry before, would take a whack at the wood, fool around with a saw and leave the table; others would get frustrated and complain or wait for help. I gradually began to give more specific supervision. That is, I would hold my hands over the hands of a child and gently guide his movements while he was hammering or sawing. I would help him get the feel of the activity. I would tell the children to keep their eyes on the nail when they were hammering and show them how they could remove a nail.

I remember one little boy who was particularly frustrated one day because he wanted to ''build a barn'' by nailing a piece of wood onto the narrow edge of another piece. The wood kept slipping and he couldn't get the nail started while holding the two pieces of wood together with his other hand. I showed him how he could start the nail in one piece of wood and hammer it in until it went through and then nail it onto the

---

OBJECTIVES FOR DEVELOPING
COMPETENCE IN THE ARTS

1. Learning to communicate internal responses graphically (paintings, drawings, and so on) and physically (dance, movement, music)
2. Beginning to be aware of differences of color, line, form, texture and how they are used to create different effects
3. Learning to use a variety of tools and equipment and recognize their properties and purposes
4. Acquiring specific skills in music such as responding to rhythm, keeping time, recognizing harmony, tone, and so on
5. Learning how to mix materials to produce new creations (mixing paints to achieve a new color, cooking, and so on)
6. Developing skills in use of materials to facilitate expression of feelings and ideas

other piece, which he could attach to a vise. He was so excited when he discovered he could indeed achieve his goal with his newly acquired skills that he went around for days offering to teach the other children how to "make a barn." I find that children are more likely to stay with a project and experiment more readily if they feel competent with the tools and materials they have at hand.

"Music is perhaps the first among all arts which children enjoy."

Berthold Lowenfeld

As children experiment with materials, the teacher can guide their natural interest and responses in a sequence of activities designed to extend experience and stimulate growth in particular areas. In music, for example, the teacher might help them learn to listen, to sing, to play simple instruments (tambourine, drum, wood blocks, bells, and so on) and to respond to different kinds of music through body movement. Here is an example of some specific goals in music:

Goal	Activity
Melody	Identify several songs or themes by name
	Indicate by difference in body response that one melody is different from another (high, low, gay, sad, and so on)
	Compose own melodies and sing or play them
Harmony	Signal chord changes they recognize while listening
	Tell whether a piece consists of only a melody or melody plus chord accompaniment
Tone	Identify various instruments by name as they are played
	Tell whether one or more than one instrument is playing
	Recognize loudness and softness in music by clapping or stamping feet in similar volume
Rhythm	Clap, beat time, rock body to different tempos
	Mark out musical accent with hand or foot movement
	Create own rhythm patterns with instruments or clapping
	Draw attention to rhythmic sounds heard in the environment and identify source (clock tick, raindrops, traffic hum, typewriter, and so on)
Form	Signal awareness of a repetition of melody or rhythm pattern

Musical goals are partially accomplished by having groups of children listen, sing, and move about for fifteen or twenty minutes each day. They are also achieved by surrounding children with music and encouraging humming, singing, dancing, and moving to sounds. Having a variety of instruments available to play, touch, and ask questions about also helps.

Most of the activities of a school can be part of the art curriculum. A group of students assigned to visit six different schools were asked to list in order of preference which schools they would like to attend if they were four years old. One student's description of the school that was the unanimous choice of all the students suggested some of the ways an imaginative staff can exploit the versatility of the school's resources.

The main room of this school was no larger than the others we had visited, but somehow it seemed more spacious and cheerful. Low shelves were neatly arranged and activities were all equally inviting so that small groups of four to six children were congregated in different parts of the room.

In one area I noticed the children helping themselves to paper and collage materials from the low shelves that were clearly labeled with pictures of the items, such as scissors, paste, crayons, and so on. The children didn't have to read in order to know where things went. The easels were designed so the children could remove their own paintings and hang them over a large drying rack without help from an adult. Some of the older children were showing the younger ones how to pour more paint from the supply shelves. Examples of the children's art work were displayed at the child's eye level.

In another part of the room two children were working at a small sink, measuring flour and water into a large plastic container. Posted above the sink at their eye level was a "picture recipe" for play dough illustrating the number of cups of flour and water, and the number of spoons of salt and powdered paint to use in mixing the dough. The children worked cooperatively without any adult supervision.

Adjacent to this area was a long low table where several children were shelling peanuts, grinding them, and making peanut butter to spread on crackers. A teacher was helping two of the children count the number of crackers needed for snack time.

I shut my eyes and listened to the sounds in the room, just as I had done at the other schools. The level of noise felt comfortable to me: muted voices coming from various parts of the room interspersed with occasional laughter, disagreement, or a plea for assistance. I was struck by the fact that adult voices in this school did not dominate the sounds, nor were there any extremes in the children's voices—shouting, screaming, crying. This school was neither too loud nor too quiet.

During a large group activity one of the adult volunteers projected some slide pictures on the wall while the teacher played some recordings, including Ravel's "Bolero" as well as a disco record. Each child whose painting or art project was shown created a dance for the group. It was a most impressive experience with the lights turned off, the large projection of a colorful painting and a child's silhouetted dance movements superimposed on his or her creation. The teacher made comments like "Jamie's painting has lots of movement to it, just the way he's dancing." "How does your painting make you feel, Rodney?" "Quiet," was the

"If I had influence . . . I should ask that the gift to each child in the world be a sense of wonder so indestructible that it would last throughout life, as an unfailing antidote against the boredom and disenchantment of later years, the sterile preoccupation with things that are artificial, the alienation from the source of our strength."

Rachel Carson (1965, pp. 42–43)

reply. "Can you do a quiet dance to show how your painting makes you feel?" "I can," volunteered Janey. "O.K. Rodney, would you and Janey both like to do a quiet dance?" Both children created a slow, gentle dance using graceful movements while the rest of the group watched intently. "I like the way you stretch your arms, Rodney. Just like they're attached to a big rubber band. Janey looks like she's slowly tossing a huge balloon up in the air and stretching on her tippy toes to catch it." When the session was over, the children rushed off to the art areas to make something for the next time.

"The child's reactions to the universe of things are also universal, constant for the human race, natural to every child. There is not one way of reaction in an American child and another in a Chinese child . . . the child's perceptual development is uniformly human. This I regard as perhaps the most significant fact established by our scientific observations of child art during the past fifty years."

Sir Herbert Read

Piaget's studies provide information as to why children produce art in the forms they do. He found, for example, that during the sensorimotor stage, children explore objects systematically, especially by sight and touch. From this visual and tactile perception they acquire knowledge of geometric forms and space relationships. Although a child does not draw before the age of two, and may not create shapes meaningful to adults before four or five, it is from perceptual learning during early years that the child eventually produces representational images.

The ability to represent what is perceived through the senses comes during later stages of development (Table 16.2). It is during the preoperational substage that children

. . . make drawings of men by attaching four lines to an irregular circle, and sometimes they put other circles inside a large one to represent eyes and eyes and other facial features. But, when the child attempts a complicated human being at this stage, it is clear that his concepts of topological relationships are not *fully* developed, because he may place the mouth over the nose or draw the ears detached from the body. Although his visual concept of proximity, separation, and enclosure is fairly well formed, his mental image of order and continuity is still poor. Thus, he cannot retain in his mind the correct sequence of mouth and nose along a vertical axis, nor can he imagine a man wearing a hat to be a continuous unit. Consequently, he draws the hat above the figure but not on it. (Lansing, 1966, pp. 35–38)

Artistic responses are based on developmental patterns. Children's competence follows several steps that are correlated with growth and development as well as experience. Rhoda Kellogg (1969) has studied these developmental patterns through her analysis of thousands of drawings of children from many parts of the world. Children everywhere scribble before they draw, and draw outline shapes before they begin to make more realistic representational drawings. Even then, children draw things the way they see them, not necessarily from an adult's perspective.

TABLE 16.2
Summary of Piaget's
Findings Regarding
Children's Ability to Draw
During the First Two
Substages of the Concrete
Operations Period

Preoperational Substage (2 to 4 years)	Intuitive Thought Substage (4 to 7 years)
Up to 3 can only scribble	From 4 to 5 begins to make straight lines, squares, triangles, houses, tables in drawings; figures have little thoughtful organization
Between 3 and 4 can indicate open and closed form figures in unorganized attempts at symbolic representation; makes irregular circles and shapes that enclose other shapes but not straight lines	From 6 to 7 begins to coordinate mental image of the world; understands topological relationships of human figure
	Spatial relationships of single objects well developed; house will be on a baseline next to other houses, people and trees, yet separate; proportions are likely to differ from reality and child does not use perspective

Adapted from K. M. Lansing, ''The Research of Jean Piaget and Its Implications for Art Education in the Elementary School,'' *Studies in Art Education*. (Publication of the National Art Education Association), 7, No. 2 (1966), 35–38.

FIGURE 16.1
Some Stages in Children's
Art

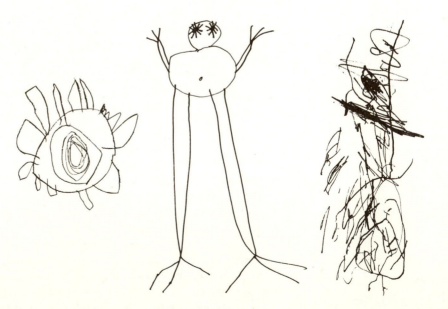

THE DEVELOPMENT OF PICTORIAL FORM

If left to develop on their own, with no formal teaching, children show growth in the portrayal of form from simple to increasingly complex patterns

1. Children's first drawings may be thought of as *recorded gestures.* As a child makes visible signs of his or her hand, arm, and even body movements, parents and teachers will first observe random rotations, sometimes called *scribbles.* Soon zig-zags will fill spaces, then circles close and shapes appear.
2. Children discover the lines and shapes they make and their control over them. They produce endless quantities of *undifferentiated shape,* mostly circular forms, the simplest possible shape. These shapes are undifferentiated in that they stand for any form at all.
3. Children add shape to shape, producing *constructed shape,* a combination of constant elements. Simple directional relationships are built. Forms become more elaborate. Still, the shapes are not so much representation as presentation.

Adapted from Arnheim (1967, p. 174).
The ideal sequence corresponds only roughly to what happens with a specific child. Different children cling to different phases for different lengths of time. Phases overlap. An older child's highly developed drawing may be followed by a scribble. Differentiation in size, color, and dimension develop in a manner similar to the development of form in children's art.

Encouraging Responses to Art Forms

A first step toward helping children develop preferences and judgment about artistic productions is to encourage recognition of a variety of patterns, forms, color, and other elements in experience. By calling attention to specifics, showing contrasts, and skillful questioning, a teacher can guide a child's initial discriminations, which form the basis for later aesthetic sensitivity. For example, questions about contrasting pictures can help a child notice that some pictures are brighter than others; some portray people, others do not. In one the lines may be mostly straight, in another they are predominantly curved; some pictures have many details, others almost none.

QUESTIONS FOR DEVELOPING
AESTHETIC DISCRIMINATION

1. How many colors do you see? Do the colors in this picture make you feel the same as the colors in that picture? Which colors do you like best? How do they make you feel?
2. What do you think the artist is trying to tell you? What does he want you to know about the people (animals, flowers, buildings, etc.) in this picture?
3. Are the people in the different pictures drawn the same way? What are some of the differences? Do they have the same kinds of hands? Of eyes? What are the differences? How are they the same?

At first, children may recognize larger, more obvious features. After repeated exposure and comparison, they will know that a Van Gogh is not the same as a Rembrandt, a Modigliani is not a Miró. They will be able to tell which artists they prefer, though it may take some time before this happens.

A traveling *gallery* of art reproductions can be prepared, with suggestions for helping children develop artistic awareness and judgment. Following are some suggested objectives:[1]

> "The teacher's responsibility is to extend personal interest, offering the child the opportunity to see what other things are being done and have been done. He is enriched by knowing that the thing he is doing has been done by others and in many different ways. . . . This makes the child a part of a great family of creators that have started with the beginning of man."
>
> *Victor D'Amico*

Objectives	Commentary
To encourage acceptance of the unfamiliar and unusual	When we look at children we see that they do not always look the same.
To develop awareness and sensitivity to feelings reflected in the face	If you are sad your face will look a certain way. (Have children demonstrate and examine expression in paintings.) What makes you feel that way?
	If you are feeling especially happy your face might look quite different. (Have children demonstrate and consider expressions in paintings.)

[1]Information used by permission of the Palo Alto Unified School District, Palo Alto, California.

Adults as Subjects

American Gothic	Grant Wood, American
Puppet Show Woman	O. Masara, Japanese
Head of a Negro	Rubens, Belgian
The Postman Roulin	Van Gogh, Dutch
Señora Sabrosa García	Goya, Spanish
People and Dog in the Sun	Miró, Spanish

Children as Subjects

Girl with a Broom	Rembrandt, Dutch
Portrait of a Boy	C. Soutine, Russian
Girl with a Watering Can	Renoir, French
Don Emanuel Osorio de Zúñiga	Goya, Spanish
Girl with Braids	Modigliani, Italian
Head of a Young Boy	Rouault, French

Young children can develop preferences concerning works of art. The two groups of portraits just described were displayed in a nursery school where children could see them at any time. At various moments individual children were brought to see them. After talking informally with each child about the first group and then the second, and attracting his or her attention to various likenesses and differences, the teacher asked:

1. Do you like the pictures?
2. What do you like about them?
3. What don't you like?
4. Which picture do you like best?

All the children were able to form an opinion; the older children, however, were more unanimous in their preferences than the younger. The choices made were as follows:

Selection	Younger Children (17) (3 and 4 Years)	Older Children (28) (4 and 5 Years)
Adult portrait most liked	Miró (7)	Van Gogh (16)
Child portrait most liked	Renoir (7)	Renoir (14)

USING THE ARTS FOR
COGNITIVE DEVELOPMENT

Art activities are a versatile part of the curriculum. They encourage social interaction, stimulate verbal exchanges, and help children become aware of their feelings. For example, if George needs help in acquiring concepts about shapes, the arts offer a natural opportunity. George likes to draw and often works at the easel. He can learn to label and observe the shapes that he is drawing; he may consider squares, triangles, and circles in other pictures.

> ## OBJECTIVES FOR DEVELOPING SENSITIVITY AND DISCRIMINATION
>
> 1. Understanding that people respond in personal (unique) ways to the arts
> 2. Becoming familiar with a variety of art forms and growing in acceptance of different modes of expression
> 3. Becoming aware of, identifying, and responding to some of the specific characteristics that comprise a work of art or expression (color, line, texture, brush strokes of paintings; timbre, pitch, melody, tempo of music; gestures, manner, tone of voice, subject matter of stories; movement, mood, gestures of dance)
> 4. Beginning to articulate and justify judgments with some specificity

At the same time, the teacher may interest him in color, brush technique, or characteristics of an artist's work.

Artistic activities can build vocabulary, develop concepts of color, of similarity, and of difference. Following are some examples:

1. "I see you're using a *wide brush* today."
2. "What *bright tempera colors* you chose to paint your picture with."
3. "Do you want me to help you move that *heavy easel*?"
4. "That is certainly *lively music*, isn't it?"

> ## TEACHERS AS LABELERS
>
> The arts offer teachers a wide vocabulary to use with children. There are terms associated with the activities involved—colors, shapes, instruments, materials, tools, methods, and techniques. In addition, many different words can be used to describe what is being done. Children need not just *put* objects together; materials can be made to *fit, match, adhere, hold, cling,* or *stick* to one another. They may join things by using string, nails, pins, dowels, thongs, rubber bands, cement, glue, solder, adhesive, scotch tape, and staples as well as paste.

"Sometimes youngsters need long uninterrupted periods of time with clay . . . rigidly scheduled sessions which are arbitrarily terminated to maintain a preplanned routine would obviously interfere with the fullest use of the material by such children. [The teacher should] regard the clay period as not just busywork or an activity to keep the children from getting into mischief, but as a legitimate channel for exploration, expression, and self-assertion, having unique meanings for each child engaged in it. . . ."

Ruth Hartley et al. (1952)

Children don't have to know they're using a *wide brush* filled with *bright tempera color* in order to paint a picture on a piece of paper that's mounted on an easel. But by labeling, teachers make it possible for children to acquire the vocabulary that helps them sort, organize, classify, and keep track of information they accumulate in art activities. The vocabulary teachers provide also aids the gradual development of concepts by which new experiences are ordered.

Children's approach to painting and clay modeling, to musical instruments and record players, to props for dramatic play is to explore first, rather than express feelings. They acquire knowledge about the physical world from contact with an art form.

Children derive a great deal of physical knowledge from the materials that are part of an arts program in a preschool; the arts lend themselves to the acquisition of logical knowledge. Many drawings involve shape and space relationships; music and finger games bring understanding of counting, adding, subtracting, and seriation; dramatic play encourages categorizing and transfer; and, as mentioned earlier, all of the arts help children acquire labels and develop concepts about in-on-under-around-over, fast-slow, loud-soft, happy-sad, up-down, and so on.

USING THE ARTS TO PROMOTE SOCIAL DEVELOPMENT

Preschools have traditionally emphasized affective and social experience as a central part of the curriculum and parents often see this as a major contribution of preschools to their children's development. The activities that fall within the arts—music, art, drama—offer excellent opportunities for children to gain social experience and to explore emotions about themselves and their interaction with both peers and adults.

The arts provide many opportunities for children to release energy. It is natural for a child to wriggle and jump and run and climb and move about. Children can be encouraged to march, skip, clap, and dance to music; to beat and stomp to the sound of drums, to recreate the gait of animals in dramatic play, to manipulate clay and other modeling materials freely, and to draw and finger paint with broad movements.

The arts also provide channels for emotional release. Young children are not always aware of their emotions, do not always know why they cry, strike out at others, are restless or feel good-enough-to-burst at times. Few have the ability to recognize feelings of these kinds or the verbal skills to express them in words.

Children's affective development needs to include opportunity for them to recognize and express feelings. Psychologist Arthur T. Jersild of Columbia University states:

GAINING PHYSICAL KNOWLEDGE FROM CLAY

If you hand young children a piece of clay, it will be a long while before they make a pot or figure with it that you will recognize if this is their first experience with clay.

They will explore its properties. That clay will be rolled, squeezed, slapped, smelled, and perhaps tasted. They will pull it, drop it, throw it, take tiny pieces from it and then put it all back together again.

Once satisfied as to how clay feels and what they can do with it, they may use it to make "balls" or "cakes" or perhaps simply roll out an endless supply of ropelike pieces for which they have no use. They are unlikely to seek labels for what they do or to talk about their activities.

Later, they may use clay to represent objects, though what they depict may or may not be recognizable to anyone else. Only after many experiences of this kind are children ready to create something of their own choosing.

If an older person wishes to understand a child's emotions and to help him cope with the conditions that arouse emotion, it is necessary to encourage the child to face feelings rather than to falsify them or run away from them. But to do this requires courage on the adult's part, the courage to permit the child to allow his feelings to show and the courage to face feelings that are aroused within himself when the emotions of someone else appear in raw form. (Jersild, 1968, p. 312)

In many countries, the most common form of self-expression by young children is dramatic play. Between the ages of three and five, children are still becoming social creatures. Dramatic play and other forms of pretending permit children to re-create for themselves what they see around them. By *trying* on a role, they learn through vicarious experience about themselves and their reactions.

The child of three participates in simple imaginative play. He or she may put a dolly to bed, cover it, kiss it goodnight saying, "Night, night," or "Baby, go to bed." By four the imaginative aspects are more detailed and complex but they remain within the same framework. Dolls are fed, talked to, and nurtured. Four-year-olds may work out aggression through spanking, scolding, and even throwing the dolls they may carefully tend at other times.

At five, make-believe of this kind often involves other children and long periods of "pretend." Typically, several children gather in the housekeeping corner, making plans for complex imaginative play involving daddies, mothers, uncles, siblings, and friends. All are an extension of the child's real world. Cultural differences appear in children's imaginative play at this level.

Children may deal with emotional problems or the need for companionship by creating imaginary playmates. During the preschool years, many of these needs are closely bound to everyday occurrences in the life of the child. The creature the child imagines accompanies him or her through all the familiar routines and has equal rights and needs.

Four- and five-year-olds frequently use imaginary people and animals to play out fears and desires that are unacceptable in real life. By five, most imaginative play is closely tied to reality; children re-enact events of their daily lives or pretend to be family members, fire fighters, grocers, and nurses.

Dramatic play takes quite different forms in different cultures. In some countries, China, for example, children are taught the values of the nation through skits, plays, songs, and dances. These forms of dramatic play socialize the young children toward national goals. In the United States, individual expressions of fantasy through play are more typical. However, even in individual play, one sees socialization.

Music has a special appeal, for both emotional and social experience. In discussing music as a universal language, Florence Foster (1965) said:

> Music has an integrating power on the individual and the group. The withdrawn child tends to relax his guard and is more ready to participate with the others, while the hostile child seems to be less aggressive, so that each is helped to become a contributing member of the group. Here is one task in which all can cooperate to produce something mutually pleasing. (p. 375)

Singing and listening to music, participating in finger games, acting out "The Wheels of the Bus Go Round and Round" or some other action song, and playing in a rhythm band may be the first group activities which young children join. Until the age of three or four, they engage in most experiences as individuals, or with an older person. Gradually, however, art activities provide opportunities for interaction. A construction project, or planning and making decorations for a "party," lend themselves to conversation and social exchange.

Every human society uses art to express the spirit, exploits, and aspirations of its people and to record historic events. The walls of cave dwellers carry a pictorial history of the prowess of their hunters. Trajan's column in Rome tells the story of his military conquests. Great works of music reflect joy and sorrow, fear and longing.

Even very young children can become aware of the art of their cultures. American children have a rich heritage to draw from; the national culture includes music, dance, and art from the many ethnic groups who settled this

---

**OBJECTIVES FOR DEVELOPING AWARENESS
OF CULTURAL HERITAGE**

1. Learning to look at details in a variety of art forms
2. Learning about artists, musicians, sculptors, and so on as occupational roles
3. Beginning to understand how artists contribute to a culture
4. Becoming familiar with some of the social, cultural rituals, celebrations and historical records through works of art (weaving stories into rugs, folk songs and folk tales and their origin, painting, carvings, and so on)
5. Learning that adults and children have been producing art for a long time

---

country and native art and music forms as well. Children learn to distinguish jazz, soul music, Indian chants, cowboy, mountain, and country songs, and modern rock music. American artists—Grant Wood, Winslow Homer, Mary Cassatt, and Andrew Wyeth portray our history and culture.

Recognizing the art of one's own culture is a matter of familiarity and can begin in the preschool. When one picture or piece of music can be recognized as separate from others, art takes on a new meaning. Identifying art and music and names of artists and composers is a useful goal in itself.

REFERENCES

Arnheim, R. 1967. *Art and Visual Perception*. Berkeley, Calif.: University of California Press.

Carson, R. L. 1965. *The Sense of Wonder*. New York: Harper and Row.

Cole, L. 1955. *A History of Education: Socrates to Montessori*. New York: Holt, Rinehart and Winston.

Croft, D. J., and R. D. Hess. 1980. *An Activities Handbook for Teachers of Young Children*. 3rd ed. Boston: Houghton Mifflin.

D'Amico, V. 1966. "On the Teaching of Art." In *Child Art: The Beginnings of Self-Affirmation*. Ed. H. P. Lewis. Berkeley, Calif.: Diablo Press.

Dimonstein, G. 1974. *Exploring the Arts with Children*. New York: Macmillan.

Douglas, N. K., and J. B. Schwartz. 1967. "Increasing Awareness of Art Ideas of Young Children Through Guided Experiences with Ceramics." *Studies in Art Education*, 8, No. 2, 2–9.

Eisner, E. W. 1978. "What Do Children Learn When They Paint?" *Art Education*, 31, No. 3, 6–10.

Foster, F. P. 1965. ''The Song Within: Music and the Disadvantaged Preschool Child.'' *Young Children,* 20 (September), 373–376.

Grossman, M. 1970. ''Art Education for the Young Child.'' *Review of Educational Research,* 40, No. 3 (June), 421–427.

Hartley, R., L. K. Frank, and R. M. Goldenson. 1952. *Understanding Children's Play.* New York: Columbia University Press.

Jersild, A. T. 1968. *Child Psychology.* 6th ed. Englewood Cliffs, N.J.: Prentice-Hall.

Kellogg, R. 1969. *Analyzing Children's Art.* Palo Alto, Calif.: National Press Books.

Lansing, K. M. 1966. ''The Research of Jean Piaget and Its Implications for Art Education in the Elementary School.'' *Studies in Art Education,* 7, No. 2, 33–42.

Lewis, H. P., ed. 1966. *Child Art: The Beginnings of Self-Affirmation.* Berkeley, Calif.: Diablo Press.

Linderman, E. W., and D. W. Herberholz. 1979. *Developing Artistic and Perceptual Awareness.* 4th ed. Dubuque, Iowa: Wm. C. Brown.

Lowenfield, B. 1966. ''Non-Visual Art.'' In *Child Art: The Beginnings of Self-Affirmation.* Ed. H. P. Lewis. Berkeley, Calif.: Diablo Press.

Read, H. 1966. ''Art as a Unifying Principle in Education.'' In *Child Art: The Beginnings of Self-Affirmation.* Ed. H. P. Lewis. Berkeley, Calif.: Diablo Press.

Stecher, M. B. 1970. ''Concept Learning Through Movement Improvisation: The Teacher's Role as Catalyst.'' *Young Children*, 25, No. 148 (January).

Stern, A. 1966. ''The Child's Language of Art.'' In *Child Art: The Beginnings of Self-Affirmation.* Ed. H. P. Lewis. Berkeley, Calif.: Diablo Press.

CHAPTER 17

WORKING WITH
EXCEPTIONAL CHILDREN

PROVIDING FOR EXCEPTIONAL CHILDREN

What should the teacher of young children know about exceptional children? Is the teacher expected to be able to adapt the curriculum to meet the needs of an autistic child or a physically handicapped child? What are the responsibilities of the preschool staff toward exceptional children? The issues raised by these questions can be approached with a review of the provisions made for treatment of handicapped people, from the past to the present.

Historical Review

Handicapped children, indeed all handicapped individuals, have most often been treated with discrimination or neglect. In some ancient societies malformed infants were killed. In the early history of the United States, neglect and abuse were predominant. No provisions were made for education or for care. Even as late as the mid–nineteenth century, more than half of the inmates of poorhouses were handicapped people (Kirk and Gallagher, 1979). Although some residential schools for the handicapped were established in the early 1800s, public school recognition of the educational needs of handicapped students came much later. The first class created for handicapped students was formed in Boston for deaf children in 1869. It was still not until around 1900 that special classes to treat various handicaps were common in the public schools (Kirk and Gallagher, 1979). Until recently, the dominant public policy was to segregate children with disabilities in special classes.

In the three decades following 1950, however, provisions and facilities for handicapped students have expanded dramatically. It is this latest phase of policy that has most direct implications for teachers in preschools and centers.

Recent Legislative Provisions

The recent and current phase of public policy for treating the handicapped involves *mainstreaming*—bringing handicapped children into regular classrooms for instruction whenever it is feasible. Mainstreaming was stimulated in part by pressure from parents, often through the courts. Some initiated class-action suits that questioned the right of school districts to exclude mentally retarded children from public schools or to put them into separate classes. Federal legislation, passed in 1965, provided support for education of handicapped children in state-operated hospitals and other institutions. The Bureau of Education for the Handicapped was established in 1967 as part of the U.S. Office of Education (Braun and Lasher, 1978).

The right of handicapped children to free public education was extended in 1974 by PL 93-380, which required states to develop plans to provide

handicapped children with education in the least restrictive environment compatible with the child's needs. *Least restrictive environment* could be interpreted to mean mainstreaming.

Provisions for education of very young handicapped children were included in legislation passed in 1972, which mandated that handicapped children make up a minimum of 10 percent of the enrollment of each local Head Start program.

In 1975, a major initiative was passed by Congress: the Education for All

"My baby sister was placed in a special class for retarded when we were in grammar school. I felt sorry and ashamed for her. I often wonder if she would be different now if she had been in regular classes. I wonder if I would be different!"

Brother of a Retarded Child

Parents have the right under PL 94-142 to examine all records, including tests, related to the education of the child, and can initiate due process procedures if there is disagreement with the program.

Handicapped Children Act (PL 94-142). The purpose of the act was to extend the right of free public education to all handicapped children. By September 1978, all handicapped children between the ages of 3 and 18 were to be covered. The federal government authorized the spending of up to $3 billion by 1982 to facilitate implementation of directives included in this act (Kirk and Gallagher, 1979).

Some provisions of PL 94-142 affecting early education programs require each state to develop an individualized education program (IEP) for all handicapped children. According to the law, an *individualized education program* is

a written statement for each handicapped child developed in any meeting by a representative of the local education agency or intermediate educational unit who shall be qualified to provide, or supervise the provision of, specially designed instruction to meet the unique needs of handicapped children, the teacher, the parents or guardians of such child, and whenever appropriate, such child; which statement shall include (a) a statement of the present levels of educational performance of such child; (b) a statement of annual goals, including short-term instructional objectives; (c) a statement of the specific educational services to be provided to such child, and the extent to which such child will be able to participate in regular educational programs; (d) the projected date for initiation and anticipated duration of such services; and (e) appropriate objective criteria and evaluation procedures and schedules for determining, on at least an annual basis, whether instructional objectives are being achieved. (PL 94-142, p. 4)

The IEP for each handicapped child must be reviewed annually by a committee. The law also requires inservice training for teachers and annual evaluations of program effectiveness in meeting the needs of the children.

Legislation requiring the mainstreaming of handicapped children into the regular classroom thus brings teachers of young children into contact with youngsters who have needs that are different from the majority. Teachers can expect to have exceptional children in their classrooms at some time during their career. They need to know about exceptionality and how to plan for it.

WHO ARE EXCEPTIONAL CHILDREN?

Individual Differences

If you could gather in one room a large number of children of exactly the same age, say four years old, and arrange them according to height, you would see an interesting display of individual differences. There would be

WRITING AN IEP

Preparing an IEP is very much like developing a plan for any child, except that it is likely to be more specific and more specialized. Following are the major steps in writing an IEP.

1. Discover the child's present level of functioning and indicate as precisely as possible what his or her skills and abilities are. This requires a diagnosis and testing that will usually be done by a specialist. The level of functioning should be summarized in each of several areas: (a) cognitive (the child can recognize colors, but cannot discriminate shapes visually); (b) social-emotional (the child is friendly but cannot engage in most group activities requiring rapid mobility, may often play alone); (c) linguistic (no indications of language difficulties).

2. Select the goals for the child, and determine how much he or she can be expected to learn within a year. These may include goals such as learning how to use crutches to aid mobility, or an optacon to learn letters, and so on.

3. Choose the strategies to help the child progress toward the goals that have been selected. These may include teaching strategies such as behavior modification or special training with a device, or specific methods in teaching concepts, or supervision in play activities in order to help the child become involved more often in play groups.

4. Assess progress. The law requires yearly evaluation. This step may include formal tests of competence in specific skills, teacher judgments, and parent reports. It is usually necessary to keep careful records of the child's behavior and accomplishment.

The parents and staff work together in all these steps. Collaboration is much easier if the plan is specific and observable and if progress is evident to the parents, the staff, and the child.

a relatively large number of children who were average for the group or slightly taller or shorter. There would be a few children very much shorter and a few very much taller than the average. If you were to draw a graph that represented the number of children at different heights, it would form a curve similar to the shape of a bell, with small numbers of children at either end and more and more children at each height moving toward the average for the group.

If you were to line the children up according to weight, or intelligence, or strength, or other human skills and characteristics, they would show a similar distribution. Children who fall at the extremes on one characteristic, however, might be at the middle on another. The shortest child might be of average intelligence, for example. Individual differences appear in observable characteristics, including rates of growth, visual ability, and behavior.

The children at each extreme of the line are *exceptional*, that is, they are

The intellectually gifted are considered exceptional, just as the mentally retarded are exceptional.

unusual. If you think of individual differences in terms of abilities—intelligence, hearing, vision, and the like—the children at the "low" end of the distribution will have diminished capacity and will have difficulty functioning in many routine life situations. The general terms *impairment, handicap,* and *disability* are used to describe these conditions. Illnesses, accidents, and genetic defects may create specific disabilities. The term *handicapped* thus refers to a broad category of persons who, for one reason or another, cannot function in daily life without assistance of some kind. At the opposite end of the line will be those who are far above average in ability—the gifted or talented children. They may be gifted in one ability but not in others, just as some children may suffer disability in only one area of functioning. However, some children have multiple handicaps and some are gifted in several abilities.

Labeling: Pro and Con

Much controversy has arisen from the issue of labeling exceptional children. The stigma of terms such as *slow learner* or *retarded* is difficult to overcome. Less negative terms have come into use: *exceptional children, children with special needs.* However, these are not technical terms; even professionals do not agree on their exact meaning.

"Unless you have a retarded child of your own, you can't truly understand why I prefer to use a vague label like 'minimal neurological dysfunction'—even if it is jargon."

Parent

Those who object to labeling argue that because terms are not clear, children can be easily mislabeled. Furthermore, they contend that educationally helpful programs do not result from labeling. In addition, labeled children suffer from lower self-esteem.

Proponents of labeling feel that classification is necessary to plan and provide special programs. Legislation to support such programs depends on identifying the special needs of exceptional children who qualify for services; money for programs is made available based on the number of children identified as exceptional.

There are thus both negative and positive effects of labeling. Efforts to find ways to maximize the benefits of labeling continue.

CATEGORIES OF EXCEPTIONAL CONDITIONS

The terms *handicap* and *exceptional* will be used interchangeably to refer to children who deviate from the average in one or more of the following characteristics or abilities: mental, physical, sensory, communication, or behavior. Exceptionalities in these areas must be such that the child requires special services to develop to his or her maximum level of ability (Kirk and Gallagher, 1979).

Exceptional children are often grouped into the following categories:

1. *Mental deviations,* including children who are gifted as well as mentally retarded
2. *Sensory handicaps,* including children with hearing and vision impairments
3. *Communication disorders,* including children with learning disabilities, speech, and language disorders
4. *Behavior disorders,* including emotional disturbance and social maladjustment
5. *Health impairments,* including neurological defects, orthopedic conditions, birth defects, and diseases such as muscular dystrophy and sickle cell anemia (Kirk and Gallagher, 1979; Haring, 1978)

Mentally Retarded

The American Association on Mental Deficiency (AAMD) describes *mental retardation* as significantly subaverage general intellectual functioning existing concurrently with deficits in adaptive behavior, and manifested during the developmental period (Grossman, 1973).

Adaptive behavior is defined by the AAMD as the ''effectiveness or degree with which the individual meets the standards of personal independence and social responsibility expected of his age and cultural group'' (Fallen and McGovern, 1978, p. 5).

Retardation is classified according to different levels of severity: *mild, moderate, severe,* and *profound.* The two most widely used IQ tests, the Stanford-Binet Intelligence Scale and the Wechsler Intelligence Scale for Children, provide the following corresponding scores for each level:

Level	Stanford-Binet	Wechsler
Mild	68–52	69–55
Moderate	51–36	54–40
Severe	35–20	39–25
Profound	19 and below	24 and below

Mildly retarded children can usually be educated in the regular classroom with individualized instruction and with the help of a resource person. Mildly retarded children, if given proper education, can care for their own needs, communicate well enough to live independently, and hold semiskilled and unskilled jobs.

Moderately retarded children are obviously delayed in development and

"After you've worked with children for a few years, you get so you can spot the youngster who may be having problems. Then you learn to talk with the parents about your concerns just because you *care*."

Teacher

usually need specialized programs. Classes for the trainable mentally retarded teach the child to take care of his or her own needs, to carry out simple daily tasks—dressing, helping with household chores—and to get along with others. A moderately retarded person will most likely require help and supervision throughout life. Some are capable of working at unskilled jobs but most adults will do best at simple repetitive tasks under supervision in a sheltered workshop.

Severely and profoundly retarded individuals are likely to have sustained damage to the central nervous system. They require highly supervised care. The profoundly retarded generally are not able to care for themselves; they have complicated medical needs. Some are restricted to bed and need help in learning to walk or feed themselves.

Recognition and Assessment   Tests have been developed to measure adaptive behavior in young children who are suspected of being retarded. These measure sensorimotor skills, communication, self-help, and socialization abilities. It is important to note that the scores of minority and/or low-income children may be lower on such tests.

Generally, the child who is moderately or severely retarded will be identified during the preschool years. It is the mildly retarded youngster who may appear essentially normal and may not be identified until later in school.

The teacher of young children will most likely be working with the mildly retarded in the nursery school or child care center. Most causes of mental retardation are unknown, and, if known, are usually complex. The condition is generally the result of multiple elements. The majority of mildly retarded cases are cultural or familial retardates, that is, conditions caused by environmental (cultural) and hereditary (familial) factors (Dunn, 1973).

Sometimes children who appear to be mildly retarded are only exhibiting developmental lag. They are simply slower in the maturational process than others. Poor auditory discrimination with resulting speech problems is one such lag frequently noted in children. The child usually catches up with others when experiences and activities are structured to his or her needs. Teachers cannot assume, however, that children will outgrow developmental problems without help. Thus, the mildly retarded child and the one suffering from developmental lag can both benefit from a curriculum designed to enhance learning skills. IQ scores can and do change. That change is most likely to occur during the early years when the quality of a child's interaction with his or her social and physical environment can have a powerful influence on cognitive development.

What the Teacher Can Do   Equally important to the method of teaching retarded children are the teacher's patience, skill, and personal feelings toward what he or she is doing for the child. Weikart (1970) states, "As far as various preschool curricula are concerned, children profit intellectually and socioemotionally from any curriculum that is based on a wide range of experience'' (p. 4).

Many teachers find that some form of behavior modification is effective with slow learners. Strategies that appear to be helpful include making simple contracts, distributing tokens, or using any method that helps the child identify a goal to see how he or she can reach it in a systematic way. Simplifying a task by breaking it into smaller units and sequencing the steps, rewarding and reinforcing small successes, setting clear limits, and eliminating distractions all help a child learn more quickly.

Field trips and practical life experiences are also good ways to teach retarded children. Socialization should be started early so youngsters can learn appropriate behaviors—taking care of themselves physically, keeping clean, practicing good hygiene habits, and generally learning how to get along with others.

Mentally Gifted

According to the U.S. Office of Education, ''Gifted and talented children are those identified by professionally qualified persons who, by virtue of outstanding abilities, are capable of high performance. These are children who require differentiated educational programs in order to realize their contribution to self and society.''

Recognition and Assessment Lewis B. Terman described the gifted children he studied as fast learners who have an early interest in reading, scientific inclination, good abstract reasoning, good command of language, and poor handwriting. They tend to be well-adjusted, imaginative, have a high energy level, and are often only children, eldest children, or children born to older parents (Terman and Oden, 1959).

What the Teacher Can Do A gifted child may come to preschool at age three or four already able to read, tell time, and do arithmetic. The teacher's task is to select challenging experiences suited to the child's level of ability.

Gifted children can be ''trouble makers'' and distracting when teachers do not recognize and plan for individualized projects that challenge the learner. Special resources, enrichment experiences, accelerated projects all require extra teacher time and the help of those who have had experience with gifted youngsters. The child with a high degree of creativity and curiosity will require as much of the teacher's time and talents as the slow learner. Gifted children do well if left to work at their own pace within flexible limits.

Hearing Impairment

Many programs screen preschoolers for possible hearing loss. An *audiometer* is used to measure hearing, using standards that have been accepted world wide.[1] Hearing loss is measured by decibels (dB).

The Conference of Executives of American Schools for the Deaf has adopted the following definitions:

> A *deaf* person is one whose hearing is disabled to an extent (usually 70dB ISO or greater) that precludes the understanding of speech through the ear alone, without or with the use of a hearing aid.
>
> A *hard of hearing* person is one whose hearing is disabled to an extent (usually 35 to 69 dB ISO) that makes difficult, but does not preclude, the understanding of speech through the ear alone, without or with a hearing aid. (Moores, 1978, p. 5)

There are different degrees of hearing loss ranging from slight (losses of 27 to 40 dB) to extreme or profound (91 dB or more).

Recognition and Assessment   Early identification of youngsters with hearing loss is needed to plan educational intervention. In some communities, high-risk infants (such as those whose mothers had measles during pregnancy) are screened and observed.

It is easy to overlook a mild hearing loss of a preschooler. Classrooms are often noisy, groups of children may participate in activities together, and the hard of hearing child may be overlooked because the hearing loss is not apparent.

Restlessness and inattentiveness signal the teacher to be alert to hidden causes. The child may try to force his or her way to the front of a group in order to hear, or may sit quietly and not respond. At times he or she may be restless and appear disinterested. A child with hearing loss may speak more loudly than others and have to be reminded frequently to use a "quiet voice." The teacher who suspects a hearing loss can test these children by speaking to them when they are not watching.

In 1967, an amendment to the Social Security Act was passed to require early and periodic screening, diagnosis, and treatment (EPSDT) of all children on Medicaid to identify young handicapped children so they could be given proper assistance early in life.

What the Teacher Can Do   Children with hearing impairments diagnosed as minimally dysfunctional can fit into the regular classroom. Emphasis is placed on preparing these children to fit into the normal activities of daily living. The hearing-impaired child should be seated in a place that will enable him or her to hear. Speak to the child when he or she is looking at you. Enunciate slowly and clearly. Watch and ask for feedback to be certain the child is hearing your words.

[1]The International Standard Organization (ISO) and the American National Standards Institute (ANSI) are the recognized organizations that establish these standards.

**CLUES TO POSSIBLE SPEECH
AND HEARING PROBLEMS**

1. The child is silent much of the time, does not volunteer to speak; often does not respond to questions.
2. Speech is unclear, jumbled. Child mumbles or speaks very softly.
3. Responses are sometimes not related to the subject or question.
4. The child has difficulty finding the right words to use.
5. Intonations and voice quality seem unnatural.
6. The child may be disruptive in a group by pushing to be in front of others.
7. The child may hesitate to join in with or approach others; may choose to be on the fringes of a group, appearing to be disinterested in what is going on.
8. The child seems generally dull and slow.

Many preschoolers with hearing losses are also deficient in language. The teacher needs to build competence in both speech and language. In more severe cases of handicap, children will need the help of a tutor for training in sign language, lip reading, and finger spelling.

Visual Impairment

Visually handicapped children are those who require special educational treatment because of problems with their vision. This group is divided into three general categories: blind, low vision, and visually limited (Barraga, 1976).

Blind refers to individuals who have no vision or who can distinguish light only. A legal definition of blindness is central visual acuity of 20/200 or less in the better eye after correction (the person can see at a distance of twenty feet things the average person could see at two hundred feet). Only legally blind persons are eligible to receive materials from the American Printing House for the Blind. Blind children who cannot read print learn to read through Braille or other aids.

Low vision includes children "who have limitations in distance vision but are able to see objects and materials when they are within a few inches or at a maximum of a few feet away" (Barraga, 1976, p. 14).

Visually limited includes children who are limited in their ability to use

SOME THINGS A TEACHER CAN DO WITH
SPEECH- OR HEARING-IMPAIRED CHILDREN

1. Talk a lot to and with the child.
2. Verbalize actions as you work with the child.
3. Encourage conversation.
4. Listen attentively to the child's speech.
5. Speak normally and at a natural rate of speed.
6. Be sure the child sees your face when you speak; squat or sit at the child's eye level; make eye contact.
7. Help the child focus on important stimuli and filter out distracting influences.
8. Use imitative games and songs directing the child to repeat sounds or make movements.
9. Phrase comments or questions to encourage maximum verbal response from the child.

vision under average conditions. They need special lighting to see learning materials and may be unable to see distant objects unless they are moving. They may need optical aids and special materials.

Recognition and Assessment   A child with faulty vision may exhibit some of the same behaviors as one who is hearing impaired—inattentiveness, restlessness, and nonresponsiveness. Sometimes the child may rub his or her eyes excessively and tilt or thrust the head forward. He or she may blink more than usual or squint and frown when looking at a book. Dizziness, headaches, and recurring sties are also clues to vision problems.

Children with visual loss often dislike activities that require eye-hand coordination—using scissors to cut designs, working puzzles, coloring in detail. They may be irritable when doing close work. Some are physically awkward; they are poor at tasks requiring visual judgment, such as catching balls. Because young children lack the experience and ability to recognize their own problems, teachers have to be particularly sensitive to cues; any abnormal or asocial behavior may indicate more serious physical disturbances.

Treatment during the early years is much more effective than later attempts at correction. When a child is suspected of having visual problems, the teacher should arrange with the school to seek the assistance of local agencies and specialists for further evaluation.

What the Teacher Can Do   Children with visual handicaps may suffer more from being denied opportunity than from their limited vision. Adults tend to overprotect handicapped children and restrict them from activities

Nursery schools and child care centers can and do enroll blind, deaf, and physically handicapped children. Early education facilities are good places to provide a "least restrictive" environment for such children.

"I always make a point to provide lots of sensory materials at our collage and art area so Jeff, who is partially blind, can touch the materials."

Teacher

that would bring them into contact with peers and experiences of a normal environment.

Teachers should encourage the visually handicapped child to engage in a variety of sensory experiences—climbing, riding, throwing and catching balls, cutting with scissors, and the like. Fear that children may hurt themselves should not limit mobility. This means risking bumps and bruises. Knowing they can control many aspects of their daily routine is important to the development of partially sighted children. If they do not explore their surroundings, they lose control of their activities and become more dependent on others.

The degree of residual vision guides the planning of activities suited to the child. Techniques to help totally blind children differ from those for children who have some vision. Children who were born with sight that is lost after age four or five are more educable than those who were born blind. This is also true of children who lose their hearing after language and speech have begun to develop.

Learning Disabilities

The category of *learning disabilities* is perhaps the most ambiguous of all handicaps. The National Advisory Committee on Handicapped Children (1968) of the U.S. Office of Education offers the following definition:

Three out of four LD children are boys.

> Children with special (specific) learning disabilities exhibit a disorder in one or more of the basic psychological processes involved in understanding or in using spoken or written language. These may be manifested in disorders of listening, thinking, talking, reading, writing, spelling, or arithmetic. They include conditions which have been referred to as perceptual handicaps, brain injury, minimal brain dysfunction, dyslexia, developmental aphasia, etc. They *do not* include learning problems which are due primarily to visual, hearing, or motor handicaps, to mental retardation, emotional disturbance, or to environmental disadvantage. (p. 14)

"When Martin gets tense and tired, he has a difficult time making himself understood. He stutters and stammers and gets frustrated. I try to get him off to a quiet corner where we can both sit in a rocking chair and relax. I can feel his body relaxing as I sing and talk quietly to him. It's great for both of us."

Teacher

Such a definition serves the need to identify the circumstances under which funds can be used to educate learning disabled (LD) children. To many critics, however, it underscores the overinclusiveness of the definition. Learning disabilities include minimal brain damage, mild forms of retardation, language difficulties, perceptual and motor problems, social-emotional maladjustment, hyperactivity, and just about any other condition that falls within the category of special education.

The lack of specificity, however, need not deter the teacher of young children from identifying and working with learning disabled youngsters.

Abilities range along a continuum; some children are in a gray zone between "normal" or "typical," and some are clearly disabled. The use of categories tends to force us to think of disabilities as something a child either has or hasn't. This is misleading.

Additionally, the distinction between developmental lag and disability is a troublesome one. Perhaps the major concern is to help a child who is lagging behind his or her peers. The child who has problems of coordination needs more of the teacher's time, quite apart from any labeling that may come to the teacher's mind. If problems are severe, there may be ways that a specialist can help, and diagnosis is important. But whether or not a child falls into a diagnostic category, he or she deserves the attention of the teaching staff.

A distinction can be made between *correctable* disabilities and those that are less responsive to ameliorative devices. Impaired vision, for example, can often be corrected with glasses or surgery, and the sooner, the better. Early correction gives the child the opportunity to learn and to do things that otherwise may have been beyond his or her ability. Learning disabilities, however, may require long-term, continuing efforts.

Recognition and Assessment   According to Haring (1978), some of the most common characteristics of LD children in the preschool are (in order of frequency):

1. *Hyperactivity*   The child is in constant motion, moving aimlessly, rocking back and forth, tapping fingers, pushing, and engaging in disruptive kinds of behavior.

2. *Perceptual-motor impairments*   The child has difficulty discriminating differences among visual and auditory symbols, and does not distinguish among shapes and letters, or among different sounds. These defects in discrimination do not come from sensory problems in vision or auditory ability. Perceptual disorders may occur in children with normal eyesight and hearing.

3. *Problems in physical coordination*   The child is awkward, poorly coordinated, clumsy. He or she has difficulty performing physical activities, such as throwing and catching a ball, jumping, running, and walking.

4. *Inattentiveness*   The child has difficulty attending to a task, or switching attention from one object to another.

5. *Impulsiveness*   The child has difficulty filtering out certain stimuli; he or she may react suddenly and inappropriately to a wide variety of events.

6. *Memory disorders*   The child has difficulty remembering events. Some cannot recognize visual symbols or spoken words that they have learned in the past. Others may not be able to recall either recent or distant events.

7. *Specific learning disabilities*   The child has difficulty performing specific kinds of tasks. For example, he or she may appear to be normal in all

aspects of work except writing, or reading, or speaking certain words. The disability is specific.

8. *Language disorders*   The disorder may be manifested in one or more of several ways: a very limited vocabulary, clumsy speech, articulation or voice problems, or incomprehensible speech.

The child with learning disabilities is often recognized as one who behaves or performs differently from the others. The teacher may administer simple tests, asking the child to recall a short series of words or numbers, to hop on one foot, to sort shapes according to a pattern, and so on.

Early screening *may* help identify perceptual disorders and minimal brain damage.

Many schools conduct developmental screening tests when youngsters start kindergarten. Tests for reading readiness, visual motor, and visual perception help detect and place children with special needs. There are also developmental and kindergarten readiness tests that can be purchased and administered to five-year-old children in the preschool.

It is not always easy to identify learning disabilities in the preschool. Diagnostic testing depends in part on the child's response to questions and instructions. For various reasons, the child may misunderstand or misinterpret what is expected. Also, during the preschool years, children are learning rapidly and one child may be far ahead of another in vocabulary, motor coordination, and ability to attend. The child who is "different" may simply be behind his or her peers. Developmental lags may easily be mislabeled as learning disabilities. It is essential not to rush to a diagnosis; individual differences in growth rates and difficulties in diagnosis must be taken into account.

"I worry about Martin cutting himself or coloring on the walls, so I never allow him to have scissors or crayons."

Parent

There are guidelines that can be used. Some authorities suggest a rule-of-thumb criterion of "differentness." Experience with young children is a

---

SUGGESTIONS FOR WORKING WITH CHILDREN WITH LANGUAGE DISORDERS

1. Create a relaxed environment for the child.
2. Give the child plenty of undivided attention.
3. Let the child know he or she is accepted.
4. Look directly at the child; attend to his or her speech without correcting or asking for repetitions.
5. Do not complete a child's sentence or verbalize for him or her.
6. Encourage efforts to talk.
7. Build the child's confidence in his or her abilities.
8. Protect the child from interruptions by youngsters who are more articulate.

necessary requirement to use this standard. Signs that a child is different from others is not a diagnosis, only a clue that alerts the teacher to observe more carefully.

An example might be a child who is average or above in intelligence but cannot pay attention, is easily distracted, appears bored, and displays erratic body control. He or she may be more disruptive than other children of comparable age. Any of these conditions is only a clue. The teacher might ask the child to skip. In comparison with normal children, the LD child may show unequal development—an ability to hop on one foot but not the other.

Another good test for clues is to watch the child on a balance beam; there is often an obvious lack of coordination and motor control. (See the section on "Sensorimotor Activities" in the companion handbook.) Parents and teachers may overlook clues in small muscle coordination because they are less obvious. A child may avoid activities such as cutting with scissors and coloring within defined spaces, or may be unable to follow the movements of a finger play. The teacher may not notice these signs among a large group of children. Another clue is failure to establish handedness, that is, the child will switch back and forth from the left to right hand when others the same age are already showing a definite preference.

In the perceptual areas, children may have difficulty distinguishing figures from background. They may appear to have trouble interpreting visual images by inability to concentrate on what is important. The total environment seems to overwhelm them so that they cannot focus on one aspect. For example, they may have difficulty finding their names or identifying markers on lockers; they often complain of being unable to find clothing without help. They usually have difficulty dressing because they cannot visualize how the body

"I never noticed Martha's problem until I had the children do some simple paper folding. She simply could not fold a piece of paper in half."

Teacher

JAMES—A HYPERACTIVE CHILD

(A Report by His Mother)

At age four, James was so hyperactive we were ready to send him to an institution. He was obviously a bright child, but he was so destructive—breaking things, having tantrums, sleeping as little as three or four hours a night. We were all worn out just trying to keep up with him. His older sister got so frustrated that she often cried. She even suggested that we put him in a special school. We couldn't do things like normal families, such as eating out or taking trips, because James was just too much to handle. His dad and I almost broke up our marriage because of James.

I had read about the use of amphetamines like Ritalin and the possible harmful side effects, but I was torn between wanting to do what was least harmful to James and getting a good night's rest for myself. Some experts insist there is no harm in drug treatment while others feel there is a disruption of the growth hormones from use of drugs. Our pediatrician put James on Ritalin to calm him down, and for a while it worked. Then, as the drug wore off, he got worse. I finally decided, with the help of our doctor, to try a drug-free nutritional program.

We took James off all foods that had additives, food coloring, and salicylates.* It wasn't easy, but the change in his behavior was so dramatic that even he noticed the difference. Since then, we have kept him on an educational and nutritional therapy program; we're all sleeping through the night and behaving like a normal family.

*See Ben F. Feingold, M.D., *Why Your Child Is Hyperactive* (New York: Random House, 1975).

fits into clothing. They may not be able to tie shoes, even at age six or seven.

The teacher may also notice that such children perseverate in their perceptions; they will continue to see a given shape even when other shapes are presented. Their poor eye-hand coordination will inhibit ability to interpret and copy shapes; drawings will show poor spatial relationships. When other youngsters are drawing fairly clear representational pictures of themselves, LD children may continue to use a scribble to indicate a person. Right-left discrimination and other such motor skills often lag.

Sometimes LD children have problems expressively, that is, they may be able to understand what they hear, but have difficulty transmitting a response, either verbally or physically. Four-year-olds, for example, should be able to attend to a simple song or finger play, repeat the words, and coordinate them with the appropriate movements. Learning disabled five- and six-year-olds may not be able to follow instructions to "stand in front of," "walk in back of," "sit next to," and other such statements requiring the ability to make connections between what they hear and do.

Teacher: Tell me a word that starts with the sound "B."
Child: Cat. Dog.

What the Teacher Can Do   Many of the materials in the preschool can be used for remedial activities. Working with LD children is not so much a matter of providing a specialized environment as it is the use of teaching methods and individualized instruction. For example, children with problems in physical coordination will benefit from activities that engage them in tasks requiring practice in ball throwing and the like. Activities are planned so that they start at their level of ability. As they progress and improve, the staff introduces increasingly difficult tasks. Perceptual-motor impairments are handled in much the same way with sequentially planned activities to provide children with opportunities to practice and increase their skills in visual and auditory perception.

Emotionally based problems—hyperactivity, impulsiveness, and such—require control, rechanneling, and setting clear limits on behavior. The teacher needs to pinpoint the specific behavior he or she wishes to modify and to set about in a methodical way to change that behavior.

The most effective program for a young child with a learning disability is one that integrates the work of a specialist with the parents and teachers of the child.

Behavior Disorders

Children with behavior disorders are usually easy to spot. They disrupt the group, are difficult to handle, and invite rejection and anger by teachers and peers. They invade the social world around them, and are unhappy and disliked. They may also be withdrawn, living in a fantasy world. The signs of their problems are their words and actions. Their handicap is the way they behave.

SUGGESTIONS FOR TEACHING LD CHILDREN

Develop a lesson plan in advance to suit the needs of the child.

Eliminate unnecessary distractions.

Avoid wearing bright clothing or jewelry because it may be too distracting for some children.

Involve the child actively—plan the lesson to allow for maximum participation.

Maintain control at all times.

Use materials the child likes; for example, if a child likes cars, use them to teach concepts.

If the child loses interest, stop or change to an alternate plan.

Know your subject matter so you can be flexible about teaching it in many different ways.

There appears to be no generally accepted definition of *behavior disorder*. A child is emotionally disturbed if he or she is so labeled by an authority. This lack of clarity is due to the fact that behavior disorders cannot be measured in the more precise ways that tests might measure IQ, visual acuity, or physical ability. It might be more accurate to define an emotionally disturbed child as one who is *not* emotionally healthy.

According to Bower (1969), a child is considered to have a behavior disorder if he or she exhibits one or more of the following to a marked extent over a period of time:

1. An inability to learn that cannot be explained by intellectual, sensory, or health factors
2. An inability to build or maintain satisfactory interpersonal relationships with peers and teachers
3. Inappropriate types of behavior or feelings under normal conditions
4. A general pervasive mood of unhappiness or depression
5. A tendency to develop physical symptoms, pains, or fears associated with personal or school problems.

Recognition and Assessment   The young child's behavior changes rapidly during the formative years. Something that seems like a major problem one month might be gone the next. Phrases such as, ''She's just going through a phase,'' or ''He'll grow out of it,'' indicate this rapid growth and change. Sometimes, however, the needs of very young children can be overlooked because the teacher is not sensitive to their problems or is reluctant to seek further evaluation. Observations of teachers and parents are the most likely sources of identification during the early years. As the child matures, the persistence of behavioral or emotional problems makes them easier to identify.

What the Teacher Can Do   There is no generally accepted curriculum for young children who have behavior problems. The familiar argument still exists as to whether a highly structured, teacher-directed program or a child-oriented approach is superior. Therapists may use strategies in the clinic that do not work well in a child development center. Parents may recommend successful techniques from experience at home that teachers cannot adopt. The emotionally disturbed child will almost certainly need more individual attention than normal children. The kind of attention depends on the particular problem and degree of severity. Thus, teaching techniques and curriculum modification reflect the needs of each situation. In some instances, the solution is to refer the child to a specialist.

Health Impairments

The term *crippled and other health impaired* (COHI) commonly applies to children who are physically disabled. "The COHI population is comprised of those children and adults who as a result of permanent, temporary, or intermittent medical disabilities require modifications in curriculum and instructional strategies" (Wald, 1971, p. 95).

Historically, children with polio or tuberculosis were usually identified as health impaired. Special educational programs were merely extensions and supplements to medical treatment services. It was only later that groups such as the Easter Seal Society for Children and Adults, the United Cerebral Palsy Association, the National Hemophilia Foundation, and the Muscular Dystrophy Association pressed for legislation and research to improve educational programming. In 1976, the National Advisory Committee on the Handicapped identified 255,000 crippled and other health impaired children between birth and 19 years of age being served in special programs; there were an additional 73,000 identified but not yet served (Haring, 1978).

Recognition and Assessment   The crippling nature of physical disorders include, among others, cerebral palsy, orthopedic handicaps, muscular dystrophy, epilepsy, hemophilia, cystic fibrosis, sickle cell anemia, cancer, and heart conditions.

The most common physical disability among children in special education programs is cerebral palsy, a condition that affects muscle coordination caused by damage to the motor functioning area of the brain. Depending on the degree of impairment, the child has difficulty maintaining normal postures and performing normal movements that require motor coordination. He

"It's fine to say teachers ought to be patient and enthusiastic, but just try to work with a group of normal preschoolers and some mainstreamed children without extra help. No way!"

Teacher

"I admit I was very much against having handicapped children in my son's class. I was afraid they might be upsetting to the other children and require more of the teacher's time. But I have noticed how my son has become more cooperative and sensitive to the needs of others, offering to help, and generally being much more comfortable about the realities of interacting with handicapped people than I."

Parent

or she is also likely to have motor speech defects. Associated with cerebral palsy are related problems of emotional coping, behavioral disturbance, and intellectual functioning. Problems before, during, and after birth can cause cerebral palsy. Premature birth, difficult labor, lack of oxygen, drugs, childhood trauma, and such can be related to this crippling disease.

Muscular dystrophy is a sex-linked disease, generally transmitted through the mother to the son. It is rarely found in female children. The childhood form causes progressive weakness of the skeletal muscles so that the young child has difficulty running or climbing. The disease often progresses rapidly to the point where the child is confined to a wheelchair. Death usually occurs in middle or late teens.

What the Teacher Can Do   Children with physical handicaps may be of low, normal, or superior intelligence. Their difficulties in school may relate to problems with mastering the physical environment. Preschoolers, especially, learn best when they can interact physically with their environment—playing, swinging, sliding. A child who is confined to a wheelchair or who must use crutches or braces needs help and encouragement to master the physical environment.

The primary consideration in adapting a curriculum for physically handicapped children is accessibility: wide paved paths in the play yard to accommodate wheelchairs; flat surfaces with gentle slopes (not to exceed a rise of one foot over a distance of twenty feet); and handrails and ramps to provide access to slides, playhouses, and bridges. Sand and water play structures should include a raised area to accommodate the child.

There may be a tendency to protect physically handicapped children from potential injury. This is reasonable, but they have the same needs as normal

Typically, children in COHI programs are capable of academic learning. If not, they may attend programs for the severely or profoundly handicapped.

BIOLOGICAL SPEECH DISORDERS

Speech disorders due to cleft palate, cerebral palsy, and other such causes, require the attention of speech therapists and clinicians who are specially trained. Specific methods in oral drill, correct tongue placement, breathing exercises, and therapy are used in conjunction with language motivating experiences. The therapist may suggest that the teacher use puppets, flannel boards, and other props to encourage the child to speak. Mirrors may be placed in strategic locations to help the child see how he or she should move his or her tongue and mouth. Singing and other music activities might also be prescribed.

children to play, explore, interact with one another, and master challenges. The teacher does not have to go to great expense to buy special toys or equipment for the classroom. Provide familiar activities and adapt them to extend and enhance the child's curiosity, learning, and independence.

WORKING WITH PARENTS

PL 94-142 requires parent involvement in individualized education planning.

The teacher who wishes to involve parents in carrying out a curriculum for a child with a disability will deal not only with the disability itself but with the adjustment that the parents and the family are making to their situation. Working with parents calls for unusual sensitivity and reflection.

Family Adjustment

"My husband and I were on the verge of divorce because our child's hyperactivity interfered with every aspect of our lives. I needed marriage counseling before I could spend any extra energy on learning how to teach my child at home."

Mother

"To add to our guilt, there is also the fact that we did not want Noah. . . . So perhaps Noah sensed chemically in the womb that he wasn't welcome. Perhaps that's why he even frequently vomited his milk during his first few weeks of life—as if to reject the life that had initially wanted to reject him."

Josh Greenfeld

The response and adaptation of a family to the presence of a handicapped child depends very largely on the nature and degree of the disability, and whether the handicap is obvious when the child is an infant or becomes apparent only as the child begins to deal with more complex cognitive or physical tasks. The problems faced by a family of a child with a mild hearing loss are obviously less compelling than those of a family with a child who has cerebral palsy or Down's syndrome.

Parents of infants with Down's syndrome report that it took months for them to get used to the idea that their babies were not normal and some said that it took years (D'Arcy, 1968). The most common and predictable parental reaction to the birth of a handicapped child is depression, a sense of grief and loss similar in some ways to mourning the death of a child. But in this case, the mourning process is not complete; the infant has survived (Solnit and Stark, 1961). These feelings may be followed by shame and the expectation that the parents and the child will be met with rejection by the community. Parents see their children as extensions of themselves and thus may take on some of the response that they expect the child to receive. Parents may also blame themselves and feel that in some way they were responsible for the disability or handicap. If they did not want the child, the handicap may be seen as a punishment. Some parents refuse to accept the reality of the problems they will face. They try to believe that the child will eventually outgrow the handicap. Occasionally, they may blame one another, the hospital, or medication for their child's condition.

Apart from their emotions about the child and the handicap, parents also may be apprehensive about the long-term effects of the disability on the family and on their other children. The intensity of feelings related to the impact that disability has on a family are vividly portrayed in *A Child Called Noah,* a father's account of the family's learning to deal with an autistic child:

Somehow the rhythm of our lives, the good fortune of our marriage, seems to have dissipated. It is hard for Foumi to believe in me and for me to believe in Foumi anymore. Successful monogamy, of course, must be based on a faith in the union if nothing else. And how can we have faith in a marriage that has biologically backfired? . . . she teems with guilt toward herself and accusations toward me. And I guess I act the same way toward her. In any event, our house of good cards has fallen apart. At first I thought the news of Noah would stabilize and fix and reaffirm our marriage. Now I'm not so sure. (Greenfeld, 1972, pp. 56–57)

Some families are unable to cope with the child who is severely handicapped and place him or her in an institution. Others accept the child and adapt their schedules and family life to the constraints that may be involved. There is a lessening of emotion and anxiety, but these may be reawakened as the child reaches a new developmental stage and the family realizes more fully the implications of the child's difficulties.

One aspect of parental reaction is the effect of the child's disability on their behavior as parents. For example, the usual process of attachment may be disrupted if the child is deaf or has a severe visual impairment. A young infant normally will respond to the parent, following the voice and face and maintaining communication with nonverbal movements and through babbling. The failure of a deaf child to respond puts the interaction out of phase; the parent may feel dissatisfaction and may make fewer overtures to the child (Howard, 1978). Parents of a blind infant sometimes appear to be indifferent to their child, perhaps because the child has little facial expression and does not smile in response to actions by others (Fraiberg, 1974).

What Is the Teacher's Role?

If the child has been diagnosed before coming to the center, your task is to develop a working relationship with the parent and with specialists in the disability. If the disability becomes apparent for the first time while the child is in your class, your interaction with the parents includes two additional phases: assisting in the diagnosis of the disability and working with the parents during the initial phases of their own response to the knowledge that their child is not normal in some way.

It is not unusual for teachers of young children to be involved in the diagnosis phases. Your responsibilities include

A program for working with parents of handicapped children is most beneficial when the parent-teacher relationship is formalized; that is, meetings, discussions, evaluations—involving both individual parents as well as groups of parents—are planned systematically.

1. Being sensitive to the indicators that suggest a child may have a disability
2. Communicating with other staff members to decide what the next step will be
3. Discussing observations with the parents to see if they have additional information

4. Making referrals or seeing that they are made by the director or other appropriate persons
5. Following the diagnosis and becoming informed about the child's status
6. Discussing the next steps with the child's parents

When a diagnosis has been made or if the child comes as one to be mainstreamed into your center (that is, with the diagnosis already made), your task is to work out with other staff members, specialists, and the parents a program of activities and a curriculum for teaching/learning that are individually suited to the needs of the child. This will include an initial conference in which information about the child and about any educational procedures will be discussed with the parents. You should discover what the parents or others are now doing in working with the child. The parents should be told of the school's philosophy and the approach that you and the staff expect to take.

Parents of children with disabilities often are very well informed and are an important resource for the teacher. They are highly motivated and often know much more about the disability than you or the director may know, and they certainly know much more about their child. You are dependent on them to develop a successful program; this is indeed a situation in which the school and home are partners.

The program to be worked out for any given child depends on the nature of the disability and its severity. There will be resources to help you. You probably will have taken a course in special education by the time you begin to work in a center as a regular staff member. In most instances, there will be local specialists to help with the planning. Other staff members may have had experience developing IEPs. The local school district may also have resources that will be available to you for consultation.

REFERENCES

Barraga, N. C. 1976. *Visual Handicaps and Learning: A Developmental Approach.* Belmont, Calif.: Wadsworth.

Bower, E. M. 1969. *Early Identification of Emotionally Handicapped Children in School.* 2nd ed. Springfield, Ill.: Charles C Thomas.

Braun, S. J., and M. G. Lasher. 1978. *Are You Ready to Mainstream?* Columbus, Ohio: Charles E. Merrill.

D'Arcy, E. 1968. "Congenital Defects: Mothers' Reaction to First Information." *British Medical Journal,* 3, 796–798.

Dickerson, M. G., and M. D. Davis. 1979. "Implications of PL 94-142 for Developmental Early Childhood Teacher Education Programs." *Young Children,* 34, No. 1, 28–31.

Dunn, L. M., ed. 1973. *Exceptional Children in the Schools: Special Education in Transition.* 2nd ed. New York: Holt, Rinehart & Winston.

Education for All Handicapped Children Act (PL 94-142). 1975. 20 U.S.C. 1401.

Fallen, N. H., and J. E. McGovern. 1978. *Young Children with Special Needs*. Columbus, Ohio: Charles E. Merrill.

Farnham-Diggory, S. 1978. *Learning Disabilities*. Cambridge, Mass.: Harvard University Press.

Feingold, B. A., and C. L. Bank. 1978. *Developmental Disabilities of Early Childhood*. Springfield, Ill.: Charles C Thomas.

Feingold, B. F. 1975. *Why Your Child Is Hyperactive*. New York: Random House.

Fraiberg, S. 1974. "Blind Infants and Their Mothers: An Examination of the Sign System." In *The Effect of the Infant on Its Caregiver*. Ed. M. Lewis and L. A. Rosenblum. New York: John Wiley & Sons.

Greenfeld, J. 1972. *A Child Called Noah: A Family Journey*. New York: Holt, Rinehart & Winston.

Grossman, H. J., ed. 1973. *Manual on Terminology and Classification in Mental Retardation*. 1973 rev. Washington, D.C.: American Association on Mental Deficiency.

Hare, B. A., and J. M. Hare. 1977. *Teaching Young Handicapped Children: A Guide for Preschool and the Primary Grades*. New York: Grune & Stratton.

Haring, N. G., ed. 1978. *Behavior of Exceptional Children*. 2nd ed. Columbus, Ohio: Charles E. Merrill.

Howard, J. 1978. "The Influence of Children's Developmental Dysfunctions on Marital Quality and Family Interaction." In *Child Influences on Marital and Family Interaction: A Life-Span Perspective*. Ed. R. M. Lerner and G. B. Spanier. New York: Academic Press.

Kirk, S. A., and J. J. Gallagher. 1979. *Educating Exceptional Children*. 3rd ed. Boston: Houghton Mifflin.

Lerner, J. W. 1976. *Children with Learning Disabilities*. 2nd ed. Boston: Houghton Mifflin.

Moores, D. F. 1978. *Educating the Deaf: Psychology, Principles, and Practices*. Boston: Houghton Mifflin.

National Advisory Committee on Handicapped Children. 1968. *First Annual Report, Subcommittee on Education of the Committee on Labor and Public Welfare, U.S. Senate*. Washington, D.C.: Government Printing Office.

Solnit, A., and M. Stark. 1961. "Mourning the Birth of a Defective Child." *Psychoanalytic Study of the Child*, 16, 523–537.

Terman, L., and M. Oden. 1959. *The Gifted Group at Mid-Life*. Stanford, Calif.: Stanford University Press.

U.S. Department of Health, Education, and Welfare, Office of Education. 1972. *Education of the Gifted and Talented*. Washington, D.C.: Senate Subcommittee on Labor and Public Welfare, March.

U.S. Department of Health, Education, and Welfare, Office of Education. 1976. *The Unfinished Revolution: Education for the Handicapped, 1976 Annual Report*. Washington, D.C.: Government Printing Office.

Wald, J. R. 1971. "Crippled and Other Health Impaired and Their Education." In *Professional Preparation for Educators of Crippled Children*. Ed. F. P. Connor, J. R. Wald, and M. J. Cohen. New York: Teachers College Press.

Weikart, D. P., D. Deloria, S. Lawser, and R. Wiegerink. 1970. *Longitudinal Results of the Ypsilanti Perry Preschool Project*. Ypsilanti, Mich.: High/Scope Educational Research Foundation.

PART FIVE

GATHERING AND USING DATA ABOUT CHILDREN AND THEIR FAMILIES

A PROLOGUE   Throughout this book we have echoed the principle that learning and teaching begin at the child's level and that planning for individual children requires an understanding of their particular stage of development. In this section, we describe some of the methods that make these goals reasonable.

Assessment, evaluation, diagnosis—these terms conjure up batteries of tests, computers, statistics, books, and written reports with lengthy tables and appendixes. But assessment and evaluation need not involve complex methods. They are merely systematic ways to get information about children, programs, and schools. *Systematic* means that information is gathered regularly about ordinary behavior, using procedures that avoid as much as possible the personal bias of the individual gathering the data. Several kinds of assessment are easily within the time and resources of the staff of the preschool.

The key to assessment is to get accurate information about the topic you are interested in; this calls for tactics that are appropriate to the task. If you want to know whether Susie can count to ten, the best way is to ask her to count to ten. You would not ask for her opinion about how far she could count, you would ask for performance. You would not, however, ask her to count when she was angry or absorbed in a game; these factors would affect her willingness to try to do what you requested. You would not ask her to perform in a situation that would embarrass her if she did not succeed. Ideally, you would not want Susie to think that she was being assessed, but you would want her to do her best. These are common sense rules that help get accurate information about Susie's ability. Assessment and evaluation procedures reflect common sense of this sort.

In the previous section, we discussed the growth of skills and competence in several areas. This kind of knowledge is easier to apply in planning for individual children if you can keep track of each child's progress. There are enormous differences among children at any given age level; age norms alone can give a rough idea of what to expect but cannot substitute for data on individual children. This section describes some of the methods available to the preschool teacher and some that may be used by specialists.

The right to gather information about children and their families invokes a responsibility to use such data wisely. This means not only incorporating information in plans for each child, but also protecting the privacy of the children and parents whose lives have become a part of the files of the preschool.

CHAPTER 18

METHODS FOR GATHERING AND RECORDING DATA

THE PURPOSES OF ASSESSMENT

"Teacher! Teacher! Look what I can do!" calls Jennifer from her perch atop the swing and trapeze area. She is hanging upside down by her knees, arms dangling toward the ground.

"That's great, Jenny," acknowledges Mrs. Crane. "How did you learn to do that? I know you couldn't do it yesterday because you were asking me to show you."

"Mary showed me how. Do you want to see how she taught me?"

Jennifer untangles herself and proceeds to show Mrs. Crane how Mary taught her to shimmy up the side of the bars, pulls the trapeze toward her, puts one leg over the bar and then the other, finally ending in her upside-down position.

"Jenny, I want to write this down so we won't forget what an important day this is."

Mrs. Crane takes a small pencil and piece of paper from her pocket and notes:

4/27/80—10:30 a.m.: Jennifer H. succeeds in straddling the trapeze and hanging upside down with no help. Mary B. taught her how to climb up the bar, pull the trapeze toward her and climb on by herself. J. very proud of herself.

R. C.

"Sometimes the children will come up to me and ask, 'Did I just do something important enough for you to write in my folder?' They like to have me read out loud to them what I have written."

Teacher

This bit of "history" is an anecdotal record that will be filed away in Jennifer's folder along with other forms of information. This is one of the many records of Jennifer's behavior that will be made and filed away during the time she is in preschool. What is the purpose of such records? Why are they made, and how are they used? What do they tell about Jenny?

Planning for Individual Children

The activities of a preschool program can be adapted to the needs of individual children only if their developmental progress is assessed in a systematic way and on a regular basis. Specific up-to-date knowledge about the child is useful in situations where the teacher is able to respond to a child's effort, plan activities, encourage and reward achievement. It is also essential in planning a curriculum for a child who is significantly behind other children in competence or social development or who is disabled in some way. Planning for individual children requires careful assessment of their stages of development, growth patterns, and strengths and weaknesses.

Planning for Program Development

Information about the children in a center gives the staff a basis for curricular development and selection. Data accumulated for a group of children can reveal areas of strength or weakness that suggest special emphasis and indicate themes or field trips that may be particularly relevant. Information about the standing of the group in educational goals—concepts, vocabulary, recognizing letters, and the like—is especially critical for planning. Early in the school year, the teacher needs to have some sense of the level of accomplishment of the group in order to make decisions about the curriculum. Program planning during the year is then adjusted to accommodate the progress of the group.

Longitudinal Records for Children

A child's progress at any specific time is understood best in reference to his or her progress in the past. In planning for individual children, knowledge of areas that may have been particularly outstanding or troublesome can be especially useful. Accumulative records give a comprehensive picture of individual development. They aid in designing curricula and selecting activities for individual children.

Collaboration with Parents

Information about children is essential for joint planning with parents and for informing them about their child's progress. Conferences with parents are much more useful if the teacher's knowledge about the child is complete and detailed.

Parents welcome specificity in assessment of their children. To tell parents that a child is doing fine or performing well is not as useful as reporting that Paul can successfully put together a twenty-piece puzzle without any help or that he can reassemble a depth perception puzzle blindfolded in less than three minutes. It is informative to say that he is able to do this task faster than about half of the children in the class.

The legal requirement that parents and teachers work together to develop a curriculum for a disabled child illustrates one way in which specific developmental information about children may be used.

TYPES OF ASSESSMENT

Descriptive and Anecdotal Records

The notes Mrs. Crane made for Jenny's file are an example of a *descriptive assessment* of Jenny's development. They describe a skill, a behavior, an accomplishment. This note does not compare Jenny with any other child. It does not suggest that Mrs. Crane had been trying to teach Jenny how to climb and so showed that her teaching method was successful. It is information about Jenny's growth and development and is related only to her age.

Descriptive developmental assessment goes on continually in the preschool. It is not always written; sometimes it is shared in conversation or simply remembered. It gives the teacher specific information about individual children and shows their progress in areas of development during the course of the school year.

By recalling that Jenny was not able to climb on the bar the day before, Mrs. Crane is able to make Jenny aware of her progress, and is able to report the accomplishment to Jenny's parents. The awareness of ''where the child is'' developmentally gives the teacher opportunities to help children recognize their progress. Such specific instances contribute to the child's self-concept and self-esteem. They also provide a basis for individual planning.

Gains in physical skills such as Jenny's are easy to observe and record. Other types of behavior can also be included in the written file or in the teacher's memory: a child stops crying when the parent leaves, begins going to the bathroom without asking for help, learns the names of other children, and talks more in a group. In all of these areas of behavior, descriptive assessment is specific and applies only to the child being assessed. It does not indicate how other children would perform in a similar situation; it does not suggest what would be expected of most children of the same age. The standard of comparison is what the individual child has been able to do in the past. Jenny is compared to herself, not to Mary or George.

Criterion-Referenced Assessment

Another purpose of assessment is to see if a child is making progress toward a specific goal that has been set for him or her. If Jenny's parents or Mrs. Crane would like her to learn her home address, testing her ability to recall her address is similar to the observations previously discussed but has an added element: how does Jenny's performance compare with what her teacher would like her to do? This type of assessment does not compare Jenny with other children, but with a standard of mastery. It is not a competitive assessment in which Jenny is scored on the basis of her superiority over others only on the basis of her mastery of a task.

"I always tell the children they are coming with me to take a test—not to 'play a game.' I don't want them to be afraid of tests."

Teacher

If observations or other measures of performance are used to indicate progress toward a specific goal, they are often called *content-* or *criterion-referenced* measures. This means that the teacher (or tester) has in mind a level of performance against which the child's behavior is compared: "Mark can count to five this week. I'm going to try to get him to count to ten by the end of the month." The essential feature of criterion-referenced measures is that the performance expected is stated in explicit terms and does not compare the child with other children.

Norm-Referenced Assessment

A teacher or parent may, however, want to know how a particular child compares with other children. "My four-year-old is reading simple words already. Is this unusual? Are other four-year-olds able to do the same?" "Roger is shorter than some of the children in his class. How does this compare with 'normal' growth patterns?"

The teacher can answer such questions only by observing other children in the group. If more precise information is desired about reading ability at age four or norms for height, the teacher would compare these children against reading performance or growth charts that are developed from measurements of hundreds or thousands of children. The teacher could then tell parents more precisely how their children compare with others—for example, "Eight out of ten boys his age are taller than Roger." Assessments of this kind are called *norm referenced* because they compare the child with a large group of other children who have been measured in exactly the same way.

A NATIONAL DEVELOPMENTAL SCREENING PROGRAM

Since 1969, the Social Security Act has included an amendment that provides for federal funds and requires, as part of the Medicaid program

> such early and periodic screening and diagnosis of individuals who are eligible under the plan or are under the age of 21 to ascertain their physical and mental defects, and such health care, treatment, and other measures to correct or ameliorate defects and chronic conditions discovered thereby as may be provided in the regulations of the Secretary [of the Department of Health, Education, and Welfare].

This program was prompted by a survey which showed that 20 to 40 percent of children in low-income families suffered from one or more chronic ailments, but that less than half of them were receiving treatment. After the program began, two million assessments of children led to referrals for almost half. Fifty percent were inadequately immunized; one-fourth had severe dental problems; and over 10 percent had impaired vision.

Diagnostic and Screening Information

Mrs. Crane notices that four-year-old David is restless, often hyperactive in a group, and frequently pays no attention to what is going on. During group story time, he quiets down when she brings him up to sit with her. She has had enough experience to recognize that David may have impaired vision. A simple Lazy Eye Test can help confirm her suspicion. This is called *diagnostic assessment*. Such assessment is usually done by a specialist and the results will lead to a decision about treatment or corrective action. The teacher in a center will rarely be expected or qualified to do diagnostic testing (although aides and volunteers are often trained by professionals to give the Lazy Eye Test). However, the teacher is expected to be sensitive to the signs that diagnostic assessment might be indicated. (Some of the signs the teacher might recognize are discussed in Chapter 17, "Working with Exceptional Children.")

Diagnostic testing and examination are usually conducted in areas of suspected disability—mental retardation, physical growth problems, neurological difficulties, and emotional problems. Diagnosis is sometimes essential in identifying children who may qualify for special assistance or enrollment

---

EXAMPLES OF SKILLS THAT MIGHT BE ASSESSED IN A PRESCHOOL PROGRAM

Each of the following examples can be used to determine whether a child possesses a particular skill. More specific information, such as the age at which the skill was acquired, the speed with which it can be accomplished, and the accuracy with which it is done, may also be relevant.

Self-Care

Ties shoes
Goes to bathroom without help
Buttons or zippers clothes

Physical Skills

Hops on one foot
Walks on a balance beam
Skips

Strings beads
Draws a circle
Follows line with scissors

Social Skills

Takes turns
Cooperates with others in a task
Follows the rules of the center

Visual Skills

Matches colors
Matches letters or numbers

Cognitive Skills

Counts to ten
Names colors
Sorts objects by shape or size

in special programs. It does not always involve developmental problems. Children from homes in which English is not a first language may be tested for command of both their native language and English in order to give the teacher information about the types of activities that are most appropriate.

Screening is similar to diagnostic testing except that it is an attempt to discover problems that have not been previously identified. Screening involves relatively simple procedures and is done on large groups of children with the expectation that some difficulties will be identified for the first time, for example, hearing loss or "lazy eye." Children who are suspected of having developmental problems are then examined more carefully to see if a problem does indeed exist and to determine appropriate remedial action, if necessary.

TYPES OF BEHAVIOR AND DEVELOPMENT TO BE ASSESSED

"I think every teacher should have some experience in doing a developmental inventory; it helps you look at children much more carefully."

Teacher

The information that will be included in a child's folder will depend on the goals of the program, the interests of the parents, and the requirements of the funding agencies. The observations that a teacher makes may cover only those types of behavior that are of particular importance to him or her, or they may cover specific skills that are assessed as part of the center program. These represent only a small portion of the range of behavior that might be included in assessment. Hundreds of measuring instruments are available on the market. Since the teacher's assessment strategy reflects the objectives set for the school and for each child, the list any program will use and the tests that are adopted will be developed by the director and staff.

METHODS FOR GATHERING INFORMATION

Descriptive Methods

Informal Assessment   Teachers and parents often make casual judgments to one another about children's ability or progress on the basis of impressions rather than on careful assessment of behavior: "George doesn't communicate very well," or, "Marie avoids other children." These evaluations are not part of the written records. Such assessments are much more useful if they include specific details to illustrate the evaluation. Are there particular things that George doesn't like to talk about? Does he have difficulty pronouncing certain words or letters? Does Marie avoid certain types of activities or does she show unusual sensitivity to rejection by other children? The specific information that informal assessment can offer gives both teachers and parents knowledge that will be useful in planning activities to help children acquire competence.

Anecdotal Reports   Mrs. Crane's informal observations of Jenny's climbing ability are perhaps the major source of information for the child's folder and the teacher's evaluation of progress.

Many written observations are running records that report information about a child or group of children over a period of time. Like the quick jottings of Mrs. Crane and her report of Jennifer on the trapeze, these records can be notes made on the spur of the moment and filled in later in more complete fashion.

Diary/Journal   Another method for summarizing information about a child is to record comments—at the end of the day or after a particular activity—describing what happened, how the child reacted or performed, the child's feelings about the activity, and any other information that seems pertinent. This sort of journal makes one teacher's experience with a child available to others. It also offers a useful source for describing the child's progress to the parents. Some parents find that such notes give them a more complete picture of the activities the child engages in during the day and how he or she responds to different situations.

Case Study   The case study is an interpretive, comprehensive account of a child's behavior and life circumstances accumulated over a period of time. Case studies gather a wide range of information and use it to create a coherent picture of the child, his or her family, and his or her behavior at school. The account may include a description of the child's first day at school, comments about the parent's reaction to the separation, the staff's analysis of the child-parent relationship, descriptions of social behavior, the child's response to other children, information about areas of difficulty or achievement in the school program, or any other topics that are of interest to the staff.

The case study is not often employed because of the amount of time it requires. It does, however, contain a great deal of information that can be used for individual planning. The extensive data included in such a study helps the staff understand behavior that is not comprehensible if viewed apart from other things that are present in the child's life. Case studies are especially helpful in determining whether a child should be referred to a specialist for professional diagnosis or in planning a specialized curriculum of activities within the school's program.

Quantitative Methods

Ratings and Check Lists   Ratings call for the teacher to use his or her prior observations about a child in order to make a judgment about a particular type of behavior. Figure 18.1 shows a scale for rating children's behav-

FIGURE 18.1

Example of Scale for Rating
Children's Behavior

Instructions: Please rate the way this child behaves by circling the corresponding number.

	Very Much	Quite a Bit	Slightly	Not at All
1. Talks easily to adults about what he or she thinks and feels	1	2	3	4
2. Attempts to work out things alone rather than ask for help	1	2	3	4
3. Has little respect for others' rights: takes toys, tries to get to head of line, etc.	1	2	3	4
4. Reacts to frustration by becoming aggressive or angry	1	2	3	4
5. Shows creativity in use of materials and toys	1	2	3	4

ior. A teacher who, over a period of weeks or months, has seen a child in situations such as those described in the rating scale has formed an opinion about the child. The teacher's judgment may be biased; he or she may have seen one or two occasions early in the year in which the child's response was clearly aggressive. From these samples of behavior, the teacher may have decided (too quickly) that this was an unusually aggressive child. Ratings are therefore biased by the teacher's unique experience with a child. They are more useful if two people make a rating and both are included in the child's folder. This helps neutralize the bias that each may have.

A check list gives the teacher an opportunity to indicate items of behavior that the child displays without rating the quality of behavior. For example, a check list of preschool skills might include a list of colors. The teacher may check those that the child knows, thus indicating the specific profile of performance and showing the teacher what colors to emphasize in future activities in which the goal is to teach a given number of color concepts. Check lists usually request a "Yes" or "No" judgment, rather than an evaluation of level of skill.

Ratings and check lists are really forms for recording observations and impressions of past observations. They can be useful in directing the teacher's attention to specific bits of behavior about which he or she wants information. The trick is to choose items carefully. The best items are those that elicit specific information about a behavior that occurs often. Repeated observations give a good basis to make the judgments called for by these techniques.

Observations and Interviews Observations can be very systematic methods of assessment. For example, a staff wanting to have an accurate indication of the social behavior of a group of children could select thirty minutes each day when the children were engaged in a given activity. During this time, they could count the number of times each child participated in activities cooperatively as well as the number of occasions he or she was involved in disagreements or quarrels.

Observing children and recording specific kinds of behavior affords a new perspective on their actions and on the style of the adults who work with them. Watch, for example, the number of times one child approaches another. What is his or her technique for getting attention—verbal request, whining, smiling, touching, pushing? How does this child approach an adult? Does he or she pull at the teacher's clothing and interrupt conversation with another child? What is the teacher's response? Does he or she give the child direct, undivided attention, or try to respond while continuing to do something else? Compare the behavior of various children and the different responses they receive from the teacher.

Observation gives the new teacher a chance to analyze the behavior of individual children and the pattern of activities of the center. It may easily make him or her aware of things that were not clearly in focus before. As a method for gathering information, observation offers the advantage of specific detail. It also provides information about behavior that is relatively spontaneous—not altered by conditions that are required for many kinds of testing—thus giving it a special validity as a basis for assessment.

Observations thus give specific instances of the level of skill or of the behavior being assessed. Observations communicate to parents in ways that ratings or general assessments could not.

On the other hand, observational data can create a mountain of descriptive information that is difficult to read and evaluate. If you were to write down everything that a child did in a period of five or ten minutes, it would be obvious that hours of observation could produce a large file of descriptive material.

Although observations are indeed made of actual behavior, that behavior is influenced by the setting in which it occurs. Hitting and pushing among a group of boys will happen more often in an outdoor game than at story time. Therefore, the observer must indicate that the particular behavior described happened in response to something someone else did (aggression in response to attack), or in the context of an activity that may provoke certain behavior (running and shouting as part of a group game), or was shaped by a given expectation of the staff (sitting quietly at a table while waiting for juice to be poured).

Interviews are, at their best, carefully guided conversations. The rationale of interviewing is simple: if you want to know what people do or think, ask them!

Interviews may be quite specific, detailed, and written out in advance; or

"I like to use a tape recorder to talk with the children about their work. They evaluate their own progress, in a sense. Parents love to hear them, too."

Owner

they may be unstructured. Usually, interviews are conducted with adults—parents or teachers—to gain more information about children.

Interviews are used less frequently in assessment than other techniques, primarily because of the time and expense involved in interviewing. They also tend to be less structured than other forms of data gathering. This technique is more useful when the questions are phrased to allow for a wide range of possible answers.

Teachers will use a combination of observations and interviews in practical ways. Experienced teachers can, with a quick glance, or by overhearing snatches of a conversation, get a great deal of information that is significant. The important part of both techniques is for the teacher to have a clear idea of what he or she wants to know.

"Parents who are anxious about their child's intelligence won't be satisfied with any IQ score. If it's high, they'll pressure the child to live up to the high IQ; if it's low, they'll push to increase it!"

Teacher

Tests   The term *test* is used in many ways and has various meanings in different contexts. We use it here to refer to a situation in which several specific tasks or questions are presented to a child who is then asked to perform the tasks or answer questions. For example, a test item might be designed to measure the child's knowledge of spatial relationships (*over, under, behind, beside, in,* and so on). The child's performance on such items is scored against a standard of correct responses. The scores on test items are totaled; if the test is complex and includes several different types of items, subscores may also be provided. Tests are intended to elicit behavior of a sort that can be judged either right or incorrect.

As we use the label, a *test* is a device that produces a score based on a number of items designed to measure a particular ability—spatial skills, reasoning ability, number recognition, or conceptual knowledge.

Tests come in many forms and cover a wide range of skills and aptitudes. They are sometimes used to assess the success of an educational program; evaluations of Operation Head Start and Project Follow Through involved the use of several different kinds of tests. On the following pages, we will discuss the various types of tests that are available.

The first intelligence tests were developed by Alfred Binet in Europe to help predict which children would be likely to fail in school.

Intelligence tests   Intelligence tests are much less popular now than they were a few years ago. Tests developed recently are more likely to be designed to provide information about specific skills and abilities. The scores from these tests are useful in curriculum planning and in assessing the level of mastery of a given child so that individual teaching can take place. Tests for very young children include many items that require a motor rather than a verbal response.

Many of the tests of cognitive functioning are standardized and must be administered only by trained personnel. However, there are some tests of cognitive skills that can be administered by the teacher without special train-

---

STANDARDIZED TESTS

The term *standardized tests* usually refers to measures that have been developed by extensive testing, revision, and retesting of large numbers of children of specific ages who are chosen to represent different sexes, and ethnic and socio-economic backgrounds. The procedures for administering the tests are worked out carefully and must be followed precisely in order to make comparison valid. Such tests are given by persons trained in their use. Unless administered by qualified persons, the results are not reliable and should not be reported or made a part of a child's record. The best-known standardized tests are the Stanford-Binet Intelligence Scale and the Wechsler Intelligence Scale for Children.

---

ing in testing. For such tests, some practice is required to follow the instructions and to get some experience in giving the test.

Instruments for measuring cognitive ability may provide useful information for the child's folder. Any assessment of intelligence will be selected by and conducted under the supervision of the center director.

Even though you will not be administering tests as a regular part of your job, some familiarity with various types of test items may be useful. Figure 18.2 shows examples (some hypothetical) of items used to assess different areas of behavior and development.

Tests of social competence and behavior   Instruments designed to measure social behavior do not quite fit the category of *tests* as we have used the word in discussing measures of mental abilities. Consider an attempt to assess some familiar social behaviors—sharing, cooperating, independence, or assertiveness, for example. Items in mental tests have answers that can be reasonably judged as correct or incorrect, but assessment of social behavior calls for judgments of whether a child does or does not exhibit certain types of behavior. The standard of the evaluation may reflect the test makers' opinion about what constitutes cooperation, independence, and the like. There may be disagreement about such judgments; one person may view a particular behavior as aggression but another may regard the same behavior as an assertive or independent act.

Measures of social and emotional performance are not as well developed as tests of cognitive abilities and skills. Although many of these devices have been produced (Walker, 1971), they are less trustworthy than cognitive tests.

FIGURE 18.2

Examples of Items on an Achievement Test

Skill/Level	Setting	Procedure	Response Expected
Naming objects from memory/3- and 4-year-olds 	Child and teacher are seated across from one another at a small table. In a concealed location teacher has six different items commonly used by child and whose names he or she knows—*Examples:* doll, book, ball, spoon, car, crayon.	For a total of six different trials, teacher places any two of the objects in front of the child, side by side, and says, "This is a game where I'm going to take one of these away while your eyes are closed. Look at the objects and think what they are. Now, close your eyes and don't look while I take one away. Open your eyes. What did I take away?"	Child should *name* the object that the teacher removed. If the child simply points to where the missing object was located, teacher should rephrase question so that the child understands he or she is to *tell* the teacher *what* was taken away—*Example:* "What was here a moment ago that isn't here now?" *Score:* 1 point for each name correctly given
Knowledge of word meaning/ Preschoolers	Teacher and child seated facing one another across small table. Teacher has 10 cards each of which contains four pictures—all elements essentially alike in each set of pictures but arranged in different relationships—*Examples:* over, on, under, with, beside, around, in, through. . . .	Teacher asks child to look at each card, one by one; as he or she does so, the teacher reads a sentence describing one of the pictures—*Example:* "The cat is in the barrel." Then the teacher says, "Put your finger on the picture that shows what I said about the cat."	Child is expected to put a finger on picture asked for (or to point to it). *Score:* 1 point for each correct answer. (If child does not respond, sentence and instruction may be repeated.)

Continued on next page

FIGURE 18.2 *(Continued)*

Skill/Level	Setting	Procedure	Response Expected
Verbal facility using parts of speech/5-year-olds	Teacher and child seated comfortably together. Teacher has list of 40 questions—one for each of 40 pictures which are designed to elicit word responses containing various parts of speech.	While child looks at a picture, teacher asks question associated with it and calling for answer that contains desired parts of speech— *Examples:* "What is the girl doing?" (crying); "What is different about these two circles?" (one is bigger).	Child is to give verbal answer in appropriate word form. *Score:* 1 point for each correct answer

This is, in part, because the behavior has less clearly defined responses than a test of vocabulary. A test of "cooperative behavior" cannot be constructed with all the correct responses known in advance. There are many different ways to display cooperation, and the inclination to be cooperative varies with the situation. Interactive behavior is thus more difficult to assess than cognitive ability.

Behavior that involves attitudes or feelings presents special difficulties for test developers. The young child does not easily describe feelings. The test administrator can try to make inferences about feelings from what the child does, but such inferences are risky because they are not necessarily reliable. Self-concept, for example, is an internal process that is not easily assessed by asking young children about themselves. Although there are attempts to measure these affective areas, this type of assessment is not as well developed as others.

Readiness tests In addition to tests that measure an underlying general ability (intelligence, for example) which is assumed to develop slowly or to have a natural basis in inherited characteristics, there are tests designed to assess skills that can be taught. These measures, often called *readiness tests,* indicate preparatory skills that the child has already acquired and that will be useful in mastering a more complex pattern of behavior. The most familiar tests of readiness assess preparation for school work, especially reading and arithmetic. Such tests measure skills, or knowledge, of specific competencies

FIGURE 18.3

Examples of Items from a
Test of Social Behavior

Item no.   1

Sally is at school.

A new girl comes to the class.

At recess, the new girl comes over to talk
to Sally.

Which one is Sally's face?

Reproduced from V. G. Cicirelli, W. H. Cooper, and R. L. Granger, *Children's Attitudinal Range Indicator* (New York: Westinghouse Learning Corporation, 1968). Courtesy of Professor Victor G. Cicirelli, Purdue University.

such as vocabulary, recognition of letters and numbers, recognition of quantities (*more, less,* or *same*), ability to match shapes or numbers, and knowledge of basic concepts that involve reading comprehension or computation of problems in simple arithmetic.

Developmental tests   Devices designed to measure levels of development may cover any area of behavior. For young children, they usually include some indicators of physical maturation and motor ability. They are designed to offer information about the growth of a child in any of several areas and are thus scored according to performance or development that is expected at a given age. In this sense, they compare the child with age mates. However, the child is also assessed against a normal pattern of growth.

The previously described approaches to assessment and evaluation of development and competence share a single goal even though they use different techniques and accumulate different types of data. They help the preschool staff understand the child's current developmental needs and recent progress. The staff can use this knowledge to plan individualized programs that are adapted to the needs of each child. Such information also offers a perspective that guides the teacher in daily interaction with the children and provides specific details that are useful in conferences and in joint planning with parents.

REFERENCES

American Psychological Association. 1974. *Standards for Educational and Psychological Tests*. Washington, D.C.: American Psychological Association.

Anderson, S., and S. Messick. 1974. "Social Competency in Young Children." *Developmental Psychology*, 10, 282–293.

Beatty, W. H., ed. 1969. *Improving Educational Assessment and an Inventory of Measures of Affective Behavior*. Washington, D.C.: Association for Supervision and Curriculum Development.

Cicirelli, V. G., W. H. Cooper, and R. L. Granger. 1968. *Children's Attitudinal Range Indicator (CARI)*. New York: Westinghouse Learning Corporation.

Cohen, D. H., and V. Stern. 1958. *Observing and Recording the Behavior of Young Children*. New York: Teachers College Press.

Downing, J., and D. V. Thrackray. 1975. *Reading Readiness*. London: Hodderas Stoughton.

Gordon, R. 1975. *Interviewing: Strategy, Techniques, and Tactics*. Rev. ed. Homewood, Ill.: Dorsey Press.

Johnson, O. G., and J. W. Bommarito. 1971. *Tests and Measurements in Child Development: A Handbook*. San Francisco: Jossey-Bass.

Johnson, O. G. 1976. *Tests and Measurements in Child Development: Handbook II*. San Francisco: Jossey-Bass.

Lindberg, L., and R. Swedlow. 1976. *Early Childhood Education: A Guide for Observation and Participation*. Boston: Allyn and Bacon.

Mediax Associates. 1978. "Head Start Profiles of Program Effects on Children." *Newsletter*, 2 (November).

Walker, D. K. 1971. *Socioemotional Measures for Preschool and Kindergarten Children: A Handbook*. San Francisco: Jossey-Bass.

CHAPTER 19

THE USES AND MISUSES OF RECORDS

INTERPRETING ASSESSMENT DATA

Teachers need a great deal of information to plan a suitable program for individual children and the group as a whole. Not only do they need test scores and other assessment data, but information about the family is also necessary. The school records offer the staff a versatile source of knowledge about the child and the family that is essential for careful planning.

Nowhere is the concept of the whole child or the whole family more useful than in planning an educational program. An assessment of a child that indicates an emotional problem, anxiety, irritability, or unexpected dependency may fit with information from the records that the parents are recently divorced or that the father is unemployed. A note from Robin's mother that the child is soon to have an eye operation is crucial in planning the activities for Robin and for anticipating her forthcoming experience. Staff members need all the information they can get; records of family status and of individual developmental progress are blended together in preparing the preschool for the child and the group.

The use of records for planning also involves communicating with parents about the child and about the curriculum. These two tasks—planning the program and communicating with parents—require the staff to evaluate information in the file, to determine its meaning, and to decide a course of action for the pattern that emerges. These judgments must be based on careful consideration of what assessment scores indicate and the reliability of the results. The records contain a range of information beyond individual assessments. The personal confidential nature of much of these data places responsibility on the staff to interpret and use the data in a wise and responsible way.

What Do the Scores Mean?

Scores that are produced by tests, rating scales, check lists, observations, or descriptive accounts do not speak for themselves. They must be interpreted—given meaning by the staff or parents. The following four standards or references are frequently used in interpreting scores and deciding what to do about the information they offer:

1. *Does the information suggest a developmental problem?*   Information of any kind about a child's behavior may indicate the existence of a problem that should be investigated further. Scores that are unusually low or behavior that is a problem to the child or the staff may signal that a more complete assessment is required. Test scores are not usually precise enough to give a clear indication of problems, but they may suggest the need to consult with a specialist.

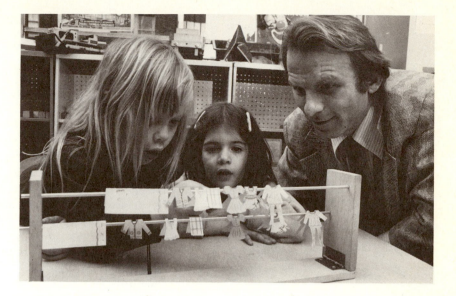

2. *How does the child compare with his or her peers in behavior or performance?* This criterion is useful in making curriculum decisions or planning for individual children. Is the child learning or growing at a faster rate than others of the same age? Scores may indicate that a child is far ahead of peers and that special attention should be considered. In using this standard, the teacher recognizes that "normal" behavior covers a wide range of possibilities. Within this range, children should be allowed to progress at their own rate.

3. *Does the child's performance meet the goals and objectives of the preschool?* Progress of any child is judged against the expectations that the staff have for the individual child or for the group. In these assessments, differences between children are not important; all children may be expected to reach a certain level of performance or acquire a given behavior. Performance is judged against these objectives, not against the scores of other children.

4. *How does the child's behavior match the objectives and goals of the parent(s)?* Parents have their own internal norms for evaluating the performance of children. They may be dissatisfied if their child is not the best or nearly at the top of the group. Others may not be concerned about assessment as long as there is no reason to believe that the child is showing serious developmental problems.

The meaning of assessment information thus depends on the expectations of the staff and the family. In all instances, the information is given meaning by the preceding standards.

Cautions for Using Test Results

Some assessment data, especially scores from tests, need to be used carefully and approached with a touch of skepticism. In the past, public confidence in testing has sometimes led parents and teachers to treat scores as statements of a child's true and lasting ability. The scores helped determine how a child was treated, not only in decisions about curriculum but also in ways that expressed the adult's belief about the child's ability and probable academic future.

Several studies in elementary schools show that teacher's expectations of the child's ability may determine how much time the child is given to respond to a question, how children are seated in the classroom, and the specific interpersonal behavior of teachers toward the child. Test scores have an impact on the child through the expectations that they create in the minds of adults.

There are two major reasons why these expectations are often unjustified.

Behavior Changes Rapidly in Early Years   Tests and other behavioral assessments should be used with caution with any age group, but they are

---

**TEACHERS' RESPONSES TO BELIEFS
ABOUT CHILDREN**

Teachers who call on a student to recite will wait a brief time for the child to respond. The "wait time" they allow for each individual seems to depend on their belief about the ability of the child. Children who teachers think are smart are given more time to come up with an answer than children they think are below average (Rowe, 1974).

Children in the first grade may be grouped in the classroom according to the teacher's estimate of their socioeconomic background and assumptions about their motivation and readiness to deal with school tasks. This grouping may take place before the children have shown their true ability in actual behavior (Rist, 1970).

Teachers who are interacting with a child they have been told is "bright" will act in a different way than they do with children they have been led to think are less able. In talking with "bright" children, teachers smile more, lean closer, use a more direct gaze, and nod their heads more (Chaikin, Sigler, and Derlega, 1974).

especially subject to misinterpretation with young children. One reason for caution is that the young child's behavior is changing at a very rapid rate. Performance one month will differ from that shown a month later because of the rapid rate at which the child is learning.

Learning is not uniform; it moves in surges and plateaus, not in an even, steady growth of skill. Test scores are statements of what the child can do at a particular time. They are not permanent testimony of an innate ability.

Scores Are Imperfect Approximations   Test scores or data from other measuring instruments are useful only if they are reliable indicators of what the child can do at the time the test is given. Many tests are relatively unreliable when used with young children partly because the rate of learning in the early years is rapid and uneven. Another reason for unreliability of scores is that tests are usually administered verbally and thus depend on the use of language at a time when the child's language competence and vocabulary are incomplete. Tests yield good data only if the subject has earnestly tried to do what the tester requested—a questionable assumption at any time, but especially shaky with young children. Tests give only rough approximations of what a child can do; they are most useful if not taken too seriously.

Factors Affecting Test Results

The response of a child to a test is affected by several conditions that may be present at the time of testing.

Skill of the Test Administrator   The response of the child is affected by the skill of the person giving the test. A skilled tester will establish trust and make the child feel at ease before presenting items of the task. If the child is not thoroughly familiar with the language of the test or with the materials used, the response may not show true ability. Some children are apprehensive about tests and may be anxious in the testing situation. Such motivational factors may alter the accuracy of the child's responses.

Cultural Bias   One of the most common sources of assessment error is cultural bias. Assessment devices call for behavior that the tester believes may have been learned. Learning depends on the child's experience in his or her family and community. If the test is developed with middle class white children in mind, it may not, indeed probably will not, be equally valid with children from other social class and ethnic groups.

Behavior of children on achievement tests differs from one ethnic group to another as well as between different socioeconomic backgrounds within each ethnic group. Research studies have shown that test responses of children in the first grade have different patterns for different ethnic groups—

"I asked one of the migrant children to tell me what a *cushion* is. He said, 'It's something to sleep on.' I had to mark it wrong, according to the test answers."

Teacher

Chinese, Jews, blacks, and Puerto Ricans. Within each group, the level of scores was different for children from high and low socioeconomic backgrounds (Lesser, Fifer, and Clark, 1965; Stodolsky and Lesser, 1967). (See Figure 19.1.)

The logic underlying most tests is, ''The child has had an opportunity to learn this information; it is part of his or her daily experience. If the child does well, it shows that learning has taken place. If the child's performance is below average, it indicates some delay in learning and thus a lower aptitude or ability.''

If the child has not had the experiences that provide an opportunity to learn the material included in the test, the items are *culturally biased*. Or, if some children have had more extended experience than others, they have an advantage. This means that they score higher on certain items and in that sense are better prepared for particular kinds of new experiences in school. It is possible, however, to construct a test that includes items that are biased in favor of children from a given ethnic group or from low-income or minority backgrounds. The items would be constructed by using experiences and vocabulary that are more familiar to a particular group.

In considering assessment devices and tests, you might ask whether the

FIGURE 19.1
Patterns of Ability by Social-
Class Level

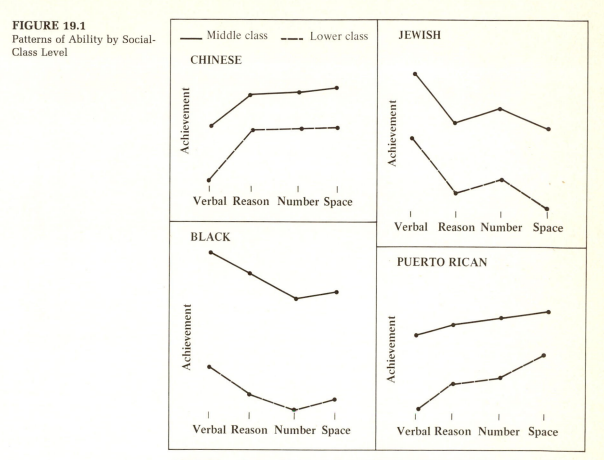

Adapted from Lesser, Fifer, and Clark, "Mental Abilities of Children from Different
Social Class and Cultural Groups." *Monographs of the Society for Research in Child
Development 30,* No. 4, Serial No. 102 (1965): 65–68.

children in your class have had the experiences that the test items call for.
Is it a culturally fair test or would other items sample the experience of some
children in a better way?

The Testing Situation   Performance on any test may be affected by the
testing situation. The mental condition of the child and the circumstances of
the setting in which the testing takes place may affect the result. Fatigue,
stress, conflict at home, or poor health may alter the child's concentration
and motivation to do well. Excessive noise while the test is being administered, outside curricular activities that may be heard in the testing room, or
the physical features of the room (lighting, distractive toys) contribute to
errors in responding to test items.

HANDLING SCHOOL RECORDS

The Preschool's Data Bank

Occasionally, a newspaper story reminds us of the vast amount of information that credit services and government agencies accumulate on private citizens in this country. There is justifiable concern about how such information is used and whether the rights of citizens are being properly protected. There is also concern about the validity of the information being collected and the secrecy with which it has been gathered and used. Recent legislation now restricts access to information about individual citizens. The Educational Rights and Privacy Act of 1974 protects confidentiality of data about citizens, except under certain conditions. The versatility of computer technology and the rapidity with which information can be stored and shared make this an important issue.

Preschools accumulate their own files of information on the children and families they serve. Although they are not usually seen as comparable to the data in the files of credit agencies, the preschool's records often contain personal and sensitive information, which is gathered at the time of admission and through other standard administrative procedures. The records may also include data from research studies and the results of assessments done as part of state or national evaluation programs.

Individual and Family Data   Planning a school experience for children requires that the parents and staff provide a significant amount of information about the family. This can be used to construct a personal picture of the family. As public agencies become increasingly involved in funding child care and education, the amount of information gathered will also increase. Many funding programs have specific qualifications; only families meeting specified criteria are eligible or are entitled to priority in admission. Many programs are oriented toward low-income and minority populations or are restricted to individuals who have demonstrated financial need. The child's family must supply the information that the staff needs to show that the child is entitled to the services provided by public funds. Evaluation of the effectiveness of child care programs or audits of the degree to which the preschool is following state or federal guidelines require that the records contain the relevant information.

The following kinds of data are used for administrative purposes—to establish eligibility, for example—and for developing a curriculum of activities for the children and their families.

Applications for admission: Names, addresses, employment status of parents/guardians; family composition; description of particular problems.

Family and child's history: Family status, occupation of parents, health history, allergies, special problems, sleep habits, toileting habits, siblings' health, immunization, illnesses.

Emergency and identification: Parents'/guardians' names, addresses, home and work phone numbers; neighbor's and friend's names and phone numbers; names and phone numbers of physician or others in event of emergency; names of persons authorized to pick up child; names of persons in car pools; information about divorce status and custody rights.

Child's performance records: Tests of motor development; diagnostic test results covering mental, social, and psychological development; teacher's comments and staff observations.

Eligibility forms: Family income, monthly expenditures, and other such information necessary to establish the school's eligibility for educational funding and food reimbursement.

Administrative records: Tuition level and record of payments; financial information; absences; special problems related to ability to pay or reliability in making payments.

Research and Evaluation Data   In addition to the information gathered by the preschool staff, there may be other kinds of data in the preschool files. If the program is publicly funded, or if research projects are conducted with the school staff or children, other information may be needed. Some additional data may be required by agency regulations.

Research data may consist of test results, reports of developmental screening, responses to studies of moral development and aggressive, cooperative, or sex-typed behavior, or observations of emotional problems. These are kept in the files of the research group but may also be in the school records of a child and family.

The files may also contain evaluation results from tests taken by children, forms filled out by parents, releases and permissions forms, evaluations of the school and staff, observations of children, interviews with parents, and comments about the program.

Providing Information for Parents

Test data and other types of information about children and parents are usually gathered to help the school prepare its program or to provide some assistance to the child. The "misuse" of information is not intentional. It may come about inadvertently or as the result of a sequence of events that were unexpected.

Consider, for example, a situation in which parents of four- and five-year-olds come to the director of a preschool to express concern about their children's readiness for kindergarten. Underlying the parents' questions is a worry about whether their children are bright enough to achieve as well as

"I won't sign a release for the center to observe or photograph or test my son. He has a speech impediment and I'm afraid the information might be used in a way that will cause him embarrassment."

Parent

the parents would like. Questions may also reflect a concern about whether the children are prepared to make a comfortable transition to the demands of the classroom. The director tries to be reassuring, but the parents press for more specific information—they want to be certain. So, in this particular case, the director decides to be more systematic.

A local college is contacted and the director requests some help from the educational psychology department. With the approval of the children's parents, arrangements are made for interns from the clinical training program to give the children a battery of tests to determine their readiness for school.

Imagine the scene. The director begins to tell parents during their individual conferences about the test results. One mother is eager to see the scores and asks to look at her child's folder—the preschool's file on the child and family. As other parents become aware that this is possible, they, too, ask to see their children's files.

Within a short time, a small group of parents are crowded into the office and are chatting about respective test scores, comparing each child's results. The next day, other parents report to the director that they have heard unfavorable comparisons made about children by some parents. They are especially concerned that this may be overheard by the children. The director realizes that the parents saw not only the school readiness scores but the results of an IQ test as well.

One mother who has discovered that her child's IQ score is lower than that of some other children makes an appointment for a conference, during which she tries to persuade the director to work intensively with her daughter. The director, who believes that IQ can't be affected significantly by such training, tries to explain without making the parent feel that the child is likely to do poorly in school.

The director has inadvertently created problems, not only for the school, but also for the families and children as well. Although nothing unethical has been done, testing the children was scarcely worth the anxiety and poor public relations it created.

Preschools and centers need to gather data for curriculum and program planning. This can be done in a way that protects the parents and children who provide the information.

Respecting the Rights of Families

"I liked having my daughter attend the university lab school, but they were constantly interrupting her play to test her."

Parent

The rights of children and their families may be compromised in two ways: first, the testing or experimental task may be uncomfortable or embarrassing, and second, the data gathered may be misused.

Most research and testing on young children carry no immediate discomfort or threat, but occasionally a child may be put in a situation that creates anxiety or fear. A scary picture or noise, a period of isolation from teacher or mother may be uncomfortable. Sometimes, research questions for parents and children may inquire about details of a personal nature or may even involve deceit for the purpose of the study. For some, the experience of being tested arouses anxiety, no matter how mild the test may be.

Once information is gathered, two precautions must be taken. One is to assure that information is kept confidential and that the names of children and families are not identified publicly. The other is to see that only authorized persons have access to the files.

Responsibility for discretion and confidentiality is not confined to those who conduct research studies. Although administrators and teachers may not be actively involved in collecting research data, they have a responsibility to handle such information in ways that protect families and children.

If parents are asked to complete forms that provide the preschool with information, they should be told why the information is required, how it will be used, and who will be authorized to see the forms. They should know, for example, if staff members will have access to files and whether volunteers or parents who help in the preschool have access to information in the preschool records.

Agencies often require the school to obtain personal family histories in order to qualify for licensing. Files are open to licensing agents who make site visits. Some schools may want to take pictures of children for publicity or educational purposes. Parents should be informed in advance of these events and asked to sign releases, which should be kept in the files. Sometimes, for personal or religious reasons, parents will object to giving certain kinds of information or to submitting to various health requirements. The administrator must see that the school's requirements for gathering information do not unnecessarily involve personal matters or violate privacy. Parents should be informed as to how information will be used and told of the procedures that will be used to assure confidentiality.

"Last year a professional photographer took pictures of my son. I was glad to see them, and I even ordered some. But this year, when an insurance salesman got my name and address from the school, I got mad. Whether it's photos or insurance, I don't think the owner of the school should have done those things without my knowledge or permission."

Parent

In most evaluation and research studies, families and children are protected by federal, state, or agency guidelines from procedures that may harm them or violate privacy. All research funded through the U.S. Department of Health, Education, and Welfare must adhere to regulations that assure such protection. Universities, colleges, and research institutes usually have committees that pass on the acceptability of each research proposal, assuring that subjects will not be harmed or embarrassed.

GUIDELINES FOR COOPERATING
WITH RESEARCHERS

Sometimes the staff of a school is invited to participate in research or evaluation. If so, the school has the legal and ethical right to set conditions by which researchers must abide. Staff members may want to draw up a philosophy of the preschool and formulate guidelines for their own particular needs. The following general principles may be useful in discussing the procedures under which research can be conducted:

1. The researcher will specify in advance the exact nature of the study, the time that will be required of those who participate, the number and approximate schedule of testing sessions (evenings, weekends, number of times in a week, and so on), and the qualifications of the research staff.
2. The director and staff of the school will have an opportunity to examine the testing instruments and to invite a group of parents to examine them if they have questions about the study.
3. The children and/or their parents are to be fully informed about the purpose of the research and the procedures involved.
4. The parents must give consent for their children to participate or will have delegated this responsibility to the director and staff.
5. The procedures of the study will not inflict physical, emotional, or mental harm on the subjects.
6. The information sought will not touch on personally offensive topics or invade the privacy of individuals or their families.
7. Information obtained about individuals or families will be kept confidential and will be protected from inspection by unauthorized persons.
8. The results of the study, if published, will not cause harm to the reputations or self-esteem of the children, families, or staff.
9. Results that identify an individual or a school will not be reported without express consent of the subjects or school *after* they or their parents have had opportunity to read or view the report and findings.
10. The participating school and parents will be provided with a report of the study and a description of the relevance of the findings for education and child development.

These guidelines are a sensible expression of the principle that research subjects should not suffer negative consequences as a result of participation in a study. When in doubt, ask yourself how people will feel when they have been through the research experience and when they see the results.

There is a potential problem with studies that give parents information about the stage of development or achievement of their children. Test scores or developmental growth charts, whether for physical, social, or mental characteristics, may serve to make parents anxious about the status and competence of their children. Especially when the children are young, parents are developing an impression of their intelligence, physical talents, and social skills. Information about the performance of their child compared to others in the class may reflect favorably or adversely on them as parents. Children are, to many parents, an extension of themselves—testimony of their background and their emotional maturity. It is difficult to overestimate the sensitivity of parents to information about the achievements of their children.

Be prepared for strong parental reaction to an assessment that compares children with one another in any significant way. Be especially cautious about letting parents know how others' children perform. This is a developmental period when parents are letting their children know, in subtle as well as not-so-subtle ways, how they perceive them. Comparisons have social significance for adults that is passed along to children.

REFERENCES

Chaiken, A. L., E. Sigler, and V. J. Derlega. 1974. "Nonverbal Mediators of Teacher Expectancy Effects." *Journal of Personality and Social Psychology,* 30, 144–149.

Keisler, S. B. 1979. "Federal Policies for Research on Children." *American Psychologist,* 34, 1009–1016.

Lesser, G. S., G. Fifer, and D. H. Clark. 1965. "Mental Abilities of Children from Different Social Class and Cultural Groups." *Monographs of the Society for Research in Child Development,* 30, Serial No. 102.

Rist, R. 1970. "Student Social Class and Teacher Expectations: The Self-Fulfilling Prophecy in Ghetto Education." *Harvard Educational Review,* 40, 411–451.

Rowe, M. 1974. "Wait-Time and Rewards as Instructional Variables: Their Influence on Language, Logic, and Fate Control." *Journal of Research on Science Teaching,* 11, 81–94.

Stodolsky, S. S., and G. S. Lesser. 1967. "Learning Patterns in the Disadvantaged." *Harvard Educational Review,* 37, No. 4, 546–593.

PART SIX

THE FAMILY AND
THE PRESCHOOL

A PROLOGUE   The job you get as a teacher may require you to work not only with young children but with their parents as well. Yet, many training programs do not provide practice teaching in parent programs. What is it like to work with parents? What happens if they disagree with your methods? And how do you deal with a parent who also happens to be your boss?

If you have never worked with parents, we suggest you volunteer in a co-op and talk with teachers in parent programs. Ask what they like most about working with parents—and what they like least. Imagine yourself in their situation. Depending on your personality and temperament, you can probably predict quite accurately whether you will like working with parents.

Remember, too, that some programs require a great deal of parent participation. Your job in such a program would mean daily interaction with parents as part of the teaching staff. Other programs may involve parents only superficially and your contact with them will be quite limited. Both situations have their advantages and disadvantages.

Part Six takes you through the various situations in which you are likely to meet and work with parents—from routine contacts during registration to close collaboration and cooperation in teaching their youngsters. There may also be situations in your job when you will be very much involved with parent policy groups and affected by the political nuances of working for a school that is controlled by the parents. Your knowledge and sophistication about such matters will be helpful.

No picture of a child in your class is complete without some knowledge of the parents' interests and concerns. Although some teachers will say they prefer to keep parent volunteers out of the classroom, most will agree that they are frustrated by lack of communication when mothers and fathers are not involved to some degree in their children's education.

As child custody laws change, you will be seeing more fathers in your classroom. The traditional nursery school and child care center has been dominated by women, and male teachers as well as father aides have been a rarity. For this reason, we have devoted a section in Chapter 20 to involving fathers, but keep in mind that all we have to say about parents and mothers applies to the fathers as well.

Whether or not you finally settle on a job requiring you to work with parents, the important thing to remember is that you are involved with parents by virtue of the fact that their child is in your classroom. You may not see much of them, and some parents may be too tired or busy to want to talk much with you, but your effectiveness in working with children depends heavily on parental support. A young child's parents and teachers are among the most important people in his or her life. Children's values and achievements depend on the kind of training they receive from the meaningful people around them. Even when parents do not work closely with you in the classroom, collaboration in reinforcing common goals determines to a great extent the success you will have as a teacher of young children.

CHAPTER 20

PARENTS IN THE PRESCHOOL

Parents play three major roles when they are involved directly with the preschool. They interact with the center as parents, in the day-to-day routines concerning their own child (providing information, picking up the child, and the like). Parents who volunteer as staff members play a supporting role by helping the center carry out its program. Some parents may interact as citizens and policy makers, sitting on advisory boards and helping in elections that may affect child care policy and funding.

PARENTAL INTERACTION IN ROUTINES
OF THE PRESCHOOL

The effective operation of a center depends on collaboration between parents and staff. The areas in which they cooperate touch both the child's life and the functioning of the school. For example, the staff needs precise information about the family and child in order to maintain a license. The center is required to gather health information about the child, to report instances of contagious diseases, and to keep an up-to-date file of other pertinent information.

The school depends on the parent to supply information that will help the teachers work effectively with each child—special health needs, home background, and other pertinent concerns. Often, parents must give permission for children to be observed, tested, or examined.

Initial Contacts and Requests for Information

Parents also need information from the staff. Initial contacts usually center around requests by parents for information about the school or center: What are the hours of operation? What ages does the school serve? What is the ratio of teachers to children? What are the costs? and so on.

The manner in which a school handles initial contacts is important. Visitors and potential enrollees gain lasting impressions and often judge the quality of a program from their first phone call or visit. In some centers, a secretary may simply answer questions on the phone and send a brochure to the interested parent. Other schools may suggest or require a personal visit from parent and child so they can see the setting and have their questions answered by a member of the teaching staff or the director. Some schools hold regularly scheduled open houses before they register new families.

Whatever the procedure, the initial contact is the time to set the tone of mutual support. In many subtle ways, the teacher can let the parent know what is valued in the school: "Our children and parents have worked very hard to plan the garden. One of the fathers helped us start the compost pile and another parent lent us a wheat grinder for our bread-baking project."

Comments and examples help parents understand their role in the school during initial visits. One parent reports her impressions of a visit:

> I called for an appointment to visit a child care center near my home and was told that I could come in anytime in the morning. They preferred that I leave my child at home, but I could bring him if I had to. I felt apologetic about bringing my son the next day, but I couldn't get a sitter. The person at the desk was busy on the phone, so after waiting for quite awhile, my son and I wandered into the classroom. Some of the teachers looked up at us, but were too occupied with the children to greet us. I finally found an adult who seemed to be less busy than others (and who smiled at me!). She told me what she knew about the program, but since she was a part-time aide, she could not answer many of my questions. I finally located the head teacher who told me to look around and pick up a brochure on the way out. I realize that children must come first, but my initial impressions were not very good. They were neither businesslike and efficient, nor were they warm and welcoming.

The manner in which requests for information are handled reflect the priorities and philosophy of a school or center. Administrators, teaching staff, assistants, and office personnel should be informed and agree on the role each will assume in giving information, welcoming visitors, and generally accepting responsibility for initial contacts.

Registration and the Initial Interview

The amount of paperwork required of a children's center demands an efficient system of registration. In some schools, volunteers help collate registration packets, which include health and emergency forms, eligibility for funding, and so on. These can be prepared in advance of registration and given to the parent at the proper time. Sometimes centers delegate responsibility for registration to one person; in others, the task is shared by administrators and staff. Those responsible need to be familiar with the forms and be able to help in completing them. They should have answers to such questions as: "How long is the TB test good for?" "What if I already have a health form on file at another school?" "Do you release this information to others?" "What if my religion does not condone medical physicals?"

Registration is also the time to help clarify concerns of parents and teachers. The initial interview should be scheduled to tie in closely with the registration procedure. This is the time to go over contracts; to explain procedures for paying and collecting tuition and other fees; and to inform parents of rules concerning illnesses—reporting them, rebates in tuition for absences, and requirements for keeping the child at home.

The school and parents will also need accurate information about emergency procedures—who is authorized to pick the child up, which doctor to call, and the routine each can be expected to follow. Parents need to understand their responsibility for keeping the school informed and up-to-date about changes in addresses and phone numbers.

Emergency and identification information should be on file from the child's first day at school. Other forms can be completed by the parents and medical people as time permits. Most licensing agencies will make allowances for late medical forms that require an appointment with a doctor, but the school is responsible for complete files when audits are held.

Interviews clarify expectations. What does the parent expect from the school? Are these expectations realistic? What does the school want from the parent by way of participation? Will the teachers be disappointed if the mother and father do not reinforce their teaching at home? How will the director feel if the parents are late in bringing their children or picking them up? These and related matters are best clarified before the child starts school. Special considerations regarding the child's needs, tuition arrangements, and family situation should be noted in the child's folder.

Orientation

This is the occasion to help parents adjust to the environment and philosophy of the school. The manner in which the staff handles orientation is a matter of administrative policy, needs of the school, and, in many instances, the personal preferences of experienced staff members. Some programs enroll large numbers of families at the beginning of a school year and find that a formal meeting of all the parents with speeches from the staff is the best and most efficient method. Other programs may elect to have small groups, each with a staff leader. In one co-op center, parents were assigned to lead a tour of each area of the school, explaining where supplies were kept, how the activities were handled, and what parents were expected to do. A private nursery school had children who had been enrolled and were familiar with school show new children around.

Whatever the method of orientation, the objective is to acquaint the parent and child with the school—its physical environment, the people in it, and some of its routines. This is a time to be relaxed, to put the new people at ease, to make them feel comfortable, and to encourage them to ask questions. Go easy on rushing through the rules and regulations. Assignments for participating parents, regulations, and requirements can be handed out in printed form for people to study at home. Be clear about responsibilities for work days, hiring substitutes, exchanging days, and so on. Group leaders can set a friendly tone by their style and reassuring manner. Serving refreshments and providing child care help create an unhurried atmosphere. Hand out lists

"Experienced volunteers designed a humorous booklet giving information about the daily routine along with suggestions about how to work with the children."

Director

of addresses so parents can form car pools; use name tags and introduce people. Have enthusiastic parents who have been in the program help the new parents.

In many respects, orientation for parents is much like the first day of school for their children. They need reassurance and plenty of time to get acquainted with their peers and to feel comfortable in their new environment. The patience and friendliness of the staff is an important element in helping parents make the transition from home to school.

The First Day

The first day is special for a variety of reasons: children, parents, and staff are encountering a new situation which may cause anxiety; parents will want information and attention; children may be afraid; teachers will be pressed to meet more than the usual number of demands.

Although some people will make a quick and smooth adjustment to the school, there will be others who feel some uneasiness and distress. Parents may be wondering: Am I doing the right thing for my child? Will he (or she) adjust well to the school? Are the teachers good teachers? Will the other kids be mean to my child? Will the teachers like him (or her)?

Teachers may have some anxiety, too. If a large number of families start on the same day, there may be more than the usual number of crying children, an increased likelihood of accidents, and more parents needing questions answered—all at the same time.

Even with the best of orientations, parents and children will need more of the teacher's time on the first day: "Where can I get some names for a car pool?" "What do you think about another philosophy of child care?" "I just wanted you to know I will be late tomorrow. How can I make up the time?"

"The first day I volunteered at school, the teacher stationed me in the yard and left for a coffee break without any instructions about what I was to do."

Parent

Some questions and comments are part of adjusting to a new environment; others reflect a need for attention and reassurance. Planning for the needs of parents and children on the first day means the teacher has to be prepared to spend more than the usual amount of time discussing, explaining, soothing, and generally attending to a variety of needs. Extra assistance from substitute teachers and volunteer parents can be very helpful in making the adjustment a smooth one. Some of these helpers can be prepared to hand out packets of information and extra forms that the parents might have overlooked or forgotten; others can be on hand to reassure parents or to comfort a child. Some parents may simply want to have the opportunity to chat with other parents.

The child's adjustment to school can be made easier if parents are clear about their options for staying or leaving on the first day. Some teachers feel a parent should stay at school until their child is comfortable. This is not always possible, especially for working parents. Other schools prefer to have the parent leave immediately, whether or not the child is crying. Some suggest that the parents stay in an adjoining room, but out of sight. Regardless of the manner of separation, parents should tell their child they are leaving— even at the risk of causing the child to cry. If parents simply disappear, young children will be puzzled and feel deceived. They may or may not cry, but their behavior may show a lack of trust in other adults or they may be distracted from their play because they are watching for the reappearance of the parent.

Parents need reassurance that their child will receive good care. "Don't worry, I'll stay with him and help him feel comfortable. Feel free to call me as soon as you get to work and any other time during the day to check on him"—such comments and suggestions go a long way to make the transition from the first day to a happy adjustment to school.

PARENTS AS VOLUNTEER STAFF

Parents come to the preschool or center with a wide variety of attitudes, experiences, and feelings about participation. Some are veterans; they know how to take part if they want to, and how to avoid commitments to anything that takes significant time or energy. Others are inexperienced and may be apprehensive or so focused on their own child that they have never considered volunteering or thought about their own role in the preschool.

Different Kinds of Involvement

There are many aspects to parental involvement in the preschool, ranging from minimal contact when the child is delivered in the morning and picked up in the afternoon to work as part-time staff in a parent co-op.

REMEMBERING MY FIRST DAY AT SCHOOL

(Reported by a Twenty-One-Year-Old College Student)

I remember sitting on the edge of the bed while my mom helped me put on my stretch socks and newly polished shoes. She braided my hair and gave me a blanket to take to school.

I remember the teacher showing me to my locker. I noticed that the color of the coat hook matched the locker. She pointed to a picture of an animal pasted over my locker and asked:

"Do you know what this is?"

"It's a pig."

"That's right. It's a pig, and your locker is the one with a pig on it."

I thought the pig was ugly. I wanted a donkey, but I was afraid to say so.

At the end of the day, the teacher told us to get ready to go home. I went to my locker and got my blanket. She said, "No, no. You leave your blanket in your locker." I wanted to cry. I was embarrassed because I didn't know I was supposed to leave my blanket at school. I felt it was my fault because I should have known.

To this day neither my mother nor the teacher knows how I felt that first day at school.

One part of parental involvement is contributing time and effort to the operation of a program. Parents have at least two reasons for participating in this way. In some schools, it is mandatory—a condition for enrolling the child in the center. Parents are asked to make verbal or written contracts specifying the kind of work they will do and the number of hours they will give to the program. The second reason is a desire to help the preschool in its task. This involvement is voluntary. In such instances, the teacher usually must take a more active role in encouraging parents to offer their services. It cannot be assumed that they will recognize the need or be eager to help.

Encouraging Participation

"During orientation, I mentioned to the parents that one of the fathers reupholstered the sofa in the parents' lounge. The next day, one of the mothers offered to make some drapes to match the sofa."

Director

You can't begin too soon! An excellent time to let parents know that participation is part of being a parent is during the initial contacts. Registration and orientation are excellent times for recruiting and for setting expectations. If your program requires parental participation, the time to let them know is when they request information about the preschool. The details can be included in packets that describe the program. If participation is voluntary, you can easily set the expectations by commenting on what other parents have done or are doing. Well before parents are asked to participate, it should be clear that yours is a school in which parents are involved and that their help is important for operating and maintaining the quality of the program.

Cooperation of new parents may also be encouraged by those who have been with the program for some time. An experienced parent volunteer can be helpful in answering questions, allaying anxieties, and generally anticipating some of the problems others are likely to face.

Newsletters, notices posted at the door, and short informal meetings can be used to let the group know what parents are doing. Providing child care during meetings is essential if maximum involvement is expected. Meetings should be held at times that are most convenient for the largest number of people to attend. Sometimes, this means arranging meetings on weekends, early mornings over coffee, or evening potluck dinners.

Some parents prefer to meet in their homes because of baby-sitting and transportation problems. In some circumstances, visiting the home is the best (and only) way to get acquainted and to make the contact a direct and personal one.

Many successful teachers prefer to find a common ground on which families can begin to share some mutual interests. Sometimes that place is the school room. Other times, the location may be less conventional. A teacher in a child care center reports:

> Seventy-five percent of our children come from one-parent families. If I relied on the old-fashioned, come-to-school parent conference, I'd never see most of the parents. Just the other day I took my car into a service station which was two miles out of my way so I could meet Jimmy's father. I took along some of Jimmy's art work and carpentry so I could chat with him while he serviced my car. I also shop frequently at a grocery store where Evelyn's mother is the checker. These parents really look forward to my informal visits and to me these are some of my most valuable parent involvement experiences. Besides, I get extra good service!

Some parents want to help but feel that they are not qualified or competent to work with children. They need reassurance and support from the teacher. They also appreciate having specific information about tasks that are clearly useful, but do not require a background of training and experience with preschoolers. Once a sense of confidence and ease has been established between the teacher and individual families, getting parents involved will be an easier task.

Perhaps one of the most important aspects of parental involvement is to give fathers and mothers a sense that this is their school and that they are in part responsible for the quality of the program. This sort of feeling comes about through the attitudes of the director and staff and the importance they attach to parental involvement.

What to Do with Parents in the Classroom

Even though parents have a great deal of experience with their young children, they cannot instinctively step into a role as volunteer staff member. They are unfamiliar with the routines of the school and may not have had experience with groups of children. If parents are to become useful members of the staff, teachers must be willing to spend time preparing them for their role.

Parents can participate in a great number of ways. Some may bring their own specialized skills and interests to enhance the curriculum. Others may contribute equipment, materials, or other resources; or they may help with administrative tasks—writing newsletters, keeping records, handling correspondence, and the like.

Whenever possible, parents should be given a choice among several tasks without having to make a long-term commitment to any one of them. For some, volunteering is an opportunity to try out new skills and to discover

> "I told the teachers that I wanted a job with some peace and quiet. They let me do the bookkeeping and filing in a corner of the office. I love it! I can be near the children in case they need me, but I don't have to deal with a bunch of noisy kids."
>
> *Mother*

THE CASE FOR PARENT INVOLVEMENT

1. *The teacher gets useful information about children from interaction with parents.* Parents provide data about home life, personal concerns, and skills that their children bring to school. This knowledge helps the teacher set realistic goals.
2. *Goals for children are best achieved if parents and staff collaborate.* Children are more likely to learn a task or exhibit a desired behavior if the important adults in their lives agree on and are consistent about the way they handle the children.
3. *Parents and teachers learn about child-rearing methods from each other.* The staff of the school is a resource for parents; they gain from seeing their children interact with others. Teachers learn from the practical experiences of parents who are more intimately involved with their children's personal preferences and habits.
4. *Parents are a resource for the school.* In many ways, parents have a great deal to offer the staff of a center. They may act as part-time staff, help with annual paint and clean-up tasks, assist in raising money, and provide transportation.
5. *Parents help shape public policy.* Child care competes with many other demands for public funding; active parent support may make the difference between a program's success or failure.
6. *Parents have a right to be consulted and involved in decisions affecting their children.* Most publicly funded programs mandate the consultation and active participation of parents, recognizing the benefits of collaboration between the home and school.

SOME THINGS PARENTS CAN DO

Telephone other parents
Help set up car pools
Check safety of playground equipment
Help with public relations
Organize fund-raising activities
Bring materials from home for school use
Paint, clean, repair equipment
Act as interpreter
Operate equipment

Supervise curriculum activities
Help with field trips
Care for a garden
Take care of pets when school is not in session
Help individual children with learning tasks
Bookkeeping, shopping
Arrange guest speakers for parent meetings

new interests. Most schools need nonteaching volunteers, and parents who do not enjoy working directly with children need not feel guilty if they choose to do administrative work or some other nonteaching task.

One of the most important aspects of training volunteers is to explain the specifics of the job to be done. A teacher's time is well spent in writing out a description of the job, with details about the kind of work, the amount of time to be spent, and helpful suggestions for carrying out the task. Volunteers report they very much appreciate specificity in descriptions of the tasks they are to perform. They want expectations to be clear.

Parents may feel unneeded when they are simply asked to stand in the play yard and supervise. They like to know where they should stand, what to look for, something about the rules and the kind of behavior that is allowed, and some idea of what to say to and how to deal with children who are breaking the rules.

"I liked working for Mrs. Martin because she always let me take charge of activities that the children enjoyed doing."

Parent

Teachers may be too busy themselves to spend time away from the children to train parents, but modeling for the parent and giving immediate feedback are very useful techniques in their training. Volunteers will be more helpful to the teacher if they are given meaningful work and if the teacher takes time to work alongside until responsibilities are clear. Many of the techniques used in working with young children also hold true for volunteers: teach in small steps, give immediate feedback, and use positive reinforcement. Tell parents when they have done a good job. Be honest and generous with praise. Avoid playing up mistakes; use redirection and make suggestions for alternative behaviors. Ask parents if they are enjoying their assignments, and let them know you could not have accomplished the day's work without their valuable help. Put them at ease with their work, let them know you support them, and assure them that their children benefit from their presence.

HELPERS IN THE ART AREA

Please plan to arrive fifteen minutes early to set up art materials for the day:

1. Take paint cans from kitchen to the easels.
2. Place one clean brush in each can.
3. Replenish easel paper (supplies are in cabinet).
4. Help children with paint aprons.
5. Help print first and last names of children on their paintings.
6. About ten minutes before snack time, remind the children they will need to finish their paintings and get ready for snacks.

Suggestions:

Do not ask the children what they are painting.
Encourage the children to do as much as they can for themselves, including putting on and taking off their aprons, writing their names, taking the paper off the easel, and so on.
Do not rush the children, or intrude on their work.
No splattering is allowed on walls and floors. Suggest that the paint be kept on the easel.

Please jot down questions you may have and bring them up at the staff meeting.

The effectiveness of parents as volunteers depends on their relationship with the staff. When they are made to feel welcome and needed and are rewarded for their efforts, they are more likely to contribute to the school's program.

INVOLVING PARENTS WITH ATYPICAL NEEDS

Some parents cannot easily fit into a traditional conception of participation. The circumstances of their lives—divorce, illness, cultural background, work schedules, and personal problems—require a different sort of involvement with the school.

Parents who work outside the home are less available and have less time to chat when they pick up or leave their children. In recent years, an increasing number of parents often cannot participate as volunteers. They have no time to take their turn and they probably don't have the energy. In these instances, "involvement" may mean that the teacher will spend extra time and make a special effort to be in touch with the parents and keep them informed of what is happening in the program.

Parents who are going through divorce or have been divorced recently are often under unusual stress. For them, child care is a vital service, a necessity

---

KEEPING PARENTS INVOLVED

Give parents useful things to do. Make them feel needed.
Plan activities that will entice them—interesting field trips,
cooking projects, tasks that involve their own child.
Hire or appoint a full-time coordinator to recruit parents.
Award door prizes to encourage attendance at meetings.
Give recognition for their work with certificates, artwork by
the children, publicity, dinners, and awards.

"During my divorce, the teachers at the center helped pull me through. They made exceptions to the co-op rules and went out of their way to help my child. They were the only family I had!"

Divorced Mother

Policies that restrict contact between the noncustodial parent and the child make that parent seem more remote and distant, intensifying the effect of the divorce for the child.

In some states, joint custody is possible and is seen as beneficial to the child.

"Things certainly have changed since I first started teaching school. We used to operate on the assumption that every child had one mother and one father."

Older Teacher

that may be the determining factor in allowing them to take a job. Their emotional and physical energy is absorbed by problems associated with marital dissolution: custody, visitation rights, property settlement, and perhaps a move to a new home. They may experience feelings of anger or guilt about the divorce or about the need to leave the child in a center. During this post-divorce period, parents are least able to give the child the support and attention he or she needs (Wallerstein and Kelly, 1975). Involving divorced parents thus presents a particular challenge to the teacher. Their personal needs are great; they have less to offer the school for the time being. It should not be a surprise if their participation is minimal.

The involvement of a parent without custody is a particularly sensitive matter. During initial stages of marital dissolution, both parents may want to see the child at the center or pick him or her up at the end of the day. After questions of custody and visitation have been settled by a court decree, there is a clear direction to follow. Until then, the teacher's task is to see that the child is not caught in the middle of the conflict. The school records should contain the vital information about the child's status and the names and addresses of both parents. It may be necessary to find out if the parent who has legal custody will permit the other parent to receive information about the child. Should the noncustodial parent be invited to meetings at the school? What should the teacher do if the parent without custody stops by to visit the child during the day? Issues of this sort are faced much more frequently now than a decade ago and the legal aspects of these situations may become clearer in the future. They present special problems in parent-teacher interaction.

Parents who have remarried also present special concerns. The child may continue to be in touch with a natural parent who does not have custody. The staff must be clear about the expectations and legal rights of *all* the adults involved—the custodial parent, the stepparent, and the parent without custody. The first principle is to be informed about the legal situation and the rights of each of the persons responsible for the child. Teachers should

HOW TEACHERS GET INFORMATION

When parents are working as aides in a program or are involved in a co-op, there are opportunities for communication and interaction focusing on a child's needs. But what about those parents who work long hours and do not have time—how does the teacher get information and what methods of communication are effective? Following are some suggestions for establishing contact with parents and obtaining information about the child and his or her family:

1. *Records on file:* Sometimes the teacher can learn more about the child's home history and background by consulting the files available to the school.
2. *Director:* There are differences in policies among schools. Sometimes the director prefers to relay concerns of the teaching staff to the parents. In other cases, the director may set up a parent-staff conference. The director will often provide teachers with additional information derived from parent conferences.
3. *Children:* The young children themselves are a valuable source of information about their lives outside the school.
4. *During drop-off and pick-up times:* The teacher can often have brief conferences with the parent when the child is checked in and out of the center. Much valuable information can be exchanged in a short period of time.
5. *Telephone:* Sometimes arrangements can be made for the parent to call the school during a work break or lunch hour. Or the teacher can get permission to call the parent at home in the evenings.
6. *Notes:* Pin a note to the child, or send a letter or report by mail.
7. *Special occasions:* Parents night, weekend work days, and family parties at the center are all times when teachers have the opportunity to talk with parents and share information.
8. *Informal occasions:* In some cases, teachers may make a point of shopping or taking care of personal business where some of the parents work so they can chat about a child.

be aware of the feelings of the parents about conferences, parent meetings, or other special occasions where both natural parents and the stepparent may want to be present.

There are other variations on the nontraditional family pattern that the teacher will occasionally encounter. A live-in boy friend or girl friend, for example, may play the role of parent by picking up the child, coming to parent conferences, and attending meetings. Again, the teacher should have clear instruction from the appropriate person about such situations. Occasionally, there will be instances in which both parents have custody. They may share the child by taking turns within a week, or the child may live with one parent for a period of time and then move to the other's home. The need to have information in accessible form is evident. Some of the issues involved are discussed more thoroughly in Chapter 9, "Keeping Children Safe."

INVOLVING FATHERS

"When my wife went back to work, I agreed to help with some of the chores at home. One of these was to go to my son's parent-teacher conference. It was such a waste of time that I suggested changing the format and, somehow, I got involved in school policies."

President, P-TA

"You really want to know why I don't visit my kid's class? I'm afraid the teacher will ask me something I can't answer. She'll see how stupid I am."

Father

You can no longer assume that fathers are secondary parents. Since the 1970s, they have become more actively involved in the lives of their children. Several forces have pushed them in this direction: the roles of men and women are being redefined; more women now work outside the home and child care is necessarily shared more often by fathers; and the proportion of fathers who seek custody of their children after divorce is rising.

Fathers may still feel awkward or embarrassed in visits to the school. Even though they are interested in their children's care and education, they need appropriate ways in which to express this interest. They may resist things they feel are childish, and may fear that the teacher will ask them for information or help they are unable or unwilling to give. They may worry about being inept in comparison with the expertise of a trained teacher or of other parents. One of the most effective beginning strategies is to ask for help in specific types of jobs—such as construction, moving of equipment, and maintenance—that are commonly considered to be "men's work." It also helps to make fathers aware that other men contribute time and talent

to the school. Men may more readily participate if they realize that they will be interacting with other fathers.

Once fathers come to the school, they often see what needs to be done to help the children. One teacher recalls such an instance:

> I noticed Jason's father arrive early each week, waiting in his car for the end of the school day. One day I invited him for a cup of coffee and asked if he would like to keep me company in the yard while I supervised the children. I left a standing invitation for him to join me for coffee any time, and as the weeks went by, he gradually became more involved with the kids and began taking an active interest in the program.

Initial contacts with fathers can sometimes be made by scheduling a home visit at a time when both parents are likely to be there and by including the father in the conversation. A teacher tells of the following experience:

> The father was at home; in fact he was the one who opened the door and invited me in. He did most of the talking because the mother spoke very little English. The visit wasn't going very well until I happened to notice some flowers he had planted. I admired them and with that he went into a long explanation about varieties and told me a great many details about their care. He cut some for me and insisted that I take them back with me. When I finally left, we still hadn't talked about his son and the boy never came into the room. But several days later, Mr. Y. brought some flowers to school for a holiday celebration. We talked to him and he returned the following week to show the children how to plant a garden. I was able to tell him how much we appreciated what he was doing for the children and he promised he would come again.

"Boy, those kids make me feel like a king! As soon as I walk into the school, they rush up to me and hang onto my hands and legs! I love it."

Father Volunteer

As with all human relationships, appreciation goes a long way with fathers. Those who feel that their efforts count and that their opinions are important will participate more than those who feel unwelcome.

PARENTS AS POLICY MAKERS

As Mrs. B., the director of Citywide Children's Center, went through the steps of setting up the large coffee pot and counting out enough measures to make thirty-six cups of coffee for the evening meeting, her mind was on a scene that she knew might take place in the next hour.

Mrs. W., president of the parent co-op group, opens the meeting: "At our last meeting we decided to settle a difference of opinion on curriculum by taking a poll. Tonight, I want to distribute the results that we have tabulated."

Responses of Eighty-Four Families and Ten Teachers of Citywide Children's Center Listed According to Order of Priority:

Parents	Teachers
1. Learning school-related skills	1. Strong self-concept
2. Good manners	2. Self-reliance
3. Getting along with other children	3. Getting along with other children
4. Strong self-concept	4. Learning school-related skills
5. Self-reliance	5. Good manners

In the past few meetings, Mrs. B. has felt more and more that her judgment was being challenged by a group of parents. The results of the survey would probably be close to what she had imagined. What then? Tonight she would have to defend her priorities or let Mrs. W. have her way. Maybe she would have to resign her job as director. "Life would be so much easier if I didn't have to deal with parents!" she thought. "I wonder if other teachers have these same problems?"

Mrs. B.'s situation is not an unusual one. Although she knows Mrs. W. personally as a parent and interacts easily with her on a one-to-one basis, tonight Mrs. W. is more than a parent; she is a member of a community group that wants to help set policy.

A conflict between parents and the preschool staff is a sensitive matter. Vigorous disagreements may last for months and the outcome may take any of several forms. On one side are the director and staff with responsibilities and rights covered in their contracts and with the influence that professional experience and training give them. On the other is a group of parents who (sometimes) have the ultimate power to make staff changes, including the directorship.

Policy making is one area in which parents can affect the life of a teacher. The specifics differ from place to place, but the issue is similar: what part will parent and community groups have in setting policy and running the school?

"Life for a teacher was simpler in the good old days."

Principal

Should Parents Help Govern Preschools?

The argument for parent participation in policy making is essentially philosophical. It is a matter of values and beliefs—a question of the right of parents to be consulted and to participate in decisions affecting their children.

Community control over the schools is not a new concept. In rural areas and small towns in this country, public schools were traditionally under the political and economic control of the community board. Over the past sixty years, however, the size and complexity of school systems has increased, education has become more professionalized, and administrators have assumed more control over the operation of districts and schools. One reason for this shift is a belief that training and experience give professionals a special competence that parents do not possess.

With the growth of professional training in early education, it is easy for teachers and administrators to act as experts and decision makers and to treat parents as clients or customers. This is based on a view that education is the business of educators or that child care is the business of child care professionals. This view, however, creates a gap in communication between the community and the school. It may lead to an educational or child care system that is divorced from the needs and values of the community it serves. In the past, separation of school and community has stimulated demands by parents for greater authority in policy making. At the preschool level, such concern applies especially to publicly funded programs in which parent advisory boards or committees may be required by law.

Teachers who are accustomed to dealing with a traditional, centralized authority and administrative structure may underestimate the influence of community groups. In many communities, the authority of the school director and board is shaped by public forces. The effectiveness of community opinion, a concerted effort by a small vocal group of parents, or the pressure from a union can exceed the teacher's expectations.

The disagreement over the curriculum between Mrs. B. and Mrs. W. might result in a compromise acceptable to both sides, but the issue itself persists: whose priorities will prevail? Parents often want to help define the goals of the school when their own children are involved. They may resent failure of the staff to consult them. A disagreement over priorities may be a symptom of poor relationships between the staff and the parents. Frustration with being ignored and brushed aside can become so great that parents may feel they need to assert their own ideas.

Conflicts between community groups and a school are less likely to develop when the communication between parents and the staff is open and positive. There usually will be early signs of dissatisfaction which the teacher will recognize in time to get in touch with parents about their feelings and objections. The chances of resolution are much better if problems are discussed as they arise rather than letting things build to a showdown. Communication with members of the community will reveal the nature of the basic problems and how they can be resolved.

"You can't assume teachers know what is best for our children. They have to be told by the parents."

Community Organizer

"Education is ineffective unless it grows out of the initiative of the people, speaks their language, and influences not only isolated individuals but the life of the whole community."

Educator

Types of Parent Power

In most situations in which you will teach, the parents' role in governance will have been decided before you become a staff member. Your first interest, perhaps, will be to find out what the structure of governance is. What form does parent participation take in making policy?

There are several distinct categories of parent power in relation to the preschool. The first of these is *personal persuasiveness*. Individual parents, or groups of parents, may approach staff members or the director, in informal conversations or at public meetings, with a request for a change in curriculum, staff, equipment, or scheduling. In some instances, parents may have no alternative to the center and must accept the decision of the staff; they have no formal power and must rely on their ability to negotiate with the director.

"Some of us overheard the volunteer talking to the children the other day, and we feel he is too directive."

Parents to Teacher

The staff may also be confronted by *spontaneous, informal groups* of parents who get together because of their common concern about a particular issue. Their effectiveness depends to a great extent on the number of parents affected, the extent to which their concern is supported by the local, state, or federal guidelines of the program, or on their own skill in creating pressure for change.

Parent advisory groups are another structure for community influence on a program. These groups may be appointed by the director-owner of the school or chosen in an election by the parents themselves. Such groups offer a forum for discussion of issues and for suggestions, grievances, and public pressure. They provide input and serve as a resource for the staff. Recommendations of advisory groups are just that—recommendations. Final decisions are made by the director, the school board, or some other agent. Advisory groups have influence, but their influence depends in part on the respect they command or their ability to arouse the community and to put pressure on elected officials.

"Sometimes advisory committees get the mistaken notion that they make policy. That's when we run into trouble."

Administrator

Other parental groups are mandated as part of a publicly funded program, which gives them more formal power. Some have authority to hire directors of programs and centers, fire personnel, set salaries, and make policy that is to be carried out by the staff. The power of these boards is often limited by their lack of specific information about the program. It is also limited by the greater professional knowledge of the staff and director and the amount of time that board members have to devote to the program.

Teachers and Policy Boards

The teacher who wants to develop competence in all aspects of the job should understand how parent boards and advisory committees work. The interaction that most staff members have with parent boards and committees falls into three general types: (1) social and routine interaction in which reports are presented, information provided on the program, and personal acquaintances and friendships established and maintained; (2) attempts to influence the board or committee to adopt a policy that represents a significant change from the present operation of the school; and (3) attempts by the board to make changes in staff, budget, or program.

The routine interaction between school staff and board will probably be handled by the director of the school. It usually follows an established procedure: reports of enrollment, description of the program, information about new equipment, announcement of special events coming up during the year, presentation of the budget, introduction of new staff members, information about trips or special events, requests for participation in clean-up day, and the like. There are some general rules that make this sort of interaction more effective and useful. Written reports should be prepared in a clear, readable form and distributed well in advance of a committee meeting; board members should not be called on to make hasty decisions. The format and content of records should be easily understood by nonprofessional board or committee members. Information about state, local, or federal guidelines that affect operation of the school should be readily available.

As a staff member who may want to *influence* board policy, you face quite a different task. Perhaps the most important first step in presenting a proposal to a board is to be certain that the board has adequate time to read and understand your proposal. Sometimes presentations to individual board members are helpful. In such sessions, the board member may raise questions or express objections more candidly than he or she would in a public meeting. This also gives a sense of what the reaction of the board members will be and how you might provide additional information that would be useful before the proposal comes to a formal discussion and vote.

In many such efforts, it is crucial to inform the parents of the children in the school or center and to get their support and backing. They should be informed well in advance of a board discussion. Again, you will learn from the parents' reactions something about the response the proposal will get. In some instances, the reaction of the parents and the board will prompt you to modify or withdraw the proposal.

The presentation to the committee should be complete but as brief as possible. Often, the best procedure is to make a brief presentation, with supporting materials available should board members request them. This is no time for complexity or confusion; clarity and good organization will help your cause. Do your homework. Allow yourself the benefit of the reactions of parents and board well before the time for public discussion. It will give you a chance to strengthen your case.

The toughest situation of all is the board or committee that is dissatisfied and is in a mood for drastic action. A confrontation, with the committee or with a group of parents bringing an objection to the committee, is the most sensitive situation. The best strategy for these encounters is to keep them from happening. Again, open communication with parents and with board members is the best way to avoid or at least to minimize conflict.

"I didn't believe serving on a board could be so exhilarating. I love the responsibility for helping make decisions."

Parent

"Every staff member should sit in on a district board meeting. There's no better way to learn how to be effective in getting what you want for your school."

District Administrator

REFERENCES

ERIC. 1978. *Parent Education: An ERIC Bibliography*. Urbana, Ill.: ERIC Clearinghouse on Early Education.

Fantini, M. D., and R. Cardenas, eds. 1980. *Parenting in a Multicultural Society*. New York: Longman.

Gordon, I. 1969. "Developing Parent Power." In *Critical Issues in Research Related to Disadvantaged Children*. Ed. E. Grotberg. Princeton, N.J.: Educational Testing Service.

Hetherington, E. M. 1979. "Divorce: A Child's Perspective." *American Psychologist*, 34, 851–858.

Honig, A. S. 1975. *Parent Involvement in Early Childhood Education*. Washington, D.C.: National Association for the Education of Young Children.

Howard, N. K. 1974. *Education for Parents of Preschoolers: An Abstract Bibliography*. Urbana, Ill.: ERIC Clearinghouse on Early Childhood Education.

Lamb, M. E. 1979. "Paternal Influences and the Father's Role." *American Psychologist*, 34, 938–943.

Miller, B. L., and A. L. Wilmshurst. 1975. *Parents and Volunteers in the Classroom: A Handbook for Teachers*. San Francisco: R & E Research Associates.

Morrison, G. S. 1978. *Parent Involvement in the Home, School, and Community*. Columbus, Ohio: Charles E. Merrill.

Stoneman, D. 1977. *A Handbook for Day Care Board Members*. New York: Day Care Council of New York.

Wallerstein, J. S., and J. B. Kelly. 1975. "The Effects of Parental Divorce: Experiences of the Preschool Child." *Journal of the American Academy of Child Psychiatry*, 14, 600–616.

CHAPTER 21

COLLABORATION IN CHILD REARING AND TEACHING

In addition to their cooperating in the activities of the school's program, teachers and parents work together in two other ways: developing parental competence in raising children and preparing children for school. These are areas of primary concern to parents, in which the teacher usually plays a supporting and facilitating role.

The interaction between parents and teachers in these areas brings up important questions. Both share responsibility for children; both are presumed to have a reasonable degree of competence in dealing with children. The boundaries between their roles are easily confused. The responsibility for handling the children during the hours they are at the center or preschool is clearly in the hands of the teachers. But parents and teachers share socialization, child rearing, and the task of preparing the child for school. How can they collaborate effectively in these tasks?

SOME DIFFERENCES BETWEEN TEACHERS AND PARENTS

Teachers are becoming increasingly important in the lives of young children. They are substitute caregivers and, in the opinion of some, they are also substitute parents. Teachers and parents often perform similar functions— discipline, nurturing, teaching, and helping.

There is sometimes confusion between the two roles of parent and teacher. Some suggest that schools should be extended families. This confuses an important distinction. The two roles sometimes overlap, but there is a fundamental difference between them.

The role of parent is unique. It is, in most cases, based on a bond between parent and child that begins in infancy and persists throughout the life of the child (Ainsworth, 1979). This tie cannot be duplicated in the preschool even though children may become very fond of a teacher with whom they have spent a great deal of time and many develop a sort of secondary attachment.

The source of confusion is the similarity and expectations in the kinds of things that teachers and parents do in caring for children. The smile, the hug, the tenderness and thoughtfulness in caring for a wounded psyche or skinned knee may look very similar. The underlying relationship, however, is different.

The two roles are different, of course, in their legal definitions. Parents have round-the-clock responsibility, whether or not they are with the child. The teacher's responsibility is limited to the hours of work and is restricted even there. This is another expression of the basic difference in the roles that parents and teachers play.

The interaction that takes place between parents and their children draws on a history of deep involvement. The response of a child or of a parent thus has its full meaning in its relationship to things that have happened before;

there is a continuity in the relationship. Teachers and young children may develop close ties, but they seldom match the meaning that comes from family bonds and a long interpersonal history.

Contrasting Styles of Interaction

Several studies describe differences between teachers and parents. Teachers tend to see the school setting as more child-centered than parents do (Winetsky, 1978). Winetsky gave parents and teachers a choice of two pictures that each portrayed a classroom scene and asked which one they preferred for the child. One illustrated a structured, teacher-directed program; the other showed an activity that was child oriented and less structured. Parents tended to select the picture showing the more structured curriculum.

Parents are also often more direct than teachers in their interaction with children. Interaction between mothers and their four-year-old children was compared with interaction between teachers and four-year-old children in their classes (Hess et al., 1979). Both were asked to teach similar tasks to the child. The difference between mothers and teachers was most obvious in their responses to errors on the part of the child. When the child made a mistake, mothers typically told their child in explicit, often gentle ways that they were wrong—"No, honey, that's not the right one. Try again. Look for the circle with only a small piece out of it." Teachers were usually less direct in response to error—"That's fine. Can you think of another way to do it?" There is other evidence from comparisons of mothers and teachers interacting with younger children (Rubenstein and Howes, 1979) that shows mothers to be more direct, often more restrictive in their exchanges with children.

Disciplinary tactics of mothers and teachers are also dissimilar. Mothers tend more often to use explicit directions in dealing with children—"Please don't do that again!" Teachers are more likely to invoke rules—"We have a rule against that. I can't let you do that." Teachers use their own authority less often, preferring to call on rules that are part of the standards and norms of the school (Conroy et al., 1980).

There is some evidence that differences between teachers and other child caregivers may be influenced by the setting in which they interact. A study by Anderson (1980) shows that teachers in full-day child care settings are more directive and expect children to master developmental tasks at an earlier age than do teachers in half-day nursery schools. A comparison of day care home mothers and teachers in full-day child care centers shows that day care home providers are more strict and structured in their attitudes and behavior than the staff of full-day child care centers (French, 1979).

Mothers who care for children in their own homes have their own style of child rearing, are more protective about the equipment and home, and have responsibilities and concerns additional to caring for children. They

"Try teaching the children in your classroom as if you were their close relative or parent. Wouldn't you interact differently with them?"

Teacher/Parent

"I have taught in both a university lab school and my own home. I interact differently in each. I am more 'professional' and 'objective' in the lab, but also less spontaneous. At home, I'm more myself. I do let the children play alone more while I attend to other tasks, but I behave more like a mother and I think the interaction is more natural."

Teacher

also have less formal training in child care and may be unaware of some of the professional attitudes and practices that prevail in the preschool.

Attitudes and behavior of caregivers thus vary from one setting to another and with the roles that the adult plays in the life of the child. If a teacher recognizes that his or her own style and preferences may be appropriate for the preschool, he or she may be able to support attitudes and behavior of parents that do not quite match what the teacher believes to be the best professional practice.

Differences in Values and Goals

Playing a supportive role is not always a simple thing to do. There are occasions when teachers may disagree with the values expressed by the family. Is it possible, in such instances, for teachers to recognize the differences in beliefs, respect the rights of families, and still not undermine the values that are contradictory to their own?

Take the case of George's father who complains that his son should not be allowed to play with dolls and dress-up clothing. The teacher's reassurances that George also participates in traditional boy-type activities like playing ball, carpentry, and climbing do not impress him. The teacher personally feels that there should be no sex-differentiated activities in the preschool, and that adults ought not to impose stereotyped roles on children.

Obviously, there are many ways to deal with this situation, some of which may have different consequences for the child and for the teacher-parent relationship. The teacher may alienate this father by refusing to accept his feelings as genuine and legitimate. But actively keeping George from the dolls and similar sex-typed activities may create different problems. Ignoring the father's concern while appearing to accept what he says seems insincere and possibly unethical. The father has a right to be involved in the education of his child. Also, the teacher has personal feelings and opinions about sex typing and the teaching of sex roles to young children, which may or may not coincide with those of George's father. In short, whatever the teacher chooses to do will not satisfy everyone involved.

There are no simple solutions to offer. Each situation carries its own considerations that change the response the teacher will give. Perhaps it is most important to evaluate such situations with sensitivity to the different roles parents and teachers play in the lives of children.

COMPETENCE IN CHILD REARING

It is not easy to be a successful parent. Parenthood has rewards and gratifications, but it is a physically demanding and sometimes frustrating role.

There is a great deal to learn: what to do about diaper rash and teething,

"I'm not used to dealing with irate fathers. They intimidate me."

Teacher

when to start solid food, when and how to start toilet training, and which sleepwear is fire resistant. There are questions about values. Should parents buy trucks and balls for boys and dolls for girls, or vice versa? How permissive should parents be about TV viewing? How should parents respond to curiosity about sexual matters? How should they deal with temper tantrums? Competence isn't delivered with the baby. Nor is parent behavior "instinctive." The task is continual; there is no union scale, no forty-hour week.

It is not surprising that parents often feel a need for help. In a national survey of parents of children between ages six and twelve, more than one-third of the parents said they worry about the job they are doing in raising their children (Yankelovich, Skelly, and White, Inc., 1977). The number of parents in single-parent households that expressed concern was even greater—almost 50 percent. The questions asked in this survey dealt with general aspects of child rearing. Even more parents want specific information about medical, educational, and psychological matters.

Where Do Parents Turn for Help?

"My parents mean well and they are a lot of help to me, but they can't be objective. They're always warning me about all the things that can happen to my baby if I'm not careful."

New Mother

The answers to parents' need for information come from many sources and in many different kinds of packages. Parents turn to books, journals, pamphlets, friends, relatives, and professionals for advice.

Whom do they trust? Professionals are high on their list, and teachers are at the top. In the previously mentioned survey, parents were asked where they would be most and least likely to seek advice. Nearly half mentioned teachers as first choice; their own parents, friends, and relatives were less popular (Yankelovich, Skelly, and White, Inc., 1977). Although this study dealt with school-age children, it very likely applies to preschoolers as well.

Publications for parents abound. Dr. Benjamin Spock's book, *Baby and Child Care,* first published in 1946, has sold more than 28 million copies. A survey of publishers estimates that 23 million books on child care have been sold in the five years between 1972–1977 and that there were more than 200 books on child care in print in 1975 (Clarke-Stewart, 1978).

The mass media—newspapers, journals, magazines, TV—offer even more advice to a wider audience. *Parents' Magazine, Ladies' Home Journal, Redbook, McCall's,* and *Good Housekeeping* (with a combined monthly circulation of well over 25 million) carry columns of counsel for the needy parent. Newspapers add to the torrent of words flowing to parents who want advice and information.

The government also publishes materials for parents. The Children's Bureau has been issuing bulletins for parents since 1914. More recently, programs for parent education through TV or home-based instruction have been supported by the U.S. Office of Education and other agencies in the recently formed Department of Education.

"I have to admit it's awfully hard to set limits, especially when my curiosity gets the better of me!"

Teacher

Parents who need help can easily come to believe that there is a "right" way to deal with the child's problems; these parents may believe that the problems are a result of their own ignorance or incompetence. As indicated by surveys, teachers can expect many of these parents to turn to them for "expert" advice. Parents will bring their problems and anxieties to the teacher, often providing confidential information that they would not share with people they have known much longer.

During an exchange of information about a child, the teacher has to determine whether the information being offered is helpful in working with the child or has gone beyond those limits. He or she must learn to use judgment and show interest in the problems, yet know when and how to use a tone of voice and phrases that will let the parent know that further details are not necessary.

There is a subtle hazard in educating and helping parents. Books, teachers, and parent education programs may create undesirable attitudes and arouse

WHEN PARENTS CONFIDE IN THE TEACHER

"Well, my mother-in-law is visiting again! Every time she comes my husband gets surly and takes it out on me. Bobby senses our tensions and starts acting up." To such a remark, the teacher might comment, "That sort of thing can be upsetting for everyone, can't it? I'll be especially careful to try to help him work out those tensions. Thanks for letting me know."

Curiosity might lead a teacher to ask, "What does your husband do when he gets surly?" Or the teacher might lead the parent on with comments like, "I know just what you mean; I have the same problems when my mom and dad come to visit." The conversation, perhaps fascinating, takes on a different tone.

In the first conversation, the teacher accepts the necessary information and uses it to help work more effectively with the child. Sometimes information can include more details than necessary, but both parent and teacher can be disappointed when the teacher uses the role of confidant to elicit unnecessary details or to mislead the parent into believing that he or she might receive some therapeutic benefits.

When a teacher plays therapist, engages in gossip, or simply encourages more details out of curiosity, the exercise may be an ego trip.

needless anxiety. Professional experts offer advice with confidence and assurance; books suggest the existence of a body of professional knowledge about child rearing. Parents might infer from all the superior knowledge at their disposal that, if only they would take the time and make the effort, they can become successful parents. Guilt feelings may lead the parent to rely more on the professional, trusting his or her own judgment even less (Hess, 1980).

The parent who feels incompetent and relies on experts expresses an uncertainty and ambivalence that is often obvious to the child. This may interfere with a basic element in parent-child relationships—a sense of confidence in the parent in what he or she is doing. Trust is critical. The parent's sense of confidence is part of his or her competence as a parent; the advice of experts is not helpful if it erodes such confidence.

How Do Teachers Help?

The questions and problems that parents bring to the staff range from items of information ("When is a good time to start my child on dental check-ups?") to severe behavior disorders. Parents have a wide variety of experience and background on which they can rely in their child-rearing responsibilities. Some will have read many of the popular titles on the library shelves; others may never have heard of Dr. Spock. Some will bring their concerns to you directly and explicitly; others will find it difficult to talk about the things that cause anxiety or may not admit to themselves that they have a problem.

How do you respond to the needs of parents, whether spoken or unspoken? A parent who asks for advice places the teacher in the position of expert. It is difficult to resist this kind of flattery or compliment, especially since the staff members in preschools usually have a background of training and experience with many different kinds of children that few parents have acquired. Even when there may not be a clear answer, the temptation is to give a personal opinion rather than solid professional advice. It is easy, also, to misinterpret an appeal for advice. Sometimes the parent is really asking for the teacher to recognize and acknowledge that being a parent is a demanding task!

When we reflect on our own experience and recall the advice we get from parents, friends, teachers, books, magazines, and other media, we recognize that advice itself does not always have an impact. We listen selectively, using bits of ideas and information to help resolve issues and problems. Advice may help, but the change, if any, comes from our own efforts.

The usefulness of counsel from someone else depends to a great extent on what sort of problem is presented. If the request is for information about the location of a good children's bookstore, a useful answer is easy to provide. If a parent wants to know how to handle a child who has chronic temper tantrums, the response may be less helpful.

The problems that parents bring to teachers usually fall into one or more of the following categories:

1. Matters of organization and management—schedules, adjusting time for work, child care, transportation, finances, fatigue, and conflicting demands
2. Specific information about child care—nutrition, clothes, sleep needs, health (for example, immunizations and symptoms of various physical problems)
3. Techniques for dealing with children—tactics to use if the child has a temper tantrum, doesn't want to stay in bed, won't eat at mealtime, and other forms of behavior the parent wants to modify
4. Values—standards of appropriate behavior in various areas, such as sex role, courtesy in dealing with others, attitudes toward authority and rules, television viewing, and so forth
5. Emotional relationship with the child—feelings of ambivalence, dependency, rejection, indulgence, anger, and the like
6. Self-confidence—feelings about competence as a parent, sense of being in control of or being controlled by events or the child

The staff of a center will, of course, have much more to offer on some problems than others. The teacher's first task is to identify the problem and decide what, if anything, can be done. We suggest a strategy that sorts out the nature of the problem and your competence as a teacher to deal with it. Your degree of competence depends on the nature of the problem.

What type of need is being expressed by the parent? Are you able to handle the request? If the concern is about a physical complaint—itching eyes, headaches, squinting—you may recognize that this could be a visual problem and suggest a referral or other follow-up. If the parent gives you permission to spank the child, the problem is very different. You can easily decide not to resort to spanking, but do you try to change the parent's method of discipline?

Your response to parental concerns might depend on determining (1) which matters you can do something about, (2) which matters you should leave alone, and (3) which matters you should refer to the director or an agency. This requires that you listen carefully to what the parent is saying. Is there an underlying plea for attention or for recognition that the parent is facing a difficult task? Is it an attempt to get more personal contact with you? Before you try to offer an answer, recognize what the question is. When you do, there may not be an answer, but you can always acknowledge

---

WHAT WOULD YOU DO IF . . . ?

A mother complains that her child has "terrible temper tantrums. She's always been stubborn. I can't do a thing with her!"

A parent asks about how to control head lice.

A mother says, "Jason is so bright! It concerns me. He gets bored just playing with other children."

A father wants help to teach his child the alphabet and the first steps of reading.

A mother says, "How do you get Danielle to mind you? She won't behave for me at home."

A mother complains that she and her husband can't agree on how to discipline their child.

A parent says, "My child seems to be slower than other children. His speech isn't developing as fast as we think it should."

A mother says, "Christina keeps using dirty words. We spank her, but she won't stop."

the parent's concerns and efforts. It may be useful to prepare for such discussions with parents by role-playing a response to hypothetical situations such as those described in the boxed insert.

So far, we have dealt with the teacher's response when parents share their problems. Another situation that calls for a decision is when a parent doesn't ask for help, even though it is needed. What is the best strategy in such a case?

There are two aspects to working with parents: the information or advice that is offered and the relationship between the teacher and the parent. It obviously does little good to confront parents with good advice if it turns the parents off, creates resentment, or makes them defensive and resistant. Ultimately, parents can only help themselves; development and growth come from their own actions. The goal is to get parents to recognize the situation and to see how a solution may be found. Several possibilities can be considered.

1. *Confront the parent*. If the relationship is good, you can share a common concern. You may not be successful in making a change, but it's worth a try.
2. *Ignore the problem*. Fine, if nothing can be done about the situation anyway.
3. *Bring up the topic in a general meeting*. Hope that the parent you have in mind will see that it applies to him or her.
4. *Distribute materials*. Pass information on the topic of concern to all parents and invite responses.
5. *Arrange a conference with the parent*. Include the item of concern in a more general discussion to see if the parent is responsive.
6. *Use positive reinforcement*. Praise the parent for things he or she is doing well; create a sense of confidence and trust. Reward the behaviors you like.

Dealing with parents' problems is not simple. But there are responses that the teacher can make. At the least, the teacher's support and recognition is itself a contribution to the child and the parents.

COLLABORATION IN PREPARING
CHILDREN FOR SCHOOL

The parents are the child's first teachers, and the home is the first school. The family's role in the child's education has long been recognized in many writings, in proverbs, and in more formal programs from Comenius' ''School of the Mother's Knee'' to the more recent Home Start programs of the 1970s.

Parents' Influence on School Achievement

"Joey is two years old and he can recognize and name the letters *O*, *P*, *R*, *T*, and *V*."

Father

Influence of parents on educational skills begins early and continues long past the time when public schooling starts. Parents affect children in three general ways. First, they foster development of cognitive skills or the ability to deal with ideas and information relevant for school, such as labeling objects, counting, naming letters of the alphabet, asking questions, using concepts, and the like. Second, parents help inspire in the child a motivation to succeed in school and a desire to learn and to acquire the skills that school experience offers. Third, parents help the child understand and accept the role of pupil. This means that the child recognizes the procedures and rules of the school, learns to interact with the teacher, develops an assertive approach to learning, and persists in working on tasks set by the school.

These attitudes and skills are learned; they contribute to successful performance in the classroom. Such behavior begins to develop in the home, especially homes in which the family has a regard for education and the school. These prerequisites for learning at school are more likely to develop if parents show that they value educational pursuits, if parents enjoy reading and read aloud to their children, and if youngsters have their own books and are encouraged to ask questions (Hess et al., 1979).

"We usually think of the beginning of public school as the time for formal teaching, but learning begins long before the actual school-term starts."

School Principal

Engaging the child in school-related activities is one of the ways parents affect children's behavior in school. Some play word games with their chil-

---

HOW PARENTS HELP CHILDREN SUCCEED IN SCHOOL

Take the child to the library; let the child select and check books out.

Read to the child.

Talk with the child; listen to the child talk.

Ask questions; make requests that encourage the child to talk and express ideas.

Point out letters and words in books, on signs, food boxes, and such.

Reinforce the child's interest in saying names of letters and words.

Help the child acquire general knowledge about the world.

Let the child know you value learning.

Buy books and records with educational concepts.

Encourage and join the child in watching educational television.

dren, challenging them with small problems to solve. Parents may also talk with the child, using language in ways that encourage him or her to speak clearly, to master the meaning of words, and to express ideas. Some parents buy books and toys that are designed to teach the alphabet, colors, numbers, shapes, and other concepts children will encounter at school. A child may be encouraged to watch television programs that are designed to teach basic preschool skills.

In a study in Israel, mothers of children from middle- and low-income backgrounds were encouraged to watch ''Sesame Street'' with their five-year-old children. As a result, youngsters from low-income backgrounds watched (and enjoyed) the show more than before and were more proficient in matching numbers, matching letters, ordering pictures to make a story, and other cognitive tasks. The mother did not engage in any tutoring activities during or after the program. The effective aspect was her interest in what the child was doing. Thus the educational elements of the program were more readily acquired by the child (Salomon, 1977).

Perhaps most important is the parent's responsiveness to the child's school-related behavior—knowledge of what the child is doing in school, concern and interest in the child's activities at home, and a desire to help the child learn. Almost any activity can become an opportunity to help children learn things that will make them ready to handle the tasks of the classroom.

The parent's expectations for the child to achieve are also an important aspect of the home environment. Some parents set high standards for their children, praising their efforts to do better. They may encourage self-reliance by teaching children to dress and feed themselves, by making them responsible for their own belongings, and by seeing that they have a chance to solve many of their own problems.

There are differences among parents in the pressure they put on young children to be independent and to acquire specific skills. Most significant, perhaps, is the warmth and trust that develop in their interactions with their children. The quality of a parent's personal relationship with the child may encourage or inhibit achievement. Parental support and affection appear to be important influences in children's ability to acquire normal developmental skills.

The staff of the center should be aware of the goals parents have for their children: this information can be exchanged as a part of the parents' learning about the goals the school has for their children. Thus, the school and family can offer material and consistent support of the child's attempts to develop competence.

Conflict between father and mother creates anxiety in children, distracting them and interfering with the development of both social and school-related skills. Conflict between parents affects the behavior of children even more than the absence of one parent.

Rutter (1979); Hess and Camara (1979)

Programs for Home-Based Learning

Since the role of the home in early learning was recognized, there have been many efforts to help parents become more effective teachers of their own children. Some focus on the role of the parent in early learning; others plan a program that involves both staff and parent in a coordinated curriculum.

There are probably more than a hundred home-based programs in this country. Many of them are local efforts that have had little publicity even though they may be very effective. Information about some of the most widely discussed programs may be obtained from references cited at the end of this chapter.

Home-based programs differ from one another in some essential ways.

Some use toys as a basis for interaction between mother and child; others utilize a more instructional approach. Some give the mother a script to use with the child; others suggest more general approaches that the mother can adapt as she likes.

A number of programs were developed by sponsors of Head Start and Follow Through. Several others were experimental efforts that grew out of university-based research in the 1960s. Some of these programs improve children's performance in both social and academic ways (Brown, 1978; Levenstein, 1978).

In 1977 more than 20,000 children were served through Home Start programs.

A national program, Home Start, emerged from this interest in home-centered learning. It was begun in 1972 through sixteen demonstration centers. It is conducted under the supervision of the Administration for Children, Youth, and Families, U.S. Department of Health and Human Services.

Home Start was designed to give mothers or primary caregivers the main responsibility for carrying out early learning activities with their children. Local centers do their own planning; parents are often involved. Trained teachers visit each family weekly for about one and one-half hours. During these visits, the parent educator demonstrates a learning activity the parent can use with the child—teaching the youngster how to count objects, to sort and classify various materials, or to do some other activity appropriate to the child's age and development. The parent then repeats the process, following the example of the parent educator, thus allowing the parent to try the teaching technique, ask questions, and learn by doing. The sessions give the parent practice in modeling, provide immediate feedback, and help prevent undesirable teaching techniques. In this way, Home Start programs seek to help parents become their children's first and best teachers.

Parents need not be involved in organized or sponsored programs in order to help prepare their children for school. The staff of a preschool can work with parents in several ways—by modeling techniques to encourage children to learn, by providing hints and suggestions for parents to use, and by letting parents know that the school has confidence in their ability to participate in their children's learning. The kinds of activities described earlier in this chapter—buying books, reading aloud to the child, using common items around the house to point out shapes, color, and the like are things any parent can do.

REFERENCES

Ainsworth, M. D. S. 1979. "Infant-Mother Attachment." *American Psychologist*, 34, 932–937.

Anderson, K. 1980. "Effects of Day Care and Nursery School Settings on Teacher Behavior." Unpublished doctoral dissertation, Stanford University.

Brown, B. 1978. *Found: Long-Term Gains from Early Intervention*. Boulder, Col.: Westview Press.

Clarke-Stewart, K. A. 1978. "Popular Primers for Parents." *American Psychologist*, 33, 359–369.

Conroy, M., R. D. Hess, H. Azuma, and K. Kashiwagi. 1980. "Maternal Strategies for Regulating Children's Behavior in Japanese and American Families." *Journal of Cross-Cultural Psychology*, 11, No. 2.

French, E. 1979. "A Comparison of Caregivers in Day Care Homes and Centers." Paper presented at the annual convention of the National Association for the Education of Young Children, Atlanta, November 9.

Hess, R. D., and K. A. Camara. 1979. "Post-Divorce Family Relations as Mediating Factors in the Consequences of Divorce for Children." *Journal of Social Issues*, 35, No. 4, 79–96.

Hess, R. D., W. P. Dickson, G. G. Price, and M. Conroy. 1979. "Different Roles for Mothers and Teachers: Contrasting Styles of Child Care." In *Advances in Early Education and Day Care*, Vol. 2. Ed. S. Kilmer. Greenwich, Conn.: Johnson Associates Inc.

Hess, R. D. 1980. "Experts and Amateurs: Some Unintended Consequences of Parent Education." In *Parenting in a Multicultural Society*. Ed. M. D. Fantini and R. Cardenas. New York: Longman.

Hess, R. D., S. Holloway, G. G. Price, and W. P. Dickson. 1979. "Family Environments and Acquisition of Reading Skills: Toward a More Precise Analysis." Paper presented at the Conference on the Family as a Learning Environment, Educational Testing Service, Princeton, November.

Levenstein, P. 1978. "Third-Grade Effects of the Mother-Child Home Program." Developmental Continuity Consortium, Follow-up Study, Verbal Interaction Project, Freeport, New York, April.

Rubenstein, J. L., and C. Howes. 1979. "Caregiving and Infant Behavior in Day Care and in Homes." *Developmental Psychology*, 15, 1–24.

Rutter, M. 1979. "Maternal Deprivation 1972–1978: New Findings, New Concepts, New Approaches." *Child Development*, 50, 283–305.

Salomon, G. 1977. "Effects of Encouraging Israeli Mothers to Co-observe 'Sesame Street' with Their Five-Year-Olds." *Child Development*, 48, 1146–1151.

Winetsky, C. S. 1978. "Comparisons of the Expectations of Parents and Teachers for the Behavior of Preschool Children." *Child Development*, 49, 1146–1154.

Yankelovich, Skelly & White, Inc. 1977. *Raising Children in a Changing Society: The General Mills American Family Report*. Minneapolis: General Mills Consumer Center.

PART SEVEN

ADMINISTRATION OF

PRESCHOOLS

A PROLOGUE   Up to this point, we have been discussing matters of central concern to the teacher—the demand for child care, opportunities in the field, the children and their families, and the evaluation and assessment roles of teachers. In Part Seven, we will look at the center from the standpoint of the director.

The items that keep the mind of a center director busy are not usually things for which you, as a teacher, will be directly responsible. But you are involved in them in several ways. The job of a teacher is linked to that of the director; you will be more competent if you understand your job from the director's perspective.

When you read this section, flip back and forth mentally between the role of the teacher and that of the director. Imagine that the director is on leave and you are responsible for the administrative tasks. Correspondence comes in about matters of licensing, a parent calls to complain that his child came home with a black and blue mark on her arm, a prospective customer wants to know what your sources of funding are and will her family be eligible for federally subsidized child care, and an advisory committee member calls to ask you to see if a piece of equipment is up to safety standards.

You won't have a quick answer for most of these questions, but an overview of the task and responsibilities of a director may help prepare you to recognize the major areas of the center's operation. Your conversations with parents will be more informed and you will need to call on the director for help less often. You will be in a better position to support the administrator, to take initiative, and to plan with other staff.

If you are thinking about opening your own school some day or applying for an administrative job, an overview of the director's duties will help you decide whether that is the direction you want to take. Your experience can also help you better appreciate what is involved in administration.

You are more than a teacher in a center, of course. You are a citizen of the community who has special skill, experience, and knowledge about the field of child care. In many situations outside of the center, you will have occasion to discuss policies, funding, taxes, and legislation that affect the field. Your continuing contact with colleagues through workshops, conferences, and local professional meetings gives you opportunity to join others in pressing for legislative changes, or in trying to persuade your representative in the state legislature or in Washington that a bill coming up for vote will benefit the field.

The topics in this section are discrete, related to one another through the importance they have in the administration of the center or preschool. We cover only the major points. This section won't transform you into a director, but it may help you see how things look from behind the desk in the front office.

CHAPTER 22

VIEW FROM THE DIRECTOR'S DESK

ORGANIZATIONAL POLICIES

    Licensing

    Zoning and Building Regulations

    Governing Boards

    Advisory Committees

PROGRAM POLICIES

    Purpose and Philosophy of the School

    Enrollment Policies

    Keeping Records

    Health and Safety Regulations

    Professional Referrals

FINANCES

    Sources of Funding

    Budgeting

FACILITIES: CREATING THE CLIMATE OF THE SCHOOL

    Impact of the Physical Climate

    Influence on the Emotional Climate

STAFF DEVELOPMENT AND MANAGEMENT

    Recruiting and Interviewing

    Inservice Training and Parent Education

PUBLIC RELATIONS

    Advertising

    Community Relations

ORGANIZATIONAL POLICIES

What does the director/principal do all day in the office? Why isn't he or she out with the children when the teachers need extra help?

To a staff member who has never had experience operating a school, the administrative responsibilities of the director may seem unnecessarily time consuming. In some cases, the director may agree.

The amount of book work and forms to complete in order to qualify for licensing, grant monies, and other such necessities can seem overwhelming. Many excellent teachers who have turned to administration complain that they regret their tasks remove them from children so much of the time.

Starting a new school can be a very time-consuming and frustrating experience for many people. Some, like the franchised schools, are planned and sponsored by business organizations experienced in such matters. But for the teacher who dreams of having his or her own school, the business of getting started can be perplexing indeed. There are licensing requirements, zoning and use permits, fire regulations, and dozens of other agencies and regulations to deal with before the school actually begins to operate.

Licensing

Licensing of family day care homes, for which there is an increasing demand, is usually regulated by the city or county. Enrollment is generally limited to about six children per home.

Most states require licenses for operating private nursery schools and child care facilities. Granting of a license indicates that the school complies with certain health and safety requirements, staff ratios, and other state and/or local agency standards considered minimum for running a preschool program. Not all states require licensing; in some areas, depending on the number of children served, the city or county may be the regulatory agency. Before buying or building a facility, the prospective owner should contact the appropriate state licensing agency and ask for guidelines regarding space, location, staff qualifications, and other such regulations. In many states, licensing is the responsibility of welfare or health departments or departments of education. Schools sponsored by federal or state funds must meet with certain standards to qualify for monies. Usually a phone call to the state agency can direct interested individuals to the right person. Some agencies have orientation classes for people who are planning to start schools.

Zoning and Building Regulations

Many people who have tried to start a school in their own homes have discovered unhappily that their project is not welcomed, either by the neighbors (who were friendly up until that point) or by the city. Most cities have zoning regulations prohibiting businesses in residential areas. Charging for the care of even a few children is a commercial venture and the owner of such a business must comply with all regulations. The owner can apply for a zoning variance to obtain a use permit, but often there are other obstacles such as size of the building, parking space requirements, ratio of building to open space, setback from street, health and fire regulations, and other such restrictions.

Leasing a commercial building or locating in a church or empty school may be a simpler and less complicated procedure. Construction is much more costly than leasing and requires more start-up capital. People wanting to start a school, either in their own homes or by constructing one from the ground up, need not be completely discouraged. The regulations and restrictions are not insurmountable, but one needs to be realistic about how to begin. Do not assume that starting a preschool facility is a simple matter. Do the necessary research and contact all state, county, and local agencies before making any major commitments.

"Nine of my preschools are located in churches; two are in buildings I own. I pay the churches a percentage of gross receipts, and my profit is much better in the churches than in my own buildings."

Owner

Governing Boards

Many schools are governed by boards, which may be made up of people representing the community, the school district, the church, or members of the school itself. Some co-op schools, for example, are owned by the group of parents that the school is serving at the time. The board formulates policies and program goals; the director must implement these policies.

Board members can be elected or selected by the owner, staff, and parents of children who attend the school, and new members can be appointed by the owner or by the existing board. Sometimes the board appoints or elects one of its members to act as liaison to the school, or the director of the school assumes the responsibility. (See Chapter 20 for further discussion about relations with parent boards.)

Advisory Committees

Some publicly funded programs require parent advisory committees (see Chapter 20). People serving on such committees are elected parents whose children are attending the school or may include interested community people who are invited to be part of the group. Unlike governing boards, advisory committees do not make policy; they give advice which may or may not result in formation of policy. Some owners of private schools find it useful to have an advisory committee of interested parents and professionals from the community.

"Some people can stir up a lot of trouble and confuse the issues. Pick your advisory committee carefully!"

Director

PROGRAM POLICIES

Every preschool and child care facility should have in writing the policies of that school relating to the purpose of the school and program, enrollment policies, goals of the curriculum, staff requirements, health regulations, and classroom procedures.

Purpose and Philosophy of the School

State in writing and make available to staff members and families the reasons for offering the program. Specify if the purpose is for education or social development of young children, if it is to serve low-income families or other special groups, and indicate how the program is to be operated—co-op, private, and so on. This statement is the basis for the description of the program. Be clear about goals and state how these goals are to be met so that people interested in attending the school can get a good idea of why the school exists and the kinds of families that will be served. If, for example, a mixed age grouping or a balance of ethnic minorities is desired, these facts should be stated as program policies. The director's philosophy about how children should be educated and the methods used to reach these goals should be made clear in the statement of philosophy.

Enrollment Policies

"I charge a small fee for placing a child's name on the waiting list. This helps to pay for mailing and processing forms."

Director

State clearly priorities in filling the places available in the school. Some owners and directors do not have to contend with waiting lists, but it is wise to state in advance (in the event that such a need may arise) all the policies determining qualification for acceptance. The license will limit the school to the ages and numbers that can be enrolled, but the director will want to make clear to interested families how acceptance will be determined: children may be enrolled in the order they sign up; equal numbers of boys and girls or a specific number from each age group may be accepted; or admission may be limited to children who fulfill special qualifications such as ethnicity, socio-economic requirements, family background, and the like. Enrollment policies provide consistent guidelines for acceptance and help avoid charges of preferential treatment. Publicly funded programs have specific, detailed guidelines covering enrollment policies and priorities.

Publicly funded programs often require documentation of program components such as parent involvement, nutrition, health and social services, and testing of children.

Keeping Records

The agency issuing the license for a school will supply forms required for keeping records on individual children. For example, some states require schools to have on file health histories, immunization records, family background, emergency and identification forms (including names of persons authorized to take the child from school).

Some schools may carry their own accident insurance, and others may require parents to pay a small fee for a blanket policy. Sometimes this fee is included in tuition charges. Usually the director is responsible for seeing that all such forms and records are kept up to date. State or federal auditors may visit the school from time to time to monitor compliance with record-keeping regulations.

Health and Safety Regulations

In addition to health certificates for children, all staff members must have negative results on tuberculosis tests or chest x-rays and have on file regular physical examination reports. The health department will provide a list of regulations covering maintenance of the facility, numbers of toilets and wash basins, and the like. Kitchen and food preparation areas must also meet health standards. Government guidelines are specific regarding the kinds of stoves, dishwashing equipment, temperature of wash water, and so forth that the school must have. Many regulations do not allow children in the kitchen area.

Other requirements include providing isolation space with a cot for sick children; adhering to lighting and ventilation standards; supplying the required number of exits with appropriately designed push bars; and following regulations for drinking water, first aid equipment, and regular fire drills. (Refer to Chapter 8 for details on children's illnesses.)

"I much prefer working in a small group with fewer teachers than in a large group with more teachers. Ratio may be important, but it is not the only criterion for a good school."

Teacher

Safety is also related to the number of adults responsible for supervision of children. Requirements vary in each state. Generally, a ratio of no more than ten children to one teacher is considered safe. Some programs serving children under three years of age need lower ratios. Some public programs require one adult (including volunteers, parents, interns) to five children with at least one certificated (professionally trained) teacher to every fifteen to twenty children. A school with large spaces and many hidden, difficult-to-supervise areas will need to have a lower ratio of children to teachers. See Table 22.1 for recommended staff ratios.

TABLE 22.1
Suggested Staff-Child Ratios in Preschool Programs

Ages	Minimum Staff Required
3	For each 12 children a trained head teacher and an assistant
4	For each 16 children a trained head teacher and an assistant
5	For each 20 children a trained head teacher and an assistant

The Head Start standard for 4s and 5s is 15 children and a trained teacher plus an assistant and community area volunteers.

Professional Referrals

In dealing with children and their parents, problems will arise that should be referred to agencies and specialists outside the school. The need to make referrals may not come up often, but when it does, it may be urgent. There are several types of situations that require the help of outside resources:

1. Emergencies, such as illness, financial problems, need for child care, child abuse, and the like
2. Suspected disabilities, such as physical or learning problems
3. Medical problems, which are many and varied
4. Emotional problems, such as difficulties that impair normal functioning of the child or parent

In most schools, the director or person in charge is responsible for making referrals. If the policy of the school is to have all problem cases channeled through one person, the teacher needs only to use his or her judgment as to when a particular problem may warrant discussion.

A referral is not always a simple matter; it may have its own impact. If a teacher suspects that a child has learning problems or a disability, parents of the child may not want to recognize the evidence. The teacher's suggestion that the child be taken to a specialist may cause strong emotional reactions. Part of the task of making a referral is to deal with its impact on the family. If the referral is for child abuse or for economic circumstances, it may begin a long chain of interaction with an agency. This type of contact can be time consuming and unpleasant and may threaten the family's sense of privacy and self-respect. Although the teacher may think of a referral as an offer of help, the family may see it as a threat of bad news or an insult. As in other types of interaction, the quality of the relationship between staff and parents is one of the most important considerations.

It is not always easy to identify specialists or agencies for referrals. Some are obvious and their phone numbers and addresses should be at hand (see boxed insert). Others, such as professional services for diagnosis of speech and hearing impairment or emotional problems, may be more difficult to locate. Specialists differ in their experience with young children, competence, fees, and accessibility.

The limits of responsibility of the school in making a referral should be clear to the teacher and the parent. Even though the school may not intend a referral to constitute an endorsement, the parent may take it as such; in some instances, it is. The school may indeed base referrals on experience and judgment. However, if a teacher knows little or nothing about the specialist, it may be best to refrain from offering a name and to suggest that the parent ask other parents or consult the phone directory.

In some instances, the school may want to establish contacts with profes-

"I would estimate more than 80 percent of my patients come to me because of the recommendations of satisfied parents and school referrals."

Pediatrician

REFERRAL AGENCIES

Poison control center   The divorce center
Parental stress hotline   Red Cross
Child abuse (protective services)   Family Service Association
Alcoholics Anonymous   Planned Parenthood
Abortion clinic   Mental health services
Legal Aid

sionals before a problem or need arises. Learning about an agency and getting acquainted with a specialist can provide the staff with useful information when referrals are indicated.

FINANCES

Much of an administrator's time is taken up with financial matters. The amount of money available and how it should be spent require careful consideration. The sources of funding for any school determine in great part how monies are apportioned. Most good schools will spend about 80 percent of their budgets on salaries. Publicly funded programs often specify amounts to be spent on teaching staff, equipment, and other items. A private school depending totally on tuition for income will generally pay lower salaries than subsidized schools. When tuition is the only source of income, pay raises and other expenditures must depend on increasing enrollment (which has a limit) and/or raising tuition.

Sources of Funding

Some schools raise extra money through nonrefundable registration fees, fund-raising activities, and donations, which can be in the form of equipment, materials, and time from individuals, or scholarships from community groups.

"It's interesting how I've become more sensitive to parent complaints since I have become an owner. I can't afford to lose any tuition!"

Owner

Schools set up on a nonprofit basis can qualify for federal and state subsidies provided they serve children with special needs, such as handicapped children, children from low-income backgrounds, those from single-parent households or whose parents both work, and children who speak no English. Some private school have become nonprofit corporations in order to qualify for grants.

Sometimes there are research grants available, and some cities offer subsidies for child care to serve the special needs of local citizens. Private schools and centers can arrange with local industries and hospitals to subsidize care for children of employees.

Budgeting

General expenses can be broken down in the following approximate percentages:

Salaries: 55%–85%
Insurance benefits: 6% (includes workman's compensation, fire, liability, and some fringe benefits)
Repairs, maintenance: 4% (varies with age of equipment)
Food: 10% (lower if no hot meals are served or if food subsidies are available)
Supplies: 4% (consumables, such as art supplies, paper, etc.; not permanent equipment)
Adverising: 1% (phone and newpaper listings, brochures)
Utilities: 3% (varies with locale)
Taxes, licenses: 1.5% (varies)
Reserve fund: 10% (for emergency expenses, like roof or heating replacement; large equipment purchase; carry on-going operating expenses if enrollment drops)
Balance: 5.5% (loans, mortgage payments, rent, miscellaneous)

The figure of 55 percent for salaries is low compared with most school budgets. In a private school, if the salaries of the owner/director and other personnel, such as janitor, groundsperson, and so on, are included, the figure can be as high as 85 percent.

Allotment of 10 percent for food may be high for some schools if federal or state food monies are available to subsidize meals. Also, many directors are able to realize great savings by purchasing items on special, participating in cooperative buying groups, or growing much of their food themselves.

Schools located in private residences, churches, or public buildings with low rents will be able to allot a greater percentage of their budget to salaries. The preceding budget is only a rough outline and is based on a program already in existence. Start-up costs for new buildings and equipment are not included. Some schools are able to spend as little as $1500 to equip a building for thirty children by using scrap or salvaged materials and doing all the construction of equipment themselves. Others spend in excess of $15,000 for the same number of children. Start-up costs vary tremendously depending on the resourcefulness and creativity of the people involved.

The director is usually responsible for all expenditures, approval of re-

"I find it very profitable to barter. I got a nurse, a bookkeeper, and a supplies manager by giving partial tuition in exchange for services from parents."

Director

quisitions, and salary payments. If no bookkeeping help is available, the director must also keep records and receipts of all transactions, post and deposit tuition monies, and generally be responsible for the total budget. Volunteers and parents who are paying partial tuition in exchange for services can be very helpful in assisting with shopping for food and supplies, collecting free materials, maintaining files, keeping books, mailing, and other time-consuming activities vital to the operation of the school.

It is useful for people starting up a new school to do a field survey of nearby facilities to determine competitive tuition charges and average costs. Engaging the services of a professional bookkeeper or certified public accountant to help set up an original budgeting and accounting system is well worth the investment.

A good school will carry on a continuous assessment of trends and needs of the community it serves.

FACILITIES: CREATING THE CLIMATE OF THE SCHOOL

A successful school depends on maintaining a consistently high enrollment. Reputations of good schools are built mostly by word of mouth. Parents are most likely to rely on recommendations of other parents they trust. Therefore, the facilities—the indoor and outdoor environment—reflect the school's philosophy about child care and education. When adults and children enter a school or center, the physical environment creates an impression of how they will interact and learn.

"It's bad business to criticize other competitive programs. School directors need to cooperate with one another to maintain consistent tuitions and salaries as well as a good reputation in general for all children's services."

Owner

Impact of the Physical Environment

Interaction with the physical environment is an important part of learning for young children. They explore and discover with their bodies, experiencing the excitement of high places, the fascination of tunnels, the motion of swings and rope ladders, the texture and shape of a multitude of objects and materials. Their senses continuously gather both general and specific knowledge of all that surrounds them. In creating their own world, they use what is in the environment to build and tear down and then to build all over again. From dealing with their surroundings, they learn firsthand to choose and judge; they find out which objects and situations they can control and which they cannot. Teachers and administrators can use the facilities of a preschool to provide a constructive as well as pleasant learning environment.

Children need room to run and jump, to wheel buggies and ride trikes, to move about freely without jostling and bumping into one another. They need quiet corners and out-of-the-way nooks as "escape hatches" and a chance to be alone. They need areas for eating, cleanup, toileting, activity, and rest.

"One of the most popular spots in our school was a closet that had been remodeled to create a small loft for children to hide away."

Parent

How space is filled has a great deal to do with whether a preschool meets the needs of the children it serves. Well-planned attractive arrangements invite exploration and minimize staff work. When related interest areas are grouped with a consideration of traffic patterns and the relationship of noisy and quiet activities, they virtually draw children to them. Arranging and rearranging movable furnishings such as shelves and bins and tables so as to create centers for "house" play, dressing up, block building, puzzles, craft projects, science, reading, and art contribute to a natural flow of activity. Flexible organization of this kind stimulates free choice and varied interests.

Needs differ widely in different kinds of programs. All-day care, for example, requires space for meals and naps not needed by schools offering half-day sessions. City schools are often more limited in outdoor area than suburban schools. In general, licensing agencies require a minimum of thirty-five square feet per child indoors, and fifty to seventy-five square feet per child outdoors. These figures vary in different states and refer to space to be used by children, not that occupied by storage units, trees, or other relatively permanent items.

"Teachers who do not plan and arrange for activities that encourage children to work independently are spending their time in unproductive ways. There's no reason to be so busy waiting on children who are capable of helping themselves."

Teacher

In addition to the tables and chairs, rooms should be designed with ample bulletin boards and display areas at children's eye level to encourage them to mount their own work and to notice what others have made. The way a room is arranged determines in part the kind and amount of supervision required. If all or most children can be seen from one or two vantage points, less patrolling and checkup is needed. This in turn means that teachers have more time for constructive, individual attention. For planning structured group projects—story hours, films, snacks, music, and the like—space

''Teachers need escape hatches and quiet places too. Our staff room is painted in soft shades and decorated to create a soothing atmosphere.''

Administrator

should be provided that requires a minimum of arranging either before or after each activity. Less supervision is needed when toilet areas are located so they can be directly entered from indoor and outdoor play areas. Also when boys and girls share toilet facilities an opportunity is provided for learning about the opposite sex.

School affairs are likely to run more smoothly for everyone concerned if the staff has some space of its own. An adjacent tastefully appointed combination office and teacher room that can also be used for parent conferences, staff training, or an isolation room is an asset to a nursery school program.

Well-planned and well-equipped outdoor areas have as great an impact on the goals of a program as their indoor counterparts. Ideally, one is simply a modified extension of the other. Smooth transition between the two can be achieved by using wide, easily opened doors and windows low enough to extend a child's vision to resources both inside and out. A wide overhang, shaded as well as sunlit spaces, and areas sheltered from the wind, make it more pleasant for children to be outdoors in all but the coldest or most stormy weather.

In such surroundings there is no reason why many activities traditionally thought of as taking place indoors cannot be enjoyed outdoors. Butcher paper tacked along a fence soon becomes a gay mural or garden decoration at the hands of eager artists; juice and crackers under a shade tree turns snack time into a picnic; in mild weather records and musical instruments can be heard as well outdoors as in. Activities in a new setting often tempt children who originally bypassed them.

Traffic patterns are as important in the play yard as they are indoors. Children's tendency to speed on wheel toys and to run without constraint can be minimized by providing relatively short expanses of unrestricted space. A cement walk that rings a grassy mound allows for distance riding with no sharp corners and therefore fewer spills.

'I've noticed how some children can climb well on a jungle gym or some other piece of manufactured equipment because the spacing is uniform, but they have difficulty climbing a tree. They need the challenge of having to use their judgment in space and distance to accommodate to natural terrain.''

Owner

Children develop judgment along with physical skills if the outdoor areas contain a variety of facilities for climbing, crawling, sliding, jumping, balancing, and hanging. Low-limbed trees often make better climbing devices than many jungle gyms because they force children into choices not needed when handholds all have identical size and mounting rungs are evenly spaced.

Children should be allowed to discover for themselves the properties and delight of a variety of surfaces and textures. Paper, wood, wire, canvas, cement, grass, sand, tanbark, gravel, hardtop, metal—all have something to impart to children acquiring knowledge about themselves and their relationships to the physical world.

Children are stimulated by their physical surroundings, and nursery school facilities planned with their needs in mind provide a safe environment in which they can explore, create, and learn in ways that prepare them for adult life.

Influence on the Emotional Climate

"Spacious rooms filled with light, color, warmth, and order appeal to children as well as adults. They make you feel comfortable and welcome.''

Parent

Two factors that influence the emotional climate of a preschool are light and noise. Natural light coming through doors and windows without glare, yet adequate to brighten the farthest corner of a room, makes for a cheerful atmosphere. When artificial light provides soft, even, overhead illumination, eye strain and fatigue are lessened. The scraping, pounding, and clicking, the humming and laughter—all the noises that accompany active children can often be muted to keep from setting nerves on edge or fraying tempers. For example, a nearly square room is a better noise absorber than a long, narrow one, especially when its walls and ceilings are made of sound-absorbing material. Floors should have a surface that can be readily scrubbed yet will not set up reverberations from every running step or pushed-back chair. Occasional rugs and mats help minimize noise. So does a quiet-voiced teacher.

Independence is encouraged when storage areas are within reach of children and they are free to use them. Cubbyholes for boots and hooks for coats and sweaters, individual compartments for personal belongings, special shelves for books and puzzles and paper, food adjacent to animal cages, water easily accessible—all these help cut down work time and encourage freer use of equipment.

Having enough—but not too much—equipment and materials for children to use fosters sharing and taking turns; having too little of popular kinds of equipment may lead to competition, frustration, and feelings of jealousy.

No listing of physical facilities and equipment can be made that insures a "perfect" setting for carrying out a preschool program that meets individual needs. Not only do choices depend on particular circumstances, but even the most favorable selection and arrangement will only be as effective as the imagination and flexibility of good teaching make them. Keeping the purposes of a program in mind will make choices a great deal easier, however, and bring about the results you want.

The illustrations that follow represent pictorially many of the specifics that go into planning the environment of a nursery school in order to achieve maximum benefit from the physical facilities.

"When you see children wandering around with nothing to do, you can be pretty certain the school environment is not well planned."

Director

"A presumed 'deprivation' in equipment does not necessarily lead to 'deprived behavior.' "

Gump (1975)

STAFF DEVELOPMENT AND MANAGEMENT

The personnel of a school—teachers, parents, volunteers—all reflect the philosophical orientation of the program. Staff competence reflects the importance that the administration places on individual qualifications, personal attributes, and amount of training. Depending on the preferences of the director and staff, the philosophical orientation of the school may create a permissive, child-centered atmosphere or a more structured and predetermined program.

Recruiting and Interviewing

Hiring a teacher may be as simple as asking an interested parent to help out on an hourly basis. Larger schools with public funds usually have to comply with specific guidelines including advertising under affirmative action regulations, screening applications, holding interviews, and submitting several names to a board that finally makes the appointment. Whether the process is simple or complex, the director should make every effort to recruit and interview as many highly qualified candidates as possible.

In addition to advertising in newspapers and employment agencies, college training programs and professional organizations are good sources for recruitment. Job specifications should be clear, including information about program philosophy, location of school, hours of work, number of children served, salary range, educational requirements, experience preferred, and a short description of what the potential employee will be doing.

Written applications should be screened and individuals who do not meet the necessary qualifications should be eliminated. In a small school, the director usually interviews and hires staff members. In a larger school, the interviewing group may consist of the director, a staff representative, parents, and advisory committee members.

It is a good idea for the applicant to visit the school and perhaps work alongside other teachers before an interview. This helps to center the discussion on a more realistic understanding of how the school actually operates.

Criteria for hiring should be established by the director and committee prior to interviews. The same set of criteria should apply to all applicants. A check list with a point system is helpful in maintaining consistency among members of the interview committee.

> "Whether or not I'm married or plan to have a baby has nothing to do with my abilities as a teacher."
>
> *Applicant*

The applicant should have a job description and information about the program as well as details concerning contracts, benefits, personnel policies, and evaluation procedures. The administration should be well versed in following affirmative action regulations where applicable. Many interview questions about ethnicity and marital history are prohibited.

Hiring procedures depend on the complexity of a school system; contracts also depend on requirements of the district or hiring agency. Some schools have only verbal agreements. Whatever the procedure, it is always wise to be as clear and specific about expectations and regulations as possible.

Inservice Training and Parent Education

> "We raised money to send two parents to the national convention along with staff members. It was the best investment we made."
>
> *Co-op Parent*

The quality of any preschool program depends on the training of its personnel. Teachers need to keep up with the field and to be inspired and motivated to do their best. Professional organizations such as the National Association for the Education of Young Children offer workshops and seminars throughout the country. Schools often include in their budgets some funds to help defray part or all of the expenses for attendance at such meetings.

Licensing agencies also require that personnel maintain certain levels of expertise by taking a minimum number of units in early education courses each year. Extension and evening classes offer many early education courses; often the school helps pay part of the fees.

Inservice training can also take the form of workshops and short seminars held in the school, both for teaching staff as well as parents and volunteers. Consultants can be brought in, or the teachers and administrative staff can plan and supervise such events. These may include workshops on music, art, nutrition, language, storytelling, and other topics related to specific areas of the curriculum.

PUBLIC RELATIONS

A good preschool or child care center does not operate in isolation from the rest of the community. Administrators need to maintain contact with the community agencies for referral purposes. They need to call on community workers to enhance the curriculum; they need professionals and lay people to serve on committees and boards. The school is a business in a very real sense, and it is the responsibility of the administration to maintain a positive image in the community through publicity and personal contacts.

Advertising

Schools need to budget a part of their income to cover costs of advertising. This can be in the form of paid ads in local newspapers, radio spots, or the yellow pages of the phone directory.

"I'm always trying to come up with new ideas for feature stories and interesting articles about our school. News stories are the best way to advertise."

Owner

Other effective means of advertising include posters placed in strategic locations such as libraries, schools, grocery stores, display windows, and other places where parents are likely to see them. Attractively designed brochures with pictures showing some of the unique aspects of the school can be distributed.

Feature stories including photos of interesting projects are often welcome additions to the local newspapers. Announcements of special events such as open house, registration day, holiday celebrations, and fund-raising activities should be sent to the papers.

Even when a school has a long waiting list, the director and administrative board should maintain an advertising program.

Community Relations

The good reputation of a school is developed over many years of service and positive interaction with the community. Satisfied parents recommend schools they like. Community workers give freely of their time because of enjoyable past experiences with the staff and children. Volunteers serve willingly because they feel needed and appreciated. Much of the success of a program depends on how well the director and teachers develop positive relations with the community.

A visit from a doctor or dentist, a trip to the fire station or local grocery store all require that others give freely of their time. Such experiences greatly enhance a school's curriculum and add to the value and desirability of the total program. Keeping in touch with these people, maintaining good relations, and showing appreciation for their contributions are all a part of administrative responsibilities.

The staff of a school should also be willing to serve in helping roles with other community groups. Advisory committees for other schools, youth-oriented groups, and related activities welcome the expertise of the staff. Giving mutual support and sharing common concerns help maintain important contacts and build supportive systems throughout the community.

"The four-year-olds painted a picture of me and put my name on it. I have it framed and hanging at the station house. I love it!"

Fireman

REFERENCES

Aaron, D., and B. P. Winawer. 1965. *Child's Play, a Creative Approach to Playspaces for Today's Children*. New York: Harper & Row.

Aikman, W. F. 1977. *Day Care Legal Handbook: Legal Aspects of Organizing and Operating Day Care Programs*. Urbana, Ill.: ERIC Clearinghouse on Early Childhood Education.

Bengtsson, A. 1970. *Environmental Planning for Children's Play*. New York: Frederick A. Praeger.

Butler, A. L., E. E. Gotts, and N. L. Quisenberry. 1978. *Play as Development*. Columbus, Ohio: Charles E. Merrill.

Cherry, C., B. Harkness, and K. Kuzma. 1978. *Nursery School and Day Care Center Management Guide*. Belmont, Calif.: Fearon-Pitman Publishers.

Dattner, R. 1969. *Design for Play*. New York: Van Nostrand Reinhold.

Gump, P. 1975. "Ecological Psychology and Children." In *Review of Child Development Research*. Vol. 5. Ed. E. M. Hetherington. Chicago: University of Chicago Press.

Haase, R. W., with D. Gardner. 1969. *Designing the Child Development Center*. Washington, D.C.: U.S. Office of Education.

Hurtwood, Lady Allen of. 1968. *Planning for Play*. Cambridge, Mass.: The M.I.T. Press.

Kritchevsky, S., and E. Prescott, with L. Walling. 1969. *Planning Environments for Young Children: Physical Space*. Washington, D.C.: National Association for the Education of Young Children.

Kruvant, C., G. Redish, D. T. Dodge, N. J. Hurt, R. J. Passantino, and R. Sheehan. 1976. *The Effects on Children of the Organization and the Design of the Day Care Physical Environment*. Washington, D.C.: Associates for Renewal in Education.

CHAPTER 23

WHO PAYS? WHO CONTROLS?: THE POLITICS OF CHILD CARE

Ledermann, A., and A. Trachsel. 1968. *Creative Playgrounds and Recreation Centers*. New York: Frederick A. Praeger.

Prescott, E., and T. G. David. 1976. *Concept Paper on the Effects of the Physical Environment on Day Care*. Pasadena, Calif.: Pacific Oaks College.

Sciarra, D. J., and A. G. Dorsey. 1979. *Developing and Administering a Child Care Center*. Boston: Houghton Mifflin.

Stevens, J. H., Jr., and E. W. King. 1976. *Administering Early Childhood Education Programs*. Boston: Little, Brown.

Stone, J. G., and N. Rudolph. 1970. *Play and Playgrounds*. Washington, D.C.: National Association for the Education of Young Children.

THE POWER OF POLITICS

The headline of the local paper read, "THREAT SEEN TO CHILD CARE IF TAX CUT PASSES." It was two weeks before the election. Mary Curtis, a teacher at the Mountain Dale Children's Center, read the headline quickly, felt a twinge of concern, but turned to her favorite columnist and comic strips. She knew there was a great deal of support for the tax cut. She also knew there was some connection between property taxes and the budget of the local school district but felt certain that the voters would not do anything that would seriously cut back support for education of their children.

Mary had graduated four years earlier with a children's center permit, a lot of enthusiasm, and the promise of a job in a church-sponsored co-op nursery school. The pay was only $3.25 an hour, but she loved to work with the kids and admired the director.

The school was supported entirely from fees paid by parents. Mary could figure out, roughly, the total monthly income of the school. She realized they could raise income only by increasing fees or taking in more children. But they had to remain competitive with other schools, so salaries remained constant even though other operating expenses went up. After three years, Mary was earning only $3.75 an hour. She was thinking seriously of changing to a different profession when the director discovered that as a nonprofit school they were eligible to apply for federal funds to help support their program.

Much of the federal money is restricted to low-income families.

The staff was excited at the prospect of additional money to purchase equipment, hire some aides, take the children on field trips, and increase teachers' salaries. However, there were strings attached to qualify; they would be required to stay open longer hours, take in more children from low-income families, and include at least 10 percent handicapped children in their total enrollment. They would have to conform to federal requirements affecting the ratio of adults to children, agree to prepare reports on their program, reapply each year for funds, and follow affirmative action to seek minorities and women for new staff positions. These guidelines did not seem unreasonable or difficult to meet.

In 1979, the poverty line established for a two-parent family with two children was $7,370. About one family in nine was below that level.

The director and Mary wrote a proposal requesting more than $38,000. They were surprised at the details required and the time it took.

The proposal was approved! Mary got a large boost in pay. The staff had to scramble to find families to fill the categories called for by the grant, but it was worth it.

Later, when the state announced that funds for child care were available, Mary's school decided it had the experience to expand its

"I was secretly apprehensive about integrating my child with low-income minority children at first. Now I see that part of our program as one of the most worthwhile and enriching components of our nursery school experience."

Co-op Parent

Monies are available for special services such as programs designed to deal with child abuse, handicapped children, and developmental screening to detect other kinds of problems.

"I used to wonder what my boss meant when she talked about funding a program with 'soft money.' Now I know."

Fired Teacher

program again. The state guidelines mandated a parent education component; a social worker was to be added to handle entry interviews; the center was to serve hot lunches, conduct educational testing, and extend its hours to full days.

The school hadn't given up the parent co-op, but it was becoming a smaller part of the program. The parent co-op children were not covered by the new grants; they did not get the hot lunches served to other children. They attended only half-day sessions and their parents were not included in the educational component. The center now operated three programs, each different from the other. The staff had grown. The need to meet guidelines on adult-child ratios had led the center to hire new teachers; it had a cook, a social worker, and a part-time nurse. The expense of providing both care and an educational component had increased the cost for each hour of child care by almost 150 percent. But the staff members were pleased with what they had done. They were offering a quality program, and salaries were more reasonable.

On June 6, 1978, Californians in a record turnout voted two-to-one to approve a constitutional amendment to cut property taxes. Budgets were reduced in almost all programs supported by tax funds. Three weeks later, Mary received her notice of termination in the mail. In thinking about it later, Mary realized that she might have taken a more active part in the election. She might have tried to make parents in her community aware of the consequences of the proposed tax cuts. Now it was too late. She had believed, a little naively, that the federal and state governments would continue to support child care.

But some of Mary's friends in other centers were not laid off; they continued to work and draw salaries. For the first time in her career, Mary began to wonder about who pays for child care and why some centers continued to get funds when others were cut off.

SOURCES OF FUNDS

What are the sources of funds for child care and early education? How can teachers and administrators whose jobs depend on these funds obtain information about them? How can they use this information to help plan their programs and careers?

Federal Support

There are several sources of support, but the biggest payroll, by far, is controlled by Uncle Sam. The federal government provides money for many services for children, including child care and early education. Funds are allocated by Congress with the president's approval. But many different agencies within the government are responsible for channeling that money to the appropriate sources.

Table 23.1 gives a general picture of the various agencies through which funds are channeled. To understand the complexities of federal spending and how preschools and child care centers finally get their funds, we would have to break the chart down even further to include many subagencies.

Money is funneled through government agencies to regional offices in various parts of the country. Salaries for Head Start teachers, for example, are authorized by Congress and allocated to the Department of Health and Human Services (HHS) and from there to the Administration for Children, Youth, and Families. The money is then distributed to the regional offices and finally to Head Start centers.

The lunch money for children in a state-funded program reaches the center by a different route. Money is allocated by the Congress to the Department of Agriculture and is routed through several subagencies to the state. The state in turn assigns funds to the contracting districts (counties, school districts, other eligible grantees) and finally from the grantee (in Mary's case, the Mountain Dale Unified School District) to the center.

In contrast to the few involved in direct payment of tuition in private schools, publicly funded programs involve hundreds of people. Even before Congress allocates money, there are those responsible for initiating legislation—preparing arguments, collecting data, developing guidelines, lobbying politicians, and carrying on correspondence just to get a bill through the House of Representatives and the Senate. When the expenditures are approved, there are hundreds more people who must read and approve proposals, negotiate budgets, check on eligibility of those receiving grants, monitor the implementation of the programs, distribute and transfer funds, and generally follow through on all the "red tape" of completing forms and required reports.

State and Local Support

The states also contribute to educational and child care programs. They usually do this by matching federal funds. For example, the state might contribute $1.00 for every $3.00 provided by the federal government.

State programs are vastly different from one state to another. One state may also get much more than another from the federal government. The specific arrangements change from time to time with new legislation. In our hypothetical example of Mary Curtis, the voters of the state demanded that taxes be cut. This action reduced or ended many programs and services. Child care and early education, as public programs that have been initiated

"The government never gave me any money to baby-sit my kids when they were young. They should put the taxpayer's money into better care for senior citizens!"

Senior Citizen

TABLE 23.1
Selected Federal Agencies and Programs That Support Child Care and Early Education

	Head Start	Other Educational	Special: Migrant, Handicapped	Child Welfare	Aid to Families with Dependent Children (AFDC)	Work Expense Allowance
Health, Education & Welfare						
Office of Education		×	×			
National Institute of Education		×				
Administration for Children, Youth & Families (ACYF)	×					
National Institutes of Health						
Social Security Administration				×	×	×
Department of Agriculture						
Department of Housing & Urban Development						
Department of Interior		×	×			
Department of Labor						
Department of Treasury						

Source: U.S. 95th Congress, 1st Session, Senate Finance Committee, *Child Care: Data and Materials*. (Washington, D.C.: Government Printing Office, December 1977).

recently, are more vulnerable at times of budget squeeze; they tend to be first in line for the fiscal knife.

Some cities also provide assistance for local child care programs. These may be combined with state and/or federal funds. In some instances, there is a sliding scale, both in amount of support from the agency and in the tuition charged. Families who can afford it pay a larger share of the cost for services.

Private Sources

In total number of dollars, a substantial part of the money for child care comes from public funds, but the largest portion is from fees paid directly

Work Incentive Program (WIN)	Other Child Care	Nutrition	Training (Including CETA & CDA)	Community Development	Research	Tax Credit
			×	×	×	
					×	
			×		×	
					×	
	×					
		×				
				×		
×			×			
						×

Note: In 1980, the Department of Health, Education, and Welfare was divided into two new agencies: the Department of Education, which now oversees the Office of Education and the National Institute of Education, and the Department of Health and Human Services, whose subagencies include the Administration for Children, Youth, and Families, the National Institutes of Health, and the Social Security Administration.

''I pay my sitter $1.00 an hour plus fringe benefits—free access to the refrigerator and unlimited use of the telephone!''

Mother

by parents, which include not only tuition to schools and centers, but also money spent on baby-sitting. The rates paid for child care vary tremendously; as rates vary, so does the income of the caregiver.

Support from institutions and corporations providing low-cost space, free use of equipment, and the like is a significant contribution often overlooked in determining child care costs. Rent can be a large expense. When a program can be located in a church or in a building belonging to a nonprofit corporation, the low or nonexistent rent is a form of assistance.

Another source of support common to many communities is the parent co-op, an arrangement in which parents contribute time as staff members for a few hours a week. This ''free labor'' helps to keep salary costs down. Contributing time works well for some, but other parents see it as an imposition and it is often an impossibility for parents who must hold full-time

"I spend three hours a week working at our child care co-op, and another four hours planning bake sales, garage sales, flea markets, and open house. If I spent the same amount of time at a paying job, I could contribute the money to the center!"

Co-op Parent

Tax credits for child care are available for single parents who work or couples who both work. In 1977, four million families—seven million children—were eligible. Cost to the government—$750 million.

jobs. Some co-ops are financially self-sufficient. That is, they exist entirely on tuition paid by parents. Others may rely on a combination of parent fees, adult education money from local and state departments of education, and fund-raising activities of parents. Some of these programs are located in rooms in church buildings or other institutions that provide space at relatively low cost.

COST OF CHILD CARE AND EDUCATION

The cost to parents of child care services varies greatly among facilities and even within a city or county. Cost is usually computed in terms of expense per child per hour. The average cost of different kinds of care and the range of cost per child hour are shown in Table 23.1.

The figures in Table 23.2 are based on reports of parents; actual costs of care would be higher for centers subsidized by public funds where parents may pay a small percentage of the actual cost. Cost per hour of child care for centers funded by state and federal programs is likely to average about $1.00 and in some instances much higher.

In addition to roughly $3 billion of federal, state, and local monies, approximately $6.5 billion is spent yearly by parents on child care and early education. Most of the money parents spend goes for home-based care—either in the child's home or the home of the provider.

PAY THE PIPER, CALL THE TUNE

In child care and education, the price for government support is government control. This seems to be inevitable; money and control are woven together.

TABLE 23.2
Cost of Child Care and Education Paid by Families for Different Types of Care

Type of Care	Average Weekly Cost	Cost per Hour
Own home by relative	10.52	.35
Own home by nonrelative	7.78	.53
Other home by relative	14.24	.39
Other home by nonrelative	16.07	.54
Nursery or preschool	14.59	.66
Day care center	19.56	.57
Overall mean	14.73	.51

Source: U.S. 95th Congress, 1st Session, Senate Finance Committee, *Child Care: Data and Materials*. (Washington, D.C.: Government Printing Office, December 1977).

In most instances, funds are awarded only to centers that meet certain conditions or agree to modify their programs to conform to guidelines. In exchange for support, centers surrender some of their autonomy.

"If I could spend as much time with the children as I have to in keeping records and writing reports, I'd be much happier."

Teacher

It is easy to be sympathetic to both sides of this issue. On the one side, the director and staff have their own ideas about how to run an educational or child care program. They know the local situation, the children, the parents, and the community. Their judgment may well bring the best care available to the children, given the resources available. On the other hand, the funding agency has a responsibility to both the taxpayers and to the children to see that the money is used in the best possible way.

So, funds are allocated with conditions and limitations attached. Part of the politics of child education and care is the process by which an agency decides the restrictions or requirements to be placed on funds. In 1967, passage of the Economic Opportunity Act authorized the official responsible for Head Start and the Secretary of Health, Education, and Welfare to establish a common set of program standards and regulations and to provide mechanisms for implementing these standards at state and local levels. As a result, a Federal Panel on Early Childhood created requirements affecting, among other things, child-adult ratios. In 1974, the Congress passed the Social Services Amendments, which prohibited the use of federal funds by centers that did not conform to the panel's requirements. The ratio for children three to four years of age was five children to one adult; for children four to six years of age, the ratio was seven to one.

This bill created an uproar. Centers that received some federal support but depended largely on parent tuition objected strongly. For example, a center that did not meet the mandated ratios could not accept a mother who used AFDC support to pay the center for care. The center could not obtain funds under the federal lunch program.

The protest from the various states was so vigorous that the Congress suspended the ratios in 1976, and in 1978 requested an evaluation of the feasibility of the requirements. The regulations had been placed in effect by the federal panel largely on the recommendations of professionals in child care and development. The struggle over their use was a controversy among professionals in the field. In the view of some, such issues are settled by a combination of forces—some based on research evidence, some on professional opinion, and some on more strictly political considerations. Controversies of this kind will continue to be associated with the use of federal and state money for child education and care.

"How can some politician in Washington know better than I what's best for my children?"

Father

Parents pay the piper, too, and they may also try to shape the program of a preschool or center. Some want educationally based programs; others want quality care at the lowest possible cost. They see no reason for expensive programs. If there are alternatives, they will shop around to see if they can get what they want. In the past, there have been few options for such parents, but there will probably be more in the future.

FORCES THAT LEAD TO FUNDING

The growth of demand for child care and education was discussed in Chapter 1. How does this demand lead to funding by federal, state, and local governments?

The press to expand child care and education through public funding comes from several directions. It is not a single, coordinated lobby or pressure group. Rather, the clamor comes from overlapping organizations of citizens, informal groups, and individuals who seek support for child care. These groups range from national organizations of women to teachers' unions to local groups of parents who meet with their city council members to gather support for a child care center.

The tactics are familiar: organized letter writing, individual phone calls, packing council chamber meetings with parents and small children, making child care an issue in an election by trying to mobilize parents to vote for a candidate who will promise to support child care or preschools, and even demonstrations have been used, often with effect. Each of these may be a relatively small effort, but when carried out over time, a climate of awareness is created that produces action. The Congress and state legislatures are sensitive to such changes in the public mood; politicians try to sense when the time is ripe for a new idea or program. A representative who can sense the right time to introduce legislation that will start a new type of popular program may gain visibility and an image that will pay off at election time.

OPPOSITION TO CHILD CARE

The concept of out-of-home child care is not universally popular. One source of opposition is simple competition for public money. Education of school-age children, welfare, medical costs for the elderly, child abuse, alcoholism, drug addiction, crime, support for agriculture, requests for research, national defense, and military operation—these and a great many more interests clamor for public funds and are supported by an elected representative's constituents. The legislator may have an interest in child care but sees other things as having higher priority; public support for the various demands is carefully weighed.

"I think it's cruel to send little children off to those crowded centers. They should be at home!"

Grandparent

Another type of opposition is more direct—an antagonism to the idea of parents' leaving young children in the care of someone else. This is a deep-seated and powerful feeling that is tied in with the concept of family and of deep convictions about what constitutes parental love and responsibility. An example of this type of opposition occurred in 1971, when Congress passed the Child Care and Family Services Act. This act would have provided billions of dollars (the estimates ranged from $7 to $30 billion) for child care, allocated directly to agencies in local cities and districts. The bill was vetoed by President Richard Nixon, who described the act as "the most radical piece of legislation to emerge from the 92nd Congress . . ." and called it "a long leap into the dark for the United States government and the American people." Furthermore, he stated that the nation's plan for developing child care programs must be "a measured, evolutionary, painstakingly considered one, consciously designed to cement the family in its rightful position as the keystone of our civilization."

President Nixon's action was consistent with the views of a number of groups opposed to child care and early education of preschool children. In California, an article claiming that early education was of no value to young children was distributed to the state legislature the weekend before a vote was scheduled on a prekindergarten educational program that had been proposed by the State Superintendent of Public Instruction. The article said, in part:

> It would be hard to find an area of educational research more definitive than that on child development and school entry age. It is difficult to see how planners can review this evidence and conclude that four- or five-year-olds generally should be in school, much less three-year-olds. . . . scientific evidence comparing the validity of the home and the school as early childhood environments clearly favors the home. (Moore, Moon, and Moore, 1972, p. 621)

In some cases, there are cries of "socialism" over the prospect of the government enlarging its support of child care, which, in the eyes of some, was a family responsibility. Comparisons were made with patterns of child care in socialistic and communistic countries.

In 1979, Senator Alan Cranston (Democrat, California) sponsored a bill, the Child Care Act of 1979, which drew this attack from a nationally syndicated columnist: "His (Cranston's) purpose is to subsidize child care services for all children up to the age of 15. His bill runs on to 26 pages, but you will find only two sentences—two sentences!—that toss a bone to the idea of parenthood" (Kilpatrick, 1979).

Behind some of the opposition to expansion of child care is the fear that it represents a dramatic advance in the liberation of women. The image of "mother" as one who cares for children while they are young, putting aside other personal goals and interests, is, for some, an essential part of family life.

The political battle over child care is thus a struggle between different values, beliefs, and personal goals of citizens of this country. These values are important to teachers also, and differences among the values of teachers are seen in their interaction with children. Political issues in various forms touch the teacher in many ways.

Teacher: "What does your mommy do?"
Adrienne: "She works."
Teacher: "Good. And what does your mommy do?"
Tim: "Nothin'."
Teacher: "Oh, your mommy is just a mommy."

THE FIGHT OVER CONTROL OF CHILD CARE

Most of the issues discussed so far have to do with the amount of funding and the kinds of programs that will gain fiscal support. There is another issue that is of central concern to professionals who work with young children. Simply stated, it is a matter of who will get the funds that are allocated.

A dramatic confrontation over this issue was the attempt of the American Federation of Teachers (AFT) to promote legislation that would put federal and state funds for child care in the public schools. Many elementary teachers have been forced out of classrooms because of falling pupil enrollments. The AFT reasoned that the public schools should be given responsibility for child care because they have the facilities, the staff (teachers that could be retrained), and the administrative and institutional organization to handle a national program of child care.

Such a move would carry with it new guidelines for staff. In order to accommodate the higher levels of training that teachers receive, compared with child care personnel, salaries would be more equivalent to those offered by the public schools and thus considerably higher than salaries earned by most child care and preschool staff. Child care professionals who had not earned teaching credentials would be replaced by certificated teachers or would be required to obtain substantial additional training to continue to hold their jobs.

This effort by the teacher's union aroused opposition. The counterarguments included concern about mingling young children with those of elementary school age; fear that the public schools would have too much control over the child's life; and a belief that the public schools might attempt to institute formal programs of education, pressing very young children to attempt to read and write. The AFT was accused of putting the interests of teachers above those of children. Early failure that might follow attempts to teach very young children to read might discourage children and affect their self-esteem as students. Other professionals in child development emphasize the need for child care staff to deal with the whole child, and not merely the mind.

The argument over who will control programs for children will continue. Often arguments of this kind are not public. Information about proposals for legislation or for certification requirements may not always be well known to teachers. Keeping in touch with professional organizations will help. They are the most likely sources of information about new programs and efforts to change, for better or worse, the ways programs are funded and controlled.

Knowledge of the patterns of funding is useful to the teacher who is looking for a position. It provides a sense of the security of the job. Keeping informed enhances his or her competence as a professional. It provides an opportunity to represent to members of the community the issues involved in decisions they may be called on to make about child care.

"Certainly, if care were all under school auspices, it would be possible to design a combination package of recreation, education, and day care which would be much better than the services of pieces and places put together separately."

Albert Shanker, President, AFT

"The schools cannot guarantee quality, only the provision of some services. They can offer no safeguard against the possibility that child care services, like schooling, will become uniform and the first step in a thoroughly institutionalized life."

James Greenman, Day Care Consultant

REFERENCES

Bruce-Briggs, B. 1977. "Child Care: The Fiscal Time Bomb." *The Public Interest*, 49, 87–102.

Butler, A. L., and N. P. LeVasseur. 1979. "Proposition 13 and Early Childhood Education: Wave of the Future or Bad Splash?" *Childhood Education*, 55, No. 3, 148–151.

Children's Defense Fund. 1976. *Title XX: Social Services in Your State: A Child Advocate's Handbook for Action*. Washington, D.C.: Washington Research Project.

Greenman, J. 1978. "Day Care in the Schools? A Response to the Position of the AFT." *Young Children*, 33, No. 4, 4–13.

Kenneston, K. 1977. *All Our Children*. New York: Harcourt Brace Jovanovich.

Kilpatrick, J. J. 1979. "Launching Another Disaster." *San Francisco Chronicle*, March 1, 1979 (syndicated column).

Kirst, M., W. Garms, and T. Oppermann. 1979. "State Services for Children: An Exploration of Who Benefits, Who Governs." Unpublished paper. Stanford University.

Moore, R. S., R. D. Moon, and D. R. Moore. 1972. "The California Report: Early Schooling for All?" *Phi Delta Kappan*, 53, 615–621.

Shanker, A. 1975. "Child Care and the Public Schools." *Day Care and Early Education*, 3, No. 1, 18–19; 53–55.

Smith, W. 1975. "The Place for the Private Provider." *Day Care and Early Education*, 3, No. 1, 20–21.

Steiner, G. Y. 1976. *The Children's Cause*. Washington, D.C.: Brookings Institution.

U.S. 95th Congress, 1st Session, Senate Finance Committee. 1977. *Child Care: Data and Materials*. Washington, D.C.: Government Printing Office.

PART EIGHT

SOME PERSONAL

MATTERS

A PROLOGUE   For some of you, the time has come to put aside note pads and books and to begin looking for a job. This is an exciting part of your training but it can bring feelings of awkwardness and a sense that you are not quite ready. These final chapters are intended to help you deal with the realities of getting a job and of being on your own.

You will learn a great deal from your first job, about both what to do and what not to do. You can make each job a new phase of learning by developing a plan for self-evaluation and self-education. You learn by identifying skills that others have but that you have not yet mastered. You learn by recognizing problems that you cannot yet handle comfortably. This is a first crucial step—identifying the things you want to learn. You can then begin to take an active part in acquiring experience or in finding the answer to a new problem.

You will learn to deal with other staff members who have a different philosophy and who approach things in ways you find difficult to accept. Some things you took for granted may require uncomfortable adjustments. For example, how do you deal with the time for snacks as a formally structured period when you are accustomed to letting children eat whenever they are hungry? Or, what do you do if the program has no rest time when you are convinced that young children need a nap, and the other teachers disagree with you? Your ability to deal with stress and burn-out on the job will be tested and tried.

Getting a job, keeping it, and being happy with what you are doing require the ability to apply the information you have to new situations. We hope these final two chapters will be of help. Good luck!

CHAPTER 24

GETTING A JOB

WHERE AND HOW TO FIND A JOB

Up to this point in the text, much has been said about doing a good job as a teacher. But not much has been written about how to get that job.

Sources of Information

One of the best sources of job information is the college or institution at which you've received your training. Bulletin boards and college placement services have the latest job opportunities listed. If you move to a new location, find the nearest teacher-training facility and ask for their job announcements.

Newspapers and "Help Wanted" columns are good sources. Sometimes, it is helpful to take out your own ad specifying your interests and specific skills as well as the hours and general locale in which you would like to work. Give your experience and expected range of pay.

Some people try to find a job simply by going through the yellow pages of a phone directory and calling all the schools listed—the success rate for this method is negligible. Some schools may take your name, but the chance of getting one that needs your services immediately is rather slim. It is better to be selective about the kind of school in which you want to work and to make a personal visit, introduce yourself to the director, and ask for information about the school's hiring policies.

Talk with teachers who hold the kind of jobs that you would like to have. Ask if you can observe and assist them in some capacity during the workday. Offer to work as a volunteer or a paid substitute. This provides you with firsthand information and knowledge about a teaching position that you cannot discover in an interview.

Following are some questions that you may want to ask in talking to teachers:

1. How did you get your job?
2. What are the good points of your job?
3. What are the negative aspects?
4. What are the most common problems?
5. What is the salary range?
6. What are the opportunities for promotion?
7. What are some of the ways to get ahead in the field?
8. How does this job compare with others in the field of early education?

People seeking jobs often are so eager to be hired that they rarely stop to think if the job actually suits them. Circumstances may be such that you simply must have some kind of employment, but remember that your long-

"I'm quite certain I got my job because I hung around the school and helped out so much that I already knew the routine and the names of the children and staff when an opening came up."

Teacher

term success and happiness with a job depends not only on how well you fit the job requirements, but also on how well the job fits your specific skills and personality.

Making Use of Your Information

After you have located a job opening and had an opportunity to find out more about the specifics, ask yourself the following questions:

1. What did I learn about the job?
2. Which qualifications do I have for the teaching position and which skills can I learn from the example of others?
3. What qualities do I need to be successful on this job?
4. Is this a job I want to be doing three years from now?
5. Should I seek the counsel of others to get more information?
6. Do I feel comfortable in the environment of that particular school?
7. Do the coworkers seem friendly and helpful?

"I try to find out why my predecessor left and how long other teachers have been on their jobs."

Teacher

The purpose of looking for a job is not simply to find one; it is also to help you become more knowledgeable about how to use the information you gather. The information you obtain can also give you a big advantage when preparing for your job interview. Job hunting and the way you gather and process information can be of vital importance to future success on the job. Remember, it's your career; you should be in control of what you do with it!

APPLYING FOR A JOB

Completing an Application[1]

Some institutions require all applicants to complete standard forms for jobs. Others may ask you to list your education and experience in a résumé. Still others may simply elicit information in an interview. Chances are likely that you will have to complete an application at some time during your career. Whether the form is designed with plenty of room to allow flexibility in writing about your background, or only limited space is given to fill in the information requested, you will want to follow some guidelines that are considered acceptable practice in completing an application.

1. Read the application all the way through before you begin to fill it out. Many applications have instructions or comments of which you should be

[1]The information for this section was adapted from *The Application,* produced and distributed by the Employment Development Department, Education/Industrial Liaison Office, 800 Capitol Mall, Sacramento, Calif., 95814.

aware that appear on the last page or they include a portion of the form that applies to earlier sections.

2. Follow directions explicitly. Some forms have directions in fine print under block headings such as "complete in your own handwriting," "please print or type," "use block letters," or "put last name first." Care in completing an application is essential as it indicates to many employers your ability and carefulness in reading and following instructions.

3. Be prepared with information that is commonly requested. Have a master application with up-to-date information about yourself, including such things as address and zip code; telephone number and area code; your social security number; driver's license; and names, addresses, zip codes, and phone numbers of references who have consented to provide you with recommendations. If you have reference letters, have machine copies readily available. Also have names, locations, and dates of previous education and employment. It is easier to complete an application carefully and neatly if you don't have to recreate the material every time you fill out a form.

4. Fill in all blanks. If they do not apply, put in a dash mark or "N/A" (not applicable) to indicate that you did not overlook the information requested.

5. Check over the completed application for neatness and accuracy. Always reread and have someone else look over your application to check spelling, correct addresses, hiring and termination dates of previous employment, and overall neatness and accuracy. Your application is all you have to represent you. How it looks reflects your conscientiousness in approaching other tasks.

Preparing a Cover Letter

A letter accompanying an application is a useful way to "speak for yourself" when your application is piled up with all the others. A well-written cover letter can do much to create a positive image of who you are. This letter should be concise, using short sentences and paragraphs, and should take no more than one page.

Address the letter to the name of the hiring authority (the director or owner of the school, the president of the board, or the chairperson of the hiring committee). Be sure you get the titles and spelling of names correct.

The first paragraph should arouse the reader's interest by presenting a simple, clear statement of accomplishment that is related to the job you are seeking. Tell why you have chosen to work for this particular school. General or vague comments, such as you would like to have a job, or you need the work, or you like little children, are not very useful. The reader should get a clear message that you will be an asset to the school.

State your career objective(s) and relate your experience to your goals. If your work experience is listed in the application, refer only generally to

"I always pick up two applications—one to practice on and one to turn in."

Applicant

"There's always someone on a committee who gets turned off by misspelled words."

Committee Member

"I like to see a picture of the applicant, even if it isn't required. A nice candid color shot of the person in action doing something with kids is impressive. Avoid the high school graduation picture. It's not very imaginative."

Chairman, Interview Committee

"Never complete an application in scrawly handwriting. Never use pencil."

Owner

the kinds of things you have done that will enhance the job you are applying for.

Impress the reader with your sense of commitment to long-term professional goals, your enthusiasm for your chosen field of work, and your eagerness to be considered for the position.

Personal data, such as the fact that you have children of your own, or that you grew up in the community, can be included if you feel this would increase your chances for employment.

Be concise, be clear, be to the point. Every sentence, every phrase, every word you use in the application and cover letter should serve to create a positive picture of you. The words you choose can enhance the impression you make on paper. When the competition is keen and many people apply for a position, the hiring agency must "paper screen" and eliminate applicants that do not appear to fill the necessary qualifications. The care with which you complete an application and what you say can make the difference.

Writing a Résumé

"I get impatient and distracted with messy, inaccurate applications. I find I don't want to interview people who are so careless."

Board Member

A résumé is a summary of personal data, training, professional interests, work experience, and special skills submitted with a job application. In order to prepare a functional résumé, cover letter, or application, it is helpful to think of your skills in specific areas pertaining to the job. For example, if the position calls for management abilities, you might want to jot down words to help you communicate your skills most effectively. Following are some suggestions:[2]

Management Skills

developing, planning, organizing, executing, supervising, directing, assigning, scheduling, coordinating, analyzing, establishing priorities, delegating, administering, evaluating, hiring, contracting, reviewing

Communication Skills

influencing, persuading, helping, leading, reasoning, developing, arbitrating, negotiating, mediating, reconciling, merging, motivating, creating

Research Skills

clarifying, investigating, surveying, gathering, synthesizing, ex-

Helping Skills

relating, guiding, leading, adjusting, servicing, referring, rendering,

---

[2]Adapted from *Clustering Your Skills,* produced and distributed by the San Francisco Job Search Techniques Workshops, Mission Employment Development Department, 2948 16th St., San Francisco, Calif. 94103.

amining, diagnosing, organizing, evaluating, critiquing, perceiving, collecting, interpreting, extrapolating, investigating, summarizing

attending, caring, listening, perceiving, understanding, monitoring, cooperating, sensitivity, maturity, intuition

Financial Skills

calculating, computing, planning, managing, budgeting, auditing, appraising, researching, analyzing, record keeping, detail, accuracy, speed, allocating, administering, solving, developing

Teaching Skills

influencing, persuading, briefing, informing, encouraging, communicating, advising, guiding, coaching, instructing, explaining, enlightening, stimulating, inventive, enthusiasm, adapting, adopting, facilitating, coordinating, developing, enabling, clarifying, conceptualizing, valuing, goal setting, deciding, initiating, creativity, imagining, innovating

THE INTERVIEW[3]

The prospect of a job interview can cause anxiety for many applicants. Although you cannot predict how the interview will proceed, some thought and preparation beforehand can help reduce much of the apprehension over such an experience.

If you have already visited the school, met some of the staff, had opportunities to ask questions and observe some of the routines, you are approaching your interview with some distinct advantages. The advance information you have can help provide a greater degree of self-confidence in discussing and questioning aspects of the program.

"A good cover letter and three or four letters of recommendation that are concise and very positive are probably the most important parts of the application."

Interviewer

Preparing for the Interview

Following are some things to consider before an interview:

1. *Nervousness is normal for most people during a job interview.* Interviewers realize this and will discount a certain amount of nervousness. However, try to remember your posture, maintain eye contact, and avoid fidgeting

[3]Adapted from *The Interview*, produced and distributed by the San Francisco Job Search Techniques Workshops, Mission Employment Development Department, 2948 16th St., San Francisco, Calif. 94103.

SAMPLE COVER LETTER

(Date)
Mrs. Jonathan Payne, Director
Oak Park Child Care Center
1121 Pine Crest Drive
Central City, New Jersey 07012

Dear Mrs. Payne:

I would like to apply for the position of head teacher at the Oak Park Child Care Center. The high standards of your center are well known in this community and it would be a privilege to be able to contribute to your program as a member of your staff.

My résumé indicates my experience in teaching, curriculum planning, supervising staff, and conducting staff and parent meetings. I know that I would grow professionally at Oak Park and believe that I would be an asset to your center.

I've enjoyed working in a variety of educational settings. After completing a thorough and stimulating program at Green Valley College, including student teaching, I gained additional training and experience in both day care and nursery school settings. In both positions, the emphasis on parent involvement gave me the opportunity to work with families from diverse backgrounds in publicly as well as privately funded centers. The different kinds of programs in these preschools enhanced my competence in all phases of teaching and curriculum planning.

I would appreciate your consideration of my application.

Sincerely,

(Name
Address
Phone number)

with objects either on the table or on your person. Be comfortable and natural.

2. *Memorize the names of your interviewers*. Find out how to pronounce names if you have doubts. Take cues from the behavior of the person(s) talking with you. Wait to be seated. Do not chew gum or smoke. Refer to interviewers by name.

3. *Be ready for common questions*. Anticipate your answers to inquiries such as, ''Tell us something about yourself,'' ''Why do you want to work for us?'' and ''Why should we hire you?'' Role-play your responses beforehand. Be definite in your answers. Tell the interviewers why you chose to apply for the job. Put yourself in their place and think about how you would want the questions answered if you were interviewing.

4. *Keep your answers to the point*. Do not stray from the topic. You need not confine responses to ''yes'' and ''no'' answers, but don't go on talking too long. Sometimes interviewers can get off the topic, limiting the time you have to make your impression. You can get the conversation back on the track by saying, ''Perhaps you have other questions you would like me to answer.''

5. *Be prepared for personal questions*. Even though affirmative action guidelines do not allow interviewers to ask questions about your plans to get married, start a family, and so on, you may find it useful to confront such issues by bringing them up yourself in order to reassure your prospective employer. For example, some employers worry that teachers who have young children of their own might have a higher absentee record because of the needs of their own children. You might want to refer to your past record and share with them your plans for child care in the event of emergency or illness.

6. *It is your job to sell yourself*. This is no time to be overly modest. Have three to six things in mind that you really believe are great about yourself. Make the opportunity to share your assets, but avoid exaggeration or the appearance of conceit.

7. *Have job-related questions in mind*. Do not be afraid to discuss the employer's expectations for performance on the job. If salary has not been discussed, give a range that would be acceptable to you.

8. *Never make a slighting remark about a former job or employer*. If you complain about someone else, you are likely to do the same about the new employer. You want the interviewers to feel you are applying for the job because of its positive aspects, not because you want to get away from a bad situation.

9. *Be honest about why you left past jobs*. You can tell the truth without making slighting remarks. If you were fired, state that you learned from that experience and that you do not anticipate it to happen again.

10. *Don't be discouraged*. Job interviews are good experience. They help

---

SAMPLE RÉSUMÉ

(*Note:* There is no one way to organize a résumé. The best format is one that highlights your strong points.)

Leslie Kneeland
580 Tenth Avenue
Central City, New Jersey 07012   October 10, 1981

<u>Occupational Objective</u>: To develop a children's center program emphasizing group cooperation, parent involvement, and team teaching.

<u>Education</u>:   Green Valley College
                     A.A. degree 6/79
                     Major: Early Childhood Education
                     Honors: Dean's Honor List

<u>Work Experience</u>:   6/79 to 9/81—Head teacher
                               Woodland Nursery
                               School
                               Amherst, Mass. 02107
                           9/77 to 6/79—Student teacher
                               Green Valley College
                               Green Valley, Ill. 60307
                           6/74 to 9/77—Day care teacher
                               ABC Center
                               Camden, N.J. 08103

---

prepare you for the next time. If you feel you have prepared adequately and done your best and you still do not get the job, don't give up. Your planning and experience will pay off if you keep trying.

Twelve Questions That Can Change Your Interview[4]

Interviewers tend to ask the same kinds of questions pertaining to job qualifications. The following twelve questions are likely to come up in almost

"You should complete every application as if your future depended on it. It just might!"

Instructor

[4]Adapted from *16 Questions That Can Change Your Job Interview* by Toni St. James, distributed by Employment Development Department, Education/Industrial Liaison Office, 800 Capitol Mall, Sacramento, Calif. 95814.

-2-

Special Skills: Play guitar
                   Experience with infants and toddlers
                   Planning parent education meetings
                   Science activities with preschoolers
                   Making cognitive materials for prekin-
                   dergarteners
                   Fluent in Spanish

Personal Data: Birth date: 7/10/59
                   Marital status: Single
                   Height: 5'6"
                   Weight: 110 lbs.
                   Health: Excellent

References: Mrs. Sally Truitt, Professor
                   Green Valley College
                   Green Valley, Illinois 60307

                   Dr. James J. Ryan
                   8544 Oak Grove Avenue
                   Camden, New Jersey 08103

                   Mrs. A. Beverly Bardet
                   668 Celestial Way
                   Marysville, California 95991

all interview sessions relating to early education positions. Role-play your answers and use them as a way to frame your replies to anticipated questions that are the same or similar to the ones listed. Here is an opportunity to plan your interview and to reflect your sense of confidence based on having done your homework.

Knowing how to answer such questions can make the difference between failure and success in landing a job!

1. *"What would you do if . . .?"* Interviewers, especially parent board members, can't resist asking hypothetical questions—"What would you do if a child bit you?" or "What do you do with aggressive children?" Remember here that the specific solution you offer is not as important as your

attitude in dealing with such questions. Approaching the question philosophically is better than saying, ''Well, I would do this. . . .'' It's far better to cushion your remarks by answering, ''One of the things I might consider would be . . .'' and then giving your response as well as some possible alternatives depending on the situation. Take this opportunity to expand on underlying reasons for such behavior. If you commit yourself too hastily to a particular method and it isn't one they like, you are in an awkward position. You will be better off to give an answer that is one of several possible choices. Be prepared for hypothetical questions. You're bound to get one.

2. *''What kinds of things can you do well?''* Use this question to reassure interviewers that you are well trained, skilled, and experienced at many facets of the job. Respond by saying, ''I like to do . . .'' or 'I'm good at . . .'' and then giving functions they may not have considered. Provide information about those things that you can do well—''When I was a student teacher, I was chosen as the best guitar player by the children.'' Don't be modest. Let them know you will add to their program with your skills. Many early education classes need people who are strong in music, creative movement, science, nature projects, carpentry, math, storytelling, nutrition projects, and curriculum planning.

3. *''What jobs have you held and why did you leave them?''* A history of many short-term positions can be detrimental to an applicant. The employer assumes that your past performance is an indication of what is likely to happen in the future. If you have legitimate reasons for changing jobs, report these facts—going back to school, moving, having to earn more money at the time. Be prepared in advance to deal with these questions and handle them calmly with rehearsed responses. If you had problems with former employers, be careful that your answers do not reflect badly on them. Be honest without being sarcastic, critical, or defensive. Practice your answers and the manner in which you respond in front of a friend or relative who can give you some objective feedback.

If you are still employed, but dissatisfied with your present position, it is appropriate to ask your interviewers to keep the application confidential. Tell them you realize they will want to speak with your present employer about your qualifications, and you are willing for them to do so if you are one of the finalists. You may want to change jobs because of greater opportunities for professional and personal growth, or because you have always wanted to be associated with a program such as theirs, or whatever your positive reasons might be.

4. *''What are your ideas about salary?''* Many people are not prepared to deal with negotiations over money. You probably want as much as you can get, but are unprepared to put it quite that bluntly. If there is an adopted salary schedule established by the district, you need only learn where you fit into that schedule. If the salary is negotiable, you can ask for their range. Have some facts about equivalent positions and what other schools in similar

''Employers are very subjective in their judgments. You can't always figure what they want. Maybe it's the way you look or the color of your hair that turns them on or off.''

Applicant

"Don't sell yourself short and undervalue your worth by saying you'd be happy to work just for the experience."

Teacher

"I like to hear what the applicant can do for us. I get tired of people who want a job for 'personal growth.' "

Owner

situations are paying their teachers. You should be candid about stating your worth without appearing to be out of line with their ability to pay.

5. *"Why do you want to work for us?"* Everyone, including your interview committee, likes to hear nice things about themselves. You will have done your homework in preparation for this question, so you will have lots of reasons to give in response. Perhaps you respect and admire the director and want to have the opportunity to learn from him or her. Or, maybe you know that there has been very little turnover in employees and you want to be associated with a staff that is committed on a long-term basis to the school. The good reputation of the school, the fairness of their policies, the opportunities for professional growth may be your reasons. Do not be insincere. If you do your homework, you will be able to come up with honest responses that reflect the positive aspects of the school and its people. Answers such as, "This is the closest place to my home," or "I need the job," won't do it!

6. *"What do you want to be doing ten years from now?"* This is a more subtle variation of "How long can we count on your staying with us?" It is costly and time consuming to hire and train new employees. Employers realize that personal situations change, and you cannot predict unforeseen events, but they need to know if their investment in you will be worthwhile. They don't want someone, no matter how good, to be always ready to take off for the next best offer. This question requires some reassurance from you that you are serious about your work and that you intend to be a professional who is committed to the field of early education. A job is not merely a convenience. Although you are not promising to stay forever, you can assure them you plan to stay as long as it is good for both of you. No employer wants someone who is no longer an asset to the program.

7. *"Tell me (us) something about yourself."* Many applicants are unprepared for such a question. It is open-ended and leaves you feeling helpless to decide just what you want to talk about. The homework and practice you do before your interview will prepare you to welcome the opportunity to let the interviewer know how your background, your interests, and your training are all good for the job. Your hobbies and personal life tell a lot about your enthusiasm, your interest in the community, and your openness, flexibility, and sense of humor. Employers want employees who are healthy, well-adjusted, wholesome people with a minimal number of personal problems. They don't need staff members who are vulnerable to disaster. In responding to this inquiry, you will seldom have a better opportunity to sell yourself.

8. *"We have many qualified applicants. Why do you think we should hire you for the job?"* If you say, "Because I think I can do the job," you can be sure every other applicant will be saying the same thing. One of the best approaches is to convey sympathy with the difficulty the interviewers will be facing in making a good choice. You are not in a position to speak to the qualifications of the other candidates, but you can assure them they will have

no reason to regret their choice if they select you. Reiterate the strengths you bring to this job, mention your skills, and speak with conviction that you honestly feel you are the best candidate for the reasons you gave.

Remember, the interviewers are responsible to others for their final selection. If your performance at work is unsatisfactory, it will reflect on their poor judgment. They need reassurance that they are not making a mistake. Take this opportunity to assure them they will be glad they chose you.

9. *"Have you had any serious illness or injury?"* Preschools and children's centers are particularly sensitive about absenteeism among staff members. Teachers who catch every cold that comes along and who often call in sick make more work for everyone else. The director has to spend time trying to find a substitute and the staff has to take on extra duties. If your health is good and your absentee record is clear, there should be no difficulty in answering this question. However, if you have had some serious illness or injury, be prepared with a signed clearance from your doctor stating that you are in good physical health and able to meet the demands of your job.

10. *"What are your weaknesses and what are your strengths?"* A variation of this one is, "In what ways do you think you can make our program better?" Smile when they ask this question. You should already have a memorized list of those things you do best. You've already used some of them to answer questions 2, 7, and 8. Stress those skills that you know they are looking for and need. If you have observed their program, and if you know why they are looking for a teacher, point out how you will bring strength to those parts of the program that are weak. "I work well in team teaching" or "I have an excellent record of success in parent involvement" are comments that may be recognizing some of their problems. Turn your weaknesses into possible strengths with comments such as, "One of my weaknesses is that I get so interested in planning a project I spend extra time after hours researching details."

11. *"How do you feel about working with other adults who are either younger or older than you?"* Many parent groups are concerned that the younger teacher might be intimidated by them, or that the older teacher might be too opinionated. They want the idealism of youth, the wisdom of maturity, and the experience of old age. Your concern, of course, is that you do the best job possible; age is not a criterion of ability for working well with others.

12. *"Do you have any questions or comments?"* Never, never pass up the opportunity to respond to this question. It usually comes at the end of an interview and gives you a chance to summarize for the committee what they should be remembering about you. Don't ever say "no" to this question. You should rehearse a short, concise statement summarizing your interest and training and how you can be a real asset to them. Touch on your awareness of their needs and how you can help them reach their goals. Do

"I have been taught all my life to be modest. Now I have to practice learning how to brag about myself!"

Student

"I reviewed this chapter just before I went in for an interview and I got the job!"

Employee

not talk too long, but do use the time to reinforce all their positive impressions about you.

Finally, remember to thank them for inviting you to an interview and express the hope that you will be working together soon. Keep that eye contact and stay calm, collected, self-assured, and pleasant.

REFERENCES

Bolles, R. N. 1979. *What Color Is Your Parachute? A Practical Manual for Job Hunters and Career Changers.* Berkeley, Calif. Ten Speed Press.

Eisenberg, A. M. 1979. *Job Talk: Communicating Effectively on the Job.* New York: Macmillan.

Fox, M. R. 1979. *Put Your Degree to Work: A Career-Planning and Job-Hunting Guide for the New Professional.* New York: W. W. Norton.

Genua, R. L. 1979. *The Employer's Guide to Interviewing: Strategy and Tactics for Picking a Winner.* Englewood Cliffs, N.J.: Prentice-Hall.

Irish, R. K. 1978. *Go Hire Yourself an Employer.* New York: Anchor Books.

Lathrop, R. 1977. *Who's Hiring Who?* Berkeley, Calif.: Ten Speed Press.

Reed, J., ed. 1977. *Résumés That Get Jobs: How To Write Your Best Résumé.* New York: Arco Publishing.

Thompson, M. R. 1975. *Why Should I Hire You? How to Get the Job You Really Want.* New York: Jove Publications.

CHAPTER 25

WHEN YOU'RE ON YOUR OWN

HOW DO YOU KNOW YOU'RE DOING A GOOD JOB?

Being on your own on your first job can be a frightening experience. The familiar surroundings of the training school and comforting voices of your fellow students will be missing. You will be faced with situations that compel you to act on your own initiative. After you have made a decision you may wonder, "How would my teacher have handled this?" or "Now, what was it that the book said about this sort of problem?" You may wish you had a chance to talk with your classmates or a faculty member about what you have done. If only your new job had the same comfortable routine of the training schedule you know so well! But things are different, and you must develop other sources of feedback.

Every teacher has been through this kind of experience. Just as they have found ways to develop greater professional competence, so, too, will you learn to rely on yourself more and to use your experience in a job to grow. In effect, you will learn to be your own teacher.

If you teach yourself, you must also evaluate yourself. How do you learn to stand aside and ask yourself how you are doing? First, you can learn to pick up cues, even subtle ones, from others that will give you valuable information about your performance. And while your former teacher's feedback and friendly criticism will no longer be there, you can learn to give yourself unwritten and unspoken grades and comments. You are now working not for grades but for long-term rewards that carry more weight than did your semester marks.

Over the years, you will develop a history of experiences that will help you determine what sort of teacher you are—you will identify your strengths and weaknesses. Already through your training experience you have developed a sense of how well you have done. Many of these impressions come from the direct feedback of the teachers with whom you have worked, grades you have received, comments on a class paper or project, and evaluations of your work with children. But you are also probably aware of more subtle cues about your performance—how the children respond, the enthusiasm of your fellow students, the behavior of parents toward you. In short, you are aware of your competence through information gained from a variety of sources, both formal (grades, direct criticism of your work, and so on) and informal. You have developed an internal system for judging your work. You take seriously what others tell you, but you also have your own evaluation of your competence. It may be somewhat tentative and cautious, but it is there.

As a professional you need to develop a more effective way to read the external cues and to set your own standards of performance. Much of the learning you will do comes directly from experience. If you begin to work out a set of goals and standards by which you will evaluate yourself, you will be aware of what you have learned from your experiences and see how they fit into your own professional growth.

SOURCES OF FEEDBACK

"Most of the time you're so busy just doing your work that you don't stop to think about how good a job you're doing. But then one day you get an indirect or subtle criticism that makes you take stock of yourself. It's rough."

Teacher

Where should the teacher turn? What are the sources of information that will tell you how you are doing? Where are the cues you will need to piece together the feedback that will show you how you look to others? The cues exist all around. There are many sources of information on how well you are doing.

The Children

First, and most available, are the children. In indirect (and sometimes almost too direct) ways they are the mirrors of your behavior. Their smiles, eagerness, reticence, and problems carry messages not only of rejection or affection but of your effectiveness as a teacher. For example:

Do the children initiate contact with you? Do they do things like touch you, climb on your lap, touch your hair?
Do they show any signs of affection—hug you, smile at you, and in other ways let you know that they are glad you're around? Are they eager to share experiences and bits of information with you?

Do the children look to you as a resource? This is more than an affectionate gesture. It is an expression of trust in your strength and helpfulness. Do they rely on you and ask for help or information?

Are you effective in redirecting the activities of children and still maintaining a positive relationship when you need to be firm?

The information you get from children's responses has to be interpreted. Your goal is not merely to be popular and have children follow you around. It is important to be liked, but your responsibility as a teacher extends far beyond this feature of your relationship with them.

"Mrs. D., I have a confession to make," confided the student teacher. "Yesterday I watched you handle Eric very firmly when he was throwing blocks and he yelled that he hated you, but a half hour later when he got frustrated with his wood collage, he adamantly refused any help from me or the other teacher and insisted on carrying all his wood and glue bottle out to you in the yard to ask your help. I was awfully curious to find out just what it is that you have

---

**CHILDREN'S ASSESSMENTS OF WHAT MAKES
A GOOD TEACHER**

A good teacher

holds you and reads to you.
sings songs to you.
doesn't slap you.
pushes you high on a swing.
goes to meetings.
puts a band-aid on a hurt finger right away.
smiles at you.
doesn't make you sit still or be quiet.
wears pretty beads.
lets you play with her hair.
helps you.
fixes bikes.
doesn't get mad.
works hard.
builds with us.
makes you laugh.

going for you, so I followed him out and pretended to be busy at the sandbox while I observed you. I watched you get down to his level and really concentrate on him like he was the most important person in the world. You looked at him and listened to him and then you suggested he do as much as he could and you would help him when he needed it. You really shared his concern and interest in a caring way. I feel like a phony when I see you in action."

"Well, I'm flattered to hear your report, but maybe I can add one more thing to your observation," replied Mrs. D. "Eric and I have had some really heavy confrontations over his aggressiveness. I have always tried to be honest with him in letting him know that I don't like his negative behavior, but I make it a point to be as supportive as possible in letting him know I intend to stay with him until we both work the problem out. He knows he can count on me and I do use lots of praise when he does good things. I have found that the children and I usually end up with a closer relationship after we have survived some battles together."

A teacher who is concerned with winning popularity contests by resorting to superficial tactics to manipulate others will be exposed as a phony in short order. The teacher who places real concerns for the mental and emotional growth of the children first will recognize that accepting and absorbing hostility is also an important part of a genuine relationship.

These bits and fragments of informal feedback from the children are a valuable source of information about some aspects of your job. As with other impressions you receive, they are most useful when assessed against a matrix of goals and objectives you have for yourself and for the children.

Colleagues

A second source of information about your performance is the opinions of other professionals. Your supervisor, the other teachers, the aides, and the volunteers with whom you work can give you quite varied and more informed opinions and reactions.

"One of the other teachers I worked with was always more popular with the parents and children than the rest of us. She seemed awfully insincere to me, but then maybe I'm jealous!"

Assistant

One way to get ideas from your peers is to ask, directly or indirectly, for comments or help. There are several ways to do this. You may ask for observation of your work. You might ask for suggestions before you tackle a difficult task. You may find it useful to ask more than one of your colleagues about some aspect of your job in order to get a different perspective.

There are ways, however, to read cues from other teachers that are more subtle. For example, what happens to the suggestions you make for changes in schedule or other features of the program or the center? Are they discussed? accepted? ignored? Do other teachers welcome your opinion? How does the director or your supervisor respond? If your ideas are not taken seriously, it may be that the other teachers cannot accept initiative from junior staff members. You may want to reserve judgment for a while to see if there is a consistent pattern in the way others react to your ideas. One or two responses are not sufficient for you to make a judgment. Again, the critical process is how you interpret the information you get from others.

Do other teachers seek you out? Do they confide in you? Do they share information about the children and the parents that will help you do a better job? When was the last time one of your colleagues asked for your opinions or ideas?

You can also learn from other teachers by watching them do things you may have difficulty with. How do they engage the children at story time? How do they greet parents? Obviously, this does not mean that you should attempt to imitate them, but sometimes there are clues that you can pick up that tell you things about what you do. Perhaps their techniques may be those you want to adopt. Or, there may be behavior you want to avoid. In any case, their techniques help you become aware of what you yourself do.

Betty watched Tim asking Nora, the other teacher, to tie his shoe. Betty felt herself beginning to reach down to tie the muddy, stepped-on shoelace. But Nora didn't move. Instead, she said, "Tim, you're a big boy now. You show me how to tie your own shoe."

TEACHERS' ASSESSMENTS OF WHAT MAKES A GOOD COWORKER

A teacher who is willing to do more than his or her share

A person who is cheerful

Someone who doesn't let his or her personal life interfere with classroom work

A person who is a good sport and knows how to work on a team

Someone who sees a need and fills it

A person who reinforces the consistency of the classroom goals

A teacher who does not contradict other members of the teaching team

A person who is emotionally healthy and able to talk through the problems all teachers face

Someone with a sense of humor

Tim did. Betty thought to herself, "Maybe I should encourage more self-reliance and independence in the children by getting them to try to do more things for themselves."

The next time one of the children asked for help with working a zipper, Betty said, "Try to do as much as you can by yourself. I'll help you if you still need me."

Betty had learned something about herself by contrasting her own behavior with that of someone else. This may mean that she will imitate, or adopt what she sees to suit her style. Or it may mean that she will congratulate herself on her own ability to do the same thing in her own effective way.

You may be aware of subtle messages that other teachers send. An oblique remark, an overheard (perhaps intentional) comment to another teacher or the director, a question or a wisp of praise about something you have done can be eloquent. The comment about a child with whom you have been working, "He requires a lot of consistency," may be a comment about the boy, or it may carry a message about your own ability to handle a child of his particular temperament. These clues are spontaneous and sometimes should be ignored. But they are information for you to gather and consider.

Parents

Parents are another good source of information about both your interactions with the children and your effectiveness in the program. How often have parents looked right past one teacher in preference for another teacher they have learned to trust and like. They will sometimes ignore new, young teachers until they prove themselves. Observe any classroom or children's center where there are several staff members. You will notice that parents may tend to confide in and chat more informally with one teacher than another. There may be outward signs of more smiling, praising, thanking, and sharing with some teachers than others.

Parents provide a good barometer of your effectiveness. Watch their subtle messages, such as knowing and calling you by name, or bypassing you to talk with someone else, or the more blatant ones of bringing gifts or inviting you to dinner. Of course, sometimes they simply tell you that they like you, or that they don't. Sometimes the most candid parent evaluations take place just outside the school doors at going home time when parents have a chance to get together and share their complaints and compliments.

Often it is a considerable task to learn how parents feel. Many parents may not have much time to come to the school to help or to respond to requests for formal written evaluations of the teacher, but their opinions are important. Teachers in all-day care centers where working parents take their children are often frustrated by the lack of communication. One teacher says,

"When I worked in a co-op, I couldn't get some of the parents to stop talking about their kids. When I was in a day care center, I couldn't reach the parents at all. For me, it was feast or famine. You have to learn to use different strategies in different settings."

Director

"They're too tired by the end of the day to do much talking. Our evening and weekend meetings are poorly attended, and we just have to resort to all kinds of ways to be in touch."

One teacher reports that it is worth the extra effort to get feedback from the parents:

I find from experience that I get the best results when I use positive examples at first. Sometimes I'll call a mother or father at home and report

---

MOTHERS' ANSWERS TO QUESTIONS REGARDING TEACHER EVALUATION

How Do You Evaluate a Teacher?

I watch to see if the teacher hears the children and gives her undivided attention while listening or speaking to a child.

I depend on the judgment of my friends if I am not able to observe for myself.

I notice whether or not the teacher treats children as individuals or always as members of a group.

I expect the teacher to talk to me as an equal and not to make me feel he or she knows much more than I do.

I wait to see if the teacher stoops down to put an arm around a child and to look in the child's eye while talking to him or her.

I don't want the teacher to tell me everything is "just fine" when I know it isn't.

I keep track of how often the teacher touches and holds the children and lets them be near.

I look to see what the teacher does with quiet children.

I count how often the teacher tells the kids what to do.

I think the teacher should punish children and not let them get away with things.

What Makes a Good Teacher?

Attends to the needs of the children

Is firm without being mean

Doesn't hold a grudge or play favorites

Gives of him or her self to every child equally

Is able to handle unexpected situations smoothly and doesn't get excited in emergencies

Makes learning situations out of every "problem"

Watches and listens and concentrates on the children

Gives me specific information about my child and helps me learn how to teach what he or she wants my child to know

Reinforces what I think is important for my child to know

Is warm and friendly and smiles sincerely

FATHERS' ASSESSMENTS OF WHAT MAKES A GOOD TEACHER

A male teacher who would handle the children differently from the way women handle them in rough and tumble play

A teacher who is not afraid to get dirty

Someone who will positively reinforce good social behavior and negatively reinforce antisocial behavior

Someone who is patient and has a lot of self-confidence

Someone physically affectionate

A man who is not afraid to be gentle and affectionate

A teacher who is not afraid to be firm and discipline the child

A teacher with a sense of humor

Someone who can create a special bond with each child

Someone with varied interests and an eager, joyful outlook on life

Someone who isn't all hung up with a sexist role

---

something amusing and clever. That often leads to questions from them about the program and how their child is doing. They may also make some comment that tells me if they like what I'm doing and how our school is run. If they say nothing about how they feel . . . well, that tells me something, too. Sometimes the most important things are those that are *not* said.

Other times I'll send home a short note and I always read it to the child first so he or she will know what it says. I try to leave them open-ended so the parents can respond if they wish. I really appreciate getting notes from the parents and I let them know that nothing is too insignificant to share with me.

"Dear Mrs. Carter,
Jason did a beautiful job of teaching some of the other children how to separate eggs today during our cooking project. He tells me you know how to bake the best cake in the world. Maybe you can share the recipe sometime. It's obvious that Jason enjoys helping you with the cooking at home. I miss not having a chance to chat with some of our parents and sharing some of these experiences, so I hope you don't mind a note from me once in a while. Please feel free to call me or drop me a note any time."

This mother called from work the next day to give me her recipe and when I asked if she had any concerns she admitted she never would have called me about it, but since I asked . . . she had some minor complaints about the routine when she picked Jason up each day. He seldom had his shoes or jacket on and his paintings and other work were often scattered so no one could find them. She felt no one really cared enough to get Jason organized when it was time to go home. She was grateful to have this opportunity to express her feelings and asked me to continue to write notes so she would have an excuse to call.''

When given the opportunity, parents provide a good source of information about teachers and programs. Sometimes a great deal of significant evaluaton takes place in the public park, the grocery checkout line, and other such places where parents are likely to meet informally. Wise teachers will help channel some of that information their way and use it to correct misinterpretations and to evaluate themselves and their program.

Supervisors

Most of the time the feedback you get from the children, colleagues, and parents will be informal; but there is another kind of assessment—a formal evaluation, usually given by supervisors. Many programs require at least an annual evaluation of the staff based on systematic, written reports and ratings (see Figures 25.1 and 25.2).

Many teachers, even those who are experienced, may be apprehensive when they know their professional skills and personal qualifications are being assessed. This is a natural response, one conditioned by years of school grading, selection procedures, entrance tests, verbal recommendations, and the like. In such a situation it is easy to raise questions about the legitimacy and adequacy of formal evaluations.

Government-funded programs are likely to be the most explicit in their evaluation requirements. Teacher ratings and written reports must be made periodically in order to qualify for funding. Evaluation practices can be very helpful to the teacher.

Linda received a written job description when she was first hired by the county to teach in a preschool serving low-income children. Along with a booklet explaining fringe benefits, holidays, sick leave, and other such information, Linda was given a printed sheet detailing exactly how and when she would be evaluated. She saw copies of check lists, rating scales, and questionnaires to be used by her head teacher, her coworkers, the parents, and her supervisor.

Twice a year, Linda has a personal interview with her supervisor who reads and discusses the evaluation forms with her. The super-

FIGURE 25.1
Example of Scale for Rating
Staff Performance

School: _____

Staff Member: _____

Observer: _____ Date: _____

Instructions: Circle the number on each line that describes most accurately the behavior and performance of the staff member in carrying out assigned tasks and duties.

1. In working with the group, the staff member is

   strict   1 2 3 4 5 6   permissive, easy going

2. With respect to racial and ethnic history and customs of children and parents, the staff member

   promotes ethnic pride and   1 2 3 4 5 6   ignores or puts down ethnic
   awareness   background and behavior

3. When with the children in a relatively free and unstructured situation, the staff member is

   warm and outgoing to the   1 2 3 4 5 6   distant, detached, stiff
   children and other staff
   members

4. In the daily curricular routine schedule, the staff member:

   selects and directs most   1 2 3 4 5 6   lets the children pick their
   activities   activities

visor may have suggestions about how Linda can improve her teaching methods and the ways she relates to the children, other teachers, and parents. She is allowed to read the supervisor's recommendations to the district board and is given an opportunity to disagree with the evaluation and to suggest changes.

The specificity of such a procedure may be intimidating to some teachers, but others appreciate knowing what is expected of them.

The field of child care is growing rapidly and is increasingly supported by public funds. With public resources comes pressure for accountability about how funds are spent. This means an increase in evaluations of both preschools and their staff. Teachers may expect to see more formal and systematic evaluations carried out in the future.

Yourself

Whether the feedback you receive about your work comes from formal or informal assessments, the best source of information about yourself is your-

FIGURE 25.2
Example of a Teacher
Evaluation Sheet

Name of Teacher: _____   Date: _____

Observer: _____   Time Observed: _____

	Excellent	Good	Fair	Poor
Performance				
Efficient	—	—	—	—
Imaginative	—	—	—	—
Maintains good control	—	—	—	—
Dependable	—	—	—	—
Attitude				
Responds well to suggestions	—	—	—	—
Happy, warm personality	—	—	—	—
Sympathetic, sensitive	—	—	—	—
Relates well to children	—	—	—	—
Relates well to staff	—	—	—	—
Personal Qualities				
Sense of humor	—	—	—	—
Self-confident	—	—	—	—
Appropriately dressed	—	—	—	—
Well-modulated voice	—	—	—	—

self. You can keep track of your own behavior and make your own opportunities for self-study and improvement. You are in the best position to see if your progress matches your goals. You are the best judge of yourself, provided you know how to make use of the feedback available to you.

One way to do this is to make a list of your priorities and then keep a log of how you spend your time when you are on the job. The ways you allocate your time reveal what your true, underlying priorities are. For example, you might start with a simple list of things you ought to do in order to be a good teacher, such as:

1. Spend time interacting with every child
2. Observe some of the problem children more closely
3. Have many positive experiences with quiet children
4. Plan more individual creative activities

The log you keep needn't be a minute-by-minute detailed account, but should give you an accurate picture of how you actually have allotted your time.

Suppose you discover that a large part of your day is spent in the kitchen preparing activities and cleaning up, another large part is spent in talking with parents or other teachers, and only a few minutes are spent in group activities with the children. The discrepancy between your list of priorities and the things you actually do can provide a means for reassessing yourself. Maybe your assigned duties do not permit you to work closely with the children, or is it possible that you have been retreating to these duties in order to disguise some of your fears or hidden motives? Most teachers have experienced times in which they frantically busied themselves tying shoe strings or wiping noses when they felt inadequate to handle a more serious situation. It happens to the best of teachers. This discomfort may be the impetus you need to sit down and redesign your work schedule or discuss with your supervisor how you can allow time for your stated priorities. In any event, the way you actually spend your time is one of the best indicators of your sense of values and competence. A sure sign of the need to reassess your goals is when there is a great discrepancy between what you do and what you say you really want to do.

If you are lucky enough to have access to a video tape machine, you can arrange to see yourself as others see you. One teacher, knowing she would be self-conscious and unnatural if the camera followed her, chose to be videotaped during a particular segment of her creative dance time with the children when she thought she was particularly effective. She replayed the tape several times and made notes that helped her improve her methods. In most cases, it may be least painful to start in areas where you feel you are most capable. Then as you begin to get helpful feedback from your self-assessment, you will be more likely to look at other areas of your teaching where you are less comfortable.

"Let's face it! Most teachers don't have the nerve to look closely at themselves. They're afraid of what they might see!"

Teacher

Use an audio tape recorder to hear yourself interact with others. One teacher used a miniature recorder with built-in microphone to tape sharing time without any distraction to the children. "I knew I would never let anyone else hear it so I didn't have to fake in order to impress someone else. I left that tape around for two weeks before I had the nerve to listen to myself. Yuck! I really sounded like an old nag. I would have hated to have me for a teacher. That first tape helped me identify lots of poor teaching strategies and I have since taped myself at least once a week and don't mind sharing and discussing the tapes with others."

Having a friend or volunteer write an observation can be helpful, especially if the observer confines the report to objective data; what you and the children actually did and said. Subjective opinions ("The child was nervous and should have been removed from the group") are of questionable value, especially if the observer is unfamiliar with your teaching situation. Suggestions can be helpful but the teacher should rely on inner standards to assess the comments offered by friends, whether they are critical or flattering.

Use your coworkers and other professional colleagues as sounding boards.

It's often helpful to toss out an idea you've been considering before you've become so committed to it or so ego-involved that you don't want to hear any criticisms. You can play around with ideas in the comfort and safety of your own imagination, but how do they appear when these same ideas are reflected against someone else's perspective? You don't have to accept their point of view, but you can learn from it.

Keeping a diary can provide an excellent basis for introspection. Like the teacher who knew she would not share her tape recording with anyone, your diary can be your private affair. Keeping a record of your discomforts and how you felt can be a therapeutic experience. Most of us try to suppress the painful things that happen to us. We want to ignore the negative signs, hoping they are not true and will go away. Usually they don't. You can utilize and exploit these experiences.

Keep a record of situations that have made you uncomfortable or seem to reveal some lack of competence. Over a period of time you may see a pattern. Maybe an honest expression of your feelings toward aggressiveness is your problem; or perhaps children who whine really turn you off. A diary can help reveal some of your vulnerable spots and help you develop ways to deal with them. Consider the following excerpt from a teacher's diary:

> Thursday, May 8—That brat, Jonathan, got me so upset today I broke down and cried! I hate him. I wish he'd drop dead, or at least move away! He seems to sense that I have a hard time handling noisy aggressive boys. Too upset to write any more.
>
> (Later, same day) I really had a good cry—took a long walk and sobbed. I felt so alone and helpless but I feel much better now. I don't recall ever crying so hard. It's a good release for my pent-up frustrations. I realized that I'm always telling the children, "It's all right to cry. It's O.K. to let people know how you feel," and here I am holding back all my feelings just because I'm afraid of being a failure as a perfect teacher! Well, I'll restrain myself appropriately, but tomorrow Jonathan is going to learn something about my honest feelings!

This teacher still had many moments of uncertainty and her teaching methods were revised many times, but she later wrote of this particular experience.

> . . . for the first time I immersed myself totally in feelings of helplessness, anger, and frustration. I came out of that experience knowing that I could deal with those feelings and I may have many more experiences in my teaching that will lead to similar feelings, but I'm stronger for having dealt with them. I guess I've lost a lot of the fear of having to confront situations that bring about those feelings of helplessness. I think I'm much more honest and sympathetic and therefore more real and effective now than a year ago.

Not all of a teacher's insights have to come from negative and painful experiences. Equally important are those times when everything runs smoothly. Too often, a teacher will lose a good opportunity to learn from a positive, rewarding situation by simply viewing it as good luck.

When the day has gone well or some activity you planned and supervised turned out to be even more successful than you had hoped, do a mental replay and try to isolate and capture the exact combination of ingredients that will enable you to do it again. Perhaps it was the combination (or separation) of certain children, or the way you introduced the activity. Maybe you made your limits clear and reinforced them at appropriate times. It could be all these things or a combination of many others, but the time you take to debrief yourself will help you be clearer about identifying your teaching methods.

Talk aloud to someone else or to yourself about the high points and the low points of the day and ask how you might have handled the situation better or what you did to make it go well. Compare in retrospect your behavior and techniques with those of others. Learn to look at yourself and to be honest in confronting your own reality. Self-assessment through systematic methods such as those described can be highly rewarding.

Information gained through these self-monitoring techniques can be helpful only if you use this information for improvement and professional growth. It's no fun to see yourself in a negative light, nor is it useful to distort your self-image so that you delude yourself into thinking you're a great teacher.

Self-evaluation is most beneficial if the teacher can share information with others who are striving to improve their teaching methods as well. Just as Weight Watchers set observable goals and applaud each other in a supportive manner for individual efforts and gains, teachers need also to share their concerns and be supportive. Too often, the work environment fosters competitiveness and individual achievement. Helping your colleagues improve is not often rewarded.

Teaching in a competitive environment can be a lonely affair and many teachers report that one of the most important factors in job satisfaction is the friendliness and cooperation of the other teachers with whom they work. Students who first enter the field report that salary is one of the most important considerations in job hunting, but after a few years of experience, they place "compatibility of other teachers" above salary.

The task of self-evaluation requires determination, consistency, and a real desire to improve, but the teacher who develops systematic techniques to aid professional growth will realize one of the greatest satisfactions in teaching—the development of his or her inner resources. A teacher who is skilled in self-monitoring will have the confidence to make decisions based on accurate self-knowledge and thus be able to rely on his or her own inner strength and self-confidence to develop and use effective teaching methods.

THREATS TO MORALE:
THE BURN-OUT SYNDROME

Teachers themselves must be the ones who take the major responsibility for monitoring their sense of success and well-being. Yet there are times when all efforts at self-monitoring and self-improvement seem not to work. When the constant demands of children, parents, and staff drain a teacher's resources, he or she is vulnerable to feelings of helplessness and a sense of failure.

Chris flops into one of the chairs in the staff room, seemingly unaware of the other teachers around him. He stares off into space, oblivious to the conversation. "Chris, it isn't like you to be so quiet. What's wrong?" asks one of the teachers.

Chris's reply comes quietly and deliberately, "I've been thinking seriously about resigning." Pleas of "The children will be heartbroken," seem not to move him.

"I know, but I've thought about all that, and I just can't take it anymore. There's never a let-up. Day in and day out the demands on me never stop. The same problems come up every day; I don't seem to get anywhere or help anyone. My resources are gone and I'm out of patience."

Chris is suffering from burn-out syndrome, a condition of emotional exhaustion created by excessive demands on energy, strength, or resources coupled with a sense of being unable to get things done (Freudenberger, 1975). For Chris, as for others, there is a feeling of helplessness.

Signs of Burn-Out

Professionals are beginning to identify symptoms of "burn-out" in a number of jobs. Staff members in human service and helping programs dealing with drug abuse, delinquency, emotional disorders, the chronically ill, child abuse, and other such problems are especially vulnerable to burn-out.

The signs of burn-out are familiar to experienced child care workers: difficulty in getting to work on time, greater absenteeism, increased susceptibility to illness or colds, lower energy levels requiring longer periods to recharge, looking at the clock more frequently, counting the days until the weekend or a holiday. At the same time, there may be an increase in complaints about children's behavior, the parents, administration, and working conditions. Staff members may be less flexible and accommodating. They are more likely to refer children with "behavior problems" to specialists. As pressures continue to mount, attitudes begin to change among staff, often

"My family says no job is worth what I go through. I'm no fun to them anymore, and now I'm reluctant to talk about my problems at home."

Teacher

taking the form of gossip, boredom, pettiness, and arguing. Tension increases among the staff, and a lower morale sets in. Often there is hostility, jealousy, and resistance to any added chores (Mattingly, 1977; Freudenberger, 1977; Maslach and Pines, 1977; Seiderman, 1978).

> In the final stages of burn-out, staff members become so negative that they either resign or are terminated. Those that hang on are so thoroughly demoralized, unhappy, or bitter that they cannot do much more than go through the motions of providing basic care to the children. It is not an exaggeration to say that some even become rather sadistic towards the children. (Seiderman, 1978, p. 7)

Many teachers and child care workers like Chris who started with idealistic goals, willing to give of themselves far beyond the requirements of their jobs, fall victims to the burn-out syndrome. Is Chris to blame for being so naïve? Are the parents to blame for leaving their children so many hours? Or is the administration responsible for his condition?

Some Causes of Burn-Out

Burn-out is not a disease. It is a reaction to three things often found in child care and other service programs: staff members who have unrealistic expectations and goals for the changes they want to bring about in the people with whom they work; a job that has relatively constant demands for emotional interaction with others; and long-term goals that are difficult to achieve or do not provide day-to-day signs of progress.

"A . . . conflict exists between the need to give and the reality that you can never give enough."

Mattingly (1977)

These circumstances often apply to the child care worker. He or she is in an emotionally giving role. The level of noise is constant and sometimes high. The demands and needs of children and parents press on staff members whether or not they are prepared for them. There is little chance to renew personal resources during the day. The interaction with children, while calling for imagination and resourcefulness, uses only a small range of an adult's social and intellectual repertoire.

Avoiding Burn-Out

What can be done to maximize job satisfaction and minimize burn-out? If it is a hazard common to people in service occupations, including child care, it is obviously worth the attention of the director and staff. A number of professionals who have studied this type of job dissatisfaction offer suggestions to help avoid burn-out. Most important of these is to recognize that burn-out is a fairly common reaction among child care workers. This helps teachers realize that it is not their own personal failure but a reaction to certain conditions of work, and also suggests that there are remedies for dealing with burn-out reactions.

The signs of burn-out tend to decrease for staff members who are moved for a part of the day to administrative tasks rather than continuing to work with children, thus suggesting that a change in routine, variety in the range of tasks, and adjustments in schedules may be useful.

Introducing variation in the job might include more flexible responsibilities so that staff members can work out hours allowing shorter workweeks with longer daily hours, trading time off, sharing job responsibilities, rotating leadership, and offering opportunities for a break from the continuous routine of contact with children.

Since burn-out may be caused in part by the feeling that little progress is being made in working with children, it may be helpful to introduce occasionally a change of tasks to things more directly under the teacher's control and that offer something specific and useful to accomplish. Working with people, whether as a parent, a public school teacher, or a staff member in a preschool, involves interaction that brings about change very slowly. Despite all that a teacher can do, Johnny's aggressiveness may seem not to change; the work of one day somehow gets undone. It is difficult for the staff to feel competent in this kind of situation. Imagine the reaction of someone who tries to knit a sweater only to find that the yarn keeps unraveling almost as fast as it is being knitted! A basic reward of work is the sense of accomplishment—the feeling of getting things done. This comes gradually in work with children.

Recognition and praise for the efforts of staff in preschool programs have special significance. They can be in the form of raises or bonuses where possible, but may also include personal reviews, compensatory time, gifts, recognition in newsletters or at parents' meetings, and attention from administrators. The feeling of being needed and appreciated is a powerful antidote to burn-out.

THE SOCIAL RESPONSIBILITY OF TEACHING

At the beginning of this book we asked you to consider your reasons for wanting to become a teacher of young children. Perhaps some of your motives included the desire to help children grow up to be better adults. Or you might have had a dream of contributing in some way to a society where people live in harmony and peace. But will your idealism and desire to "make a difference" stand up in the face of evaluations, morale problems, and staff burn-out?

As a teacher of young children you are expected to help produce better adults. You are also expected to be more patient, more nurturing, more

"When you get kids who consistently misbehave and you try everything you can to change their behavior and nothing works, you start to blame the kids or yourself. You lose your patience and everything seems futile. That's when you want to quit."

Teacher

knowledgeable, and more wise than people in many other occupations. Will you—can you—fulfill these expectations? And are they realistic?

The challenges you face are exceedingly complex. The children you teach will be living in a world requiring special abilities to deal with dwindling resources, larger populations, higher costs, and more competition than you face today. You are expected to provide them with the skills to solve intellectual and social problems in order to succeed in life. Yet, if you look around you today, you can see that our children live in a fragmented world. Family styles are changing rapidly; events in other parts of the world affect the way we live in our communities. Through the media, through political events, and through a world made smaller by sophisticated communications technology, youngsters will be exposed to many more diverse and complex influences than you were when you were young. Many of these influences will be contradictory and confusing.

Our society has always valued diversity and individualism—"Do your own thing," "Take care of number one," "Compete to succeed." The important socializing agents in a child's life—family, church, friends—also want him or her to learn to cooperate, to care for others, to be peace loving.

Faced with changing priorities, inconsistent values, and many confusing alternatives open to the young, the teacher needs more than ever to bring consistency to the child's world. The teacher of today cannot indulge in the luxury of operating in an environment designed to recognize only one set of goals. He or she must be aware of a larger society and of the events and significant people who shape the child's life.

To prepare children for the world of tomorrow, you must be aware of the larger society, continually seeking new information, sorting out what is important, establishing and re-establishing priorities based on lasting values. And through it all, you must be prepared to face the painful prospect of change.

Through expertise in the field, concern for quality in teaching, dedication to children and to the profession, you, as a teacher of young children, will indeed be a determining force in shaping the future of our society.

"Happiness comes only when we push our brains and hearts to the farthest reaches of which we are capable. The purpose of life is to matter—to count, to stand for something, to have it make some difference that we lived at all."

Leo Rosten.

REFERENCES

Freudenberger, H. J. 1975. "The Staff Burn-Out Syndrome in Alternative Institutions." *Psychotherapy: Theory, Research, and Practice,* 12, No. 1, 73–83.

Freudenberger, H. J. 1977. "Burn-Out: Occupational Hazard of the Child Care Worker." *Child Care Quarterly,* 6, No. 2, 90–99.

Maslach, C., and A. Pines. 1977. "The Burn-Out Syndrome in the Day Care Setting." *Child Care Quarterly,* 6, No. 2, 100–113.

Mattingly, M. A., ed. 1977. "Symposium: Stress and Burn-Out in Child Care." *Child Care Quarterly,* 6, No. 2, 88–156.

Seiderman, S. 1978. "Combating Staff Burn-Out." *Day Care and Early Education,* 5, No. 4, 6–9.

APPENDIX OF RESOURCES

The following agencies, organizations, and publications provide additional resources related to early education topics. Brochures, newsletters, films, speakers, and periodicals may be obtained by writing for further information.

AGENCIES AND ORGANIZATIONS

Administration for Children, Youth, and Families
U.S. Department of Health and Human Services
330 Independence Ave., S.W.
Washington, DC 20201

Adult Education Association of the U.S.A.
810 18th St., N.W.
Washington, DC 20006

American Association for Elementary-Kindergarten-Nursery Educators
1201 16th Street, N.W.
Washington, DC 20036

American Association for Gifted Children
15 Gramercy Park
New York, NY 10003

American Montessori Society
150 Fifth Avenue
New York, NY 10111

Association for Childhood Education International (ACEI)
3615 Wisconsin Ave., N.W.
Washington, DC 20016

Association for Children with Learning Disabilities
4156 Library Rd.
Pittsburgh, PA 15234

Child Development Associate Consortium, Inc. (CDA)
7315 Wisconsin Ave., East, Suite 601
Washington, DC 20014

Children's Rights, Inc.
3443 17th St., N.W.
Washington, DC 20010

Child Study Association of America
50 Madison Avenue
New York, NY 10010

Council for Exceptional Children
1920 Association Dr.
Reston, VA 22091

ERIC/ECE, Educational Resources Information Center
University of Illinois at Urbana, Champaign
805 West Pennsylvania Avenue
Urbana, IL 61801

Family Service Association of America
44 E. 23rd St.
New York, NY 10010

National Association for the Education of Young Children
1834 Connecticut Ave., N.W.
Washington, DC 20009

National Center on Child Abuse and Neglect
U.S. Children's Bureau
P.O. Box 1182
Washington, DC 20013

National Child Safety Council
4065 Page Ave.
P.O. Box 280
Jackson, MI 49203

National Committee for Prevention of Child Abuse
111 E. Wacker, Suite 510
Chicago, IL 60601

National Congress of Parents and Teachers
700 North Rush Street
Chicago, IL 60611

National Council of Organizations for Children and Youth
1910 K St., N.W.
Washington, DC 20006

National Nutrition Consortium
9650 Rockville Pike
Bethesda, MD 20014

Parents Without Partners
7910 Woodmont Ave., Suite 1000
Washington, DC 20014

Society for Research in Child Development, Inc.
University of Chicago Press
5801 Ellis Avenue
Chicago, IL 60637

U.S. Department of Education
400 Maryland Avenue, S.W.
Washington, DC 20202

PUBLICATIONS

Child Development
Society for Research in Child Development
University of Chicago Press
5801 Ellis Ave.
Chicago, IL 60637

Childhood Education
ACEI
3615 Wisconsin Ave., N.W.
Washington, DC 20016

Children Today
U.S. Dept. of Health and Human Services
Administration for Children, Youth, and Families
Superintendent of Documents
U.S. Govt. Printing Office
Washington, DC 20402

Day Care and Early Education
Behavioral Publications
72 Fifth Ave.
New York, NY 10011

Developmental Psychology
American Psychological Association
1200 Seventeenth St., N.W.
Washington, DC 20036

ERIC/ECE Newsletter
University of Illinois at Urbana, Champaign

805 West Pennsylvania Ave.
Urbana, IL 61801

Harvard Educational Review
Longfellow Hall
13 Appian Way
Cambridge, MA 02138

Human Nature
Harcourt Brace Jovanovich, Inc.
757 Third Ave.
P.O. Box 10702
Des Moines, IA 50340

Merrill-Palmer Quarterly of Behavior and Development
Merrill-Palmer Institute
71 East Ferry Ave.
Detroit, MI 48202

Report on Preschool Education
Capitol Publications, Inc.
2430 Pennsylvania Ave., N.W.
Suite G-12
Washington, DC 20037

Young Children
NAEYC
1834 Connecticut Ave., N.W.
Washington, DC 20009

GLOSSARY

Accommodation   Piaget's term for the process by which new information is handled in the mind.

Adaptive behavior   Effectiveness with which an individual meets the standards of personal independence and social responsibility expected of his or her age and cultural groups.

Affective bond   See **attachment.**

Affective education   Helping children learn to solve personal and emotional problems and understand the causes of the behavior of others.

Aggression   Unprovoked attack or hostile behavior.

Ambivalence   Mutually conflicting ideas or feelings toward the same object.

Assessment   Systematic gathering of information about performance.

> **Criterion-referenced assessment**   Comparing a particular behavior with a specific level of performance.
>
> **Diagnostic assessment**   Specialized testing, particularly in the area of a suspected disability.
>
> **Norm-referenced assessment**   Comparing some aspect of a child's growth or behavior with that of many other children.

Assimilation   Piaget's term for the process of taking in new information.

Associative play   Interaction between two or more children that does not involve group cooperation.

Attachment   Relationship (emotional bond) of the child to the parent(s) or primary caregiver.

Audiometer   Instrument for measuring acuity of hearing.

Audit   Review of financial records by an authorized agency or individual.

Behavioral objective   Statement of achievement desired.

Behavioral science   The study of human behavior in physical and social environments by experimental and observational methods.

Behavior disorders   Emotional disturbances and social maladjustments.

Budgeting   Grouping the expected uses of funds into categories.

Burn-out syndrome   Reaction to job pressures and demands leading to feelings of helplessness and a sense of failure.

Certification   Issuance of a document, such as a license, which shows that an individual has fulfilled requirements to teach.

Child Development Associate (CDA)   Credential awarded to individuals who fulfill certain performance-based competencies thereby qualifying them to work directly with preschoolers and their parents.

Cognition   Mental process by which knowledge is acquired.

Cognitive development   Growth of ability to reason and solve problems.

Cognitive developmental approach   Teaching preschoolers skills related to elementary school.

Communication disorders   Speech and language difficulties.

Compensatory education   Programs intended to make up for social and educational disadvantages.

Concept   A general idea or understanding; awareness of an object or thought and the meaning associated with it.

Conservation   In child development, the concept that some properties of material remain constant despite changes in other properties (for example, volume may be constant even though shape has changed).

Cooperative play   Rule-governed social interaction between two or more children.

Cooperative preschool   A school owned by parents or by a public agency, with parents serving as part-time teachers' aides.

Crisis   Any situation or sudden change that calls for immediate action and invokes stress.

Curriculum   A schedule of planned activities for the classroom.

> **Absent curriculum**   Whatever teachers choose *not* to teach.
>
> **Hidden curriculum**   Attitudes and values taught unknowingly.
>
> **Implicit curriculum**   Activities that are not directly stated, but exist in the teacher's mind.
>
> **Prepared curriculum**   Activities planned in advance by the teacher.
>
> **Structured curriculum**   A clear, purposeful curriculum with prearranged sequence of materials and specific goals.
>
> **Unstructured curriculum**   Free-play program in which children move at their own choosing from one activity to another.

Day care center A facility that usually provides full daytime care for preschoolers of all ages and after-school care for elementary school children.

Diagnosis Classification of an individual on the basis of observed characteristics; identification of an abnormality.

Director Person who is responsible for all aspects of a school program, including staff.

Disability See **impairment.**

Disadvantaged Lacking in social and/or economic opportunity.

Discourse Conversation between two or more individuals.

Discovery learning Learning based on direct experience.

Duo A pair of words that conveys a comprehensive message; one of the early forms of speech.

Early intervention Attempts to alter the course of educational or social development; usually suggests a program intended to raise educational achievement.

Emotional trauma An experience that causes severe emotional stress and damage.

Evaluation Measurement of the attainment of established goals or progress toward achieving goals—may apply to individuals, preschool programs, or national programs.

Exceptional child A child whose abilities or characteristics fall at either end of a normal distribution curve.

Extrinsic Outside one's self.

Handicap A condition that makes achievement difficult and dependent on assistance. See also **impairment.**

Head Start Federally funded program that provides educational and social experiences for children from low-income families before they begin school.

Head teacher Teacher in charge of classroom staff and activities.

Hierarchy Items arranged in a graded series (smallest to largest, shortest to longest, weakest to strongest, and so on).

Holophrase Single words that may express extended meaning.

Home Start Federal program that involves parents in home-centered learning.

Homogeneous Composed of similar parts.

Humanistic Awareness of one's own feelings and concern for the feelings of others.

Hyperactivity Excessive activity or restlessness.

Identity Awareness of self as member of a larger, socially identifiable group.

Impairment A defect that prevents a child from performing at normal levels. See also **handicap.**

Imprinting A type of learning that occurs rapidly and early in life and that resists extinction or change.

Individualized education program (IEP) A written statement required by Public Law 94-142 specifying the curriculum, goals, and time schedule for the education of a handicapped child.

Infant-toddler center Facility that provides care for children from birth to two years of age.

Information processing Operations by which the mind receives and organizes stimuli.

Inservice training Training on the job, either at the place of work or at other locations in workshops, conferences, and seminars.

Intrinsic Originating from within one's self.

Intrusive Entering inappropriately or without invitation; interfering.

Latch-key children Children who, because their parents work, have keys to their homes and are unsupervised after school.

Learning Acquiring information, knowledge, or skills.

Liability Legal obligation; responsibility imposed by law to compensate another for injury.

Licensing Permission given by an agency of the state or local government for operating a school; presumably indicates that the school meets legal standards.

Linguistics The scientific study of languages.

Mainstreaming Bringing handicapped children into regular classrooms for instruction.

Mandate Instruction or command given by a group or individual in authority.

Mental retardation Significant subaverage intellectual functioning usually accompanied by deficits in adoptive behavior.

Migrant families Families who move seasonally from one agricultural job to another.

Mnemonic device An aid that assists or is intended to assist memory.

Modality The pathways through which information is received; pertaining to one of the senses (visual, auditory, olfactory, gustatory, and tactual).

Modeling   Learning or teaching by demonstration and example.

Moral development   Learning behavior that conforms to a set of rules and moral judgments of a society.

Nonprofit school   A school organized to meet expenses but not to make money for its owner(s).

Nonverbal cues   Communicating meaning without use of words.

Nursery school   Facility for children two to five years of age that offers services, usually in the morning or afternoon.

Nurture   To train, to rear; to foster development.

Objective   Free from personal or emotional bias; not dependent on the judgment or opinion of an individual observer.

Object permanence   Piaget's term for the scheme or condition of knowing that objects continue to exist although they may have disappeared from view.

Object play   Activity in which a child plays alone with an object.

Observation   Systematic procedure for watching and recording behavior.

Orientation   Procedure by which teachers and/or parents become acquainted with the school environment.

Parallel play   Children playing alongside one another with little or no intentional interaction.

Perception   The process through which stimuli (information) reach the nervous system through sensory modalities.

Perseverate   To repeat an action after it is no longer appropriate; due to inability to shift from one activity to another.

Poverty   (Social Security Administration definition) Level set by ratio of annual money income to the cost of a minimum diet for persons in a household.

Practicum   Direct experience in laboratory or field settings under supervision.

Precocious   Designating unusually early development or maturity, particularly in mental ability.

Prejudice   Favorable or unfavorable belief or judgment about others made without adequate evidence.

Preoperational stage   Piaget's term for the stage in cognitive development when internal representations become a familiar part of a child's mental system—occurs between two to seven years of age.

Project Follow Through   Federal program designed to extend the educational resources of Head Start into the primary grades.

Referral agency   Private or public group that is organized to advise and deal with individual and/or social problems.

Reinforcement   Strengthening a behavior by some external or internal reward.

Résumé   Written summary of work experience, education, and personal data.

Reversibility   The mental operation, according to Piaget, by which a quantity is returned to its former state in order to check that it is the same.

Role playing   Acting in accordance with certain characteristics that are not one's own.

Rote learning   Memorizing material in a way that seemingly requires no understanding but only the reproduction of words or symbols.

Scheme   A group of activities that are organized and related to one another to accomplish a particular purpose.

School board   The governing body of a school responsible for policy and financial control.

Screening   Testing populations to discover problems not previously identified.

Self-concept   Awareness of one's own characteristics.

Self-esteem   An individual's perception and evaluation of his or her characteristics and self.

Sensorimotor intelligence   Knowledge derived from the senses and physical activity.

Sensorimotor stage   Piaget's term for the first stage of cognitive development, roughly spanning the period from birth to two years.

Seriation   Process by which unorganized objects are grouped into a certain order according to identifiable characteristics.

Social development   Learning to interact with others; growth of knowledge and understanding of the behavior of others.

Social play   Activity involving interaction between two or more children without rules.

Social system   The network of institutions, values, laws, customs, and informal expectations that make up a society.

Soft money   Funds that are provided for a limited time and dependent on reallocation or approval from an outside source; usually refers to public (local, state, federal) support.

Special education Instruction for children with special learning needs.

Sponsorship Source of fiscal support.

Subjective Reporting or evaluating based on personal judgment.

Symbol Something that is chosen to represent something else.

Teachable moment A time during normal development when a child is particularly ready to receive new information or to learn a new skill.

Team teaching Cooperative teaching by two or more members of the teaching staff.

Temporal order A time concept involving ideas of sequence.

Tenure An agreement that, after holding a position for a specified number of years, a teacher cannot be dismissed except for reasons stated in his or her contract.

Territoriality Tendency of human beings and other animals to establish and protect geographic and/or psychological boundaries.

Test A situation in which specific tasks or questions are presented for a response; a device that produces a score based on responses to a number of items designed to measure a particular ability.

Developmental test A number of items or techniques for measuring progress in any area of behavior.

Readiness test Measures skills that can be taught, usually academic.

Standardized test Instrument for performance assessment developed through testing large numbers of children by controlled selection.

Waiver Written statement made releasing holder from a stated responsibility.

INDEX